2785

68-95

PRIESTS AND PEOPLE IN F

D1589167

QMC

BX 1504
CON

PRIESTS AND PEOPLE IN PRE-FAMINE IRELAND 1780-1845

S. J. Connolly

GILL AND MACMILLAN

First published 1982 by
Gill and Macmillan Ltd
Goldenbridge, Dublin 8
with associated companies in
London, New York, Delhi, Hong Kong,
Johannesburg, Lagos, Melbourne,
Singapore, Tokyo

This paperback edition first published 1985
7171 1410 4

Printed and bound in Great Britain by
Biddles Ltd,
Guildford and King's Lynn

I. M.

Thomas Connolly

1905 – 1978

Contents

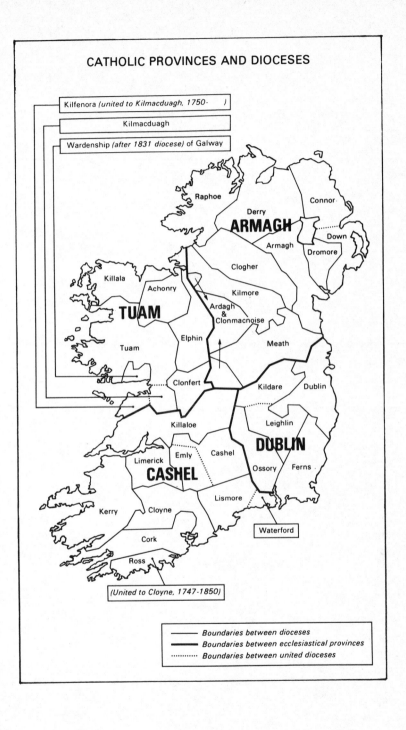

CATHOLIC PROVINCES AND DIOCESES

Kilfenora *(united to Kilmacduagh, 1750-   )*

Kilmacduagh

Wardenship *(after 1831 diocese)* of Galway

Raphoe

Connor

Derry

ARMAGH

Armagh

Down

Dromore

Clogher

Killala

Achonry

Kilmore

TUAM

Ardagh & Clonmacnoise

Elphin

Meath

Tuam

Clonfert

Kildare

Dublin

Killaloe

Leighlin

DUBLIN

Emly

Cashel

Ossory

Ferns

Limerick

CASHEL

Lismore

Kerry

Cloyne

Cork

Waterford

Ross

(United to Cloyne, 1747-1850)

—— Boundaries between dioceses
━━ Boundaries between ecclesiastical provinces
·········· Boundaries between united dioceses

Introduction

In July 1835 the French writer Alexis de Tocqueville, on a tour of Ireland to collect material for a projected book, obtained an interview with William Kinsella, Catholic Bishop of Ossory. In both England and Ireland, de Tocqueville began by observing, he had often heard it said that the Catholic population of Ireland was half savage. But this was probably false? The bishop, however, did not respond to this leading question in the way that his visitor obviously expected:

> I must admit that it is in part true. . . . The people has some of the characteristics and, unfortunately, some of the defects of savage people. This people has all the virtues dear to God; it has faith; there is no better Christian than the Irishman. Their morals are pure; premeditated crime is very rare. But they basically lack the civil virtues. They have no foresight or prudence. Their courage is instinctive; they throw themselves at an obstacle with extraordinary violence and, if they do not succeed at the first attempt, give it up.

Later in their conversation the bishop returned unbidden to the same theme: 'I say again that they have the virtues dear to God, but they are ignorant, violent, intemperate, and as incapable of resisting the first impulse as savages.'[1] De Tocqueville never wrote his book on Ireland. But the notes made during his visit contain more than one set of draft reflections on the character of the Irish clergy, and on their relationship with their congregations. 'There is an unbelievable unity between the Irish clergy and the Catholic population,' he had noted four days before his meeting with Kinsella. 'The clergy, rebuffed by high society, has turned all its attention to the lower classes; it has the same instincts, the same interests and the same passions as the people; [a] state of affairs altogether peculiar to Ireland.'[2] It was a view echoed — if not always with the same note of approval — by many of his contemporaries, and more recent writers on pre-famine society have also tended to take the view that relations between the Catholic clergy and their congregations were characterised by an exceptional harmony of sentiment and outlook. But where do Bishop Kinsella's comments fit into this general picture? What were the features of pre-famine social life which led him to stigmatise the general body of Irish Catholics as ignorant, violent and intemperate? Did other churchmen share his critical attitude to the lives and morals of their congregations and his evident sense of the distance which lay between his world and that of the ordinary Irish Catholic? If so, how do such sentiments affect the traditional picture of relations between priests and people? And what, if anything, can an examination of these issues contribute to our understanding of later developments in the history of Irish Catholicism, and of the part which Catholicism has played in the shaping of contemporary Irish society?

These are the questions which lie behind the present book. It is intended as a study of the place of the Catholic Church and its clergy in Irish society, and of relations between priests and people, in the six or seven decades preceding the famine of the 1840s. The distinguishing characteristics of this period, and the reasons which justify its treatment as a chronological unit, are set out in the first chapter. The remainder of the book falls into two parts. The first offers a general survey of the state of Irish Catholicism in the late eighteenth and early nineteenth centuries, looking at ecclesiastical organisation and discipline, the background, training and general character of the Catholic clergy, and the nature of popular religious belief and practice. The second half of the book goes on to examine three specific areas, in each of which a clear conflict arose during this period between the code of conduct which the authorities of the Catholic Church were seeking to impose and the attitudes and standards of behaviour of their congregations. The three areas discussed in this way are, firstly, the traditional practices of the pattern and the wake;

secondly, marriage and sexual behaviour; and thirdly, the problem of public order, particularly in relation to the activities of agrarian secret societies and of feuding local factions. In each case an attempt is made to examine the type of discipline which the Catholic clergy were attempting to impose, the means by which they sought to achieve this, and the extent to which their efforts were successful.

The resulting book cannot pretend to present a fully rounded picture of relations between priests and people. Its main emphasis, in the first place, is inevitably on the negative side of that relationship, on conflict, differences of outlook, and coercion or attempted coercion. Neither can it claim to deal equally with all sections of the Catholic population. Instead the greater part of the discussion concentrates almost exclusively on the poorer sections of the Catholic laity, on the labourers, cottiers and small occupiers of the countryside and (to a lesser extent) on their counterparts in the towns and cities. Yet both types of limitation have their virtues. An emphasis on areas of conflict, while inevitably yielding only a partial view of relations between priests and people, may at the same time serve to compensate for a more common bias in the opposite direction on the part both of later writers and of contemporary observers. In the same way an emphasis on the Catholicism of the poorer classes, at the expense of more sophisticated varieties, will at least have the merit of focusing attention on the distinctive features of the culture it describes. For the religion of the Catholic poor cannot be understood simply as an inferior version of the religion of their social superiors. It was the attempt of several generations of men and women to reshape and adapt the doctrines of their church into something more relevant to the world in which they found themselves. And the outcome of their efforts was a variety of Irish Catholicism so different to that which was to supersede it that its existence has been largely forgotten.

* * *

The research on which this book is based was begun while I was a postgraduate student at the New University of Ulster and completed at the Institute of Irish Studies, the Queen's University of Belfast; I am grateful to both institutions for the support which enabled me to undertake the work. I am greatly indebted to Dr A. C. Hepburn, my supervisor at NUU, whose criticisms and suggestions did much to improve the first version of this study, and who in addition read and commented on part of the present text. Dr Peter Roebuck of NUU also took a close interest in the development of the work and provided much helpful advice and assistance, while at different times I have benefited greatly from correspondence or conversations with Dr F. A. D'Arcy, Dr David Dickson, Professor E. R. R. Green, Dr Marianne Elliott, Dr Donal Kerr, Mr Peter Laslett, Professor D. W. Miller, Professor John A. Murphy, Mr. Seán Ó Súilleabháin and Dom Mark Tierney. I would also like to thank Mr Colm Croker of Gill and Macmillan for a thorough and expert scrutiny of my text. My wife, Mavis Bracegirdle, neither typed nor made the coffee, but has helped in other, far more important ways.

For permission to make use of manuscript sources I am grateful to the Director, Public Record Office of Northern Ireland; the Deputy Keeper of Public Records and Keeper of State Papers, Ireland; the Royal Irish Academy; the Director and Trustees of the National Library of Ireland; the Department of Irish Folklore, University College, Dublin; the Archbishop of Cashel and the Bishops of Clogher and Dromore; the Parish Priests of Nobber, Co. Meath, St Canice's, Kilkenny, and Slieverue, Co. Kilkenny, as well as the custodians of other parochial records not drawn on in the present study; Viscount Massereene and Ferrard. Thanks are likewise due to Mr John Curry, Mr Michael Kenny and Miss Josephine O'Farrell for permission to consult unpublished theses, and to the staffs of the different libraries and institutions in which I have worked for much courteous and efficient assistance. Like so many other students of Irish history in recent years, I must make particular mention in this respect of Mr Brian Trainor, Mr Trevor Parkhill, Dr A. P. W. Malcomson and their colleagues in the Public Record Office of Northern Ireland, and of Mr W. H. Crawford, late of the same office. Nor can I omit my own former colleagues in the Public Record Office and State Paper Office of Ireland, who I hope will before long be given the opportunity of rescuing both offices from the sad condition into which they have recently been permitted to decline.

The book is dedicated to the memory of my father, who did not live to see it completed. He would not have liked everything it contains, but I hope that he would have found something in it of which to approve.

Dublin, December 1980

NOTE

There are numerous variations in the spelling of the names of eighteenth- and early nineteenth-century Irish bishops. The spellings used in this book are in all cases taken from the lists of bishops by Benignus Millett and C. J. Woods in T. W. Moody, F. X. Martin and F. J. Byrne, ed., *A New History of Ireland*, IX (forthcoming).

In quotations from contemporary sources spelling, capitalisation, etc. have been modernised, except in one or two cases where it has seemed desirable to retain the distinctive features of the original.

1

Pre-Famine Ireland:
Religion and Society

The six or seven decades preceding the famine — the period, roughly, from 1780 to 1845 — was a time in which the Catholic Church moved from being a technically illegal organisation to being an accepted part of the structures of power and influence within Irish society. During the same period religious fears and animosities which contemporaries had begun to think of as part of the seventeenth-century past made a new and violent appearance, with consequences which remain with us to this day. Simultaneously, and in a related process, new connections were established between religious affiliation and political allegiance. It was also in this period, finally, that the economic and social development of the greater part of Ireland unmistakably and irreversibly diverged from that of the remainder of the British Isles. Whereas most parts of Great Britain moved during these years into a period of sustained industrial growth, Ireland, with the exception of its north-east corner, headed inexorably towards the massive demographic catastrophe of the famine and a social transformation of a very different kind.

All these developments are of relevance to the subject of this study. Although none can be examined in detail, a brief review will establish the context for what is to follow.

* * *

At the beginning of the 1780s the Catholic Church remained nominally subject to the comprehensive body of penal legislation introduced by the Irish parliament in the aftermath of the Williamite victory. The main provisions of this legislation are well known. In addition to severely restricting the rights

of the Catholic laity in politics, property matters and education, the laws banished all Catholic bishops, vicars general
and other persons exercising any ecclesiastical jurisdiction, as
well as all members of religious orders. Any such person found
in the kingdom after 1 May 1698 was to be deported, and
those who returned to Ireland after being so deported incurred
the penalties of death and forfeiture of possessions prescribed
for the crime of high treason. An act of 1703 extended these
same penalties to any Catholic clergyman whatever who
entered the country after 1 January 1704. There was, however,
no direct prohibition of Catholic religious practice. Ordinary
secular priests already in the kingdom were required to register with the authorities and to provide securities for their
good behaviour, but having done this they were permitted to
say mass and perform their other duties openly and legally.[1]

In the opening years of the eighteenth century a serious
attempt was made to enforce this legislation. Throughout the
country unregistered priests, members of religious orders and
the small number of Catholic bishops remaining in the kingdom were sought out and, where possible, arrested and
deported. The period of strict enforcement, however, was
relatively short. As memories of the 1690s and fears of a
Jacobite counter-attack receded the extermination of the
Catholic hierarchy no longer seemed either necessary or particularly desirable, while the course of British foreign policy
rendered a measure of practical toleration expedient. The
speed with which a more relaxed attitude was adopted varied
from place to place. Already by 1718 the authorities in
Dublin were showing little enthusiasm for the strict enforcement of the penal laws. When the Catholic Archbishop of
Dublin was arrested in that year, through the efforts of a
renegade priest turned bounty-hunter, no evidence was presented against him and he was allowed to return openly to
his episcopal duties. In Co. Limerick, on the other hand,
illegal or unregistered priests were presented at every assizes
up to 1726. By the early 1730s, however, it was clear that
the worst was over. A detailed report commissioned by the
Irish House of Lords in 1731 showed that in most parts of
the country both regular priests and bishops operated with
little or no attempt at concealment. In the following year,

when the Irish parliament introduced new measures against the Catholic clergy, the papal nuncio was reasonably confident that the matter would be forgotten as soon as parliament dissolved. The events of 1743—44, when Britain was at war with France and a Jacobite invasion force was believed to be assembling at Dunkirk, were the occasion for a fresh outbreak of searches and arrests, but this was to be the last episode of its kind. In the more serious crisis of the following year, when a Jacobite army had actually appeared in Scotland, and in the many later emergencies and invasion scares, the Irish administration made no moves against Catholic churchmen.[2]

Although by the middle of the eighteenth century the laws against regulars, unregistered priests and Catholic bishops had largely fallen into disuse, individual clergymen nevertheless continued for some time after to receive the occasional sharp reminder that their position was not entirely secure. In 1751 Bishop Sweetman of Ferns was arrested after a suspended priest had reported that he was enlisting men for the armies of a foreign power. Five years later Archbishop O'Reilly of Armagh was arrested along with eighteen of his priests because of allegations that he was engaged in collecting money for the Stuarts. In 1758 the Parish Priest of Rathkeale, Co. Limerick, was declared an outlaw after having been presented to the grand jury by a local landowner to whom he had given offence. Both Sweetman and O'Reilly were released as soon as the authorities were satisfied that the charges against them were unfounded, and the outlawed parish priest was able to return after a decent interval and take up duty in another part of the diocese. But the point had been made to all concerned: a *de facto* toleration was not something to be taken for granted. The Whiteboy disturbances of the early 1760s provoked an even more alarming reaction. Both Catholic priests and prominent Catholic laymen were arrested on charges of complicity in the agitation, and one priest, Nicholas Sheehy of Clogheen, Co. Tipperary, was executed in 1766 on what were almost certainly fabricated charges of murder. In addition, there were threats in both Cork and Tipperary to proceed against the Catholic clergy as a body by reviving the legislation against unregistered priests.[3]

At the beginning of the 1780s, then, the legal standing of

the Irish Catholic Church remained somewhat ambiguous. On the one hand its clergy had enjoyed more than three decades of practical toleration. But at the same time the laws against Catholic ecclesiastics remained on the statute book, and there were fairly recent events to show that these were not to be regarded as entirely a dead letter. In 1776 Archbishop Carpenter of Dublin, writing to a newly appointed papal nuncio, still felt it necessary to warn him to address his letters simply to 'Dr Carpenter', with no reference to an ecclesiastical title. And even in 1800 a request that the Catholic prelates should supply the government with a detailed account of the ecclesiastical establishment in each diocese, in connection with proposals for a state subsidy to the Catholic clergy, gave rise to some disquiet. 'But oh! my honoured Lord,' the administrator of the diocese of Waterford and Lismore exclaimed in a letter to Archbishop Bray of Cashel, 'the number and obvious tendency of the queries proposed appal me in the extreme. *Inimicus homo hoc fecit. . . .* May God protect us from machinations.' Bishop Coppinger of Cloyne and Ross had similar doubts: 'Are we totally beyond the reach of legal animadversion, and even legal penalty, while we give in this detail under our hands? Are we aware of all the possible consequences of such authenticated detail, in the very possible supposition of blasted hope?' He went on to explain that he was taking the precaution of not signing his name to the return which he sent to Bray for transmission to the government. Six years later Coppinger displayed equal concern over the decision of some of his colleagues to co-operate with Edward Newenham in a religious census, a project which he felt might give offence at a time when government had been alarmed by agrarian disturbances in Connacht and by fears of a French invasion.[4]

The sense of insecurity created by the penal laws, then, clearly continued long after the main restrictions on Catholic ecclesiastics had been formally repealed in 1782. However, the point should not be overstated. Fear of giving offence did not, for example, deter Archbishop Butler of Cashel from publishing a pamphlet in 1787 vigorously refuting charges of Catholic disloyalty put forward by Richard Woodward, the Anglican Bishop of Cloyne. By the end of the eighteenth

century, furthermore, anxieties of the kind expressed by
Coppinger were becoming increasingly anachronistic. Not
only was there no longer any real prospect of a return to the
penal code; it was even coming to be accepted that Catholic
churchmen had a certain social status in their own right.
The funeral in 1796 of Bishop Egan of Waterford and Lismore
provided a vivid illustration of the new respectability of the
Irish Catholic hierarchy. According to Bishop Moylan of Cork,

> Nothing could surpass the respect paid by all denomina-
> tions of people to the memory of our dear and much-to-
> be-regretted deceased friend. The funeral procession was
> attended by the principal Protestant gentlemen of the
> county, with the mayor and corporation of Clonmel. . . .
> Most of the lawyers then on circuit attended, and the
> judge declared that if he could with propriety quit the
> bench he would attend the funeral of so venerable a
> member of society.[5]

The first half of the nineteenth century saw a steady growth
in the degree of recognition offered to Catholic churchmen
by the Irish establishment. In 1831 Archbishop Murray of
Dublin became a member of the board set up to supervise
the new system of National Schools; in 1844, along with two
other prelates, he was appointed to the newly created Board
of Charitable Bequests; two years later he was offered a seat
on the Irish Privy Council, although he declined to accept. It
is true that when Murray was put forward for membership
of the Royal Dublin Society he was blackballed. But by 1868
even that episode could be triumphantly recalled by Murray's
successor, Paul Cullen, when he was invited to the same Royal
Dublin Society to dine with the Prince and Princess of Wales
and was seated immediately after the royal family: 'The poor
parsons think the world is going upside down when they see
popery in high places.' By 1887 Archbishop Walsh of Dublin
could take it as an affront when invitations to state banquets
were not sent to him as a matter of course, as they had been
(though never accepted) both to his predecessor and to himself in earlier years.[6] It was not only senior church dig-
nitaries, furthermore, who were affected by this change in
status. The ordinary parochial clergyman also found himself

increasingly accepted as a legitimate part of the structures of local power and influence. The extent to which this was so became clear in 1846, when parish priests were included among the *ex officio* members of the relief committees established by the government to deal with the famine crisis.

The new willingness of the authorities in late eighteenth-century Ireland to accord to Catholic churchmen a measure of status and respect, as well as the more tangible gains achieved in the Catholic Relief Acts of 1778, 1782 and 1793, were seen by many contemporaries as evidence of a general decline in religious prejudice and animosity. In 1792 Bishop MacMahon of Killaloe described to his Roman agent the generous subscriptions made by the grand jury of Co. Clare towards a school which he had set up in Ennis, citing this as an example of 'what liberal sentiments at present subsist betwixt Roman Catholics and Protestants'. By the time he wrote, however, events in another part of the country had already begun to make nonsense of all such claims. The first clashes between organised bands of Catholics and Protestants, operating under the names of Defenders and Peep o' Day Boys, occurred in Co. Armagh in 1784. By 1790 the conflict had spilled over into adjoining Ulster counties, and by the end of the decade it would be carried, in differing degrees, to the other three provinces.[7]

The extension to other parts of Ireland of a conflict originally born of circumstances peculiar to certain parts of Ulster has frequently been attributed solely to the short-comings of official policy — to a blind assumption that Catholicism was synonymous with disloyalty, leading to tactics which eventually turned that erroneous equation into fact. But it is difficult to believe that the outcome could have been what it was if the events of the 1790s had not brought to the surface resentments and hostilities which were already present, however deeply buried, in the minds of the Catholic population. Heavy-handed methods of repression, applied by religiously motivated militia-men, cannot by themselves explain how the original creed of the United Irishmen came to be so thoroughly translated into an aggressive Catholic sectarianism. The oath taken by a new recruit to the United Irishmen in Carlow town in May 1798 bound him, not to 'a

brotherhood of affection among Irishmen of every religious
persuasion', but instead 'to be true to the Catholic religion
and to assist the French should they land in this kingdom'.
An almost identical form of words was in use a few months
later in Co. Clare. Even in Dublin city the message of the
United Irishmen was that 'In a couple of months there will
be but one religion, and we will be the owners of the soil.'
Such sentiments were all too readily translated into action.
When the Rev. George Knipe of Co. Meath was murdered
in April 1797, the leader of his attackers 'fired a shot at the
body with a holster pistol, saying there lies the body of a
heretic which I hope to have the nation shortly quelled of
and become republicans'. The episodes of purely sectarian
killing which accompanied the outbreak of rebellion in
Co. Wexford in May–June 1798, including the execution
of 97 Protestants in Wexford town and the burning alive
of others in a barn at Scullabogue, near New Ross, are well
known. In Co. Kildare rebels killed a number of Protestant
non-combatants, while leaving loyalist Catholics unmolested.
Elsewhere too the rebellion, if not marked by actual sectarian
killings, was nevertheless very clearly a Catholic uprising. When
the rebels in Co. Westmeath seized Wilson's Hospital, a
charitable institution a few miles from Mullingar, 'they
turned all the charity boys out of the hospital, telling them
they had it long enough, that it shall be no more taken up
with heretics'. Even in Co. Mayo, where relations between
Catholics and Protestants had been regarded as particularly
good, 'the common people talked much about religion, and
made it very much a religious business, and a party of them
who were brought in for plundering justified themselves as
having attacked only Protestants'.[8]

In Ulster the recurrent sectarian fighting of the 1780s and
1790s continued into the nineteenth century, not only in
rural areas but also in the rapidly growing city of Belfast,
where the death of two men in rioting after a Twelfth of July
parade in 1813 marked the beginning of what was to become
a familiar pattern of violence.[9] Outside Ulster the hostilities
and resentment which had come so violently into the open in
1798 did not die away. A threatening notice in Cashel, Co.
Tipperary, in 1836 linked the demand 'No tithes' to an openly

sectarian message: 'Heretics prepare for death. . . . The day is approaching when we will root the bloody heretics out of the world. . . . Let them prepare to meet the flaming devils.' A notice posted on the door of the Catholic chapel of Moygownagh, Co. Mayo, in the following year, called on Catholics to deal only with traders of the same religion: 'Protestants very wisely always give the preference of their money and bargain to themselves, and why [do] ye not do the same among yourselves, if ye do not do it by fair means, ye must do it by foul means.' Popular songs and ballads from the 1820s to the 1840s were laced with references to the approaching overthrow of the 'heretics' and of 'Luther's generation', and a similar vision of the total destruction of sectarian rivals provided the dominant theme for the widely circulated prophecies of Pastorini and St Colmcille. But without the direct confrontation with an actual adversary which had occurred in the 1790s, and which continued to exist in most parts of Ulster, such sentiments were relegated to the peripheral role of spicing the language of popular protest. Wild tales of priest-led conspiracies and of a planned massacre of Protestants continued to reach Dublin Castle, but responsible observers were generally agreed that the agrarian disturbances of the three southern provinces were concerned solely with the redress of economic and social grievances, and that their targets were chosen on this basis alone.[10]

Outside Ulster, then, although there had been no apparent change in popular attitudes, the first half of the nineteenth century did not see a continuation of the violent sectarianism of the 1790s. What it did see was the installation of religion at the heart of the new forms of popular political activity which emerged during this period. The campaign for Catholic Emancipation mounted between 1823 and 1829 under the leadership of Daniel O'Connell marked a crucial innovation in Irish political life. Whereas earlier efforts to obtain the repeal of the remaining legal restrictions affecting Irish Catholics had been conducted by an elitist pressure group, the Catholic Association of the 1820s sought to obtain its goals by the mobilisation of a much larger section of the Catholic population. In doing so, however, it not only ensured that large numbers of Irish Catholics received their first experience of political activity in connection with a religious issue; it also set an important precedent in its widespread use of the Catholic parish clergy as local organisers and agents. The second major popular agitation of the period, in 1831–38, was over the payment of tithes to the Established Church, an economic grievance but at the same time a religious one. Once again the Catholic clergy took a prominent part in directing and encouraging the agitation. By the time a purely political issue came to the fore, in the Repeal movement of 1840–43, the pattern had been firmly established. Catholic priests and bishops flung themselves wholeheartedly into the campaign, recklessly mingling religious and political appeals. 'The priests of Ireland', a clerical orator declared in Enniscorthy in July 1843, 'have sounded the trumpets for the peaceful struggle — the people shouted — did you not hear them today? ... and down will fall the walls of Saxon Jericho.' The same connection was made by the rank and file of the movement, in terms less sophisticated but no less eloquent:

Since Luther lit the candle we suffered penury
But now it is extinguished in spite of heresy,
We'll have an Irish parliment [*sic*], fresh laws we will
    dictate
Or we'll have satisfaction for the year of ['98].

.   .   .   .   .

Then Luther's generation must take a speedy flight,
And go into Hanover from the lands of sweet delight,
All heretics must cut their sticks and leave this fertile land,
For it was decreed that Harry's breed should fall by the
    old command.

Repeal, of course, had its Protestant supporters, and its leaders sought anxiously to demonstrate that it was not an exclusively Catholic movement. But no amount of pious disavowal, and no handful of prominent exceptions, either in the 1840s or in later decades, were to make the slightest impression on the links which had been established between religious affiliation and political allegiance.[11]

One immediate consequence of these developments was a sharp reversal of the trend towards more friendly relations between Catholics and Protestants of the better classes which had been so much praised by observers in the late eighteenth century. 'The Catholics and Protestants of Carlow', a priest told the French traveller de Tocqueville in 1835, 'avoid seeing and speaking to each other.' A Protestant barrister in Dublin agreed: 'You cannot conceive the distance that holds these two groups apart, especially at the moment. . . . We hardly ever meet each other in society.' In some cases, it was reported, there were not merely Catholic and Protestant inns, but even separate coaches travelling on the same routes, each used exclusively by members of one denomination. This growing religious separation was also reflected in the attitudes of the Catholic clergy. A Westmeath magistrate reported in 1839 that priests no longer dined in the houses of the Protestant gentry, although they had at one time been willing to do so. In 1865 Archbishop Cullen not only boasted that he himself had never dined with a Protestant, but also identified Catholics who did mix socially with Protestants as persons uniformly hostile to the changes which he was attempting to bring about in the Irish Church.[12]

* * *

Pre-famine Ireland has often been described as a peasant society. In so far as the term can be taken as signifying a predominantly rural and agricultural society, this is reasonably accurate: in 1841 seven persons out of every eight lived either in rural areas or in towns of less than 2,000 inhabitants, and almost three-quarters of all families were classified by the census commissioners as dependent either wholly or principally on agriculture. But the term 'peasant', correctly used, implies not merely a predominance of farming occupations, but a particular type of agricultural society. A peasant farm is a holding owned or occupied by a single family and worked by members of that family with little or no outside assistance. In addition, it is generally understood that peasant farmers do not operate on a commercial basis, but use their produce primarily to pay rents, taxes and other levies and to meet the consumption needs of their own families.[13] Applied to the rural Ireland of the late eighteenth and early nineteenth centuries, this description has elements of truth, but it is nevertheless seriously misleading. The problem is not merely that a single label like 'peasant' tends to blur the considerable variations, both in social status and in levels of economic activity, which existed within rural Irish society below the rank of landlord. It has an added disadvantage in that it fails to do justice to the extent to which the members of that society were separated from one another, not merely by differences in wealth or status, but by the relationships of landlord and tenant, employer and employee.

Any attempt to fit the complexities of a real society into a single classification scheme will of necessity be somewhat arbitrary. The outline presented in Table 1 divides the rural population of pre-famine Ireland into three main groups, each of them overlapping with one or both of the others, and all three containing within themselves variations in wealth and status considerably greater than those which separate them from each other. The first of these groups consists of some 450,000 farmers, defined here as occupiers of agricultural holdings who were returned under this label in the census of 1841. This group included a minority of large occupiers: in 1844 there was a total of 17,000 occupiers with holdings of between 100 and 200 acres, 6,000 occupiers of holdings of between 200 and 500 acres, and a further 1,500 occupiers with holdings of more than 500 acres. This was the type of large farming enterprise represented a little later by the holding of the Fogarty family in Co. Limerick, a 200-acre farm equipped with a quarry, a lime-kiln, a sandpit, a turf bog and an eel weir, and employing sufficient workers to require the supervision both of a foreman and a head dairywoman. The great majority of farms, however, were on a much more modest scale: 83 per cent of all farmers occupied holdings of 50 acres or less, and 39 per cent occupied holdings of 15 acres or less. At the same time it would be a mistake to underestimate the resources of even this latter group or the place its members occupied in the hierarchy of rural society. In 1841, it has been pointed out, farms of between 6 and 15 acres possessed, on average, two cows, and there was one horse for almost every holding in this category. In addition, even these smallest farmers were commonly employers of labour. Peadar

Table 1. Social Structure of Rural Ireland, *c.* 1841—45

Farmers	453,000	Above 50 acres	70,000
		15—50 acres	207,000
		15 acres or less	176,000
Smallholders	408,000	Above 5 acres	135,000
		1—5 acres	182,000
		1 acre or less	65,000
		Unclassified joint tenancies	26,000
Cottiers and labourers*	596,000		
Farm servants	104,000		

Source: See Appendix A.
*'Cottier' here applies only to labourers receiving their wage in land. See p. 19n.

Ó Laoghaire, born in Co. Cork in 1839, recalls that his father held 'only the grass of seven cows, and bad land at that', but at the same time mentions elsewhere that the household included a 'servant boy'. The Railway Commission in 1837 confirmed that the occupiers of holdings 'from eight to twelve or fifteen acres' generally employed paid labour, sometimes for a daily wage but more commonly in the form of resident farm servants.[14]

Statistics on the size of agricultural holdings can provide, of course, only a rough guide to the structure of the farming community. The standard of living that could be derived from a holding of a particular size depended on the quality of the land it contained, and also on the use to which that land was put, whether grazing, dairying or tillage. Both the south-east and parts of Ulster contained relatively small farms which, through tillage or a mixture of tillage and livestock, yielded to their occupants a reasonable standard of life. In Tyrone and adjoining counties, it was reported in 1852, 'a holding of twenty, or sixteen, or, in some places, even of twelve or ten acres of fair land at a fair rent, is considered to be a pretty "snug" and secure condition, and would entitle the holder to the designation of "Mister" among his poorer neighbours or his equals, and a more familiar salute from the squire or clergyman of the parish'. In parts of Leinster and Munster, on the other hand, 'a much larger holding would be necessary to raise its occupant to the same grade of comfort and respectability', and a holding of three or four hundred acres in these districts 'would be no more than equivalent to the possession of about sixty acres in crowded and commercial Ulster'.[15]

Below the different grades of farmer came an almost equally large class of smallholders, here taken to be those occupiers of agricultural holdings who were not returned in the census of 1841 as 'farmers'. To some extent, of course, the division is an arbitrary one, with the smallest 'farmers' and the largest 'smallholders' separated, not by differences in social status, but by variations in personal vanity or local linguistic usage. But in the absence of other criteria it supplies a rough indication of the point at which one passes from farmers, however small, to occupiers whose holdings either yielded no more than a bare subsistence or provided only a partial living which had to be supplemented from other sources. Once again figures relating solely to the size of holdings are of only limited value. The small occupiers in Table 1 would have included weavers and other tradesmen whose earnings from sources outside agriculture kept them in a condition superior to that suggested by the size of their holdings alone. During the first half of the nineteenth century, however, domestic spinning and weaving, formerly diffused over a wide area, came to be increasingly concentrated in the north-east, with the result that the proportion of small occupiers who depended solely on the inadequate living provided by their holdings steadily increased. The very smallest occupiers, of course, the 65,000 persons holding plots of one acre or less, cannot have depended on their holdings for more than a small part of their livelihood. At this point the category of smallholder begins to merge into the third major division in Table 1, the cottiers, labourers and farm servants.

The employment of agricultural labour in pre-famine Ireland took three main forms. First there was the hiring of resident farm servants, described in 1837 as 'young men between sixteen and twenty-five years of age, who reside in the family of their employer, and hire themselves out at re-markably low wages, seldom exceeding £1 per quarter, and, in numerous instances, scarcely more than half that sum'. Employment of this kind was clearly a phase passed through by many adolescents and young men in the period between leaving their parents' homes and setting up their own families, either as day labourers, cottiers or small occupiers. A second form of employment was through cottier tenancies, in which a labourer received a cottage and a small plot of ground from a farmer, the rent being set off against work done by the labourer on the farmer's land.* Finally, there was the employ-ment of labourers for a daily wage, ranging in the 1830s from 6d or even lower to 1s, and averaging 8½d. Some agricultural labourers, particularly in the eastern counties, used their wages to purchase food and other consumer goods. In many cases, however, the labourer invested the bulk of his earnings in what was known as conacre, land let for the period necessary to sow and harvest a single crop of potatoes, so that the line between landless labourer and small occupier is once again less clear-cut than might at first appear.[16] The analysis in Table 1 suggests a total of 700,000 agricultural workers employed in these three ways in the early 1840s, of whom just under 600,000 were labourers and just over 100,000 farm servants.

Even this brief outline of agrarian class structure should make clear that rural Ireland in the decades preceding the famine contained not merely numerous gradations in wealth and social status, but more than one type of economy. Both the larger tenant farmer and the landless labourer who used his wages to purchase food and other consumer goods be-longed, in their different ways, to a system of commercial agriculture comparable in character if not in scale to that which had existed in most parts of England since at least the

---

*The term 'cottier' has been the cause of some confusion. In the early nine-teenth century the term was used in different parts of the country to mean three quite different things: (a) the occupant of a smallholding of up to 10 acres; (b) a labourer receiving his wage in land; (c) any occupant of a cabin, without reference to his mode of employment (see *Poor Inquiry* (1835–37), App. H, Pt 2, 4). In this book the term 'cottier' is used exclusively in the second and most distinctive of these senses.

middle of the eighteenth century. By comparison the cottier lived in an almost totally different world, where agriculture was practised at subsistence level and labour services were exchanged directly for land. Between these two extremes came various intermediate stages of involvement in the market economy — the small farmer, for example, paying his rent in money but otherwise supporting himself and his family almost entirely from the produce of his own holding; or the agricultural labourer, exchanging his work for conacre ground, but doing so through the medium of a cash wage. It is this coexistence of radically different ways of life which has led some recent historians to write of pre-famine Ireland as a 'dual economy', with both commercial and subsistence sectors. But to speak of a dualism tends to obscure the extent to which the two sectors overlapped and penetrated each other: even the cottier, trading labour directly for land, calculated his bargain in money terms; even the poorest areas had some retail trade. J. E. Bicheno was perhaps more accurate, in concept if not in his precise terminology, when he characterised Ireland as a peasant society similar to that which existed in many parts of Europe, but one which was being penetrated, progressively but unevenly, by a money economy — 'a country not yet emerged from the ancient territorial relation, and upon which the commercial principle has been grafted with very imperfect success'.[17]

If contemporary observers were wrong in seeing early nineteenth-century Ireland as uniformly backward and impoverished, their concern about its condition and prospects was nevertheless far from misplaced. Rural Ireland in the decades preceding the famine was a society poised on the brink of disaster. At the root of its problems lay a rapid expansion in population, from perhaps 3·6 million in 1772 to 4·7 million in 1791 and to 6·8 million in 1821. A similar increase in numbers had been recorded elsewhere in the British Isles, but in Ireland, unlike England or Scotland, a growing population could not find employment in the new factories of the industrial revolution. Instead it remained in the countryside, steadily swelling the ranks of the rural poor. By the early 1840s the farmers had become a minority group in rural Ireland, outnumbered more than two to one by the small occupiers, the cottiers and the landless labourers (see Table 1). Up to 1815 the strains resulting from this massive increase in numbers, and the resulting shift in the balance of social classes, were partly relieved by two factors. High agricultural prices, and in particular good prices for the products of labour-intensive tillage, permitted the subdivision of holdings to support a larger number of occupiers and also provided employment for increased numbers of labourers and cottiers. In addition, the diffusion of domestic spinning and weaving, not only in Ulster but also in Connacht, north Leinster and parts of Munster, provided an important source of supplementary employment. After 1815, however, the end of the French wars brought a sharp fall in agricultural prices, while the early nineteenth century, as already mentioned, also saw a general decline in domestic textile industry outside the north-east. Population meanwhile continued remorselessly to expand, rising from 6·8 million in 1821 to 7·8 million in 1831 and to 8·2 million in 1841.[18]

These developments of the period after 1815 had disastrous implications for large sections of the rural poor. The fall in agricultural prices meant that many small holdings which had previously yielded an adequate living now provided only a bare subsistence or less, while the decline in domestic industry deprived thousands of families of a major source of income. In these respects, however, the post-1815 depression merely intensified the hardship resulting from a wider problem: the failure of Ireland, outside the north-east corner, to follow other parts of the British Isles in developing new sources of support for a rapidly growing population. What this meant in practice was that Irish agriculture, in spite of a steady growth in output in the period 1815–45, could not provide either the land or the employment required by the constantly growing number of persons who depended on it for a livelihood. By the 1830s the agricultural labourer was generally without work for a substantial part of every year: the Poor Inquiry commissioners calculated in 1836 that agricultural labourers had on average only 135 days of paid employment in each year, with an additional 48 days' work on their holdings for those labourers who held small plots of land, and an additional 14 days on their conacre ground

for those who did not. As the number of labourers continued
to grow, furthermore, it became increasingly difficult for
many of them to find the small amounts of land on which—
either as cottiers or takers of conacre — they grew the potatoes
which fed themselves and their families. Much of the agrarian
violence of the early nineteenth century, as will be seen in a
later chapter, reflected, not the dissatisfaction of farmers
over their rents or conditions of tenure, but rather the
desperation of a rural poor excluded from the land on which
their way of life depended.[19]

These problems were felt in different ways, and to a different extent, in the various economic regions which made
up pre-famine Ireland. Along the western seaboard, where
population growth had been most rapid and where the poor
quality of land had provided little reason to refrain from
subdivision, there were few medium-sized or large farmers
and few landless labourers. Here the crisis was one of small
occupiers cultivating holdings which provided only a bare
living, and conditions came closest to the uniform poverty
sometimes attributed to pre-famine Ireland as a whole. The
north-east, by contrast, was generally regarded as the most
prosperous region of Ireland, a prosperity which — thanks
to the continued presence of domestic industry and to the
absorption of surplus population by the rapidly growing
towns — was shared in even by the small occupier and the
rural labourer. In other parts of the country — in Leinster,
eastern Connacht and most parts of Munster — the population
was divided into a minority of reasonably solvent farmers and
a large group of cottiers, labourers and small occupiers whose
condition, though somewhat better in the eastern counties
than elsewhere, was generally poor and in many cases bordered
permanently on the desperate.[20]

The remainder of the story is well known. In 1845 and in
subsequent years the potato crop, the staple diet of the rural
poor, was attacked by a destructive fungus. Repeatedly during
the previous thirty years, in 1817, in 1821—22 and more than
once in the 1830s, localised food shortages following failures
in the potato crop had demonstrated just how precarious was
the margin which separated large sections of the population
from disaster. But the crisis of the 1840s reduced all that had

gone before to comparative insignificance. By 1851 a total of one million people had died of starvation or fever, and a further million had emigrated to Britain or America. The loss of population was concentrated, as one might expect, among the poorer sections of the rural population. Precise statistics, for reasons already discussed, are impossible to provide, but a rough calculation suggests that between 1845 and 1851 the total number of persons below the rank of farmer — that is, smallholders, cottiers, landless labourers and farm servants — was reduced by something like one-third.[21] By contrast the farming class, apart from its poorest segment, escaped largely untouched: between 1845 and 1851, in fact, the number of holdings of more than 15 acres actually increased slightly, from 277,000 to 290,000. The resulting shift in the balance of social classes was reinforced in the decades that followed, as continued emigration further reduced the numbers of the rural poor. Whereas in 1845 farmers had been outnumbered more than two to one by poorer sections of the rural population, by 1881 the two groups were roughly equal.*

Strict chronological divisions, in social history at least, can rarely be entirely satisfactory. In many respects, as is often pointed out, the effect of the famine was merely to precipitate changes which would have taken place even without it, or to accelerate developments which had already begun before 1845. There can be no doubt, equally, that a detailed study of the 1850s and 1860s would reveal much continuity with what had gone before, as well as much change. At the same time the famine, initiating as it did a major change in the class structure of rural Ireland, remains a natural turning-point for many subjects of inquiry, including an investigation of the Irish Catholic Church and its place in Irish society. Both in the resources with which they had to work and in the problems they confronted, the Catholic clergy of the second half of the nineteenth century were to find themselves in a world very different to that of their pre-famine counterparts.

*The census returned a total of 198,579 agricultural labourers and 94,737 indoor farm servants, but added that most of the 134,085 persons returned as general labourers could be assumed also to be employed in agriculture. The number of occupiers of less than 5 acres returned in 1881 was 67,071, and the number of farmers 382,342. (See *Cen. 1881, Pt II,* 22, 112, 117.)

2

The Catholic Church

1. *The Laity*

In the eighteenth and early nineteenth centuries considerable time and ingenuity were devoted to the problem of discovering, from incomplete and dubious statistics, the relative numbers of Catholics and Protestants in Ireland. Attempts at an official census of religious affiliations were made in 1732–33 and in 1766, while various individuals attempted private computations. The purpose behind such exercises was in most cases openly polemical, and discussion proceeded along predictable party lines. A Cork priest, writing in 1807, was confident that a private census then being planned 'will prove that, instead of two to one, *we* shall be found in the exalted situation of eight to one'. On the other hand John Leslie Foster, an opponent of Catholic Emancipation, used figures relating to school attendance to calculate in 1825 that the proportion of Catholics was just over 70 per cent and so remained 'within a very minute fraction the same as is suggested by Sir William Petty to have been the case in 1676'.[1]

In spite of all this debate, however, and despite so many rival exercises in denominational arithmetic, the changes which took place during the eighteenth and nineteenth centuries in the relative numbers of Catholics and Protestants were of minor significance. In the period before the famine, when the population as a whole was expanding rapidly, Catholic numbers increased somewhat more quickly than those of other denominations. But the change in their share of total population was a gradual one, from perhaps three-quarters in 1732–33 to 81 per cent in 1834. During the long period of declining population which began in the

1840s it was the turn of Catholic numbers to fall more rapidly than those of other denominations. Between 1834 and 1861 the number of Catholics in Ireland declined by 30 per cent, compared with 19 per cent among Anglicans and Presbyterians. But the change in relative numbers was once again a gradual one, with the Catholic share of total population falling from 81 per cent in 1834 to just under 78 per cent in 1861 and to 74 per cent by 1911. At all times, of course, the relative strength of the different denominations varied from region to region, with Catholics least numerous in the north-east and most numerous in the south and west. In 1834 Catholics made up a minority of the population in three Ulster dioceses, Down, Connor and Dromore, and accounted for roughly half the population in Ulster as a whole. In the ecclesiastical province of Dublin, on the other hand, Catholics made up 85 per cent of total population, while in Cashel and Tuam they made up 96 per cent in each case.[2]

Of greater importance to a discussion of the character and situation of the Irish Catholic Church in this period than the number of its adherents is the social composition of the Catholic laity. Catholics were represented, though not in equal numbers, in all the major social groups which made up the Irish population in the eighteenth and early nineteenth centuries. At the top of the social scale there was a small Catholic landowning nobility and gentry. In the course of the seventeenth century successive confiscations and forfeitures had reduced the amount of land owned by Catholics from an estimated 59 per cent in 1641 to 22 per cent in 1688 and to 14 per cent by 1703. This proportion was further reduced during the eighteenth century as a result of the restrictions imposed on the acquisition, and still more the inheritance, of land by Catholics. By 1776 Arthur Young estimated the amount of land in Catholic hands at only five per cent of the total. The Catholic families who kept their estates intact during this century did so through the conformity of individual members to the Established Church, through being lucky enough to produce only one male heir in each generation, or through some other stratagem or good fortune. In 1777 the Catholic landed class still included seven peers: the Earls of Fingall and Kenmare, Viscounts Dillon, Gormanston and Netterville, Lord Caher and Lord Trimleston. By 1809 the Dillon and Caher titles had passed to Protestants, but their places had been filled by two other titles, ffrench and Southwell, whose latest holders were Catholics although their predecessors had been nominal Protestants while the penal laws remained in force. The remainder of the Catholic landowners were gentry like the Bellews of Co. Louth, the Butlers of Co. Kilkenny and the Blakes, Kirwans and Brownes of Galway and Mayo. Among these Catholic landed proprietors there were two, Kenmare and Caher, who possessed substantial estates. In 1780 the income of the former was reported to be £8,000 a year, and the income of the latter £6,000. By 1814 the gross rental of the Kenmare estates in Kerry and elsewhere was over £21,000, and by 1850 over £28,000, while in 1812 it was estimated that the Caher estates in Co. Tipperary (by then, as we have seen, no longer in Catholic hands) could be relet for £36,000. The incomes of other Catholic landowners were more modest. A report in 1780 put the annual income of the Butlers of Ballyragget, Co. Kilkenny, at £3,000, that of Lord Fingall in Co. Meath at £2,500, and those of Gormanston and Trimleston at £4,000 each. In 1812, according to Edward Wakefield, the ten Catholic landed proprietors in Co. Galway had incomes ranging from £2,000 to £7,000 per annum.[3]

Ownership of land was, for historical and political reasons, a major concern of contemporaries. But it would be wrong, in a discussion of wealth and social structure, to concentrate too narrowly on this aspect. For landed wealth, as Wakefield pointed out in 1812, was not solely a matter of outright ownership of land. There was also the important category of leasehold interest, where land was leased for a fixed term at a rent lower than its current letting value, as well as the substantial amounts of capital which could be represented by livestock. Next to the Catholic landowning class, therefore, one must set the other levels of rural property ownership, from the largest graziers and holders of profitable leases, whose fortunes might equal or exceed those of the lesser gentry, down to the smallest grades of farmer, separated from the propertyless poor only by the possession of minimal capital resources. When property in the form of leasehold and livestock was taken into account, Wakefield suggested, the amount of personal property owned by Catholics might be found to exceed half the total. The figure is impossible to verify, and Wakefield, as a supporter of Catholic Emancipation, may well have been tempted to exaggerate the extent of Catholic wealth. But at least he was correct in emphasising that the Catholic share of landed property should not be seen solely in terms of the five per cent of outright ownership suggested by Arthur Young.[4]

The other group within the Catholic laity possessing substantial wealth was the commercial and professional middle class. The limits of this group are impossible to define exactly, ranging as it did from extremely rich merchants, like the Dublin sugar baker and distiller, Edward Byrne, who at the time of his death in the early nineteenth century was reputed to be worth £400,000, to the point where the world of the lower middle classes merged imperceptibly with that of the shopkeeper, the tradesman and the skilled worker. Throughout the eighteenth and early nineteenth centuries the extent of Catholic mercantile wealth was a subject of constant comment, with Catholics using it to support their claims for political representation, and Protestants to demonstrate the need for new penal enactments. In Kilkenny city, a local Catholic maintained in 1825, the capital 'is almost exclusively Catholic. . . . All the heavy business, distilleries, breweries, and so on, are Catholic, with the exception of one flour mill,' and similar claims were made for other towns. Recent research, however, has established that Catholics were in fact under-represented in most sections of the commercial middle class. In Dublin around 1780 they made up about three-eighths of all merchants, in Cork and Waterford in the 1820s little more than one-third. Catholics were also under-represented in the professions. In 1861, the first year for which statistics on occupation and religion become available, Catholics made up only 32 per cent of physicians and surgeons, 34 per cent of barristers, attorneys and solicitors, 29 per cent of civil engineers, and 31 per cent of architects. But under-representation should not be confused with exclusion. A one-third share or thereabouts in commercial and professional life, however low in relation to the size of the Catholic population, amounted to a far from negligible proportion of the country's middle-class wealth.[5]

Below the possessors of urban and rural property came what for want of a better term must be described as a lower class. The classification is once again a somewhat arbitrary one, threatening to blur or obliterate distinctions as important as those it emphasises. The circumstances and status of the tradesman or the occupier of a small agricultural holding, for example, were very different to those of the unskilled worker or the landless labourer. But all four were linked by the fact that they possessed little or no property, so that the resources which separated them were both slender and precarious. The superiority of the tradesman was easily wiped out by illness or unemployment, that of the small-holder by losses of crops or livestock. This section of the population contained both the greatest number and the highest proportion of Catholics, and the proportion increased as one moved down the social scale. Thus in 1861 98 per cent of both agricultural and general labourers in the three southern provinces were Catholics. In Ulster, where Catholics made up only half the population, there was a more substantial Protestant lower class, but it was generally agreed that the Catholics of the province were the least prosperous section of the population, concentrated among labourers, cottiers and smallholders in the countryside and among unskilled workers in the towns. The preponderance of Catholics at the bottom of the social scale in all parts of the country was also revealed in the cross-tabulation of religion and literacy provided in the census of 1861. Of the 39 per cent of total population returned as unable to read or write, 92 per cent were Catholics.[6]

The Catholic population of the eighteenth and early nineteenth centuries, then, must be seen as a pyramid, similar in its basic structure to the somewhat larger pyramid made up by the population as a whole, but narrower at the top and broader at the base. This difference in the outline of the two pyramids, the under-representation of Catholics in the middle and upper levels of society and their increasing over-representation as one approaches the propertyless poor

at the bottom of the social scale, should not be permitted
to conceal the fact that there was a Catholic rich, and a
substantial Catholic middle class, as well as a Catholic poor.
What is true, however, is that the rapid growth in population
during the late eighteenth and early nineteenth centuries,
concentrated as it was at the bottom of the social scale,[7]
inevitably meant a growth in the number of Catholic poor
relative to more affluent sections of the Catholic population.
If, therefore, the decades preceding the famine saw mounting pressure on the resources of the Irish Catholic Church,
the explanation is to be found in this growth in the proportion of its adherents who could contribute little or
nothing to the support of a religious establishment, not in
a condition of overall poverty engulfing the entire Catholic
population.

These social divisions within the Catholic laity of the
eighteenth and early nineteenth centuries did not exist
solely on paper or in the disembodied categories of an
analysis of social structure. No matter what aspect of the
history of the period one chooses to examine, from age at
marriage to religious beliefs and practices or political development, it is necessary to separate the experiences and attitudes
of different social groups. Neither can we overlook the extent
to which the Catholics of this period were themselves conscious
of these social divisions. Thus Wakefield observed in 1812
that the Catholic landed gentry and aristocracy seldom
associated with those Catholics who since 1782 had purchased land with money acquired in trade or as graziers
and middlemen. It is true that Wakefield also suggested that
these old Catholic proprietors 'possess a very peculiar influence over the common people, which is not enjoyed by
Protestants of the same rank'. But such deference had its
limits. It did not, for example, protect Catholic landowners
like the Butlers of Ballyragget from the attentions of the
Whiteboys and other agrarian secret societies. When a group
of Catholic gentry in Clonoulty, Co. Tipperary, addressed
an appeal to the farmers of the area in 1835, seeking their
assistance in resisting demands for tithes, they made no
attempt to appeal to vertical ties based on a common religious
allegiance. Instead, after complaining that the authorities

had realised 'that there is no strong union, no patriotic, no faithful fellow-feeling, between the farmers and those above them in society', they appealed to simple self-interest, warning the farmers that their immunity from the process-servers would continue only until the more respectable Catholics had been dealt with. Similar social divisions and conflicts of interest existed lower down the social scale, in the disputes between farmers on the one hand and cottiers and labourers on the other which accounted for a substantial part of the agrarian violence of this period. The existence of such divisions is easily overlooked in view of the remarkable success of the campaigns for Catholic Emancipation and Repeal in uniting different sections of the Catholic population behind a common political goal. But even here social divisions emerged from time to time – notably in the secession of the gentry from the Catholic Committee in 1791 – and it remains doubtful how far down the social scale either movement really penetrated.[8]

But all these disputes revolved around matters of politics or economics. Religious affairs, it might be suggested, would have been conducted in a different spirit. If so, however, the abandonment of social distinctions found remarkably little expression in the external arrangements of Catholic public worship. A respectably dressed traveller, visiting a chapel in Cashel in 1777, found that 'the people made way for me, and some of them offered to conduct me to where the *quality* sat'. His experience was not unique. In both urban and rural areas during this period it was common for Catholic churches to have private seating reserved for the more respectable members of the congregation. In some cases this seating was erected by the church authorities themselves, then sold to members of the congregation to raise funds for the cost of building and maintaining the chapel. In others prosperous parishioners were permitted to co-operate in erecting a gallery at their own expense, in which they would then have seats reserved for themselves and their families. Nor was it only the 'quality', the Catholic gentry and middle classes, who were set off in this way from the more plebeian sections of the congregation. When the vicar general of the diocese of Cashel discussed the erection of a gallery in a new chapel in 1808, it was the 'decent farmers' of the area whom he assumed would come together to build it. The family of Mary Fogarty, prosperous farmers in Co. Limerick in the 1860s and 1870s, held the two front pews on each side of the local chapel, close to the steps of the altar.[9]

This institutional recognition of social distinctions was a matter of considerable importance to those involved. In 1833 one bishop, Michael Blake of Dromore, attempted to do away with what he regarded as 'the abuse of having purchased family seats in the church', proposing instead that the seats to be erected in the new chapel in Lurgan should be paid for by being made available to the first-comers each Sunday at a charge of a halfpenny a time. But when the would-be purchasers of family seats threatened that they would in that case stay away from services altogether, he was forced to capitulate. In other cases too the issue of private seating gave rise to bitter disputes: in one Co. Waterford parish in the early nineteenth century an attempt by a newcomer to the district to take a seat in the most select of the three galleries in the parish chapel is reported to have given rise to bloodshed within the chapel walls. Such episodes, and indeed the whole issue of private seating in Catholic chapels, provide further illustrations of the extent to which a consciousness of social distinctions ran through all levels of Irish society in this period. They also make clear that there was no question of those distinctions being left behind when the congregation passed through the doors of the parish church.[10]

2. *The Clergy*

The formal administrative structure of the Catholic Church in this period was fairly simple. Ireland was divided into twenty-six dioceses, grouped into the four ecclesiastical provinces of Armagh, Dublin, Cashel and Tuam. Each diocese was administered by a bishop, assisted by one or more vicars general or vicars forane. In some cases there was also a diocesan chapter, drawn from the parish clergy, but the only significant power possessed by this body was the election of a vicar capitular to administer a vacant diocese until a new bishop could be appointed. In theory the archbishop who ruled the principal diocese within each province had powers of supervision over the other bishops of that province. In practice, however, this counted for very little. Disputes which could not be settled within a diocese almost invariably ended up being referred to Rome, even if the parties first went through the motions of an appeal to the archbishop. During the nineteenth century the Irish hierarchy gradually evolved procedures for consultation and joint action in matters of common concern. But the individual bishop within his own diocese remained almost entirely independent of his colleagues, answerable only to Rome for his conduct of affairs.

For most purposes, then, the Catholic clergy of the eighteenth and early nineteenth centuries can be seen as a body of parish clergy acting under the direction of bishops. This section will be concerned with some fairly concrete questions concerning that parish clergy: their numbers in relation to the population they had to serve, the backgrounds from which they were drawn, the training they received, and the standard of living and social status they enjoyed. After this a further section will look at some wider issues concerning the state of internal discipline within the Irish Church and its effectiveness as an organisation.

* * *

The lower ranks of the Catholic clergy in this period were made up of two groups: the seculars, who acted as parish priests and curates, and the regulars, who were theoretically dedicated to a communal life under a specific religious discipline, but who in practice undertook a wide range of parochial duties, either by serving as parish priests or curates or by acting as auxiliaries to the parochial clergy of the district in which they lived. In 1731 an incomplete return made to the Irish House of Lords suggested that there were 1,445 priests and curates serving in Ireland; the number of regulars at this time is not known, but it probably amounted to at least 700 monks and friars. It was frequently maintained in the first half of the eighteenth century that this was a

Table 2. The Catholic Clergy, 1731–1871

Date	Number of priests (parish priests and curates)	Catholic population	Number of Catholics for each parish priest or curate
1731	1,445	2,293,680	1,587
1800	1,614	4,320,000	2,676
1840	2,183	6,540,000	2,996
1871	2,655	4,141,933	1,560

Source: See Appendices B and C.

greater number of clerics than the population could support. After 1750, however, such criticisms gave way to the opposite complaint — that the number of priests was too low. By 1800 Catholic bishops in all parts of the country were reporting that the number of clergymen available to them was totally inadequate to their needs. That their complaints were not unfounded can be seen from the figures in Table 2. Between 1731 and 1800 the number of priests serving in Ireland increased by only 12 per cent, compared with an 88 per cent increase in population. Between 1800 and 1840 a 35 per cent increase in clerical numbers still failed to keep pace with a 51 per cent increase in population. As a result, the number of Catholics for each parish priest and curate increased from 1,587 in 1731 to 2,676 in 1800 and to almost 3,000 in 1840. Neither was it possible to look for increased support to the regular clergy. By 1800, owing mainly to restrictions imposed on the reception of novices in Irish religious orders, the number of regulars had declined to 400, and it does not appear to have increased substantially in the decades that followed.[11] The result was a constant shortage of clergymen to administer what was, as one bishop of the period pointed out, 'a very ritual' — and therefore very labour-intensive — religion.[12]

The main reason for the failure of clerical numbers to keep pace with rising population was the inability of the Irish Church to provide facilities for the education of a sufficient number of priests. The Irish bishops at the beginning of the nineteenth century blamed their problems on the closure of the continental colleges at which priests had formerly been educated and the failure of the newly founded Maynooth to replace them. The continental colleges, Archbishop Troy maintained in 1800, had between them supported more than 400 students, while Maynooth had only half that number.[13] In fact clerical numbers had probably begun to lag behind an expanding population while the continental colleges were still in operation.[14] At the same time the shortage of priests in the early years of the nineteenth century appears to have been particularly severe. 'Some of our prelates', the President of Maynooth reported in 1806, 'are obliged to ordain persons without any ecclesiastical education, and occasionally to employ them in the functions of the ministry, while other prelates are struggling to give a very mutilated education to many whom the wants of their districts oblige them to employ.' Owing to 'the imperious demand of clergymen', he added, the course of studies at Maynooth was a restricted one, 'and many are called away before that confined course is completed'. After 1815 the supply of new priests improved, as the continental colleges reopened, although on a smaller scale than in the eighteenth century, and as facilities in Ireland were expanded. By 1826 there were 391 students attending Maynooth, about 120 in other seminaries in Ireland, and about 140 on the continent. By 1840 the total number of clerical students at home and abroad was probably between 700 and 800. But an increase from more than 400 students in the 1780s to 800 or less in 1840 would not even have managed to keep pace with the doubling of population over the same period, much less provide the basis for an improvement in the ratio of priests to people.[15]

Limited facilities for a clerical education were not the only restriction on the supply of Catholic priests. Bishops also attributed their problems to the inability of the Catholic population to support a greater number of clergymen.[16] A growing population, all things else being equal, should have been able to provide sufficient extra revenue to sustain a proportionate increase in the number of priests. But in fact, as was pointed out in the preceding section, the increase in population was concentrated among those groups which could contribute little or nothing to the support of a church establishment. In this situation an improvement in the ratio of priests to people could have been achieved only by one of two methods: by increasing the share of a declining Catholic *per capita* income which went to the Church, or by reducing the incomes of the Catholic clergy. Neither alternative was very realistic. Even under existing conditions, with the number of priests relative to population declining steadily, the financial demands of the Catholic clergy gave rise to recurrent outbreaks of popular anticlericalism, while clerical incomes at the beginning of the nineteenth century were already fairly modest. Even if the Irish Church had been able to train enough priests to restore the manning levels of the early eighteenth century, therefore, it is difficult to see how the extra personnel could have been supported once ordained.

While the shortage of clergymen affected all parts of the country, its effects were more severely felt in some areas than in others. In 1834—35, the only year for which figures are available relating to individual dioceses, the number of Catholics for each parish priest or curate ranged from 1,941 in the diocese of Ferns to 4,199 in the diocese of Tuam. The shortage of priests was most acute in the dioceses of the north-west, west and south-west, where the rate of population growth was faster than in other regions, while at the same time a largely impoverished population were unable to support even the same inadequate rise in clerical numbers which was achieved elsewhere (see Table 3).

The social origins of Irish Catholic priests were a matter of considerable discussion among contemporaries, particularly in the first half of the nineteenth century. The Catholic clergy, it was generally agreed by observers of otherwise very different views, were taken 'from the inferior and uneducated classes', 'from a very low class', 'generally speaking from the lower orders'. One reason which was suggested for this lowly social status was the poor and uncertain income generally enjoyed by Irish Catholic clergymen, along with the degrad-

Table 3. The Supply of Priests to Irish Dioceses, 1800–40

Diocese	Number of parish priests and curates (% increase since 1800 in parentheses)			Number of Catholics per priest, 1834–35
	1800	1835	1840	
Armagh	71	114(60%)	115(62%)	2,715
Derry	45	80(78%)	73(62%)	2,458
Clogher	52	87(67%)	85(63%)	2,991
Raphoe	34	43(26%)	43(26%)	3,381
Down & Connor	45	58(29%)	47(4%)	2,656
Kilmore	52	80(54%)	81(56%)	3,007
Ardagh & Clonmacnoise	52	84(61%)	83(60%)	2,322
Meath	105	125(19%)	129(23%)	3,020
Dromore	21	26(24%)	34(62%)	2,934
Armagh province	477	697(46%)	690(45%)	2,805
Dublin	123	152(23%)	154(25%)	2,572
Kildare & Leighlin	85	108(27%)	110(29%)	2,685
Ossory	58	85(46%)	80(38%)	2,469
Ferns	60	89(48%)	92(53%)	1,941
Dublin province	326	434(33%)	436(34%)	2,451
Cashel & Emly	81	108(33%)	108(33%)	2,747
Cork	n.a.	73(n.a.)	72(n.a.)	4,164
Killaloe	n.a.	122(n.a.)	116(n.a.)	2,947
Kerry	75	78(4%)	81(8%)	3,809
Limerick	52	97(86%)	96(85%)	2,539
Waterford & Lismore	66	89(35%)	102(55%)	2,844
Cloyne & Ross	83	121(46%)	130(57%)	3,608
Cashel province	n.a.	688(n.a.)	705(n.a.)	3,188
Tuam	100	98(−2%)	115(15%)	4,199
Clonfert	34	33(−3%)	37(9%)	3,608
Achonry	32	37(16%)	39(22%)	2,941
Elphin	80	84(5%)	74(−8%)	3,688
Galway	17	24(41%)	22(29%)	2,354
Kilfenora & Kilmacduagh	22	24(9%)	28(27%)	3,402
Killala	29	33(14%)	37(28%)	4,133
Tuam province	314	333(6%)	352(12%)	3,675
Ireland	n.a.	2,152(n.a.)	2,183(n.a.)	2,991

Source: See Appendices B and C.

ing system of 'ecclesiastical beggary' implied by their dependence on supposedly voluntary offerings. More frequently, however, the promotion to the priesthood of such humble persons was blamed on the existence of a seminary at Maynooth. Before the foundation of this college, it was argued, the cost of travelling to and attending a university in France, Spain or the Low Countries had ensured that the Catholic clergy had been persons of respectable backgrounds. The expenses involved in an education at Maynooth, on the other hand, could 'form no obstacle to the pretensions of the lower orders', whose great ambition was to have a son ordained to the priesthood.[17]

Comments of this kind were, not surprisingly, rejected by supporters of the college. 'I conceive my parents', one student testified in 1826, 'to belong to that state of life which we call the middle class of society; and with regard to the generality of the students at Maynooth, it is my opinion that their parents belong to the same order of persons.' By 'the middle class of society', he explained, he meant those persons, both in commerce and in agriculture, 'who can live independently and who, perhaps, could provide for their children a situation that could be more lucrative than the priesthood'. A Dublin priest, educated at the college between 1848 and 1853, reported that his fellow-students had been 'the sons of persons in business and trade in the cities and provincial towns, and the sons of the comfortable, middle and humble farmers in the country'. Bartholomew Crotty, the president of the college, took a similar view in 1826: 'Our students are generally the sons of farmers, who must be comfortable in order to meet the expenses I have already mentioned; of tradesmen, shopkeepers; and not a very small proportion of them are the children of opulent merchants and rich farmers and graziers.' Other comments, not arising out of the debate over Maynooth, suggested a similar picture. Bishop Power of Waterford and Lismore, writing in 1808, maintained that 'The majority of our priests are the sons of honest farmers . . . generally of the better sort of farmers.' And a young Catholic interviewed by the French traveller de Tocqueville in 1835 lamented that the Catholic clergy were not the sons of gentlemen, but rather 'of large tenant farmers', adding that 'We call a man a large farmer if he cultivates 150 acres.'[18]

Those who argued against the image of a student body drawn exclusively from the lowest levels of society had in general a vested interest in doing so. At the same time they were able to support their claims by pointing to the far from insignificant expenses involved in a Maynooth education. In 1806 Andrew Dunn, then president of the college, estimated that attendance there, exclusive of fees, would cost £20 per annum, to which had to be added an initial expenditure of £20 on furniture. In addition, he pointed out, the student paid for in this way would normally be only one of four or five children for whom some provision had to be made. Crotty, twenty years later, estimated the normal expenses of a student in his first year at college, again exclusive of fees, at £50 — made up of a deposit of £8, £17 for clothes and travel to the college, £10 for furniture and college dress, £12 for washing and repair of clothes, and £4 for books — and at a minimum of £12 for every subsequent year. Both Dunn and Crotty also drew attention to the expenses involved in educating a boy to the standard required for admission to Maynooth and in supporting him until he reached the age of eighteen or twenty. Education to the required standard, Crotty believed, would normally require three years' attendance at a school teaching Greek and Latin. This involved not only the payment of fees to the school (normally at the rate of one guinea a quarter), but also the cost of board and lodging for the pupil in cases where, as frequently happened, there was no suitable school of this kind near his home. Preliminary education was also important in securing a bishop's nomination to a place in the college, so that students who could afford to pay for the best tuition available enjoyed a definite advantage. When Peadar Ó Laoghaire, son of a small farmer from Co. Cork, sat the examination through which such places were allocated in his diocese, his rivals were boys who had boarded in the diocesan seminary, paying £30 a year to do so, and receiving extra tuition not given to pupils like Ó Laoghaire who attended less expensively as day boys.[19]

The expenses outlined by Dunn and Crotty were exclusive of college fees. Critics of Maynooth in the early nineteenth century were not correct in suggesting that the college provided aspiring priests with the necessary education free of charge. As well as students maintained without charge 'on the establishment', there were 'pensioners' who paid a sum of 20 guineas a year for their maintenance; in 1826 the number of pensioners was 110, compared with 250 on the establishment. The two categories, furthermore, were not mutually exclusive. About half of the students admitted to the college entered as pensioners and continued to pay fees for one, two or three years, although relatively few had to pay for their maintenance throughout their career in the college. In other cases places on the establishment were divided between two students, who were then classified as 'half-pensioners'.[20]

The most direct evidence on the social status of the students educated at Maynooth is that provided in a return drawn up in 1808 by the trustees of the college, in which they showed the occupation of the fathers of all 205 students then in the college. The results can be summarised briefly:

(A) 11 graziers, 148 farmers (total 159)
(B) 7 merchants, 2 flour factors, a corn factor, a linen manufacturer, an architect, a clothier, a ship's captain, a land surveyor, a land agent, a clerk of coalmines, a collector of taxes (total 18)
(C) 10 grocers, 2 innkeepers, an apothecary (total 13)
(D) An ironmonger, a glover, a tallow chandler, a chandler, a wine cooper, a dyer, a maltster, a truss-maker, a ship's carpenter, a house carpenter, a shoe- and boot-maker, 2 tanners, a nurseryman, a baker (total 15)[21]

By far the most common occupation listed in the return is 'farmer', a term which could be made to cover such variations in income and social status that it can tell us little about the background of the students concerned. The occupations of the 46 fathers not involved in farming or grazing, however, are more revealing. The picture they suggest is of a student body whose origins ranged from the level of the tradesman and shopkeeper up to that of the lower professions and the small-scale business, with the distribution weighted in favour of the lower end of the scale. It is easy to see how students drawn from such backgrounds might have appeared to many contemporaries to be of humble origins. Certainly it would be misleading to refer without qualification, like one of the Maynooth students quoted above, to 'the middle class of society'. But it is even more misleading to refer simply to a 'low' social class. A clear superiority of both income and social status separated even the fourth of the groups set out above from the real lower orders of the towns and cities, just as it did the farmer from the smallholders, cottiers and labourers of the countryside. Both the trustees' return and an account of the expenses involved in a Maynooth education suggest that the majority of students at the college must have been the sons of men who, in the context of their own community, were persons of some substance. The contrary observations of contemporaries must be seen as the result, partly of bias, and partly of a failure to appreciate that the social gradations of Irish society did not end with the simple distinction between gentlemen and others.

There are also some grounds for questioning the other recurring feature of contemporary comment on the social origins of Irish priests, the contrast which was alleged to exist between those educated at Maynooth and those educated at seminaries on the continent. The cost of travelling to a college in France, Italy or Portugal was clearly a major item to add to a student's total expenses. At the same time the difference in cost between a Maynooth and a continental education should not be exaggerated. In 1840 the total charge for attendance at the Irish College in Rome, including both tuition and maintenance, was £25 a year, while prospective students were informed that £25 was sufficient for travelling expenses from Ireland to Rome. There were also other mitigating circumstances. Some of the burses set up for the support of students at the continental seminaries included an allowance for travel, which could be forwarded to Ireland, while in other cases financial help was provided by the bishop. Students might also be helped on their way by contributions from relatives and neighbours. A newspaper account in 1774 describes a 'priest's wedding' in Co. Down: 'What they call a priest's wedding is when any young man intends going into orders, he gives an entertainment and every one of the company gives money to enable him to prepare himself for his church.' Once he had arrived at his college, a student might be supported by one of the burses that had been set up by benefactors for this purpose, or by funds provided by the colleges themselves. The Irish College in Lisbon, for example, offered its vacant places to each Irish diocese in rotation, charging each student only what he could afford to pay. In addition, students, particularly in the first half of the eighteenth century, were frequently ordained before leaving Ireland, so that they could support themselves by the fees they received for celebrating masses. One report, apparently drawn up for the information of the government in the first decade of the nineteenth century, suggests that out of a total of 476 clerical students educated on the continent before the French Revolution, 168 were supported by foundations established for that purpose, and 260 were ordained priests who could support themselves by the exercise of their clerical functions. These different types of assistance appear to have made it possible for young men of limited personal resources to obtain a clerical education. In at least one case a student who had attended the Irish College in Paris with the assistance of a burse, but who was forced to return to Ireland after the outbreak of the revolution, was unable to provide the money needed to continue his training at Maynooth.[22]

These particulars suggest that contemporary observers exaggerated the difference in cost between a clerical education on the continent and that which was available at home, and with it the contrast in the type of person who could aspire to each form of training. Comments on the humble social origins of the Catholic clergy, it should be noted, did not begin with the foundation of Maynooth. Already in 1788 the *Dublin Evening Post* could write of the 'couple-beggar' Patrick Fay, whose parents 'were in poor circumstances in the county Meath, and actuated by a vanity which usually possessed the lower class of people [the time referred to is the 1740s or 1750s] . . . had their son educated for a Romish clergyman'. In 1806, when the total number of men ordained from Maynooth would have been about 250, a priest in Co. Cork was lamenting that the Catholic clergy 'spring from the inferior orders of society'. One strongly anti-Catholic writer in 1809 maintained that the social origins of Catholic priests

had actually improved over the previous thirty or forty years
in parallel with the increasing prestige and wealth of the Irish
Catholic Church. Such comments make it easier to accept the
opinion of Daniel O'Connell in 1825. The Maynooth priests,
he believed, were 'most of them the sons of very low persons',
but he went on to explain that he did not intend to suggest a
contrast between them and the priests educated abroad: 'The
former were taken from the same, or nearly the same class; I
should think perhaps a little superior; but the difference not
very great, and by no means for any public purpose could I
say it would be essential.'[23]

When applied to the Catholic clergy as a whole, then, contemporary comments on the increasingly humble social origins
of the Irish priest must be treated with caution. This is not to
say that they were entirely without foundation. Contemporaries may have been encouraged to think along these lines by
two quite genuine developments, each affecting a minority
group within the clerical body. In the first place, even if the
social origins of the average priest had not altered significantly, there may have been a decline in the number of persons
recruited from the most affluent sections of the Catholic
population. Respectable Catholics, it was reported in the mid-
nineteenth century, preferred to send their sons into the more
socially prestigious religious orders rather than the secular
clergy.[24] In addition, there is some indication that by the
early nineteenth century individuals drawn from the Catholic
upper classes were less likely to achieve prominence within
the Church, as internal reform and a changing social and
political climate combined to diminish the weight given to
birth as a qualification for ecclesiastical promotion. A detailed
statistical analysis would be necessary before one could speak
with certainty, but the churchmen of gentry or aristocratic
backgrounds who figured prominently in the eighteenth-
century hierarchy, men like Archbishop Blake of Armagh,
Lord Dunboyne, Bishop of Cork, or the three successive
Butler Archbishops of Cashel, do not appear to have had
many counterparts after 1800. So contemporaries who
lamented the low social origins of the Catholic clergy of the
early nineteenth century may have been influenced by a
genuine decline either in the number or in the prominence

of churchmen drawn from the best Catholic circles. In that case, however, they would have done better to recognise that what was at issue was the disappearance of an elite group, and not, as they suggested, a dramatic change in the character of the clerical body as a whole.

Apart altogether from the question of social origins, contemporaries professed to find a great difference between the type of Catholic clergyman produced by Maynooth and the type which had been produced by the continental seminaries. A priest of the older generation, it was argued, had received the education of a gentleman. On his return to Ireland 'he almost invariably brought with him a knowledge of the world, some acquaintance with all "universal" topics, a polished demeanour, a relish for "good" society, an improved taste, and an appreciation of the refinements and delicacies of life'. An education at Maynooth, by contrast, was vastly inferior — 'inferior as to learning and manners and professional utility, as well as to liberal sentiments and adaptation to society'. The student pursued a narrowly defined course in a restricted setting, surrounded exclusively by persons of the same background as himself. As a result, he emerged less cultured, less polished in his manners, and more intolerant in his attitudes. Henry Inglis, writing in 1834, summed up the complaints of many observers:

> I found the old, foreign-educated priest a gentleman, a man of frank, easy deportment and good general information; but by no means, in general, so good a Catholic as his brother of Maynooth; *he* I found either a coarse, vulgar-minded man, or a stiff, close and very conceited man; but in every instance Popish to the back-bone; learned, I dare say, in theology, but profoundly ignorant of all that liberalises the mind; a hot zealot in religion; and fully impressed with, or professing to be impressed with, a sense of his consequence and influence.

Others maintained that the older priests were more ready to support the authorities in the maintenance of law and order, while the Maynooth-educated priests were those who took the lead in popular agitation.[25]

Much of this comment betrays an obvious prejudice. To

contrast the politically active clergy of the 1820s and 1830s so unfavourably with their more quiescent predecessors was both a useful polemical device and a comforting indulgence in nostalgia. At the same time there are indications that, in this case, the contrast contemporaries drew between the Maynooth priest and his foreign-educated counterpart was not entirely unfounded, and that the training given to the former was in fact of a particularly functional and restricted character. Students at Maynooth were kept as far as possible isolated from the outside world. They did not mix socially with the inhabitants of the area, and their superiors dis- approved of them spending more than a couple of vacations during their academic career away from the college. They were forbidden to receive newspapers or periodicals (although the authorities confessed that they found this rule impossible to enforce strictly), and all books brought into the college had to be submitted to the dean for examination. The president of the college reported in 1826 that during his time in office he had had to dismiss two students for possessing unapproved books, one of them Smollett's novel *Roderick Random* and the other, 'still more objectionable', Rousseau's *Émile*. Further- more, the kind of teaching given at Maynooth was unlikely to broaden the restricted horizons thus imposed. In 1825 it was reported that a shortage of books was made up for by the professors dictating lectures which were taken down by their students word for word. And a newly appointed pro- fessor, thirteen years later, complained that the study habits of the students were still bad, and in particular that their practice of returning their lecture notes almost verbatim was much to be regretted.[26]

If contemporaries were mainly concerned with the intel- lectual breadth of the teaching given at Maynooth, later writers have placed more emphasis on its doctrinal content, particularly in the field of moral theology. The official his- torian of the college, writing in 1895, conceded that the teaching given there in its early years was strongly influenced by what he described as 'rigorism', 'the moral system of those who draw too tightly the reins of law in restriction of man's natural liberty of action; who are inclined to make precepts out of counsels, and mortal sins out of venial ones'. Evidence of such an outlook is also to be found in the nature of the discipline under which students lived during their time at the college. Maynooth, O'Connell admitted in 1825, 'has a good deal of a monastic discipline'. To Mr and Mrs Hall, writing in 1842, it represented 'the iron rule of St Bernard revived in the nineteenth century'. The student's day began at 5 a.m. in summer and 6 a.m. in winter. Between this and the time he retired — around 10 p.m. — he had at most four hours of free time — two periods in the morning of about half an hour each, somewhat less than two hours up to 5 o'clock in the afternoon, and one hour in the evening between 8 and 9 o'clock. The rest of his time was taken up with lectures, study, meals or religious observances. During these activities, furthermore, a strict rule of silence was to be observed. Wednesdays and Saturdays were half-holidays, on which this requirement was somewhat relaxed, but on five days of the week the students were forbidden to speak to each other except during the four hours of each day allowed for recreation. There were also regular periods of retreat during which the regime became even more stringent. The strictness with which the rules of the college were enforced is suggested by the case of the young Theobald Mathew, who left Maynooth in 1808 to avoid being expelled after he had been caught entertaining a few friends in his room.[27]

The severe discipline imposed on students at Maynooth and the rigorist nature of the doctrines taught there have led some historians to suggest that the establishment of the college was responsible for the introduction of a new and more puritanical tone into the teaching of the Irish Catholic Church. It may be agreed that these aspects of life in the college would almost certainly have influenced the character and outlook of the priests it produced and the type of discipline which they in turn attempted to impose on their congregations. But the argument that priests trained at Maynooth had thus been exposed to influences radically different to those which had shaped priests educated elsewhere is less convincing. 'The discipline maintained in the college', the Maynooth inquiry concluded in 1826, 'is stated to differ very little from that which is observed in other institutions for the education of the Roman Catholic clergy.'

The rule of silence, according to the senior dean, was stricter than that enforced in the other Irish seminaries, but less so than that demanded in some seminaries on the continent. A rigorist bias in the teaching of moral theology, also, was by no means confined to Maynooth. The early professors there had brought their ideas with them from France, and the textbooks used in Maynooth were also standard works in continental seminaries. Students, then, were probably as likely to come under the influence of rigorist ideas in a continental college as at Maynooth. It was at Coimbra in Portugal, for example, that the future Bishop Doyle 'adopted some strong opinions in favour of what is technically called "rigorism"', so that he regarded the Jesuits as over-lenient confessors and for a time restricted their activities in his diocese.[28]

One further point must be made about the influence of Maynooth on the character of the Irish Catholic clergy in the first half of the nineteenth century. The tone of some contemporary comment might lead one to believe that within a few years of the foundation of the college its graduates were to be found disseminating the baneful effects of their inferior background and education in every parish in the country. In fact the spread of the Maynooth clergy was a much less dramatic process. The generation of priests who had received their training in continental seminaries in the years before the French Revolution did not die out overnight. Even after 1815, furthermore, only a proportion of those priests who took up duty for the first time in Ireland had been trained in Maynooth. In 1826 the college supplied only 50 of the 80 or 90 priests required every year for Irish parishes. And even in 1853 it was found that of the 2,262 parish priests and curates serving in Ireland only 1,199, or 53 per cent, had received their training in the college.[29]

In considering the background and training of the Irish Catholic clergy of the late eighteenth and early nineteenth centuries, therefore, it is necessary to qualify in a number of ways the generalisations of contemporary observers. The claim that the Catholic clergy of the early nineteenth century, and in particular those educated at Maynooth, were drawn from the very poorest section of the population appears to have been the result partly of simple prejudice and partly of a failure to understand the complex social distinctions which existed within that population. Accounts of the contrast which existed between the social origins of priests educated at Maynooth and those of earlier generations of clergymen also appear to have been greatly exaggerated. Where the type of training given at Maynooth and elsewhere is concerned, the belief that a priest educated at Maynooth had received a narrower and more functional training than one educated abroad probably had some foundation. It is also true that the doctrines taught at Maynooth and the discipline to which the students of that college were subjected were of a kind calculated to foster severe moral attitudes and a puritanical outlook on human life in general. But the training given at Maynooth does not appear to have differed significantly in this respect from that received by priests educated in other institutions. Finally, in all discussions of the influence of Maynooth it must be remembered that for most if not all of the first half of the nineteenth century it was only a minority of the priests serving in Irish dioceses who had received their training in the college.

The remaining question to be considered concerns the incomes and standard of living enjoyed by Catholic churchmen in this period — a point which, like the question of the background from which churchmen were drawn, has obvious implications for any discussion of relations between priests and people. The most detailed information on this subject comes from the returns drawn up by the Irish bishops for submission to the government in 1801 in connection with proposals for a state subsidy to the Catholic clergy.[30] Interpretation of the figures presents some difficulties: in one diocese the return is said to show the sums to which the Catholic clergy were entitled, rather than those they actually received, while in another case there is a note suggesting that certain expenses, such as the cost of wine and candles for the chapel, had to be met out of the income shown. But assuming that the figures relate in most cases to sums actually received, and to net rather than gross incomes, the picture suggested by the returns is fairly clear. The figures in Table 4 summarise the information given about the incomes derived from 573 parishes in eighteen dioceses. Of those parishes

Table 4. Parish Incomes in 18 Dioceses, 1801

Income	Parish priest only	Parish priest and one curate
Less than £50	78	11
£50–£100	179	157
£100–150	24	90
£150–£200	1	17
£200+	0	16
Total	282	291

Source: Castlereagh Correspondence.

Note: This table is confined to the two most common types of parish: those served only by a single priest, and those served by a parish priest and one curate. It excludes mensal parishes and parishes in which a pension had to be paid to a retired parish priest, and also parishes marked 'curate wanting', since it is not clear whether these were parishes which would normally have a curate, or merely parishes in which it would be desirable to have one.

served by a single priest, the great majority had incomes of between £50 and £100, and most of the remainder had incomes of less than £50. Of those parishes in which a parish priest was assisted by one curate, the majority of incomes were once again between £50 and £100, but a greater proportion of the remainder, and more than one-third of the total, had incomes of over £100. In the seven dioceses in which the returns gave only a single figure for average incomes these ranged from £55 for a parish priest in Raphoe to between £100 and £120 for a benefice in Cloyne and Ross. The abstract which accompanies the return suggests that the average income of a parish priest, exclusive of the cost of keeping a curate, was £65, and this seems to be a reasonable estimate. It is clear from the figures in Table 4 that there were no very great inequalities of income concealed behind this average: relatively few parish priests, once the cost of keeping a curate is allowed for, can have had an income much in excess of £100. There were, however, variations between dioceses. Tuam, for example, had a higher than average share of poor livings — 15 of the 19 parishes in which the parish priest officiated alone had incomes of less than £50 a year, while only one of the 26 in which there was a single curate brought in more than £100 a year. At the other end of the scale incomes appear to have been significantly higher than elsewhere in the dioceses of Cloyne and Ross, Meath, Ossory, and Kildare and Leighlin.

All these figures relate only to cash incomes. In order to obtain a true picture of the standard of living of the Catholic clergy in this period it is also necessary to take into account a number of important customary entitlements. Priests in different parts of the country regularly received payments in kind in addition to those made in cash. Thus it was noted in the return of 1801 that priests in Kildare and Leighlin, Ferns and rural parts of the diocese of Dublin received gifts of hay or corn from their more prosperous parishioners. In 1835 priests in one parish in Co. Donegal were reported to receive from each family 'two shillings a year, one stook of barley and one hank of yarn', while in Errigal Truagh, Co. Monaghan, collections of oats appear as a regular item in the parish register, not only in the 1830s but into the 1860s and 1870s.[31] In some cases such donations were in lieu of cash payments, and as such may have been included in the incomes returned in 1801, but in other cases it seems clear that they were an additional, and quite valuable, prerogative. Priests also commonly received the labour of their parishioners free of charge. According to a priest of the diocese of Cork, writing in 1806, it was the custom 'that his turf should be cut, his corn reaped, his meadow mowed etc., gratis'. Evidence given to the Poor Inquiry commissioners in the mid-1830s confirmed that labourers who could not afford to pay dues frequently performed unpaid work for the priest instead. Apart from its importance as a further levy on parishioners for support of their clergy, this practice reminds us that a priest's revenue from his parish was often supplemented by some kind of agricultural holding, if only a meadow or potato garden.[32]

Finally, and most important of all, priests were entitled by custom to the hospitality of their parishioners, not only in the celebrations which might follow a christening or a marriage, but also after what was known as a 'station'. In most parts of rural Ireland at this period it was customary for the parish clergy to go once or twice each year to selected private houses throughout their parishes to hear confessions and administer communion, and on these occasions they generally dined afterwards with the family of the house in which the station had been held. 'In large populous parishes', the Bishop of Kildare and Leighlin explained in his return, 'the stations . . . generally exceed, sometimes considerably, one hundred in the year, from which, of course, results a very capital saving in the article of house-keeping, especially in times like the present.' The importance of this item in the domestic economy of the Catholic clergy can be seen from the fact that when station dinners were abolished in the diocese of Cloyne and Ross the Christmas and Easter dues — which made up one half of the total revenues of a parish — were doubled as compensation.[33]

The first quarter of the nineteenth century appears to have seen a general improvement in the incomes of the Catholic clergy. Thus a priest in the diocese of Cloyne and Ross estimated in 1825 that the average value of benefices in that diocese was between £220 and £250 a year, compared with the average value of between £100 and £120 reported twenty-five years before. In the same way the Archbishop of Armagh reported that there was no parish in his province that was worth less than £100 a year, although in 1801 it had been only a minority of parishes in the province which had been worth so much. Some of this growth in parish incomes must have been absorbed by the concurrent increase in the number of Catholic clergymen among whom it had to be distributed. Thus the revenues of the parish of Maryborough, which in 1801 had amounted to £200 per annum, were said in 1831 to vary between £200 and £300 a year, but by this time there were two curates in the parish instead of one. At the same time it seems clear that the financial position of parish priests improved substantially during this period. John Leslie Foster in 1825 put the average income of an Irish priest at £150 per annum. Daniel O'Connell, slightly more cautious, described £150 as 'a high average' for a parish priest. But in either case this represented a distinct improvement on the £65 suggested twenty-five years before. Details of incomes in the twenty years after 1825 are more difficult to come by, but there is some contemporary comment to suggest that the 1830s and 1840s saw a further improvement in the financial position of the Catholic clergy.[34]

All these details, it must be stressed, relate solely to parish priests. The financial position of the curates who assisted this group was very different. Where a curate lived apart from the parish priest, the arrangement most frequently mentioned in the return of 1801 is that he received one-third of the revenues of the parish. More frequently, however, the curate lived in the same house as the parish priest, receiving his keep and an annual salary. The figure suggested by the return for Waterford and Lismore, and repeated in the general abstract which accompanies the returns, is £10 a year. O'Connell in 1825 suggested an average salary of £20 or £30 a year, suggesting that the position of curates improved along with that of their superiors during the first quarter of the nineteenth century. At the same time contemporaries continued to comment on the poverty of this class. The Catholic curate, Foster maintained in 1825, 'is very scantily maintained, and very severely worked. His inducement to enter upon such a course is the certainty that it will lead to his becoming a [parish] priest.'[35]

The Catholic bishops derived their incomes from three main sources: the revenues of one or two mensal parishes, which were reserved to the bishop (although he normally had to pay a curate or curates to administer it); a yearly levy on all the clergy of his diocese; and the fees charged for licences granted to couples who wished to marry without publishing banns. The average bishop's income was estimated in 1801 at a little over £300. The richest dioceses, like Cork (£550 per annum) and Cashel (£450 p.a.), were well above the level of even the most profitable parish, while the poorest, like Kilfenora and Kilmacduagh (£100 p.a.) and Clonfert (£116 p.a.) were worth considerably less. 'There are some parishes that I would prefer to a diocese,' the Bishop of Kilmore observed in 1828, 'certainly to the diocese of Kilmore.' In the case of Kilfenora and Kilmacduagh it was generally agreed that anyone appointed bishop should have some private means which would supplement the meagre income which it yielded. The income of bishops, like that of parish priests, appears to have increased in the years after 1800. By 1825 the Archbishop of Armagh believed that no bishop in his province had an income of less than £500 a year, while the income of the Bishop of Kildare and Leighlin had increased from £300 in 1801 to between £450 and £500. In 1835 the French traveller de Tocqueville was informed by the President of Carlow College that the income of the Bishop of Kildare and Leighlin was £500 a year and that the incomes of the other Irish bishops ranged from that figure up to around £1,000 per annum.[36]

In order to give meaning to these different figures it is necessary to ask what the incomes being discussed would have meant in terms of standard of living and social status. One obvious comparison is between the incomes of Catholic priests and those received by clergymen of other denominations. The clergy of the Church of Ireland were, as one might expect, considerably better paid for their services than their Catholic counterparts. In 1832 there were 488 Anglican benefices in Ireland with incomes of under £200, 544 with incomes of between £200 and £500, and 365 with incomes of over £500. A comparison with the Presbyterian clergy attached to the Synod of Ulster, however, yields somewhat different results. The clergy of this denomination, the Moderator of the Synod explained in 1825, could be divided into three groups of roughly equal size. The first of these included a few incomes of between £250 and £300, with the remainder averaging about £160 or £170 per annum; average incomes in the second group were between £125 and £145, while average incomes in the third were from £90 to £100. The average income then being attributed to Catholic parish priests, it will be remembered, was £150 per annum or slightly less, and this cash income was supplemented by payments in kind, in labour and in hospitality. Catholic churchmen may have resented the wealth of the Established Church, but by other standards of comparison it is difficult to see them as having been poorly rewarded for their services.[37]

A second, and perhaps more important, comparison is between the standard of living enjoyed by the Catholic clergy and that enjoyed by their parishioners. Here the comments of contemporaries suggest that the lifestyle of most parish priests would have been somewhere, but not very much, above that of the more prosperous members of their congregations. Their houses, Major Willcocks informed a parliamentary committee in 1825, were 'generally thatched [i.e. rather than slated]; snug little cabins most of them, some not very good'. A magistrate from Co. Cork maintained that the priests were better off than the richer farmers, but that at the same time they did not live in what he would have considered comfort. De Tocqueville's account in 1835 presents a similar picture. The parish priest he visited near Tuam, Co. Galway, lived in 'a little house, built of stone, with four windows in front and two stories. This building was covered in thatch like the others, but the thatch was new and the rafters in good repair.' It was a day of abstinence, and they dined adequately but modestly on salmon and potatoes.[38]

* * *

This section has discussed the numerical strength of the Irish Catholic clergy, the backgrounds from which they were drawn, the training they received, and the incomes and standards of living they could expect to enjoy. The broader questions of the relationship between these priests and their congregations, and the degree of influence which they could hope to exercise, are the main concern of this book, and a general discussion at this stage would be of little value. However, this may be the place to make three specific points.

The first concerns the implications for the potential influence of the Catholic clergy of the conclusions just presented concerning their social origins and standards of living. This was an issue raised by more than one contemporary observer. Gustave de Beaumont, writing in 1839, invited his readers to imagine how the Irish lower classes must compare the clergy of the Church of Ireland, wealthy, supported by the power of the state, and concerned only with personal advancement, with 'the Catholic priest, who has no family, no fortune, and no estate, who is the child of Ireland, and has sprung from the popular ranks, [who] lives only for the people, and devotes himself entirely to its service'. Major Warburton, somewhat more soberly, suggested to a parliamentary committee in 1825 that people preferred the clergy trained in Maynooth 'because they are generally more immediately acquainted with them; they go from amongst themselves and come back directly to them, and therefore they know them better, and as far as that goes, I think that influences them'. Similar arguments have been put forward by more recent writers. 'The priests' power', Professor K. H. Connell suggests, 'was the greater for their being drawn themselves from the peasantry, sharing peasant prejudices.'[39]

Arguments of this kind clearly contain a certain amount of truth. Occasionally, in some of the churchmen of the early nineteenth century, one catches a glimpse of the very different path which relations between priests and people might have taken if the circumstances or the aspirations of the former had been higher. When Dr Walsh of Cork diocese, writing in 1806, discussed the disadvantages arising from the custom of having stations in private houses, one of the objections, in his view 'of no small weight', was that 'The clergyman, by his uninterrupted intercourse with the lower orders of the community, may lose that polish which by education or observation he may have attained, and be by degrees totally unfitted for more select society.' Almost twenty years later another priest in the same county could still refer disapprovingly to 'the indecorum of the priests consorting at dinner indiscriminately with the common people'.[40] The backgrounds of these censorious clergymen are unknown. Perhaps they had been born to such refined attitudes, members of that elite among the Catholic clergy whose passing contemporaries were lamenting at this period.[41] Or perhaps they had seen the education and status which came with their entry into the priesthood as carrying with it the obligation to adopt the manners and attitudes of a gentleman. But in either case it was clearly as well for the future influence of the Irish Church and its servants that they did not become the representative type of the Irish Catholic priest.

At the same time the importance of this point should not be overstated. The first section of this chapter drew attention to the social distinctions which existed within the Catholic laity of this period, and to the extent to which a consciousness of these distinctions permeated all aspects of life, including the religious. This section has argued that contemporary comments concerning the humble social origins of the Catholic clergy are misleading, that the social groups from which they were drawn cannot realistically be regarded as the lowest levels of Irish society. What we have, then, is not a homogeneous 'peasantry', from which was drawn both the Catholic clergy and the great bulk of their congregations, but rather a stratified society, whose members were very conscious of the divisions which existed within it, and a clergy drawn predominantly from a particular, relatively favoured stratum. In this situation it would be unrealistic to attribute too much importance to a solidarity based on common origins. Neither should too much be made of the modest incomes enjoyed by the Catholic clergy. The gap between the standard of living of the Irish priest and that of the majority of his parishioners, like that between the farmer and the cottier or labourer, may not have seemed to outside observers a matter of great significance. But the members of this society were not so ready to see themselves as part of one undifferentiated mass, united in a common poverty. At times of severe economic pressure the labourer and cottier struck out not merely at the landlord or the tithe proctor but also at the tenant farmer. At such times, also, as will be seen in a later chapter, the financial demands of the Catholic clergy could become a cause of resentment, and the priest himself the target of popular agitation.[42] A broad similarity of social origins and incomes which were not excessive may well have helped to prevent the development of certain forms of potentially dangerous conflict. But to argue that these factors alone were capable of creating an automatic solidarity between priests and people would be to ignore the social context within which both existed.

A second point concerns the way in which the status of the local priest was affected, and his potential authority enhanced, by the absence in so many communities of alter-

native social leaders. The extent to which the Catholic population of the eighteenth and early nineteenth centuries really
lived in a state of permanent alienation from their landlords
and from other members of the middle and upper classes, as
well as the extent to which things would have been significantly different under a predominantly Catholic aristocracy and bourgeoisie, must remain open to question. At the
same time it can be agreed that the Catholic priest was in
most cases the educated man to whom his parishioners could
most easily and most confidently turn for advice and assistance. Thus the priest was frequently called on to act as an
intermediary between his parishioners and those in authority,
for example by soliciting aid from the government in times
of famine or economic crisis or by appealing to landlords on
behalf of their tenants. 'If a poor man wants a favour asked
of some great man,' a Catholic lawyer reported in 1839, 'he
gets the priest to ask that favour for him; if he is in distress
or difficulties, he goes to his priest, and looks upon him as
his friend and protector.'[43] In other ways too the priest's
position gave him a central role in the lives of his parishioners,
extending far beyond religious matters. 'Besides being their
spiritual comforters,' Bicheno observed in 1830, 'the priests
are their physicians in remote districts, and the lawyers
everywhere. . . . In addition to this, they are very competent
advisers in matters of business.' When the Catholic Association
allocated to the Catholic clergy a major part in the campaign
for Catholic Emancipation, it did so not because of their
ability to impose political views or policies on their congregations, but because no other group was so strategically
placed to occupy the role of local organisers and agents.[44]

A final point concerning the potential influence of the
Catholic clergy has received less attention. This is the implications for that influence of the authoritarian tone which
appears to have characterised social relationships in general
in most parts of Ireland both before and after the famine.
Visitors from England, with its limited but vigorous tradition
of popular rights and liberties — the heritage of the 'freeborn
Englishman' — were struck by the absence in Ireland of anything remotely comparable. Arthur Young, writing in 1779,
commented on 'the subordination of the lower classes,

degenerating ito oppression', which seemed to him 'a perfect contrast to their situation in England, of which country, comparatively speaking, they reign the sovereigns'. In the same way Edward Wakefield, thirty years later, recalled having seen a gentleman lay open a man's cheek with his whip on a racecourse in Co. Carlow and contrasted the submissive reaction of the bystanders with what would have been seen in the same circumstances in England. Even in more recent times authoritarianism has been identified as a prominent feature of Irish rural family life, and more recently still as a characteristic of contemporary Irish political culture.[45]

This general willingness to defer to authority was inevitably reflected in relations between priests and people. An Irish priest, describing his experience in a rural parish in the late nineteenth century, notes revealingly that

> Although they may like the pleasant, 'gallas' man who somewhat descends to their level in his conduct and conversation, the peasantry reverence and respect more the priest who, whilst being kind, considerate and humble, yet, in his intercourse with them maintains a dignity and a discreet reserve and aloofness. Him they style a 'grand man'; the other, perhaps, a 'nice man'.

The tone which such a background gave to relations between priests and people is seen even in the friendly comments of de Tocqueville, describing an excursion in company with a priest in the west of Ireland:

> On seeing him the women curtseyed and crossed themselves devoutly, the men respectfully took off their hats. He saluted nobody and did not seem to notice the respect with which he was received, but, walking on without stopping, spoke a word to each: 'How is your old father today, Mr X?' he said to one. 'When is your wife to be churched, John?' he said to another.

Even the willingness of social superiors to resort to blows — and the willingness of inferiors to accept them — which so impressed both Young and Wakefield, appear to have played a part in relations between priests and people. Accounts of priests making use of manual chastisement to discipline parishioners came not merely from Protestant polemicists like the Rev. Mortimer O'Sullivan but from relatively unbiased observers like John O'Donovan and Wakefield himself. In addition, such episodes more than once became the occasion of legal action. In Co. Sligo in 1825 a jury failed to agree on whether a priest had struck a man for refusing to pay the 'Catholic rent'. In Co. Galway in 1838 an inquiry was held into the case of a youth who died some months after his parish priest had caught him taking part in a boxing match and given him several blows with a whip. In the same year the Catholic curate of Achill Island, Co. Mayo, was fined 2s 6d for similarly taking his whip to a teacher from the local Protestant colony during a dispute over whether he should be left alone with a dying woman.[46]

These different factors — the social origins and lifestyle of the Catholic priest, his lack of connection with the political and social establishment, the absence of alternative social leaders, the atmosphere of an authoritarian culture — all helped to ensure that the priest would occupy a prominent place in Irish society. But whether they were sufficient to give him the unique degree of social influence claimed for him by many contemporaries is another matter, and one which is best dealt with at a later stage in this study.

3. *Abuses and Reform*

In the summer of 1753 Nicholas Sweetman, Bishop of Ferns, carried out a visitation of his diocese. The visitation was a bishop's main opportunity to discover how the parishes under his supervision were being managed, and the notes which Sweetman made on this occasion indicate that he found much to criticise. In the case of one priest he noted: 'His ornaments were indifferent, except his alb was very dirty; and the veil of the chalice scandalously broken and ragged; and the chalice itself very bad.' Of another, visited three days later: 'His vestments and missal ordinary and indifferent, and his altar stone without consecration, being broke quite across the middle, and covered with dirty greasy leather, and his chalice scandalous.' Elsewhere too the bishop noted instances of altar equipment damaged or not properly cared for. In one case he went so far as to tear up a dirty purificatorium in order to ensure that it was not used again. In addition, Sweetman received complaints about some of the priests themselves. Several, he recorded, were negligent or careless in the matter of preaching and giving religious instruction to the congregations committed to their care. Two were on bad terms with their parishioners, another was not 'very zealous or diligent in his duty', and a fourth was 'neither very instructive or edifying to his flock'. In the parish of Rathgarogue the bishop was informed 'that the pastor minded dogs and hunting more than his flock, and also that he did not give mass at Rathgarogue on holydays'. In all Sweetman had an adverse comment of some kind to make about nearly half of the thirty-two priests whose parishes he visited in this year.[47]

Nearly thirty years later, in 1780, another bishop, Patrick Joseph Plunkett, carrying out his first visitation in his new diocese of Meath, encountered very similar problems. He too reported instances of parishes in which the altar linen and vessels or the vestments were dirty or damaged, and in which the chapel itself was not clean enough or was in poor repair. Like Sweetman, he complained of priests who failed to preach on Sundays and holydays or to ensure that the children of their parishes were adequately instructed in Christian doctrine. In two instances he refused to perform any confirmations because none of the children presented to him were sufficiently instructed in their religion to receive the sacrament. In several of the chapels he inspected Plunkett also complained of the irreverent and disorderly behaviour of the congregations.[48]

The experiences of Sweetman in Ferns and Plunkett in Meath were not in any way unique — except, perhaps, for the care with which these two prelates carried out their visitations and for the extent of their concern over what they found. Their findings reflected a general weakness of ecclesiastical discipline which affected all sections of the Irish Catholic Church in the eighteenth and early nineteenth centuries. This section will be concerned, firstly, with the causes and consequences of this weakness, and secondly, with the efforts which were made in the first half of the nineteenth century to replace old habits and attitudes with a new and stricter discipline.

*　*　*

The problems revealed in the visitation records of Sweetman and Plunkett can in part be attributed to the effects of a long period of restrictive legislation and intermittent persecution. Irish Catholicism on the eve of the Reformation had been as backward as that which existed in other underdeveloped parts of Europe. It was not until the first four decades of the seventeenth century that a sustained attempt was made to bring church government and popular religious practice into line with the new standards and practices of the Counter-Reformation. This period of reform was halted and its achievements partly reversed by the civil war of the 1640s and the severe repression which followed. After 1660 the work of reform was begun again in the more tolerant climate of the Restoration, only to be brought to an equally sudden halt by the deposition of James II.[49]

The effects of this lengthy period of disruption, and of the incomplete introduction into Ireland of the new discipline of the Counter-Reformation, were perpetuated into the eighteenth century by the penal laws introduced in the aftermath of the Williamite victory. The sections of these laws relating to Catholic ecclesiastics were, it is true, allowed to fall fairly rapidly into disuse: after 1720, in spite of some lapses into stricter enforcement, a *de facto* toleration appears to have been increasingly the rule, and by 1750 it could be largely taken for granted. By this time, however, there had been at least a partial collapse in the structure of church government. In 1697 there were only eight bishops in the country. A number of sees were vacant altogether, while the occupants of others had retreated into exile on the continent. By 1703 the number of bishops had been reduced to three, and four years later it was reported that there were only two, one of whom was in failing health and the other in jail. The first steps to remedy this situation were taken in 1707 with the appointment of five new bishops. In the years that followed other appointments were made to fill up the vacant Irish sees, but it was not until 1747 that the last long gap in the episcopal succession was brought to an end with the appointment of a bishop to the see of Dromore, vacant since 1716. By this time a number of dioceses had been without a bishop for periods of several decades. The see of Achonry was vacant, apart from one brief reign of less than three months, from 1603 until 1707, Kilmacduagh from *c.* 1653 to 1720, Kerry from *c.* 1650 to 1720, Raphoe from *c.* 1657 to 1725, and Kilmore from 1669 until 1728.[50] Even where there was a bishop to supervise the affairs of a diocese, furthermore, the climate of the early eighteenth century posed obvious obstacles to efficient administration. An Irish Catholic bishop in the first half of the eighteenth century had strong incentives to live as quietly and inconspicuously as possible, and none whatever to add to his problems by attempting to impose too strict a discipline on his clergy.

It would be unrealistic, however, to see weakness of internal discipline solely as a consequence of the penal laws. It is also necessary to take account of the effects of poor communications and of the backwardness and isolation of many parts of eighteenth-century Ireland — conditions which made it difficult for even the government to control the activities of its local agents and which, even in the absence of restrictive legislation and official hostility, would have prevented many bishops from exercising a very strict control over their subordinates. When it came to the next stage in the hierarchy of control, supervision of the bishops themselves by the Vatican and its agents, the practical obstacles to effective administration were magnified enormously. When a bishop became incompetent through age and persistent drunkenness, as the Bishop of Ardagh was said to have done in 1729, or when the fees he received for performing ordinations led him to admit unsuitable candidates to holy orders, as was alleged against the Bishop of Achonry five years later, there was no authority with the effective power to do very much about it.[51] In this sense the problems of the Irish Church can be seen as one more example of a triumph of the local over the central which affected both church and state in many parts of eighteenth-century Europe.

This aspect of the problems of church government in

eighteenth- and early nineteenth-century Ireland was illustrated in the matter of the appointment of parish priests.
Theoretically such appointments were entirely in the hands
of the bishop, but in practice concessions were made in more
than one way to local interests and sensibilities. In a few
cases, where Catholic families remained in possession of
landed property, the church authorities continued to recognise a right of presentation to particular parishes: thus Lord
Kenmare enjoyed the right of presentation to the Catholic
chapel of Killarney, as well as to both the Catholic and
Protestant livings of Hospital, Co. Limerick. Even where a
formal right of presentation was not recognised, the wishes
of local landowners, both Catholics and sympathetic Protestants, received consideration. Attention was also paid to the
wishes of the local congregation. The Catholic spokesman
Richard Lalor Sheil observed in 1825 that 'The Roman
Catholic hierarchy, though absolute in name, are greatly
under the influence of public opinion; they generally select
the individual whom the parishioners wish to nominate.'[52]

Sheil may have been overstating his case. But there is
plenty of evidence to show that on those occasions where the
church authorities did choose to disregard or override local
preferences in these matters the consequences could be very
serious. Throughout the eighteenth and early nineteenth centuries, in all parts of the country, there were instances of parish
rebellions in which local clergymen, supported by their congregations, defied the authority of their bishops. Some of
these incidents arose when the clergyman in question was
suspended for some misdemeanour and refused to surrender
control of his parish. For example, Patrick Scanlan, Parish
Priest of St Munchin's in the city of Limerick, was suspended
in 1755 after two women had allegedly borne children by
him, but continued to officiate in the parish with the support
of a section of his congregation, and other clergymen who
attempted to enter the parish, including the bishop, were
forcibly driven out by his supporters. In Aughnamullen East,
Co. Monaghan, the curate, Edward O'Callaghan, was suspended in 1835 or 1836, but remained in the parish, performing his priestly duties under the protection of an armed body-
guard provided by his local supporters and forcibly excluding

from the parish chapel the clergyman appointed by the bishop. Other disputes arose out of the refusal of the bishop to appoint to a particular parish a clergyman popularly regarded as having a claim on it. Thus there were various cases of parishioners supporting the claim of the curate of a parish to succeed to its management on the death of his parish priest and refusing to accept other clergymen appointed by the bishop. In Kells, Co. Meath, in 1790 parishioners excluded the parish priest appointed by the bishop in favour of Patrick Smyth, a native of the parish. In Beach, Co. Galway, in 1816 the congregation supported the man nominated by the Clanricarde family, whose claim to present to the living was denied by the Bishop of Kilmacduagh, and the parish remained in rebellion for five years, in spite of having been placed under an interdict. In these and similar cases attachment to the familiar figure of a local clergyman clearly took precedence over the more remote and impersonal authority represented by the bishop. It is not surprising, in these circumstances, that bishops generally preferred to defer where possible to local wishes in the way that Sheil suggested.[53]

Finally, there is the question of to what extent the problems of the Irish Church reflected not merely the practical difficulties created by the penal laws and the character of the society in which it operated, but also a certain lack of zeal on the part of its servants. The eighteenth century was not on the whole a period of great religious enthusiasm. In both Britain and Ireland, it has long been recognised, the established churches of this period were dominated by a religious outlook which can best be described as rational rather than enthusiastic. In the case of Irish Catholicism the research has not yet been done which would enable us to generalise with confidence about the several thousand clergymen who served in Ireland during the eighteenth and early nineteenth centuries. At the same time there are some grounds for suggesting that a similar religious outlook, and the relaxed approach to clerical duties which went with it, was also to be found in the ranks of the Catholic clergy. Thus while the Banishment Act might have been responsible for temporarily depriving Irish Catholicism of its bishops, it cannot be offered as a full explanation of why after the

1720s, when it was clear that legislation against Catholic ecclesiastics was not going to be seriously enforced, the Roman authorities should have complained so frequently about the difficulty of getting Irish bishops to reside in their dioceses. In particular great concern was caused during the 1730s by three Irish bishops who insisted on spending all or most of their time on the continent rather than in the districts entrusted to their care. These were Richard Piers, Bishop of Waterford and Lismore, who had at least the excuse of old age and a close identification with the exiled James II; Ambrose O'Callaghan, Bishop of Ferns, who was not a permanent absentee, but whose visits to the continent were so frequent that the nuncio commented in 1735 that he might truly be described as a prelate in perpetual motion; and James O'Daly of Kilfenora, who attempted to be an absentee twice over, forsaking Ireland for France and then insisting on his right to live in Paris rather than in Tournai, where he was a canon. In addition, there were cases of internal absenteeism, where bishops spent all or most of their time in Dublin or in some other part of Ireland which they preferred to the diocese for which they were responsible. In 1749, for example, the clergy of the diocese of Ossory complained that their late bishop, Colman O'Shaughnessy, had spent most of his episcopate with relatives or fellow-Dominicans in his native Connacht, while as late as the 1770s Archbishop Anthony Blake provoked grave discontent in his diocese — and ultimately his own suspension by Rome — by his insistence on residing in his family home near Galway rather than in his diocese of Armagh.[54]

Other cases can also be mentioned in which the conduct of eighteenth-century bishops was such as to suggest that any deficiencies which might have been found in the administration of their dioceses would not have been altogether the fault of the difficult circumstances in which they worked. Archbishop Blake's one-time protégé, Dominic Bellew, Bishop of Killala from 1779 until about 1812, emerges from the correspondence of his episcopal colleagues as a dedicated ecclesiastical careerist, ready to provoke major internal disputes solely for the purpose of furthering his own prospects. When John Butler, Bishop of Cork since 1763, succeeded in

1785 to the family estates and to the title Lord Dunboyne, he chose to put family duty and the necessity of producing an heir before his ecclesiastical commitments: he resigned his see, conformed to the Church of Ireland, and married a distant cousin. Both Bellew and Butler were, of course, extreme cases. A more representative figure was perhaps Daniel Delany, Bishop of Kildare and Leighlin from 1787 to 1814, an active promoter of education but — according to the mild assessment of the biographer of a later bishop of the diocese — 'somewhat dilatory in performing the various arduous duties of episcopal life. Passionately fond of the society of intellectual and sincere friends he often forgot, in the charm of their presence, to execute some long-advertised visitation.' The description is one we would not be surprised to find applied to an Anglican churchman of the period in either Ireland or England. And it suggests that the Catholic Church and the Established Church, in spite of their very different legal situations, may perhaps have had more in common, in terms of religious outlook, than has generally been recognised.[55]

The Irish Catholic Church of the eighteenth century, then, was characterised by a general laxity of internal discipline, reflecting both the absence of effective control from above and a certain lack of religious zeal. The results of this laxity can be considered under three main headings. The first of these, the manner in which the Catholic clergy performed their routine pastoral duties, has already been illustrated from the visitation comments of Bishops Sweetman and Plunkett. Similar problems existed elsewhere. 'Notwithstanding our zealous endeavours to render our clergy sensible of the great end of their mission,' Archbishop Carpenter of Dublin observed in 1770, '. . . we find to our great concern that some are deficient in the discharge of these essential duties. The consequences of this neglect are truly lamentable, and demand from us an exertion of our authority, by proceeding with canonical rigour against the indolent and the slothful.' In the early nineteenth century reforming bishops like James Warren Doyle in Kildare and Leighlin were to devote a great deal of their time to the task of ensuring that their clergy paid proper attention to preaching, catechising and other routine pastoral duties, and that they maintained a reasonable standard of outward display in their religious services.[56]

The effects of lax internal discipline could also be seen in the everyday behaviour of the lower clergy. The most prominent problem here was that of clerical drunkenness. Sexual immorality had, of course, greater potential for scandal, but instances appear to have been relatively rare. 'Although I took many opportunities of inquiring respecting the purity of the priests' lives,' the English traveller Bicheno reported in 1830, 'I did not hear, even from their opponents, that the violation of their vow in this respect was imputable to them; on the contrary, they are signally exempt from the charge.'[57] Clerical drunkenness was another matter. Both Bicheno and Wakefield, in the course of otherwise favourable accounts of the Irish Catholic clergy, mentioned drunkenness as a fault to which some of their number were prone. The Archbishop of Baltimore, writing in 1788 to Archbishop Troy of Dublin about priests who might be willing to emigrate to his diocese, felt it necessary to add the warning that in his part of the world sobriety in drink was expected from clergymen 'to a great degree', so that what in many parts of Europe would be perfectly acceptable would be regarded in his diocese as 'unbecoming excess'. 'Your Lordship', he added diplomatically, 'will excuse this detail, and know how to ascribe it to its proper motive, that gentlemen applying to come to this country may know what to expect.'[58]

Apart from the problem created by individual drunkards, reform-minded churchmen in the early nineteenth century found cause for concern in the extent to which the parish clergy as a body participated in the social activities of the laity. Hunting, for example, appears to have been popular with many priests. The Rev. David Croly, writing in 1834, saw it as evidence of the improved social status of the Catholic clergy that 'the country priest now copes with the country squire [and] keeps sporting dogs'. In the diocese of Kildare and Leighlin, it was later asserted, there were priests 'who ejaculated "Tally Ho" as often as "Pax Vobiscum"'. In other ways too the parish clergy of this period appear to have had little hesitation about mixing socially. Thus the diary of the Co. Kilkenny schoolmaster Humphrey O'Sullivan is full of casual references to pleasant evenings spent in the company of his parish priest. In November 1830, for example, he dined with the priest, six gentlemen and five ladies. 'We passed the night merrily and comfortably till ten o'clock, eating, drinking, singing and enjoying ourselves.' A week earlier he 'spent some of the night merrily with the priest at a christening'. On another occasion 'a merry group' of fourteen, again including the parish priest, had dinner. 'We drank enough punch', O'Sullivan records, 'and came home nice and comfortable.'[59]

A regular occasion for clerical sociability of this kind was provided by the practice of holding stations in private houses. On these occasions, as already mentioned, it was customary for the household to entertain the priest to a meal after confessions and mass were over, and this had in many cases developed into a lavish entertainment, involving not only the priest but a select gathering of neighbours. 'A station dinner', according to the aspiring priest in Carleton's famous story, 'is the very pinnacle of a priest's happiness. There is the fun and frolic; then does the lemon-juice of mirth and humour come out of their reverences like secret writing, as soon as they get properly warm.' The comment is a satirical one, but it receives unexpected confirmation in the minutes of a synod held in Carleton's own diocese of Clogher as late as 1861:

> Big dinners at stations [are] most injurious to priest and people. Bishop most solemnly forbids dining at a station if any but the family of the house be present at table; and forbids dining at all if any intoxicating [drink] (even wine) be introduced at table.

Elsewhere too in the first half of the nineteenth century bishops prohibited the practice of dining at stations, partly because of the burden which it imposed on the householders concerned, but also because they regarded it as improper that priests should take part in such entertainments.[60]

Finally, the effects of lax internal discipline can be seen in a third feature of the Irish Church of the eighteenth and early nineteenth centuries: the willingness of its clergy to engage in damaging and divisive internal disputes. In the 1720s, for example, the clergy of Dublin were divided into two hostile factions over the appointment of a dean to St Patrick's

Cathedral (a purely nominal appointment, since the cathedral had long been in the possession of the Church of Ireland), and later of a coadjutor to the archbishop. Earlier, around 1710, the rivalry of the Bishop of Dromore and the Vicar General of Armagh for the succession to the latter diocese was reported to have done great damage to religion. In 1744 it was claimed that the diocese of Ferns had been the scene of serious scandals over the previous thirty years, owing to resentment on the part of the clergy at the appointment of two successive bishops from outside the province of Dublin. Disputes of this kind continued to take place in the second half of the eighteenth century and after. In some cases, as with Archbishop Blake of Armagh in the 1770s, opposition to a bishop by the priests of his diocese was primarily the result of his own maladministration. In other cases, however, it was on more questionable grounds. Thus the sustained obstruction which Bishop James Murphy of Clogher encountered from a section of his clergy between 1801 and 1817 owed something to the bishop's hot temper and his harsh treatment of subordinates, but it also involved a conflict between two family groups and the disappointed aspirations of a rival candidate for succession to the see. Francis O'Finan, appointed to the see of Killala in 1835, found himself opposed and finally overthrown by a section of the lower clergy who had been favoured by the previous bishop, John MacHale, and who felt that one of their number should have been chosen to succeed him. Another dispute, even more unequivocally concerned with the pursuit of ecclesiastical power and privilege, had taken place in the province of Tuam in 1809–12, when Bishop Bellew of Killala, who hoped to succeed to the archdiocese of Tuam, induced the other bishops of the province to join with him in refusing to recognise the appointment of his chief rival, Oliver Kelly, as vicar capitular.[61]

The extent of clerical factionalism can be seen not only from those instances in which it gave rise to open conflict, but also from the way in which its importance was acknowledged in other cases. When the Bishop of Waterford and Lismore died in 1796, there was general agreement among his colleagues that the man chosen to succeed him should be a priest from outside that diocese. 'The ferment of party', one bishop in the province reported, 'is not subsided there yet, and would likely gather fresh strength from the promotion of either of the candidates of the diocese, which in all likelihood would render the administration of the successful one troublesome to him.' In 1827 William Coppinger, Bishop of Cloyne and Ross, proposed to his clergy that they should hold a ballot among themselves to choose the person who should be called for as his coadjutor and eventual successor. His motive, he explained to a colleague, was that he 'had reason to apprehend, should my death intervene, that disedifying divisions and consequent injury to religion would be the probable consequence'.[62] If it had not been for this type of preventive action, it is likely that disputes of the kind seen in Armagh, Clogher, Killala and elsewhere would have been even more frequent.

This problem of clerical factionalism, along with the deficiencies already mentioned in the everyday conduct of the lower clergy and in the manner in which they performed their pastoral duties, continued into the first half of the nineteenth century. By the end of that period, however, the importance of all three problems had been diminished by the progress in most parts of the country of a general movement for internal reform. Several reasons can be suggested for the appearance of such a movement at this time. The formal repeal in 1782 of the penal laws affecting Catholic ecclesiastics removed the main excuse — whether genuine or otherwise — for a degree of laxity in ecclesiastical affairs. The appearance and early successes of a Protestant missionary movement dedicated to the conversion of Irish Catholics may have helped to make Catholic churchmen more aware of the deficiencies — and the vulnerability — of their organisation. But the main stimulus to internal reform was not something confined to any one religious group. The late eighteenth and early nineteenth centuries also saw the emergence, in both Britain and Ireland and among Protestants of all denominations, of a new seriousness with regard to religious duties. There were, of course, some important distinctions. The reform of Irish Catholicism was primarily an administrative one, concerned first with imposing new standards on the Church's servants, and secondly with a more thorough and a more effective regimenting — within a strict institutional framework — of the religious practices of the laity. It involved none of the emotional extremes displayed by the Methodists or other revivalist groups which flourished in Britain in the same period. A closer parallel is provided by the major reforms — again mainly administrative in character — introduced in the Church of Ireland during the early nineteenth century.[63] But all denominations, whatever the differences in their response, were clearly reacting to the same broad shift in religious attitudes and outlook.

Internal reform was in part a matter of individual bishops seeking to impose new standards in their own dioceses. The best known of these reformers was James Warren Doyle, Bishop of Kildare and Leighlin from 1819 until 1834. In a regime totally different from those of his easygoing predecessors Doyle set about imposing new standards of behaviour on his parish clergy, reviving the practices of regular theological conferences and spiritual retreats, forbidding priests to appear at horse-races, hunts or other places of amusement, prohibiting station dinners, and insisting that priests adopt a distinctive clerical dress. He also introduced fixed tables setting out the fees which were to be charged for baptisms, marriages and other services, and as a further deterrent to clerical avarice he decreed that all moneys accumulated from ecclesiastical offices should be bequeathed solely to charity or for religious purposes. On one occasion he refused to permit the customary 'month's mind' commemorative service for a deceased priest who had ignored this rule, declaring that he wished 'to mark that man's grave with my reprobation'. Regulations such as these were backed up by a close personal supervision of the clergy under his control. Doyle's visitations, his biographer's account suggests, were dramatic occasions, on which vestments and altar equipment which failed to meet the bishop's requirements might be summarily destroyed and priests rebuked for their shortcomings in front of their assembled congregations.[64]

The activities of Doyle in Kildare and Leighlin are particularly well known, mainly because of the existence of a detailed and well-documented biography, published thirty years after his death by W. J. Fitzpatrick. But very similar reforms were being introduced in other dioceses at about the same time. In an almost equally well-known letter to Propaganda, written in 1826, Bishop George Thomas Plunket of Elphin described his efforts to improve the administration of his diocese, including the introduction of a distinctive clerical dress, the establishment of regular theological conferences, and the reclamation of 'drunken, immoral and disorderly clergy'. Similar efforts were made by James Murphy in Clogher and by Daniel Murray, Archbishop of Dublin from 1823 until 1852. In Tuam Edward Dillon, appointed archbishop in 1798, also found much to criticise. 'Could I afford', he wrote to a fellow-bishop in 1799, 'to hold out a sufficient enducement to six or eight priests to engage them to retire to some distant country, things would go on tolerably well.' No Irish prelate was in a position to resort to such sweeping remedies. But Archbishop Troy of Dublin, writing after Dillon's death in 1809, considered him to have achieved 'a great deal in the way of reform in the archdiocese' and recommended Oliver Kelly, Dillon's vicar general, as the person best acquainted with his plans 'to effect a complete reform had he lived'.[65]

In addition to the efforts of prelates such as these to introduce a stricter discipline within the confines of their own dioceses, the movement for internal reform involved a degree of co-ordination and co-operative effort. Thus Archbishop Murray of Dublin and his suffragan bishops of Ferns, Ossory and Kildare and Leighlin came together in 1831 to work out a uniform code of ecclesiastical discipline for the entire province, the resulting legislation being ratified at separate synods of each of the four dioceses. Over the next twenty years the legislation enacted in this way provided a model for the statutes introduced in other Irish dioceses, so that already by 1850 there was a certain degree of uniformity in Irish ecclesiastical law. A more formal provincial synod was held in Tuam in 1817, and its legislation was ratified by Rome in 1825. Co-operation of this kind was taken a stage further in 1850, when the Synod of Thurles, the first national synod of the Irish Church for almost seven hundred years, provided the opportunity for the introduction of a uniform body of ecclesiastical legislation for the country as a whole.[66]

The regulations introduced at Thurles in 1850 were similar in many ways to those which reform-minded individuals had been introducing in their own dioceses over the previous fifty years. Thus priests were forbidden to take part in dances, horse-races and other social gatherings, and were obliged to read religious books regularly and to attend periodic theological conferences and spiritual retreats. They were also cautioned against giving any cause for suspicions of simony or avarice. Offerings for extreme unction, the sacrament administered to the dying, were prohibited altogether, and priests were forbidden on pain of suspension to withhold any sacrament on account of non-payment of fees. The rites of the Church were in future to be administered with the full ceremonies prescribed for them, and the administration of sacraments in private houses was to be abolished wherever possible. Clear and uniform rules were provided on such issues as the powers and duties of bishops, parish priests and curates, and on administrative matters such as the custody of ecclesiastical property and the preservation of diocesan records. New procedures were also laid down whereby the bishops would consult together and arrive at an agreed response to any measures introduced by government which affected the position of the Church, instead of fighting out their disagreements in public as they had done over the National Schools and the Queen's Colleges.[67]

The legislation of the Synod of Thurles summed up and consolidated the achievements of a half-century of reform and reorganisation. At the same time it would be wrong to see this gathering as marking the end of the campaign to introduce new and higher standards. In the years after 1850 laxity of ecclesiastical discipline, and the problems that went with it, remained a cause for serious concern. When Bishop O'Higgins of Ardagh died in 1853, Archbishop Cullen of Dublin still felt it necessary to urge on Rome the necessity of making an early appointment. If this were not done, he warned, the priests of the diocese 'will begin to divide themselves into parties and to make trouble, and discipline will become more relaxed than it is'. From the time of his arrival in Ireland in 1850 Cullen was the main force behind a continued effort to impose a tighter and more uniform discipline on the Irish Church. Yet even at the time of his death in 1878 his programme of reform had failed to penetrate the archdiocese of Tuam, still governed by the formidable John MacHale. Accounts of the condition of Tuam in the late 1870s recall the problems encountered elsewhere forty years before: priests engaged in factional squabbles; preaching, supervision of local schools and other pastoral functions widely neglected; the best parishes monopolised by relatives of the archbishop. John MacEvilly, the coadjutor finally forced on MacHale in 1878, but whose existence the octogenarian archbishop stubbornly refused to recognise, commented in the following year that it would take generations of archbishops to reform Co. Mayo.[68] Already by 1850 the Irish Church had come a long way since the days of Sweetman and Plunkett, and even since those of Doyle. But the progress of internal reform was both gradual and uneven, and old habits and attitudes persisted — in some areas at least — until well into the second half of the nineteenth century.

3

Popular and Official Religion

1. *Belief*

'We live, most reverend sir, in wretched times, when too many of our people are ignorant of or forget their real principles, or, what is worse, are ashamed to profess them.' Archbishop Troy of Dublin, writing to the Warden of Galway in 1792, expressed an unease which must have been shared by many European churchmen as the eighteenth century drew to a close. For several decades the basic doctrines of Christianity had been under mounting attack as deist and atheistic writings circulated throughout the greater part of Europe. Now the spirit of infidelity had assumed more concrete and more menacing forms in the aggressive secularism of the French Revolution and in the policies of Enlightenment rulers in other European states. It is not surprising, then, that Troy and other bishops should have been ready to see in events around them, and particularly in the spread of popular support for the United Irishmen, evidence that similar doctrines were about to appear in Ireland. Yet before very long it was clear that they need not have worried. A few middle-class Catholics might take up deist or sceptical ideas (as, for a brief period, did Daniel O'Connell). These ideas might even spread, as Troy complained, to 'some ignorant, lukewarm or temporising clergy'. Yet Ireland had never been likely ground for the emerging spirit of religious indifference to put down roots, and its impact even among intellectuals was both transient and superficial. In the census of 1861 a total of 146 persons returned themselves as deists, atheists, freethinkers or persons of no religion.[1]

The main threat to the position of Catholicism in Ireland during this period came, not from social change or Enlightenment ideas, but rather from developments within Irish Protestantism. The eighteenth century had seen a steady stream of defections to the Established Church from the ranks of the Catholic gentry and middle class. But among other sections of the population, in the absence of any serious missionary efforts from a lax and worldly Church of Ireland, the number of losses through conformity had been negligible. The losses which did occur, furthermore, had probably been balanced if not exceeded by the absorption into the majority religion of lower-class Protestants, either through intermarriage or through pressures for conformity of a different kind.[2] From the early years of the nineteenth century, however, all this was to change as the growing influence of evangelical ideas among both Anglicans and Nonconformists resulted in a new interest in missionary efforts, both foreign and domestic. The years between 1820 and about 1860 were the period of the 'Second Reformation', when a whole range of dedicated and well-supported Protestant societies devoted themselves to the task of the conversion of the Catholic Irish.

If the Second Reformation was the major test of its internal stability faced by Irish Catholicism in the first half of the nineteenth century, then the test was passed with surprising success. The missionaries showed a good instinct for the weaknesses of their adversary, concentrating their attack in areas like Kerry and Connemara, where social conditions were exceptionally harsh and where the resources of the Catholic Church were at their lowest. The investment of money and human effort was considerable: when the founder of the Protestant colony in Dingle, Co. Kerry, applied for assistance to the Irish Society in 1836, he was sent no less than twenty Irish-speaking preachers to assist him. In the short term such concentrated efforts achieved results. By 1845 the colonies at Dingle and Ventry contained some 800 converts, while in Achill four years later the Anglican bishop confirmed more than 400 converts during a single visit. But none of the missionary groups succeeded in achieving the crucial breakthrough by which the Second Reformation could be carried beyond these artificially created islands of Protestantism to the population as a whole, and the gains which were made were largely wiped out by an energetic counter-attack by the Catholic Church, spearheaded by Redemptorist missionaries, in the early 1850s. The failure of the missionary effort can in part be attributed to the personal failings of some of the individuals involved, and to the lack of enthusiasm, amounting at times to positive hostility, which local Protestant incumbents displayed towards what they regarded as disruptive intruders. But the main reason was undoubtedly the resistance encountered from the great majority of Catholics even in these backward and neglected areas of their church's domain.[3]

In striking contrast to this impressive display of internal cohesion is the casual and in many cases openly derisive attitude which Irish Catholics could on other occasions display towards their church and its teachings. Satire directed not only at the Catholic clergy but also at basic religious doctrines remained a notable feature of popular literature up to at least the early nineteenth century. Thus the famous *An Sotach 's a Mháthair*, composed around 1815, consists of a dialogue in which a beggarwoman's pious exhortations that worldly suffering should be met with prayer and patience in expectation of a reward in heaven are mercilessly debunked by her disgruntled son. The joys of heaven are dismissed with the comment that they are of little use to a man with an empty stomach, and the threat of hell with the claim that if everyone who shared his views was sent there, then the place was full to overflowing years before. Stories and ballads describing the debates between Christianity, represented by St Patrick, and a sceptical paganism, represented by the mythical hero Oisín, with the latter being allocated a good proportion of the best lines, were also a favourite genre. Neither was this willingness to satirise confined to songs and poems. Among the features of the traditional wake which attracted the repeated condemnation of the church authorities, as will be seen in a later chapter, was the enactment of mimes and games in which Christian sacraments and rituals, and in particular marriage and confession, were mocked and parodied.[4]

Students of Irish popular literature and folklore have not in general chosen to take this tradition of religious satire at face value, preferring to see it as the application to religious matters of a broader comic tradition. In this they are probably correct. In the light of recent work on popular irreligion in sixteenth- and seventeenth-century England it is no longer possible to assume that widespread scepticism and indifference were a new development of modern industrial living and that pre-famine Ireland, as a 'traditional' and predominantly rural society, would not have had its unbelievers. Indeed, John O'Donovan, discussing the Catholic families of Clones, Co. Monaghan, in 1834, noted the existence of 'the only atheist in the parish, who believes that the devil is a bugbear got up by the clergy to make money'. But in the absence of other evidence one can only conclude that such individuals were rare and that for the majority of Irish Catholics this tradition of mockery reflected, not a lack of belief, but rather a lack of reverence. In this it not only draws attention to an aspect of popular religious attitudes which the solidarity of Irish Catholicism in the face of attack from without might lead one to overlook. It also provides a timely reminder that what we are setting out to examine is a world of beliefs and attitudes in which modern concepts of the elements which make up a religious outlook will at best be inappropriate and at worst may prove gravely misleading.[5]

2. Education

For the greater part of the Catholic population of Ireland in the eighteenth and early nineteenth centuries, instruction in the doctrines of religion was conveyed exclusively by word of mouth. In 1861 only 35 per cent of Catholics aged five years and over were returned as able both to read and write. A further 19 per cent, it is true, were returned as able to read though not to write; however, it may be surmised that they did not do so often or with very much ease. In earlier decades the proportion of literate persons would have been substantially lower — in 1841 it was found that more than 50 per cent of all males born between 1741 and 1760 were unable to read or write, compared with only 38 per cent of those born between 1811 and 1820, and 35 per cent of those born in the 1820s.[6] A popular religious literature did exist in pre-famine Ireland in the cheaply bound lives of the saints and devotional works which were sold throughout the country by travelling pedlars and small-town shopkeepers.[7] But for the influences which shaped the religious outlook of the great majority of the population it is clearly necessary to look to other forms of communication.

Two main methods were adopted by the Catholic Church of this period to provide its laity with a knowledge of the doctrines of their religion. The first of these was the preaching of the parish clergy. Diocesan statutes regularly insisted on the obligation of pastors to deliver a sermon at mass on all Sundays and holydays. To assist them in this task priests could draw on a wide range of manuals and collections of printed sermons. One survey lists a total of seventeen such works printed in Ireland during the eighteenth century, while the visitation book of Archbishop Butler of Cashel in the 1750s shows that there was a volume of sermons prescribed for use in the diocese, referred to as the 'prone', which all priests were expected to produce for inspection during the visitation. Most of the books available were in Latin or French, with a few by English authors. However, there was one outstanding work designed specifically for Irish pulpits, the *Sixteen Irish Sermons in an Easy and Familiar Style* published in 1736 by Bishop James Gallagher of Raphoe, and the end of the eighteenth century saw the publication in rapid succession of several other sermon books by Irish authors. Bicheno in 1830 was favourably impressed with the preaching of the Irish Catholic clergy, contrasting their vigour and energy with the 'cold, official reading of the established clergy'. At the same time there are indications that the obligation of preaching regularly, like other aspects of ecclesiastical discipline, was not always strictly observed. Bishop Sweetman's complaints about neglect of this duty in the diocese of Ferns have already been quoted. And the situation in the diocese of Dublin at the time of the succession of Daniel Murray in 1823 was described thirty years later in terms which even the circuitous and euphemistic language of a funeral oration could not altogether weaken:

From the unexampled calamities that had overtaken religion in these countries — from local abuses, that when once introduced it is so difficult to eradicate — from the scanty numbers and overpowering calls upon the priesthood, the announcement of the sacred word in the city, and still more in the rural portions of the diocese, had become rarer, unfortunately, and less efficient, than the sacred canons would have permitted in less afflicted portions of the Church.

If this was the situation in Dublin after nearly forty years under the rule of the formidable Archbishop Troy, it is hardly surprising that in other parts of the country reforming prelates like Doyle in Kildare and Leighlin and Plunket in Elphin should have made better and more regular preaching a prominent part of the new regime which they sought to impose on their parish clergy.[8]

A second potential constraint on the effectiveness of the preaching of the Catholic clergy, apart from neglect on the part of pastors, was the problem of language. This is a matter which it is easy to overlook. From at least the beginning of the nineteenth century the Irish language had been in decline. By the time of the census of 1851 less than five per cent of the population were monoglot Irish-speakers, and contributions to Mason's three-volume parochial survey in 1814—19 suggest that even at that date there were relatively few areas in which more than a minority of the inhabitants were unable to understand English. But if we are to be concerned not merely with whether preaching was understood but also with how it was received, then the language which was used remains an important consideration. Many of those returned as capable of understanding both Irish and English (a group which even in 1851 made up more than one-third of the population in both Munster and Connacht) would have been more at home in the former than in the latter. In Clonmore, Co. Louth, in 1814 'most of the inhabitants speak the English language, but they prefer the Irish among themselves'. In the neighbourhood of Carrick-on-Suir, Co. Tipperary, similarly, English was universally understood but was spoken only when necessary and with 'evident reluctance'. In areas such as this an English-speaking preacher might well have been understood by his congregation and yet have found the language he used a barrier between him and them. In the eighteenth century, when Irish was the only language of a much larger section of the Catholic population, the problem was, of course, still more serious.[9]

The church authorities of the eighteenth and early nineteenth centuries were aware of the danger of an English-speaking clergy being partly or wholly cut off from an Irish-speaking congregation. In 1764 Bishop O'Brien of Cloyne and Ross explained to Propaganda that he had been led to compile his Irish dictionary because 'the necessity . . . under which our young priests are placed of studying in the Catholic schools on the continent for many years exposes them to the danger of forgetting their mother tongue, which is so necessary for them in their work'. Bishop Kernan of Clogher, sixty years later, noted that an otherwise satisfactory priest or seminarian did not know Irish, adding the blunt injunction 'Let him lay down his shoulders to acquire it.' Nicholas Archdeacon, Bishop of Kilfenora and Kilmacduagh from 1800 until 1823, grew up 'an utter stranger to the Irish language', yet 'by application and industry, but particularly by secluding himself from his family and boarding himself at the house of a country parish priest, who was master of the language, during eighteen months, he learned it radically and now exhorts and catechises with ease'. But it is doubtful whether every priest whose knowledge of Irish was deficient could have been induced to follow such an example. And even Archbishop Bray was prepared to subordinate the question of language to other matters, arguing implausibly in 1802 that ignorance of Irish did not affect the suitability of the candidate he favoured for the position of Coadjutor Bishop of Cork.[10]

The second principal means by which the church authorities of this period attempted to maintain a reasonable standard of religious education was through the provision of a measure of formal instruction for the young. In some cases this was provided in schools set up by the Catholic clergy themselves. In 1792, for example, Bishop MacMahon of Killaloe opened a school in Ennis, supported by public subscriptions, replacing a smaller establishment which he had financed out of his own pocket for twenty-five years. Bishop Hussey of Waterford and Lismore claimed in 1797 to have founded a free school in each of the principal towns of his diocese. In other cases schools were set up in or beside Catholic chapels, under the supervision of the local clergy. In addition to such individual efforts, this period saw the rise of two great teaching orders, the Presentation Sisters, who began work in Cork in 1777 and who by 1830 had a total of twenty-eight schools in different parts of Ireland, and the Christian Brothers, founded in 1802. Some provision was also made for secondary education, in schools like Clongowes Wood College, opened by the Jesuits in 1814, and the Ursuline convent, Cork, 'long celebrated all over the continent for its method and success in giving a moral, religious and genteel education to young females of the higher class'. The diocesan colleges established in different dioceses from the late eighteenth century onwards were intended primarily to prepare students for entry into Maynooth and other seminaries, but they also provided a grammar school education for the more affluent sections of the Catholic laity. Thus St Finian's College, Navan, founded in 1802, was intended 'for the education of the genteeler class of society . . . in which many respectable gentlemen, from various parts of the kingdom, have studied the ancient and modern classics, and most of the present generation of our clergy were prepared for the Royal College of St Patrick, Maynooth'.[11]

Considering the limited financial resources available to Catholic churchmen in this period, this investment in elementary and intermediate education represents a substantial achievement. But the number of pupils catered for in these establishments accounted for only a tiny proportion of the younger Catholic population. In 1824 there was a total of 5,541 pupils being educated in the 24 schools run by the Christian Brothers and other male religious orders, 7,575 being educated in the 46 female schools attached to convents, and a further 33,847 attending 352 Catholic day schools supported by the subscriptions of the Catholic inhabitants of certain parishes and under the supervision of the local priests. Even in 1861 there were only 25,803 pupils attending elementary schools managed by Catholic religious communities, of whom more than 15,000 were pupils of the Christian Brothers. The numbers receiving a specifically Catholic secondary education were even smaller: 1,649 attending the 20 schools run by the religious orders, 2,469 attending 51 convent schools, and 1,202 attending 15 diocesan colleges.[12]

A much larger number of Catholic children received an elementary schooling in the institutions known with increasing anachronism as 'hedge schools' or alternatively, since the master received a fee from his pupils, as 'pay schools'. In 1824 about 300,000 Catholic children were attending private, elementary day schools of this kind.[13] The type of teaching provided in these institutions varied considerably, but most seem to have concentrated on an elementary instruction in reading, writing and arithmetic, with perhaps a smattering of other subjects, such as history and geography. In addition, the majority of these private schoolmasters appear to have included some instruction in religious doctrine in their curriculum. The visitation books of Archbishop Butler of Cashel show that even in the 1750s he took it for granted that the schoolmasters in his diocese would teach the Catholic catechism, and that teachers who did not do so were summoned to appear before the bishop, reprimanded for their neglect, and forced to promise to teach catechism in future. In Ulster, the Rev. Henry Cooke reported in 1825, schoolmasters of all religions commonly taught the pupils under their care the catechism of whatever denomination they belonged to, purely as an exercise in rote learning. He himself recalled being taught the Presbyterian catechism in this 'automaton' manner by a Catholic teacher. The private pay schools thus provided a valuable service to the Catholic clergy, and many of them operated with the sanction and co-operation of the local priests. At the same time not all churchmen were completely satisfied with their contribution. Bishop Doyle, writing in 1821, dismissed the teachers of his diocese as 'in many instances . . . extremely ignorant', adding the complaint that in their schools 'the children are piled on each other, and the sexes promiscuously jumbled together'. More important, the religious education provided in these schools was received by only a proportion of the Catholic population. The Catholic authorities, in a memorial submitted to the government in 1821, claimed that half of their laity never received any formal schooling. A comparison between the total figure of

400,000 Catholic children attending day schools in 1824 and the number of children aged between 5 and 15 recorded in the census of 1821 (1,749,000, of whom about four-fifths, or 1,400,000, would have been Catholics) suggests that this estimate was a reasonable one.[14]

The final means by which provision was made for the religious instruction of the young was through the establishment of special catechism classes in the parish chapels. Diocesan statutes regularly noted the obligation of all parish priests to provide facilities for such classes, and this obligation — by the early nineteenth century at least — appears to have been fairly generally fulfilled. According to the commissioners of the Irish Education Inquiry in 1824, 'there are . . . but few chapels in Ireland in which religious instruction is not imparted on Sundays to the Roman Catholic children of the parish'; one of the commissioners had himself seen more than 4,000 children assembled for this purpose in four chapels in the city of Limerick. The instruction provided at these classes, exclusively concerned with religious doctrine, was not usually given by the clergy themselves, but by suitable lay persons recruited for the purpose. The Rev. James Hall, visiting a Catholic chapel in Enniskillen on a Sunday morning in 1813 'found a tall, sensible-looking young woman examining a number of girls, of various sizes and descriptions, on the Roman Catholic catechism; and, at the same time, in a different part of the chapel, a young man catechising a number of boys, some of them nearly advanced to manhood'.[15]

In many dioceses by the early nineteenth century this lay participation in religious instruction had been given a more systematic basis through the setting up of Confraternities of the Christian Doctrine. 'These confraternities', Doyle explained in 1825,

> consist of young men and young females of a religious character, who assemble at an early hour on Sundays, and dispose the children in classes and teach them the rudiments of the Christian religion; they read before mass to them some pious lecture or instruction; and in some chapels after mass resume the same business, and continue it for an hour or two; they conclude these instruc-

tions by some form of prayer, after which they disperse and go home.

The movement for the establishment of these confraternities had begun towards the end of the eighteenth century. They had first appeared in Kildare and Leighlin in 1788, and in the following year the bishops of the province of Cashel had reommended their establishment in every parish where it could be effected. In 1796 Bishop Plunkett of Meath set up branches in the parishes of his diocese, seeing them 'as a remedy for the ignorance of the common people, and their degeneracy, causes which had contributed to the late depredations of Defenderism'. By 1824 the Irish Education Inquiry found that confraternities existed 'in many of the towns and most populous parishes of the south and west of Ireland, and appear to be daily extending themselves to other parts of the country'.[16]

What was the standard of religious education imparted in these catechism classes? The requirements for confirmation outlined in 1780 by Archbishop James Butler II of Cashel presumably reflect what he regarded as the minimum acceptable knowledge of Catholic religious doctrine:

> I announced . . . that I'd confirm no children under seven, and none past seven who were not well instructed in the principal mysteries, the commandments, the seven sacraments, particularly confirmation and the dispositions for a good confession, and who did not know the acts of contrition, faith, hope and charity.

But it is open to question whether even this fairly modest standard was always achieved in practice. We do not know, in the first place, what proportion of children actually received the catechetical instruction prescribed in diocesan statutes. At a time when the Catholic clergy were unable to enforce universal compliance even with the more fundamental obligation of attendance at Sunday mass, it is difficult to believe that there were not at least some children who attended only irregularly or not at all. In addition, there is the possibility that not all priests were equally conscientious in ensuring that regular catechetical instruction was provided. There may even have been areas in which this obligation was altogether ignored — as in Kilmore Erris, Co. Mayo, where a newly appointed parish priest in the 1830s was said to have found only seven of the inhabitants capable of repeating the Lord's Prayer correctly. And even if it is assumed that the majority of Catholic children did attend at regular catechism classes, there is the question of the quality of the instruction they received. In particular it is difficult to see how, even with the use of lay auxiliaries, the numbers involved could have been catered for without a heavy reliance on rote learning. Archbishop Butler's own summary of his requirements betrays elements of that emphasis on an ability to repeat certain formulae and prayers which was later to be parodied by William Carleton: 'the three thriptological virtues . . . the four sins that cry to heaven for vengeance, the five carnal virtues — prudence, justice, temptation and solitude, the seven deadly sins, the eight gray attitudes . . .'[17]

This is not to suggest that the four or five decades before 1830 did not see substantial improvements in the religious education of Irish Catholics. Schools wholly or partly controlled by the Catholic clergy had been established in different areas. Reforming prelates in various dioceses had insisted on a greater degree of attention to preaching and to religious instruction generally. The establishment of Confraternities of the Christian Doctrine had helped to provide badly needed lay auxiliaries to assist in the provision of regular catechetical instruction. As a result of these developments, the laity of the 1820s were probably better instructed in the doctrines of their church than any previous generation of Irish Catholics. But this superiority was entirely relative. Even in the 1820s it was only a small proportion of Catholic children who attended a school under the direct control of the Catholic clergy. The great majority of school-goers attended private schools, where they received a religious education which may in some cases have been perfectly satisfactory to the church authorities but which must have varied considerably in quality. And something approaching half of the Catholic population still received no education beyond, at the most, a rudimentary grounding in the catechism at a Sunday school and the weekly sermons of the local priest.

In the case of many of the problems which hindered the operations of the Irish Catholic Church in the first half of the nineteenth century — for example, the shortage of priests and the lack of adequate church accommodation — the beginnings of an improvement had to wait until the famine and its aftermath had radically altered the structure of Irish society, and with it the financial circumstances of the Irish Church. Where education is concerned, however, the change must be dated from a point almost two decades earlier, the establishment in 1831 of the National System of Education. Historians have devoted considerable attention to the dissatisfaction of Irish churchmen in the second half of the nineteenth century with aspects of the National System, and to their lengthy campaign to bring about the changes they desired. But the pleasures of disentangling this complex chapter in church–state relations should not permit us to forget that the main result of the introduction of the National System was to bring about a dramatic increase in the educational resources of the Irish Catholic Church, by creating a network of schools funded by the state but under the direct control of its clergy. It is true that this was not the result envisaged by the founders of the scheme, who had sought instead to create a system in which pupils of all denominations would receive a common secular and a separate religious education, the two being kept scrupulously apart. Indeed, this declared preference for non-denominational schooling led some churchmen, notably Archbishop MacHale of Tuam, to advocate the complete rejection of the National System. Archbishop Cullen, on the other hand, dismissed the ideal of a common education as impossible to achieve. The National System of Education, he pointed out in a report to Rome in 1851, 'is very dangerous when considered in general, because its aim is to introduce a mingling of Protestants and Catholics, but in the places where in fact there are no Protestants this mingling cannot be achieved'. Within a few years it was clear that this brutally realistic assessment was correct. By 1870 there were 807,330 Catholic pupils on the rolls of National Schools. Of these more than 400,000 attended schools in which there were no pupils of any other denomination and in which the teachers were Catholics. A further 364,154 attended schools which were returned as denominationally mixed, but where the teachers were Catholics and the number of pupils of any other denomination — 25,076 — was so small that they could in practice be regarded as Catholic schools. The number of Catholic pupils exposed to the hazards of the mixed education favoured by the original authors of the scheme was 42,441, just over 5 per cent of the total. And by 1867 85 per cent of the schools attended solely or predominantly by Catholics were under the sole management of Catholic priests.

It is in this perspective that one must view the criticisms of the National System of Education voiced by Catholic churchmen in the second half of the nineteenth century. No doubt their dissatisfaction with the restrictions imposed on the display of religious emblems and the time of classroom prayers, and their opposition to the non-denominational 'model schools', were genuine enough. But these were the complaints of men who took for granted the essentials of a state-supported denominational system under their control. A more accurate reflection of what the establishment of the National System had meant to the Irish Catholic Church of the mid-nineteenth century may be found in the comments of Bishop Moriarty of Kerry after a visitation in 1859: 'The children were admirably instructed wherever there were National Schools, and where there were not, the children are in ignorance of the catechism.'[18]

3. *Practice*

'No one can visit Ireland without being impressed by the intensity of Catholic belief there, and by the fervour of its outward manifestations.' Louis Paul-Dubois, writing in 1908, was commenting on what has remained one of the most striking features of twentieth-century Irish Catholicism, the remarkably high level of religious practice among all age groups and social classes. In other predominantly Catholic European countries it has long been accepted that the Catholic whose religious practice meets even the minimum requirements laid down by his church is the exception rather than the rule. In modern Austria, for example, the proportion of

Catholics attending weekly mass has been estimated at about one-third, in urban Italy at 28 per cent, in France at a little over one-fifth. Yet in Ireland in the early 1970s it was found that 91 per cent of adult Catholics claimed to attend mass at least once a week, and only slightly lower proportions claimed to make at least a yearly confession and communion. The proportion of Irish Catholics whose religious practice exceeded this canonical minimum was if anything even more striking. Almost one person in four claimed to attend mass more than once a week, and a full two-thirds to receive communion at least once a month.[19] It is against this modern picture of an unparalleled popular piety that we must examine the Catholic religious practice of pre-famine Ireland.

One obvious point of comparison is the level of attendance at Sunday mass, an obligation binding on all Catholics on pain of incurring mortal sin. Already by the early nineteenth century Irish Catholics were generally regarded as particularly scrupulous in fulfilling this obligation, their concern to do so being interpreted as evidence either of superior virtue or of abject subjection to their clergy. 'No distance of place,' an English Catholic ecclesiastic maintained in 1808, 'no badness of the road or of the weather, prevents them from attending divine worship on the days prescribed.' The poorer classes, a Co. Wexford rector agreed six years later, 'are in extreme subjection to the priests and attend chapel in all weather alike'.[20] However, the statistics on church attendance collected in 1834 for the Commissioners of Public Instruction show that the proportion of Catholics regularly attending Sunday mass fell well below that indicated by modern surveys. Professor David W. Miller, in a detailed examination of the commissioners' figures, concludes that average attendances in rural areas ranged from 60 per cent of the Catholic population to as low as 20 per cent, and that it was only in some of the medium-sized towns that the numbers attending Sunday mass were in any way comparable to those observed today. Professor Miller's figures relate to individual parishes or groups of parishes in which the data collected by the commissioners appear fairly unambiguous, and he does not suggest a single figure for overall church attendance in pre-famine Ireland. But if the twenty-three areas he selects are in any way representative, then it is difficult to believe that average attendances at Sunday mass can have greatly exceeded 40 per cent of total Catholic numbers.[21]

In any assessment of these figures it is, of course, necessary to make allowances for those persons to whom the obligation of attendance at Sunday mass did not apply — children, the old, the ill and persons housebound by inescapable domestic chores. The size of this group is impossible to estimate exactly, but it probably made up something like one-quarter of the total Catholic population.[22] Of the remaining one-third of Irish Catholics, who should have attended mass on any given Sunday but failed to do so, there were some who were kept away primarily by social pressures. There were frequent reports of persons being unwilling to attend church because they did not have decent clothes to appear in. 'When a man has nothing but rags on him,' a Co. Cork labourer explained to the Poor Inquiry commissioners in the mid-1830s, 'he has not courage to go among the people. If he went in among the clean and decent congregation on a Sunday, all the eyes in the chapel would be on him, and he could never stand it.' In addition, some chapels had compulsory collections, with those who did not contribute being refused admission, and even where this was not the case there were probably those who preferred to stay away rather than suffer the humiliation of allowing the collection plate to pass them by untouched.[23] However, embarrassments of this kind could of their nature affect only a minority conspicuously more impoverished than their neighbours. For a much larger group, it seems clear, the supposedly strict obligation of attendance at Sunday mass was simply being ignored.

The data collected by the Commissioners of Public Instruction reveal not only an unexpectedly low overall level of church attendance but also significant variations in that level. Professor Miller presents this variation in terms of a contrast between predominantly Irish-speaking and predominantly English-speaking areas, pointing out that attendances in the former ranged from about 20 per cent to about 40 per cent of total Catholic numbers, and attendances in the latter from 30 to 60 per cent. This contrast, he argues, reflects the different strength of the traditional beliefs and practices which in his view weakened the hold of orthodox Catholicism on the minds of Irish Catholics before the famine. A simpler explanation, however, would be that the areas in which church attendance was at its lowest, the north-west, west and south-west, were also the areas in which church accommodation was most restricted and in which the parochial clergy were most thinly distributed. In addition, as was seen in an earlier chapter, these were the areas in which internal reform and re-organisation had as yet had least effect on the character of Catholic religious life. From this point of view the findings of the Commissioners of Public Instruction can be seen as reflecting the uneven progress in different parts of the country of a general movement for the tightening of internal discipline and the improvement of pastoral services, a movement which was still in its early stages at the time of the commissioners' survey. Even in the city of Dublin Archbishop Murray's biographer, writing in 1853, dated what he considered 'the amazingly increased frequentation of the sacraments' only from the jubilee of 1826, conceding that before that date the attention of Dublin Catholics to their religious duties 'had been, in fact, for a long time, anything but edifying'.[24]

The second major religious obligation binding on all Catholics was to confess and receive communion at least once a year, in the period around Easter. In this case there are no statistics comparable to those concerning church attendance. However, there are indications that this obligation too was frequently neglected by Irish Catholics in the decades before the famine. Bishop Plunkett of Meath, inspecting his new diocese in 1780, was 'scandalised to find so many grown-up young people of both sexes who had never been at confession'. Bishop Troy of Ossory, writing in the same year to the clergy of his diocese, complained of 'the very little attention paid to the important obligation of receiving the holy eucharist at least at Easter'. But it is indicative of the extent of such neglect that Troy did not attempt to apply the strict rule of the Church, according to which persons who failed to perform this duty were to be excommunicated and deprived of Christian burial. Instead he confined himself to announcing that offenders would not be married in church, permitted to act as godparents, or, in the case of women, churched after childbirth. In the diocese of Cashel by the early nineteenth century the obligation had been extended to a twice-yearly confession and communion, at Christmas as well as Easter, but complaints about widespread neglect continued. In 1818—19, it is true, the coadjutor archbishop, Patrick Everard, appears to have mounted a minor campaign for stricter enforcement of this regulation, with some success. In one parish which he visited in September 1818 about two hundred persons who had neglected to perform their Easter duty came forward and declared their penitence, and similar reconciliations of large numbers of offenders were recorded in three other parishes in the following May. But the visitation records of Everard's successor, Robert Laffan, in 1824—28 show that he remained far from satisfied with the level of compliance with this basic obligation.[25]

Where the other sacraments of the Catholic Church are concerned, there appears to have been a distinction in popular attitudes and practice between those marking rites of passage and those which lacked this fundamental significance. Thus it would seem that there were relatively few Catholic children from this period which were not taken by their parents for baptism, and it was generally agreed that to die without extreme unction was regarded by Irish Catholics as a major tragedy. On the other hand attitudes to marriage, which will be dealt with in a later chapter, appear to have been mixed, a general intolerance of extra-marital sexual intercourse being combined with a widespread disregard for regulations on consanguinity, consent of parents and similar matters. The sacrament of confirmation appears to have been held in little regard and to have been frequently neglected, at least up to the early nineteenth century, when accounts from different regions of large numbers of adult confirmations suggest that the church authorities were beginning to take a stricter line. In Portarlington, Queen's County, one of the first parishes he visited after taking over the diocese of Kildare and Leighlin, Doyle is reported to have confirmed a total of 1,000 persons, some of them in their sixties or older, out of a total Catholic population of 9,000. The confirmation of large numbers of adults was reported in Waterford and Lismore in 1840 and in the diocese of Derry in the following year. In Cashel and

Emly, as late as 1876, Archbishop Croke confirmed a total of 10,345 persons, of whom 1,753 were adults. In Connacht during the early 1850s adult confirmations were a prominent by-product of the counter-attack against the forces of the Second Reformation. At Cong in 1853 a Vincentian mission was followed by the confirmation of 1,000 persons, of whom 800 were adults, while two years earlier Cullen had reported to Rome that the Bishop of Clonfert, inspecting the diocese of Kilfenora and Kilmacduagh on behalf of the aged Bishop French, had confirmed almost half the population.[26]

The aspects of Catholic religious practice with which we have so far been concerned — Sunday mass, a once- or twice-yearly confession and communion, the sacraments of baptism, marriage and extreme unction — represented no more than the obligatory religious observances binding on all members of the Catholic Church. There were some Irish Catholics, even in the early nineteenth century, whose religious practice went well beyond this canonical minimum. 'We do have great work here on festivals,' a schoolmaster in Rathangan, Co. Wexford, told a priest friend in 1822:

> On Corpus Christi we have a procession of the Blessed Sacrament, on Palm Sunday a procession of palm, on 15th of August, our patron day, a grand solemn mass and procession of candles. Every Sunday in Lent we sing round the stations, and on other festivals we have a benediction of the Blessed Sacrament, all which serve very much to excite devotion in the people.

In Loughrea, Co. Galway, by 1847 the obligatory mass on Sundays and holydays was supplemented by the public recitation of the rosary on Sunday evenings, as well as by benediction after the midday mass on the first Sunday of each month. In addition, the authorities in different dioceses had begun to encourage more frequent attendance at confession and communion through the establishment of lay societies and confraternities. Thus as early as 1778 Archbishop Butler of Cashel established a Confraternity of the Blessed Sacrament, whose members had as their principal duty to receive communion on the third Sunday of each month. In Dublin, in the parish of St Audeon's, an Association of the Sacred Heart of Mary was established in August 1840, its members receiving indulgences for taking communion on the second Sunday of each month and on the different festivals dedicated to the Virgin, as well as for attending mass on Saturdays at a particular altar in the parish church. Elsewhere too there were accounts of Purgatorian Societies, Rosary Societies and similar lay confraternities.[27]

Innovations of this kind anticipate the major developments of the second half of the nineteenth century. At the same time none of these moves towards a pattern of more frequent and more elaborate religious practice affected more than a minority of Irish Catholics. Processions, benediction and the like may have become familiar sights in the larger towns and in a few other districts, but in most parts of the country they remained unknown. An Austrian Redemptorist, carrying out a mission in Enniskillen in 1852, discovered that the people there 'had never even witnessed benediction of the Blessed Sacrament, never seen incense rise from a thurible', and elsewhere too it is clear that such refinements did not become common until well into the second half of the nineteenth century. Furthermore, in spite of the establishment of Confraternities of the Blessed Sacrament and similar associations dedicated to the encouragement of a more frequent attendance at the sacraments, the great majority of Catholics continued to confess and receive communion only once or twice a year – and in many cases, as has already been seen, they fell short even of this. This general adherence to the bare canonical minimum was recognised, and indeed institutionalised, in the practice of holding stations once or twice each year in private houses throughout each parish. In 1853 a synod of the province of Cashel reported to Rome that an attempt to do away with stations had had to be abandoned, because in their absence so many persons had failed to make even an annual confession. The reason why so large a proportion of Irish Catholics in America fell away from the Church, it was suggested in the same year, was 'their being accustomed [*sic* – unaccustomed] to go to the churches to have an opportunity of receiving the sacraments, and the priests in America being so few they cannot *wait on* the people with religion as they do in Ireland'.[28]

All the evidence, then, suggests that the religious observances of pre-famine Irish Catholics were more restricted in range, and considerably less frequent, than those of their counterparts in later decades. In order to appreciate the full extent of the gulf that separates the Catholic religious practice of the two periods, however, it is necessary to look not merely at the content of that practice but also at its physical circumstances. A noticeable feature of the pre-famine period was the considerable variation in quality of the church accommodation available. In some areas, even in the early nineteenth century, there was still no Catholic chapel of any kind, and mass continued to be celebrated in the open air. In the diocese of Tuam in 1835 there were nine places where Sunday mass was celebrated without a chapel. In Portrush, Co. Antrim, in the same year mass was still celebrated in a private house in winter and on some rocks by the shore in summer, and open-air altars were also found up to the mid-1830s in some parts of Co. Tyrone. In other districts, by contrast, there was evidence, even in the early years of the century, of an increasingly ambitious approach to church-building. This was particularly the case in Dublin, where a Catholic pro-cathedral was completed in 1825 and a further six new churches were erected between 1830 and 1845. But elsewhere too major projects were undertaken: the cathedral in Carlow, completed in 1829 at a cost of £30,000, and the cathedral in Tuam, completed in 1840, as well as others begun in Ennis in 1831, in Armagh in 1839, and in Killarney in 1842. However, building on a large scale was possible only where the Catholic community was relatively prosperous or where, as in the case of cathedrals, the resources of an entire diocese were concentrated on the erection of a single prestigious edifice. The majority of Catholic parish chapels remained unimposing buildings, frequently unable to accommodate the full number of persons attending them, and in some cases seriously defective. Of the 106 Catholic chapels in the diocese of Tuam, the archbishop reported in 1825, 18 or fewer had slate roofs, and a local Catholic gentleman confirmed that the chapels of the area were 'extremely wretched'. The Bishop of Ardagh and Clonmacnoise conceded that the chapels of his diocese were, with some exceptions, 'miserable enough'. In Cork and Waterford the agent to the Duke of Devonshire described 'very wretched thatched chapels, so irregular in the line of their roof, that they looked like several cabins joined together'. In Skibbereen the parish priest admitted that his chapel was 'in such a state that I daily fear some accident may occur whenever the people are assembled in it, in consequence of the decayed state of the roof and the walls'. In addition, there were frequent reports of chapels too small to accommodate their congregations, so that a large proportion had to remain outside during services. 'Any body travelling through Ireland on a Sunday', a landlord confirmed, 'will see them kneeling all about the chapel-yards and in the streets.'[29]

The physical unimpressiveness of the majority of church buildings was matched by a general lack of the backcloth of embellishment and visual display which normally makes up an integral part of Catholic public worship. Bishops of the eighteenth and early nineteenth centuries, as was seen in an earlier chapter, appear to have found it difficult to ensure that their clergy maintained a reasonable standard of display even in the altar equipment and vestments which they used in their religious services. In the diocese of Kilmacduagh the use of any kind of distinctive garb for ecclesiastical functions is reported to have become so uncommon that a parish priest who appeared in his chapel wearing a soutane saw his congregation walk out in a body. They had done so, one of them explained later, because they were 'opposed to Protestantism in every form'. The chapels themselves were in most cases almost entirely bare of ornamentation. Edward Dillon, arriving in the administrative centre of his new diocese of Tuam in 1799, found 'a large chapel, with a very bad roof, without a single article of sacerdotal ornament that would be fit for the most obscure country chapel'. De Tocqueville, visiting a chapel in the same district more than thirty years later, described a similar bareness: 'The floor was of beaten earth; the altar was of wood; the walls had neither paint nor pictures, but remained as the mason had left them.' In Co. Limerick, as late as the 1860s and 1870s, Mary Fogarty attended mass in 'a poor plain little chapel. There was an altar with a large crude statue of the Blessed Virgin on it and two vases for flowers. . . . There was no singing, no incense, no candles, no pictures nor stations of the cross.'[30]

Accounts of this kind contrast sharply with the lavish display which was to become such a prominent feature of Catholic public worship in the second half of the nineteenth century. But it was not only in their outward appearance that the Catholic chapels of the pre-famine period differed from those of later decades. They were also to a much lesser extent the centre of the religious life of the parish. Whereas the modern Catholic chapel is the location for almost all the organised observances and ceremonies of the district it serves, the pre-famine chapel appears frequently to have been little more than, in the literal sense of the word, a mass-house — a place where mass was said on Sundays and holydays but which had no particular claim to be the scene of other religious functions. The practice of stations, where confessions were heard and communion administered in a private house rather than in the chapel, has already been mentioned. In addition, it remained customary throughout the first half of the nineteenth century for both baptisms and marriages to take place either in the home of the persons concerned or in the house of the parish priest rather than in the chapel. Severe restrictions on both stations and baptism and marriage in private houses were imposed by the Synod of Thurles in 1850, but in each case the reformers, led by Archbishop Cullen of Armagh, encountered strong resistance not only from the laity but also from their fellow-churchmen. As late as 1875 Cullen complained that the decrees of the synod, particularly those relating to baptism and confession in private houses, continued to be widely ignored.[31]

This restricted range of functions helps to account for the final important difference which must be noted here between the Catholic chapels of the first half of the nineteenth century and those of later decades. In modern Ireland a Catholic church building is consecrated ground, and this status is acknowledged even at times when formal religious services are not in progress. Persons entering the chapel genuflect in front of an altar; men uncover their heads, and women until recently covered theirs; visitors speak only in whispers. The reasons for this outward display of reverence are theological: the Catholic doctrine of transubstantiation and — as a result of this doctrine — the permanent presence in the tabernacle of the consecrated host. The same reasons explain why Catholic chapels are commonly used for private prayer in a way that the churches of other denominations are not. However, it was not until the second half of the nineteenth century that this practice of retaining the host permanently in ordinary chapels became customary in Ireland. As late as 1880 Archbishop Croke of Cashel reported to Rome that 'Generally speaking the blessed sacrament is not reserved in small churches.' This circumstance, along with the transference to other locations of a large proportion of the public religious observances of the parish, had important consequences for the status of the local chapel. It meant in effect that its character as a sacred building was intermittent rather than permanent. Outside the times of Sunday and holyday mass the chapel could and did become a building like any other. In Monasterevan, Co. Kildare, the local Catholic church, built in 1729 and up to 1788 the only Catholic place of worship in the parish, was used between Sundays by the local farmers as a threshing-floor. Elsewhere the parish chapel was frequently used on weekdays as a schoolhouse. This lack of any permanent status as a building set aside for religious purposes was further reflected in the conduct of the worshippers who attended these chapels. William Carleton describes how a rural congregation awaiting the arrival of the priest and the beginning of mass 'collect together in various knots through the chapel, and amuse themselves by auditing or narrating anecdotes, discussing policy or detraction'. A similar casual attitude was noted by Bishop Plunkett of Meath, who complained more than once during his first visitation in 1780 that people spoke aloud and misbehaved during mass and other ceremonies, and that in general they seemed unacquainted with the respect due to a place of worship and unused to being instructed in the matter. Even in the second half of the nineteenth century the attitude of elaborate reverence towards Catholic chapels with which observers of modern Irish society are familiar developed only slowly. As late as 1910 the practice of raising the hat or cap as one passed a Catholic church was presented as a recent development which was spreading from Dublin to other parts of Ireland.[32]

A survey of Catholic religious practice in the first half
of the nineteenth century and earlier, then, presents a very
different picture to the remarkable popular piety which has
been such a notable feature of twentieth-century Ireland.
Throughout the decades before the famine the religious
practice of the great majority of Irish Catholics remained
severely limited, in frequency of attendance, in the range
of devotional observances, and in the degree of ceremony and
external display with which public worship was conducted.
By the end of this period, it is true, one can detect the
beginnings of a movement for the imposition of new habits
and standards, but this affected only a small minority. Real
changes in the pattern of Catholic religious practice did not
come until the two or three decades after the famine. It was
in this period that the resources of a newly prosperous
Catholic laity were mobilised by a reformed and energetic
Church to bring about what Professor Emmet Larkin has
aptly described as a 'devotional revolution' within Irish
Catholicism. One aspect of this revolution was a change in
the physical circumstances of Catholic public worship. In
church-building, to begin with, the plainness and occasional
squalor of earlier days were more than compensated for in a
nation-wide orgy of extravagant construction. By 1908 even
a sympathetic observer like Paul-Dubois could not help being
struck by the contrast between the size and splendour of the
churches he encountered in every part of Ireland and the
general poverty and economic backwardness of the society.
Within these new and ostentatious structures, furthermore,
the tone of Catholic religious services was transformed by
lavish ornamentation, by the introduction of more elaborate
vestments and altar equipment, and by the use of music and
incense. Secondly, and more important, the 'devotional
revolution' involved a change in the character of popular
religious practice. During this period attendance at mass,
confession and communion became more regular, while at
the same time the routine devotional repertoire of Irish
Catholics was extended to include such novel elements as
retreats, benediction, the 'forty hours' devotion and stations
of the cross, and participation in all religious observances
was encouraged by the spread of sodalities, confraternities

and other organisations of the laity. It was also during this period that private devotional aids such as medals, scapulars and beads became common for the first time. Within a generation of the famine, Professor Larkin concludes, 'the great mass of the Irish people became practising Catholics, which they have uniquely and essentially remained both at home and abroad down to the present day'.[33]

In the first half of the nineteenth century, however, all this had still to come. Inevitably the restricted scope and impoverished circumstances of popular religious practice affected the position and influence of the Catholic Church and its clergy. It would, of course, be naïve to suggest that a population which regularly attends church will in all cases listen obediently to the voice of its clergy, and that a population which attends only infrequently will always ignore it. Too many other variables intrude for any such simple equation to hold good. But the position of the Catholic Church in pre-famine Irish society can hardly have failed to be affected by the fact that a large proportion of its adherents confined their religious observances to the obligatory minimum prescribed by canon law, and frequently fell below even that minimum standard; that the whole public image of the Church, as it presented itself to the faithful through the forms of public worship, was such an impoverished one; and that the doctrines and concepts it sought to embody lacked the reinforcement of concrete symbols. Pious historians might wish to idealise the simplicity of popular religious practice in an earlier time. But the rapidity with which elaborate devotional aids and new standards of external magnificence were adopted once circumstances permitted suggests that the churchmen of the nineteenth century had a different perception of that simplicity. For the majority of Irish Catholics in the period before the famine, religion was something which intruded on their lives with considerably less frequency than was to be the case in later decades. When it did so, furthermore, it was generally in circumstances which did little to inspire in them that awe and reverence by which religion, or its representatives, could hope to intimidate and persuade.

4.   *The Non-Christian Supernatural*

This discussion of the religion of pre-famine Irish Catholics
has so far been conducted entirely according to the definitions
of the Catholic Church itself. We have looked at the extent of
belief and disbelief in orthodox Catholic doctrine, at the
means by which that doctrine was transmitted, and at the
degree of participation in officially sanctioned religious rituals.
For a real understanding of Irish Catholicism in this period,
however, it is necessary to look beyond these doctrines and
rituals to another set of beliefs and practices, some of them
identifiable as survivals from earlier religious traditions,
others examples of the type of magical or supernatural
belief which can be found at any time in societies below
a certain threshold of economic and social development. Any
discussion of this non-Christian supernatural is complicated
by an evident predisposition among contemporary observers
to highlight any aspect of Irish Catholicism which could be
treated as evidence either of ignorance or of superstition. In
addition, there is the ever-present danger of mistaking the
products of a lively popular culture for seriously held magical
beliefs; most of the topics considered here will in fact be more
familiar to students of Irish folklore than to students of Irish
social history. At the same time even a brief examination
should make clear that what is involved is not merely a colourful folk tradition but a body of beliefs and practices which
made up a very real part of the mental world of large numbers
of Irish Catholics in the decades before the famine.

A case in point is the matter of belief in fairies. Contemporaries were in no doubt about popular attitudes to
these powerful beings. 'The fairy mythology', Thomas
Campbell maintained in 1778, 'is swallowed with the wide
throat of credulity,' and later observers also commented on
the extent of belief in fairies and on the care which was commonly taken to avoid incurring their displeasure — for example,
by speaking of them respectfully as 'the good people' or salut-
ing an unusual eddy of dust that might mark their passing.
Even with the most reliable of such accounts it is impossible
to be sure how much genuine popular belief lay behind the
customs described. But there are at least two aspects of the
fairy mythology which one cannot interpret other than as

manifestations of serious and deeply held beliefs. It was frequently noticed, in the first place, that certain types of bush
which were regarded as sacred to the fairies, as well as the
circular mounds which were believed to be their dwelling
places, were left severely alone by the common people, often
at the cost of considerable inconvenience. Thus observers from
the Ordnance Survey working in Counties Antrim and
Londonderry in the mid-1830s noted bushes of this kind
standing alone and untouched in the middle of cultivated
fields. In Westmeath in 1842 the German traveller Johann
Kohl noted that the local people, although they frequently
robbed plantations for firewood, never ventured near the
wood growing wild on reputed fairy mounds. A second aspect
of fairy beliefs, and one even more difficult to relegate to
the category of a harmless folk tradition, was the idea that
the fairies sometimes abducted a person, generally a young
child, concealing the theft by leaving in its place a 'changeling'
which resembled the stolen mortal but which would pine
away and eventually die. As a result of this belief, children
suffering from unexplained illnesses were subjected to various
forms of ill-treatment in an attempt to drive away the changeling and restore the real child. The case of Bridget Cleary of
Co. Tipperary, burned to death in 1895 by a group of relatives
and neighbours whch included both her husband and her
father, was merely the latest and best known of these incidents. In 1826 a woman was indicted at Tralee assizes for
drowning a four-year-old child while attempting 'to put the
fairy out of it'. Eight-year-old Anne Moorhouse, of Rathvilly,
Co. Carlow, died in 1837 as a result of bluestone administered
to her by a servant who believed her to be a fairy, while in
Tipperary in 1840 a sickly child died after being threatened
with a red-hot shovel and forced to admit that he was a
changeling.[34]

In addition to this belief in fairies and other supernatural
beings such as the banshee and the pooka, there was a wide
range of popular tradition relating to the exercise of occult
powers by humans. One common belief of this kind related
to the theft by magical means of dairy or other agricultural
produce. A person skimming the dew from a field on the
morning of 1 May, for example, would have the butter of

the cows grazing there in their own churn, while the owner's milk would mysteriously fail to churn at all. By similar means it was possible to obtain a double yield of corn or twin calves, while the victim's own crops failed or his cows aborted. Another common belief was that certain persons had the 'evil eye', so that, either willingly or unwittingly, they brought bad luck on whatever they complimented. For this reason it was customary for persons who praised a child or an animal to ensure that no harm was done in the process by adding 'God save him' or by spitting as they did so. 'Few things are considered more dangerous or unfriendly,' Crofton Croker wrote in 1824, 'or are longer remembered, than the omission of such ceremony,' and feeling on this matter was so strong that 'even people of education and above the ordinary rank' found it better to comply with popular custom rather than give offence. Popular tradition also prescribed methods of laying a curse on an enemy, by making a circuit of a holy well from east to west (instead of from west to east as was generally done) or by turning the stones known as 'cursing-stones' which were to be found in certain graveyards and other sites.[35]

Traditions of this kind are similar in many ways to the witchcraft beliefs found in other countries at this time and earlier. However, there is one important difference to be noted. In continental countries, and to some extent in England, the witch had, from the late middle ages, come to be defined primarily as a worshipper of Satan, a person whose occult powers were received in exchange for their allegiance to the devil. No trace of this concept, with its attendant paraphernalia of infernal pacts, familiar spirits and witches' sabbaths, appears in Irish popular tradition. In most of the beliefs relating to the use of occult powers for malevolent purposes, in fact, the actual perpetrator remains a remarkably shadowy figure. In some cases, it is true, a known individual was credited with possessing the evil eye, and there may have been other situations in which a particular person was blamed for harm done by magical means. But in most cases the witch seems to appear only as a generalised threat, the 'someone' or the 'hag' who might steal the luck of the farm or the value of its produce unless certain precautions are taken. Thus whereas witchcraft beliefs in sixteenth- and seventeenth-century England have been interpreted as legitimising the hatred and fear arising out of certain types of social tension, no similar function can be attributed to Irish popular tradition. Instead the attraction of Irish witchcraft beliefs was that they provided an explanation for the otherwise incomprehensible disasters of rural life, as well as the comforting sense that one could take some precautions against the occurrence of these disasters. It is not surprising that it was milk and butter — at a time when techniques of dairying were based more on custom than on science — which were regarded as particularly vulnerable to witchcraft, as well as to the malice of the fairies.[36]

If pre-famine Ireland did not have witches — at least not in the normal European sense — it did have its known practitioners of white magic. These were the men and women generally known as 'fairy doctors', who were frequently resorted to in cases of illness among both animals and people. In some cases what these offered was a folk medicine based on herbal remedies and a claim to special anatomical knowledge. A Co. Kilkenny practitioner who in 1836 undertook to set a dislocated hip did so by having two assistants pull on the patient's leg while he attempted to ease the joint into its proper place, a procedure which succeeded only in breaking the man's thigh and rupturing a blood vessel, so that he died the following day. In 1842 a Mayo man named Pat Bowls, described by a local magistrate as having 'hurried many to an untimely grave by his total ignorance of compounding medicine', undertook to bleed and blister an ailing patient, as well as preparing a medicine for him, again with fatal consequences. In other cases, however, both illness and cure were seen as magical in character. Thus fairy doctors were frequently called on to treat cows which were believed to have been injured by darts maliciously fired at them by the fairies, so that they lost weight and failed to give milk. In Co. Armagh such animals were treated by fixing to their tail a charm consisting of a prayer transcribed onto a piece of paper, or of herbs, nails and other talismans, and by giving them a drink of water, salt and pounded herbs while repeating a formula of exorcism over them. In other cases fairy doctors treated calves believed to be suffering from intestinal knots by the sympathetic magic of untangling a piece of string twisted into a complicated knot and laid over the animal's back.[37]

One reason for not treating the various popular beliefs described by observers of late eighteenth- and early nineteenth-century Ireland merely as colourful folk tradition is that so many of these had an obvious social utility. Thus a common use of popular magic in this period was to determine the truth or falsehood of disputed statements, a matter for which society has always had to provide procedures of some kind. In pre-famine Ireland, as in pre-industrial England and in many primitive societies today, the means favoured was an ordeal in which persons swearing falsely would incur some dreadful punishment, while those telling the truth would remain unharmed. In Grange Silvae, Co. Kilkenny, it was reported in 1839, persons accused of theft were asked to drink a glass of water from a certain well, in the belief that anyone who did so after swearing a false oath would be punished by having his mouth leave its proper place and open under his left ear. In other cases there were reports of croziers said to have belonged to certain saints, or of boxes believed to contain sacred relics, being used to swear on. The consequences of swearing a false oath on one of these objects varied. The most common punishment mentioned was once again the displacement or grotesque distortion of the offender's mouth, but one crozier used in Co. Mayo was believed to react to false oaths by a melancholy rolling of the gems resembling eyes set in its cover, and another in Co. Galway by glowing with such intense heat that the offender could not hold it. (In this last case, however, the custodian of the relic claimed to be able to detect from certain signs that a person intended to swear falsely and prevented such individuals from coming forward — an interesting example of the way in which such talismans could be used to intimidate suspected wrongdoers into betraying their guilt without the more extravagant claims concerning them ever being put to the test.) In Co. Tyrone the consequences of swearing falsely were said to be 'some dreadful calamity, probably the more terrific from the nature of it not being ascertained'. But whatever the exact nature of the claims surrounding them, the power of these relics to deter potential perjurers was clearly taken very seriously — so much so that their custodians were generally able to charge a fee for making them available to be sworn on. In the case of a crozier used for this purpose in Co. Galway up to the early nineteenth century the fee was 5s, while for a similar talisman still in use in Co. Roscommon in 1837 it was 2s 6d.[38]

The utility of popular magic, at least as far as psychological comfort is concerned, may also be seen in the case of many of the numerous beliefs and observances which can be grouped under the heading of calendar custom. Dr Kevin Danaher, in the most systematic study of this topic, has listed a total of thirty days to which some significance was attached in Irish popular tradition. These ranged from such minor landmarks in the yearly cycle as St Swithin's Day (15 July), when portents could be detected of the weather to be expected in the succeeding forty days, to major festivals like 1 May and 23 June. As in the case of other societies in which calendar custom remained a prominent part of popular culture, clear connections existed between many of the most important festivals and the turning-points in the agricultural year. Thus the feast of St Bridget, celebrated on 1 February, marked the start of preparations for the spring sowing; 1 May, similarly, represented the beginning of summer, the day on which tenancies began or ended, workers were hired and cattle transferred from their stalls to the fields or from the home fields to rougher pasture; and St John's Eve (23 June) was the festival of midsummer, the point at which the power of the sun began to grow weaker and the days shorter. The observances surrounding these feasts were to a large extent festive in character, involving the lighting of bonfires, dancing and a variety of other amusements, and in many cases this was probably the main reason for their perpetuation. In at least some cases, however, these observances continued to have a magical character and function. The crosses woven from rushes or straw on St Bridget's Day, for example, were hung in dwelling-houses, and sometimes in stables and cow-sheds as well, to provide protection both from accident and from evil spirits. The bonfires lit on both May Eve and St John's Eve, similarly, were believed to have a protective function. Cattle were driven through the smoke or ashes or were singed with the burning brands, individuals leapt over the flames in the belief that this would bring them good luck and protection, and embers from the fires were used to bless crops growing in the fields. Rituals of this kind, performed at strategic points in the annual cycle, permitted men to feel that they exercised some control over the mysterious forces which governed the uncertain fortunes of life in general and farming life in particular.[39]

Observances designed to secure supernatural protection or assistance were not, however, confined to particular days of the year. Day-to-day life in pre-famine Ireland was crowded both with minor rituals which could ensure good luck or ward off harm and with omens predicting future events. In Co. Longford, for example, the first day of the month or the year was regarded as the best time to begin any new undertaking, and it was considered that no one should move to a new home on a Friday. In Co. Cork, similarly, 'the doctrine of omens . . . has still a large class of disciples. . . . Good and bad luck are supposed to attach to particular days, and many trifling things have the credit of a similar designation.' The fishermen of Galway, Aran and Connemara, O'Donovan reported in 1839, 'cannot bear to hear the name of a fox, hare or rabbit pronounced, and should they chance to see either [*sic*] of these animals, living or dead, or hear the name of either expressed, before setting out to fish in the morning, they would not venture out that day'. In Co. Limerick, even in the 1860s and 1870s,

> 'God be between us and harm' was forever on their lips — if a red-haired stranger came to the door; if the cock crowed during the day; if a heedless girl swept the floor towards the door; if she lit a candle without first crossing herself, or forgot to nip the cake [i.e. to break off a small piece from a newly baked loaf or cake].

Observances of this kind were less dramatic than those surrounding St John's Eve or 1 May. But for this very reason, because of their routine, everyday character, they penetrated all the more thoroughly the lives and minds of those among whom they were current.[40]

Beliefs and practices of the kind described here were not confined to any one region. Customs and terminology varied from place to place, but the same general set of rituals and traditions was found in all areas, not only in what one might be disposed to think of as the more primitive areas of the west coast but also in prosperous counties of Munster and Leinster. 'It is not in the west,' Sir William Wilde observed in 1851, 'or among what is termed the true Celtic population alone, that superstitious and mystic rites are still practised. We have fortune-tellers within the circular road of Dublin, and fairy doctors of repute living but a few miles from the metropolis.' As might be expected, however, the extent of belief in traditions of this kind varied between social groups. Thus the schoolmaster Humphrey O'Sullivan recorded but did not share what he clearly regarded as the ridiculous superstitions of his neighbours. In the same way Mary Fogarty, daughter of a prosperous Co. Limerick farmer, was assured by her parents that the stories she had been told of ghosts and fairies were not true. Nevertheless, as she later recalled, 'We could not help knowing that the maids, and most of the untaught people round Lough Gur, believed that a third world, fraught with danger, was going on all around them.' The third world to which she referred was the universe of fairies and other supernatural beings that existed side by side with the human world on the one hand, and the world of the Christian supernatural on the other.[41]

Widespread belief in different forms of magic continued up to at least the middle of the nineteenth century. By the 1830s, it is true, observers were beginning to detect the first signs of decline. 'All those notions are dying rapidly,' O'Donovan wrote from Roscommon in 1837, 'and in fifty years hence the Connacht man will not believe in giants, fairies, ghosts, blessed wells, stations or prophecies.' In other counties he commented in similar terms: in Galway, for example, a holy well was visited only by some old persons 'who are laughed at for their credulity'; in Offaly the people 'are now getting too sensible etc.' to visit wells in search of bodily cures. A few years later Mr and Mrs Hall remarked — in less regretful tones — on the same abandonment of traditional beliefs: 'In Ireland superstitions of a grosser or more unnatural character have almost vanished. Prejudices will soon follow them. The rational is making rapid way.' The process of decline was accelerated by the famine, with its wholesale disruption of social relationships, its demoralisation of the rural poor, its decimation of the social groups among which beliefs of this kind had been most popular. The traditional beliefs of the Irish countryside, Sir William Wilde maintained in 1849, 'are going fast, and will soon be lost to us and our heirs for ever', their disappearance being the result of 'depopulation the most terrific which any country ever experienced on the one hand, and the spread of education and the introduction of railroads, colleges, industrial and other educational schools on the other'. Even at this point, however, the abandonment of magical beliefs was less dramatic than these comments, written in the immediate aftermath of the famine, would suggest. Mary Fogarty's memories of the 1860s and 1870s, not to mention the case of Bridget Cleary in 1895, make clear that even in the second half of the nineteenth century there was still a substantial section of the population for whom the third world of the non-Christian supernatural remained an important reality.[42]

* * *

This survey of magical beliefs and practices could profitably be expanded at many points. However, our primary concern here is not with these traditions themselves, but rather with the relationship between popular magic on the one hand and the orthodox doctrines and rituals of the Catholic Church on the other.

It would be a mistake to think of this relationship as something which can be summed up in a single formula. The various forms of popular magic did not make up a coherent whole in the way that Catholicism did; consequently there could be no single, all-embracing accommodation between two broadly comparable traditions. Some of the beliefs and practices of the non-Christian supernatural — for example, the observances connected with May Eve and Hallowe'en (descended from the Celtic festivals of Bealtaine and Samhain) and many of the gatherings which originated as celebrations of the festival of Lughnasa, the beginning of harvest – had remained largely or entirely untouched by Catholic doctrine. Others had acquired Christian labels while their content remained largely unchanged. Thus the Celtic festival of Imbolc, the beginning of spring, continued into the nineteenth century and beyond as St Bridget's Day, and a similar process can be seen in the case of the strange festival known as St Martin's Day (11 November), when an animal or bird was killed and its blood sprinkled in different parts of the house and smeared on the foreheads of members of the family. However, the assimilation of popular magic into Christianity was not always so superficial in character. The annual pilgrimage to Croagh Patrick, Co. Mayo, on the last Sunday in July was originally one of the many celebrations of the festival of Lughnasa, but continues today as one of the most famous manifestations of Irish Catholic piety. Another example of complete or partial assimilation, the conversion of magical springs into holy wells dedicated to Christian saints, will be discussed in detail in the next chapter. Finally, there are instances of the reverse process, where aspects of Catholic doctrine and practice were modified to suit the popular need for magical solutions and remedies. This occurred, for example, when croziers and other alleged relics of Christian saints were used as a means of verifying oaths.[43]

In all these ways elements drawn from orthodox Catholic doctrine and practice came to be inextricably linked with others whose origins lay in the circumstances and psychological needs of the Catholic poor. Perhaps the most striking illustration of this process was in the case of the different prophecies which circulated widely among this section of the population in the late eighteenth and early nineteenth centuries. An interest in texts appearing to foretell major upheavals, disasters and victories, and a general susceptibility to millenarian excitement, were by no means confined to Irish Catholics during this period. In England at about the same time prophets like Richard Brothers and Joanna Southcott became the centres of large-scale popular cults, while a recent study has emphasised the role of prophecies and millenarian expectations among Ulster Presbyterians in the period immediately preceding the rebellion in 1798. What distinguished the prophecies favoured by Irish Catholics was their concentration on the theme of the conflict between the Catholic Church and heresy. The prophecies of Pastorini, derived from an analysis of the Apocalypse of St John first published in 1771 by an English Catholic churchman, Charles Walmesley, foretold a violent overthrow of the Protestant churches in the year 1825, and achieved mass circulation in Ireland in the early 1820s. The prophecies of Colmcille, circulating in different versions from at least the 1790s, were more closely tied to the particulars of Irish sectarian conflict. The version published in 1844, for example, foretold a general massacre of the Catholics of Ulster (organised by the Protestant clergy of that province), after which a league of Catholic nations would intervene to destroy heresy in both England and Ireland. Such fantasies provide a useful corrective to the inevitable emphasis in the preceding pages on the presence in popular Catholicism of a strong non-Christian element. If Irish Catholics freely adapted official doctrines and symbols into something more relevant to their needs, it was nevertheless in the total triumph of their church over its rivals that they found a symbol for their aspirations.[44]

If the degree of interaction between the beliefs and observances of the Christian and non-Christian supernatural varied from case to case, then, it seems clear that the relationship — at least where the Catholic laity were concerned — was rarely one of conflict. Where the two did not coexist peacefully, they overlapped and provided mutual reinforcement. Pilgrims visiting a holy well combined the sympathetic magic of a piece of cloth tied to a nearby bush or tree with prayers learned from the Catholic Church; the crosses woven on St Bridget's Day were sprinkled with holy water or taken to the priest to be blessed; the lighting of the bonfire on St John's Eve might begin with the recitation of prayers. In Irish folklore also, traditional beliefs were translated into Christian terms. Ghosts became souls of the dead who were confined in purgatory, while the fairies were identified as angels who had fallen to earth during Satan's rebellion against God and who had been permitted to remain there rather than being banished with the other fallen angels to hell.[45]

If the Catholic laity of the eighteenth and nineteenth centuries had little difficulty in reconciling popular magic and orthodox Catholic doctrine, the attitude of the church authorities was, as might be expected, somewhat different. As early as 1614 synods of the provinces of Dublin and Armagh, meeting a few months apart, had passed resolutions calling for the reform of 'certain abuses and superstitious usages practised by ignorant persons assembling at wells and trees'. The Dublin synod had also condemned as 'savouring more of superstition than piety' the practice of laymen carrying round with them croziers, bells and other relics of the saints, with which they sprinkled water on cattle and people. Condemnations of this kind were regularly repeated during the eighteenth and early nineteenth centuries. Regulations against witchcraft, spells and other forms of superstition were enacted in Limerick in 1721, in Dublin in 1730, in Kerry in 1747, in Cloyne and Ross in 1755, in Cork in 1768, and in Cashel in 1813. The Rev. Martin Marley's handbook, *The Good Confessor*, published in 1743, invited penitents to examine their consciences as to whether they made use of 'vain observances' about lucky and unlucky circumstances or of superstitious cures for diseases in men or cattle, and whether they had recourse to magicians, sorcerers or witches. Archbishop Butler's catechism, compiled in 1775, also contained a comprehensive list of prohibitions:

Q. Is there any thing else forbidden by the first commandment?
A. Yes; all dealings and communications with the devil; and inquiring after things lost, hidden or to come by improper means.
Q. Is it also forbidden to give credit to dreams, to fortune telling and the like superstitious practices?
A. Yes; and all incantations, charms and spells; all superstitious observations of omens and accidents; and such nonsensical remarks, are also very sinful.[46]

Prohibitions of this kind were backed up, in some cases at least, by positive action against offenders. The visitation records of James Butler I of Cashel, in the 1750s, show that he inquired regularly about the existence of 'necromancers', 'fairy men or women' and other evidence of superstitious practices. The archbishop, it is true, noted only one case of an actual offender being detected, a man 'that goes about curing people with his bottle of witchcrafts'. His successors in the diocese, however, were either more diligent or better informed. In one Co. Limerick parish in 1819 Archbishop Everard discovered 'a very decent respectable congregation, but much inclined to superstitious practices', while in Ballingarry, Co. Tipperary, in the following year a fortune-teller was induced to make a public submission to the archbishop and promise to amend her life. In a different parish visited by Everard's successor, Robert Laffan, in 1828 'a great many gave themselves up to the archbishop for fighting, witchcraft, not attending their duty, &c. &c.'.[47]

These, however, were the attitudes and statements of the church authorities. The rank and file of the Catholic clergy, in some cases at least, adopted a less critical approach to the customary observances of their flocks. Thus Nicholas Madgett, Bishop of Kerry, complained around 1758 that 'Certain priests do not exert themselves in instructing the people against these vices. I have even seen some of them simply laughing at these vices, but not chiding or paternally correcting their flock who are being defiled by this pagan infection.' The regulations drawn up in 1771 by Bishop Sweetman of Ferns suggest that in some cases priests not only failed to suppress such practices, but actually lent them their support:

> No pastor, priest or ecclesiastic whatsoever, in the diocese of Ferns, must presume, *sub poena suspensionis et privationis beneficii*, to read exorcisms or gospels over the already too ignorant, and by such ecclesiastics too much deluded people, or act the fairy doctor in any shape, without express leave in writing from the bishop of the diocese. Under the foregoing article I comprehend all those who bless water to sprinkle sick persons, cattle, fields with.

A similar concern over the possible inability of the Catholic clergy themselves to distinguish between legitimate and illegitimate forms of supernaturalism is reflected in the statutes drawn up in 1768 for the diocese of Cork, in which preachers are warned not to relate stories from apocryphal parts of the scriptures, to tell of miracles that had not been properly authenticated, or to predict the future.[48]

Not all of the parochial clergy, then, held themselves as much aloof from the customary observances of their congregations as the tone of formal diocesan legislation would suggest. In one Co. Limerick parish during the early nineteenth century the parish priest attended at the lighting of the midsummer bonfire and led the people assembled there in prayers. In Co. Longford it was recalled in the 1950s that in the past 'the priest was usually called in, in cases of butter being taken [i.e. by occult means], and that the clergy long ago looked upon the butter-taking as a fact, and not due to natural causes, such as a dirty churn or something like that'. In Taughboy, Co. Galway, the custodian of a crozier used for validating oaths always brought the relic to the chapel after it had been sworn on 'and got it prepared for use again by the priest's reconsecrating it after such profane use'. Some time before 1838, however, a new parish priest not only refused to co-operate in this ceremony of reconsecration, but publicly condemned the family for allowing the relic to be sworn on at all.[49]

This instance of a change in clerical attitudes was not an isolated one. Sir William Wilde, writing in 1849, quoted the opinion of 'one of our most learned and observant Roman Catholic friends':

> The tone of society in Ireland is becoming more and more *'Protestant'* every year; the literature is a Protestant one, and even the priests are becoming more Protestant in their conversation and manners. They have condemned all the holy wells and resorts of pilgrims, with the single exception of Lough Derg, and of this they are ashamed; for, whenever a Protestant goes upon the island, the ceremonies are stopped.

Twelve years earlier John O'Donovan, reporting on the abandonment of traditional observances at a cave in Co. Roscommon, had commented in very similar terms: 'The priests, I am sorry to see and to say, inclining very much to Protestant notions, are putting an end to all those venerable old customs.' In Co. Donegal, similarly, it was noted in 1834 that 'The priests are endeavouring to get rid of as many

superstitions . . . as possible.' Other reports testified to the
same general change in attitude. At Lough Keeran, Co. Mayo,
people were accustomed to assemble on the last Sunday in
July to protect their prosperity in the coming year by swim-
ming their horses in the lake, by throwing in offerings of
butter, and by attaching to a nearby tree the ropes they had
used to tie up their livestock. By 1838, however, the bishop
of the diocese had had the tree cut down, and the local clergy
were attempting to suppress the other observances connected
with the lake. In Kilcummin in the same county the parish
priest had removed a cursing-stone from the local church-
yard. Elsewhere there were reports of attempts to suppress
the customary practices at holy wells. Even the claim that
the Catholic clergy, or at least a section of them, were becoming ashamed of Lough Derg receives some support from
Bishop Doyle's evasive answers to a parliamentary committee
in 1825: 'Some in the neighbourhood of Lough Derg do
strange things, but I do not know it.'[50]

Several reasons can be suggested for the growing hostility
of the Catholic clergy to the traditional observances of their
flocks. To some extent the clergy were merely responding to
the same general influences which had also begun to produce signs of a more critical attitude to such practices among
sections of the Catholic laity — their superior educational
opportunities and relatively favoured social background ensuring that in this respect they were in advance of the majority
of their congregations. Furthermore, improvements in internal ecclesiastical discipline would have meant that the higher
clergy were better able to ensure that their subordinates did
not tolerate or connive at practices of which they disapproved.
Most important of all, perhaps, the Catholic clergy of the
early nineteenth century were a more prestigious body than
their predecessors, acceptable in circles where the latter had
not moved, and prominent as never before in public affairs.
It is not surprising that some of them felt obliged to live up
to their new-found status by displaying a more fastidious
attitude to the cruder elements of their religious heritage.
Already by 1819 a perceptive observer commented on the
opposition to keening shown by the Catholic clergy, 'whom
circumstances have rendered more objects of consideration,

and therefore more sensitive to ridicule'.[51]

At the same time the extent to which priests turned against the traditional beliefs and observances of the laity should not be exaggerated. By the 1830s the Catholic clergy were clearly more ready to take action against obvious examples of non-Christian ritual practice, but the suppression of such observances, and of the beliefs out of which they grew, never became a major element in their programme of social control. The only traditional observances which might be said to have become the object of an all-out attack were the wake and the pattern, both of which, as will be seen in the next chapter, were opposed partly as examples of popular magic, but primarily as threats to popular morals.

One factor which inevitably affected the policy of the church authorities towards traditional beliefs and practices was that they were themselves, as religious leaders, committed to propagating a whole series of doctrines relating to the supernatural and its intervention in men's lives. Bishop Madgett of Kerry in 1758 was not prepared to deny that milk and other farm produce could be affected by witchcraft. He had, after all, been informed by two trustworthy priests of his own diocese that they had themselves known instances of cream and butter being mysteriously replaced by thick, congealed blood. The most he could say was that real witchcraft was less common in Ireland than in other countries, and that where it did occur people should have recourse to the exorcisms and prayers of the Church and should not appeal to the devil to undo his own works. In 1791, when Bishop Plunkett of Meath was having trouble with a rebellious priest and some of his supporters, he received a letter from Archbishop Butler of Cashel, inviting him to avail himself, 'as an undoubted fact I can vouch for', of an incident in Butler's own diocese, in which God had intervened 'in the most striking manner' to bring about the sudden accidental deaths of the four men responsible for a similar rebellion. No doubt the archbishop was able to distinguish clearly between authentic miraculous intervention of this kind and the 'superstitious practices' and 'nonsensical remarks' which he had so clearly condemned in his catechism a few years before. But it is to be doubted whether that distinction was quite so clear to the lay population to whom Plunkett was invited to recount this cautionary tale.[52]

The continued willingness of the authorities of the Catholic Church to lend their support to the concept of direct supernatural intervention in everyday life was clearly demonstrated in 1823, when two bishops separately endorsed cures alleged to have been brought about through the agency of the German priest and supernatural healer, Alexander Emmerich, Prince of Hohenlohe. On 10 June 1823 Maria Lawlor, an eighteen-year-old girl who had been unable to speak since an illness six years before, attended mass at Maryborough, Queen's County, at exactly the same time that Hohenlohe in Germany celebrated a mass for her recovery. At the moment she received communion she heard a voice announce: 'Mary, you are well,' and her powers of speech were instantly restored. The bishop of the diocese, James Warren Doyle, investigated the incident and on 26 June published a pastoral letter announcing it as an authentic miraculous cure. In Dublin city two months later a similar cure was effected for Mary Stuart, a nun who had been both paralysed and unable to speak. This time it was Archbishop Daniel Murray who, after careful investigation and supported by the unanimous opinion of his clergy, published a pastoral letter declaring 'that the cure which was effected in the person of the said Mary Stuart on the 1 August instant is the effect of a supernatural agency, an effect which we cannot contemplate without feeling in our inmost soul an irresistable conviction "that this is the finger of God"'. Both Doyle and Murray were much criticised for the encouragement thus given to popular superstition, but in fact it is unlikely that their actions could have contributed very much to long-standing and deeply held traditions. At the same time their willingness to endorse miraculous cures of this nature not only shows how the enunciation of orthodox Catholic doctrine could weaken or nullify clerical condemnations of non-Christian supernaturalism, but also suggests that even in the 1830s the reduction of popular credulity was not the consideration uppermost in the minds of the church authorities.[53]

Finally, there is the question of how the continued existence of this non-Christian supernatural, and the place it occupied in the lives of Irish Catholics, might have affected the position of the Catholic Church and its clergy. One possibility, favoured by many contemporaries, is that popular credulity served to enhance the prestige and authority of both. The priests, according to one of their number who had defected to the Church of Ireland, 'arrogate to themselves the power of performing miracles, and the generality of the people are fully impressed that the priests are possessed of that power'. The Rev. David Croly, writing in 1834, also maintained that it was 'a prevailing notion' that the Catholic clergy 'can at their will and pleasure make sick or make well, give prosperity or adversity, damnation or salvation'. Comments of this kind may often have been exaggerated, but they nevertheless had an undoubted foundation in fact. There were well-documented instances, for example, of healing powers being attributed to the clay taken from the graves of certain priests; the grave of one Co. Tyrone curate in the second half of the nineteenth century had to be cemented over to prevent the coffin being exposed by pilgrims taking away soil for this purpose. The powers of miraculous healing attributed to the temperance reformer, Father Theobald Mathew, are equally well attested. There was also one much more dramatic illustration of the readiness of Irish Catholics to credit their clergy with far-reaching magical powers. This occurred in 1824 when John Carroll, Catholic Curate of Killinick, Co. Wexford, attempted to perform an exorcism on Catherine Sinnott, a girl of three and a half, whose possession apparently took the form of recurrent fits. Evidence at the subsequent trial revealed that a large crowd of onlookers had watched as the priest first jumped up and down on the child as she lay in bed, and then sat for more than three hours on an inverted wooden tub which he had placed over her. The father of the girl, who arrived home when the exorcism was already in progress, attempted to approach the bed, but 'some of the people desired me to be quiet, and kneel down, as the priest was going to perform a miracle'. He knelt down with the others and joined in the prayers. The next time he saw his daughter she was dead:

What did you do when you found that the child was dead?
I took her up in my arms and showed her to the priest.
What did he say to you?
He desired me to lay it down again on the bed.
Did you make no observation to Father Carroll on his conduct?
I did not, as I thought he would return and bring the child to life again.
Did you think he could bring the dead to life?
It was my opinion that he could.

Carroll was later acquitted of murder on grounds of insanity. Five of his parishioners, tried at the same time for complicity in the murder, were found not guilty.[54]

It is scarcely possible, in the light of this evidence, to deny that the Catholic clergy were in some cases credited by their congregations with possession of magical powers. At the same time the extent to which this might have contributed to their authority should not be exaggerated. The only clear-cut evidence of magical powers being attributed to Catholic priests, in the first place, relates not to the clerical body as a whole but to particular individuals. Both Theobald Mathew and John Carroll were regarded as having powers not possessed by other priests, and it was only certain clergymen whose graves were stripped of clay by pious seekers after cures. (There was also a widespread belief that 'silenced' priests — men who had been suspended from the exercise of their priestly functions on account of some misbehaviour — had powers of healing and other magical abilities not possessed by ordinary priests — a tradition which presumably reflects the element of mystery which inevitably attached to such individuals, to men who were priests and yet not priests.)[55] It is certainly possible that, in addition to these special cases, the clerical body as a whole was also credited with certain, more limited magical abilities, and that these added something to their prestige and influence. But the extent to which this was so remains impossible to determine. Furthermore, the notion that the Catholic clergy as a whole were significantly helped to maintain their authority over their congregations by a widespread belief in their supernatural powers is difficult to reconcile with the evidence of those repeated occasions, to be discussed in a later chapter, when Catholic priests became the targets of intimidation and even of violence directed at them by their flocks. Whatever belief there was in the magical powers of the Catholic clergy, it did not render them immune to open demonstrations of popular hostility or even, on occasion, to physical attack.

Finally, against the questionable gains which the Catholic Church and its clergy derived from popular credulity, one must set a consideration of the way in which the existence of this non-Christian supernatural served to diminish their influence and prestige. One aspect of this point has been developed by Professor Miller, who has linked the low levels of orthodox religious practice in pre-famine Ireland to the continued importance of the ritual observances of popular tradition. Professor Miller's argument is framed in extremely schematic terms, with popular magic (which is interpreted almost entirely in terms of calendar custom) serving the single function of guaranteeing the prosperity of agriculture and so relieving 'stress related to the uncertainty of future food supply'. The crudeness of this interpretation becomes apparent when Professor Miller goes on to argue that the famine, with its successive crop failures, shattered popular faith in the effectiveness of the customary rituals and so paved the way for the devotional revolution of the post-famine decades.[56] But the point can be restated in broader and more realistic terms. Popular supernaturalism in all its forms — not calendar custom alone, but also belief in fairies, in witchcraft and magical healing, in charms, omens and protective rituals — provided an explanation for what would otherwise have appeared as a meaningless pattern of good and bad fortune, while at the same time enabling people to feel that they exercised some control over that pattern. In this way, by catering for psychological and emotional needs which would otherwise have been met by religion, the beliefs and observances of popular tradition inevitably reduced the extent of men's dependence on the Catholic Church and its rituals.

There was also another way in which the influence of the Catholic Church and its clergy was affected by the existence of these different traditions and observances. It can reasonably be suggested that because there were supernatural forces, and even supernatural beings, which were not part of Catholic doctrine, the importance of that doctrine was to some extent reduced. This is not to say that men were led to doubt the truth either of the Church's teaching or of their magical beliefs. The overlapping and mutual accommodation of the two traditions made any such outcome unlikely. At the same time the prestige of the Church and the place it occupied in the lives of its members can only have been diminished by the fact that it did not have a monopoly either of the interpretation of the supernatural world or of the manipulation of the forces it contained. And even if an awareness of the non-Christian supernatural did not affect the way in which the Church was consciously perceived, it must have detracted from emotional and psychological involvement in Catholic doctrine and practice. Mary Fogarty describes how vividly the world of saints and angels was presented to herself and other children — 'the world of faith,' as she puts it, 'which to Catholics is almost as real as the earthen world in which we live'. She, however, was the daughter of a prosperous farmer. The maids employed in the same household

> did not get into the other world in the way we did who knew more about it. Although they were thankful for holy days and went to mass, they were really more interested in an old Irish world where fairies, witches and banshees took the place of our angels and saints.[57]

5.   *The Machinery of Discipline*

The remainder of this study will be concerned with the efforts of the Catholic Church authorities to suppress or discourage different forms of behaviour of which they disapproved. It might be helpful, therefore, to conclude this chapter by looking briefly at the principal means by which the Catholic Church in the pre-famine period dealt with offences against the code of conduct it prescribed, and at the potential effectiveness of the sanctions available to it.

The central ritual by means of which the Catholic Church dealt with offences against its discipline was the sacrament of

confession. Confession was conceived of primarily as a process through which an offender expressed his sense of repentance and his determination not to repeat his transgressions
and was then formally absolved of the guilt he had incurred.
But it was also important in a number of other ways. It provided both for a regular and thorough scrutiny by the parish
clergy of the behaviour of individual members of their congregations and for an important personal confrontation
between priest and parishioner, with the former in a position
of unquestioned authority, able to interrogate, exhort or reprimand the penitent as he saw fit. To conceal an offence in
the confessional invalidated the whole process, while a person who had not received absolution could not receive the
other sacraments without committing sacrilege and risked
damnation in the case of sudden death. A priest was not permitted to reveal or make use in any way of information he
had received under the seal of confession, but he could withhold absolution until the offender had met with any conditions he might impose regarding the performance of penance
or the making of reparations for injury done to others.

The confessional, with its aura of secrecy and its intimate
personal disclosures, had a peculiar fascination for Protestants
in both Ireland and Great Britain. A pamphlet issued in
1838 from the mission station on Achill Island ransacked
Catholic theological manuals for details of the way in which
women were to be interrogated about their sexual lives.
'Shall young and lusty bachelors, hot from Maynooth . . .
dare any longer thus to catechise your young women, your
modest and virtuous daughters and sisters?' And even more
moderate observers were ready to credit the confessional
with a remarkable effectiveness. Thanks to the confessional,
Edward Wakefield believed, the priests were regarded by
their flocks 'as the depositories of their private thoughts',
and both he and Thackeray attributed the superior chastity
of Irish women to the existence of 'that great terror-striker
the confessional'. For confession to act as an effective
deterrent, however, it was necessary that it should be taken
seriously, that people's anxiety to obtain absolution should
be sufficient to lead them to go to a priest and admit all their
offences. In the eighteenth and early nineteenth centuries,

as was seen earlier, Irish Catholics did show considerable concern about confession, but only in the context of not dying
without absolution. Among the healthy, confession was frequently confined to the canonical minimum of once or twice
a year, and in many cases attendance fell below even this
minimum standard. Confession, in other words, appears to
have been primarily conceived of, not in terms of the theology of repentance and amendment, but as a wiping of the
slate to be accomplished before death. The implications of
this outlook for the effectiveness of confession as an instrument of social discipline were made clear in 1825, when
clerical witnesses examined before a parliamentary committee
agreed that persons involved in agrarian secret societies
stayed away from confession while disturbances were in progress. According to the Parish Priest of Skibbereen, Co. Cork,
persons involved in recent disturbances had been bound by
their oath of combination not to attend confession, 'first,
lest the consciences of those going to confession would be
acted upon by the priest; secondly, as it would be altogether
useless to them whilst they were in that state'. If a member
of a secret society wished to be married, he might come to
confession first, 'but I should apprehend that it would be a
matter of form on his part' — the penitent, in other words,
would not make a full confession.[58]

The imposition of a suitable penance was a recognised part
of the process of confession and absolution. In the majority
of cases this would have involved no more than a token performance, such as the saying of a prescribed number of
prayers. For certain offences, however, penances were imposed which were clearly designed to be a genuine penalty
and to act as a serious deterrent both for the penitent himself and for others. In some cases, it appears, this could take
the form of a physically painful performance. Wakefield reported an incident in 1808 where the Bishop of Ferns had
made the persons involved in a brawl do penance by going
round the parish chapel twice on bare knees. The Rev. James
Hall, a few years later, claimed to have seen a man walk on
his bare knees across the rough floor of the Catholic chapel
at Athy, Co. Kildare, drawing blood in the process, and to
have been told that such penalties were common. Other

accounts suggested that the physically painful performances frequently seen at holy wells were sometimes imposed on penitents by their confessors. Bishop Madgett of Kerry, discussing a technical point relating to penance in 1758, made use of the hypothetical example of a man who was required to climb Mount Brandon every week for a year. The church authorities of the early nineteenth century, while clearly disapproving of such penances, appeared to admit that they were not unknown. The statutes for the diocese of Cashel, drawn up in 1813, spoke unfavourably of 'public penances or pilgrimages to be performed at wells, old churches and such places' and strictly forbade their imposition on women. Archbishop Kelly of Tuam in 1825 conceded that 'In some instances pilgrimages may be imposed as penances; it is not a general practice.'[59]

If the extent to which painful physical performances were imposed in the confessional remains unclear, there can be no doubt about the frequency with which sinners of a certain type were required to make an act of public reparation. 'Articles of General Discipline' drawn up by the bishops of the province of Cashel in 1777 laid down that persons who had been involved in riots and brawls were 'to be punished with the utmost rigour, part of which punishment is that they shall come barefooted to the ordinary or vicar general, there to be ordered proper penance. A general penance is that they shall stand *in albis* three Sundays at the church door of the parish where they gave scandal.' In the city of Cork in 1791 eleven persons who had attended a wedding in a Protestant church were made to do penance in white sheets in the parish chapel. In the diocese of Ossory in 1782 any person who struck another at a fair was to be denied the sacraments 'until the offender shall publicly acknowledge his crime, ask pardon of God, and solemnly promise amendment before the congregation assembled on a Sunday in each respective parish chapel'. In the diocese of Kildare and Leighlin in 1826 persons who had allowed themselves to be temporarily recruited by evangelical missionaries were made to do penance kneeling in the chapel yard, while in one Co. Monaghan parish in 1832 persons who attended wakes and dances were to be excluded from the sacraments 'until they first give public satisfaction in the chapel one Sunday'. In the diocese of Elphin public penance remained in use into the second half of the nineteenth century. According to a local folklorist, 'I have heard old people stating that they were present in the church when a young man and woman were ordered up by the priest to the altar before mass, and there on their knees made a public confession of what they had done and begged forgiveness for the scandal caused.'[60]

Public penance of this kind can be seen as a straightforward sanction against breaches of the Church's law. An offender was punished by being made to go through an unpleasant and humiliating performance, and potential wrongdoers were warned of the consequences of misbehaviour. But it had a further significance also. Public penances, the statutes of the diocese of Cashel laid down in 1813, were not to be inflicted except 'where a reparation of public scandal requires them', and a similar restriction was laid down in other diocesan regulations.[61] The examples given above confirm that it was in fact only in the case of a public offence, such as brawling, attendance at a wake or pattern, or contracting a runaway match, that this type of penance was required. Public penance, then, was not merely a punishment but also an act of submission, where the man who had been seen to behave contrary to the rules of the Church cancelled out the scandal he had given by affirming his return to obedience and his repentance for having misbehaved.

Public penance, like the confessional, could be used as an instrument of discipline only where the offender was willing to submit to it in order to obtain absolution. Where an individual was not prepared to submit in this way, sanctions of a different kind might be invoked. These took three main forms: the offender might be publicly denounced, he might be excluded from the sacraments, or he might be expelled from the community of the faithful through the ritual of excommunication.

Public denunciation of certain types of offender had a recognised place in the armoury of the Church. The statutes of the diocese of Cashel, for example, laid down that heads of families who permitted wake-games to be played in their houses and persons who assisted at elopements were to be

reprimanded from the altar. At the same time such denunciation was clearly regarded as something to be used with caution.
Priests were instructed to avoid maledictions and abuse and
not to make use of expressions which would give offence to
the faithful or sound out of place on the lips of a priest. This
caution was shared by prelates elsewhere. 'Maledictions from
the altar', Bishop Plunkett of Meath observed in 1780, 'are
too awful to be made use of, except upon most extraordinary
occasions, when all the rigour of ecclesiastical authority is to
be exerted by the bishop's direction.' In Dublin in 1831 and
in Ardagh and Clonmacnoise in 1834 it was similarly laid
down that public denunciation should be used only with the
permission of the bishop or his representative. However, it is
possible that the lower clergy were not so scrupulous in their
use of this weapon. One of the complaints which the Whiteboys
made against the clergy of Munster in 1786 was their use of
'shocking curses and imprecations' delivered from the altar.
In 1804 Bishop Coppinger of Cloyne and Ross complained
that a priest with whom he was in dispute over the siting of a
new chapel had publicly given his curse to all those who supported or subscribed to the erection of the chapel in the place
favoured by the bishop. 'Such cursing or ringing bells in this
diocese, without express permission,' Coppinger declared,
'involves suspension *ipso facto*; for at my entrance here it
was too common.' Certainly priests appear to have had no
hesitation in naming from the altar specific individuals who
had been guilty of offences. Thus in 1837, when an inhabitant
of Kilworth, Co. Cork, found parts of a sheep that had been
stolen from his property buried on a neighbour's land, he told
the parish priest, who repeated the story from the altar the
following Sunday.[62]

Exclusion from participation in the sacraments was a second
sanction which could be invoked against offenders. In the
diocese of Ossory it was used against persons who had participated in the custom of collecting May balls, in the diocese of
Clogher against persons who distributed drink at funerals, in
Cashel against userers, prostitutes, fortune-tellers and others.
Once again the Cashel statutes distinguished between public
and private offences. Even where persons guilty of the former
had been to confession, they were to be refused communion

unless they had improved their behaviour and given public satisfaction for the scandal they had caused. Where persons who were guilty of sins that were not publicly known, and whom the priest did not know to have reformed their lives, applied privately for communion, they too were to be refused. Where they applied for it publicly, however, and could not be refused without scandal, such persons were to be allowed to receive communion, in spite of the priest's uncertainty about their spiritual state.[63]

The last and greatest of the sanctions which the church authorities could employ against offenders was excommunication. This was of two kinds, major and minor. Minor excommunication was a limited sanction, excluding the offender from participation in the sacraments during the period that he was subject to it. Major excommunication, on the other hand, was in its full form a complete expulsion of the offender from the community of the faithful. A person incurring such a sentence was excluded from the sacraments, ineligible to take any part in the internal affairs of the Church, and deprived of the society of other members of the Church. The effect of this last provision — summed up in the Latin mnemonic *os, orare, vale, communio, mensa* — was that the faithful were forbidden to speak to the excommunicant, to join with him in prayer, to salute him, to have any civil intercourse with him, or to eat with him. The penalty for disobeying these different prohibitions was a minor excommunication (the only offence for which this sanction was applied). The full provisions of a major excommunication, however, were invoked only in certain circumstances. A sentence of excommunication could be incurred in two ways — either by performing an act that had been prohibited under a penalty of automatic excommunication, as was the case in certain dioceses with persons who contracted clandestine marriages or who became members of secret societies, or else by an individual sentence of excommunication pronounced against the offender personally. It was only when a sentence of excommunication was of the latter kind, and when it was pronounced in public, that it carried the effect of exclusion from the society of the faithful. An excommunication incurred *ipso facto* or a specific sentence which was not made public involved only exclusion from the sacraments.[64]

The penalties attached to a full sentence of excommunication, then, were of two kinds. By excommunication, in the
first place, a person ceased to be regarded as a member of the
Catholic Church. He was excluded from participation in the
sacraments and from all the other spiritual benefits that were
believed to come with membership of that body, and was in
effect written off as a lost soul, doomed to eternal damnation
unless he repented and was reconciled to the Church. The
ceremonial which accompanied a public excommunication
was designed to drive home this aspect of the sentence to all
who witnessed it:

> The ringing of the bell proclaims that the excommunication
> has been published. The closing of the mass-book signifies
> that excommunicated persons, unless they repent, shall
> forfeit all title to the promises contained in the gospel of
> Jesus Christ. The shutting of the chapel doors denotes that
> persons under excommunication are excluded from the
> house of God, and from Catholic communion; and, as
> rotten, infectious members, are cut off from the body and
> society of the faithful and 'delivered over to Satan, for the
> destruction of the flesh; that their souls may be saved, in
> the day of our Lord Jesus Christ'. And by extinguishing
> the candle-light, you are instructed, that excommunicated
> persons who die impenitent shall be for ever deprived of
> the light of heaven, and condemned to the horrors of ex-
> ternal darkness.

A similar message was conveyed in the sentence of excommunication pronounced against the Whiteboys by Bishop
Troy of Ossory in 1779:

> We exclude them, their accomplices and abettors, from the
> participation and communion of the precious body of our
> Lord, from the society of all Christians, and from the
> threshold of the Church in heaven and on earth, declaring
> them by these presents excommunicated, accursed and
> condemned to the everlasting fire of hell, there to burn with
> the devil and his angels and all the wicked.

To this exclusion from the spiritual community Troy added a

remarkable string of maledictions, consigning not only the Whiteboys themselves but also their descendants to a comprehensive temporal doom:

> Set thou, then, O Lord, a wicked sinner over them, and let the devil stand at their right hand. When they shall be judged, may they be condemned and may their prayers be turned to sin; may their days be few and others take their places. Let their children be carried about vagabonds and beg, and let them be cast out of their dwellings. May the usurers search all their substance, and let strangers plunder their labours. May there be none to help them, nor none to pity their fatherless offspring. May their posterity be cut off in one generation. May their names be blotted out. May they be continually before the Lord, and may their memory perish from the earth.[65]

It was not only the lower clergy, it seems, who sometimes passed from condemnation or reprimand to what an uninformed observer might mistake for the laying of a curse.

The other effect of excommunication was social, the exclusion of the offender from intercourse with his fellows. This exclusion, as already mentioned, was to take place only in the case of major excommunications publicly pronounced, and it is possible that even here this part of the penalty was not always applied. But in some cases at least public sentences of excommunication included a specific prohibition of communication with the persons concerned. When Archbishop Carpenter of Dublin excommunicated a couple for living together in sin in 1779, he forbade the faithful 'to speak to, or to salute, or to receive into their houses, or to have any dealings or connections whatever' with the couple. Those who disregarded this prohibition, he warned, 'will themselves incur an excommunication and expose themselves to the anger of almighty God and his holy Church'. In 1831 a Co. Limerick priest was successfully sued by a woman named Mary Wright, allegedly the mistress of the Knight of Glin, whom he had excommunicated. Prosecution witnesses claimed that the priest had 'cautioned the people against having any intercourse or dealing with Mary Wright, pronouncing her to be a common prostitute, the outcast of a barrack, and worse than the devil; the priest further said that the butcher or baker or others may say they could not refuse to supply her with necessaries; but he (the priest) said they could'. The defence did not attempt to challenge this part of the evidence, resting its case instead on the argument that the sentence imposed on Mary Wright had been justified by her misbehaviour. The dean of the diocese, questioned about the meaning of excommunication in the law of the Catholic Church, denied that it was intended to prohibit commercial dealings with the person involved, but at the same time he admitted that it prohibited 'all unnecessary communication'.[66]

In its most extreme form, then, excommunication was a penalty explicitly designed to isolate the offender from other members of the Church. Bishop Doyle in 1825 conceded that a full sentence of excommunication, pronounced against an individual in public, 'would do him serious injury', but he claimed that 'We are generally very careful, for our own safety's sake, even in cases where the criminal is most obstinate and wicked, and scandalous, not to denounce him so as to bring upon him any of those temporal evils which would follow from his being so denounced.' In this, however, Doyle, was being less than frank. Only one year earlier, in 1824, he had excommunicated a man in Tullow, Co. Carlow, warning those present, in the words of an eye-witness, 'not to eat or keep company with the unclean man, and to put him away from amongst them'. And in 1826 he instructed the Parish Priest of Graigue to exclude from the parish chapel a couple who had been excommunicated for living together, adding that he should take care 'from time to time to warn the neighbours to hold no unnecessary communion with them'.[67]

Even in cases where an excommunication did not include an explicit prohibition of intercourse with the person concerned, there are indications that the sentence may have had social as well as spiritual effects. In 1809 Bishop McLaughlin of Raphoe was sued, again successfully, by Peter Boyle, a shoemaker resident in his mensal parish of Ballyshannon, whom he had excommunicated after disturbances in the parish chapel over a proposed allocation of pews. Counsel for the plaintiff alleged that the bishop had forbidden the parishioners to have any dealings with Boyle and that as a result the latter had been ostracised and his business affairs had suffered. In this case the defence denied these allegations, claiming that the sentence had been intended only to exclude him from the sacraments. The truth of the matter is impossible to decide. But it was noticeable that even witnesses for the defence, who claimed that there had been no mention of communication with Boyle, conceded that excommunication would affect their social relations with the person concerned. The local doctor considered himself 'perfectly at liberty' to associate with Boyle, but at the same time he pointed out that 'No Catholic could entertain a good opinion of that person who, by his irreligious conduct, had brought such a sentence upon himself. . . . In my commercial or money transactions I would hold myself as much at liberty [to associate with him] after as before; but would not consider one capable of incurring such a censure as a proper person to associate with.' Another witness, asked if he would consider himself entitled to associate with an excommunicant, replied: 'I would not like it. . . . I consider that if a man would bring an excommunication on himself, it would not be right to hold any communication with him.' In the case of Mary Wright the dean of the diocese of Limerick, while denying that excommunication was intended to prevent all communication with the person at whom it was directed, conceded that 'it might otherwise be understood by the weak or ignorant portion of society'.[68]

*　　*　　*

This section has been concerned with the formal procedures available to the Catholic clergy in their dealings with offenders. The way in which these procedures were employed, and the extent to which they proved effective, should emerge more clearly in the chapters that follow. There are, however, three general points which can be made here.

Firstly, a survey of the machinery of church discipline reveals something of the way in which the Catholic clergy of this period perceived the society in which they operated and the task on which they were engaged. Ecclesiastical legislation and policy distinguished clearly between public and private offences, regularly providing, in the case of the former, either for a public demonstration of submission and repentance or – where offenders remained obstinate – for the formal exclusion of the sinner from the Catholic community. These principles were applied with a regularity and consistency which indicates that what was involved was not merely a lingering inheritance from the medieval past – as was the case, for example, with the public penances still imposed from time to time by the courts of the Church of England.[69] Instead the idea of public reparation for public offences remained an integral part of ecclesiastical policy. As such it suggests that Irish churchmen, in their efforts to impose a measure of discipline on their congregations, continued to think in terms of a community, a unit within which people were very conscious of each other's behaviour and in which the successful maintenance of a set of rules depended largely on these being perceived as the generally accepted norm. The extent to which this perception was a realistic one is something which cannot be gone into here. But it may well be that techniques which, in the greater part of Britain, were becoming increasingly anachronistic, remained both appropriate and effective when applied to the Catholic population of pre-famine Ireland.

The second point which must be made about the sanctions commonly employed by the Catholic Church authorities is the extent to which these relied on external deterrents. If public penance and excommunication were devices to repair or minimise the damage done by open breaches of the Church's laws, they were also punishments designed to deter would-be offenders. In the case of physical penance and denunciation from the altar the element of straightforward punishment was even more pronounced. Contemporaries generally described the infliction of such penalties in order to stress the extent of the power and influence enjoyed by the Catholic clergy. But it might be more accurate to see resort to such methods as a sign of weakness. It implied that religious influences alone, the internal constraints and imperatives of guilt, fear and emotion, were not sufficient to shape the behaviour of the great majority of Irish Catholics. Instead these had to be supplemented by external pressures, by the threat of being forced to perform an unpleasant penance, of being denounced from the altar, or of being exposed to the social consequences of a major excommunication.

The difference between these two types of influence, internal and external, may be seen in the anecdotes that circulated in early nineteenth-century Ireland concerning the legalistic manner in which Catholics treated the obligation of an oath, particularly in the case of temperance pledges. According to Mr and Mrs Hall in 1841,

> We recollect a man swearing he would not drink for a month — he soaked bread in spirits and ate it; another, who swore he would not touch liquor while he stood 'on earth', got drunk amid the branches of a tree; another, who vowed not to touch a drop 'in doors or out', strode across his threshold, placing one leg inside and the other outside — and so, persuading himself he did not break his oath, drank until he fell.

Anecdotes of this type were common,[70] and they should not perhaps be taken literally. At the same time there is other evidence to suggest that the attitude being satirised here, a disposition to take the obligations of religion seriously enough but to conceive of those obligations in terms of adherence to a certain more or less arbitrary set of rules, was a genuine one. Elements of such a disposition can be seen, for example, in the calculating attitude to confession discussed above, in which salvation by means of absolution became a matter more of timing than of repentance. It appears even more strikingly in the case of Mary Higgins of Co. Sligo, taken ill and eventually dying on her way to Lough Derg about 1840, who from her death bed asked a companion 'to do penance for her on the island, as she was concern[ed] in the murder of the late James Fairbanks'. For John O'Driscol, writing in 1823, this type of behaviour could be blamed on the insistence of the Catholic clergy on dogmas and ceremonials rather than on the teaching of the true gospel: 'The Church of Rome insists upon forms, and accumulates external observances, until the people are encumbered, and the priesthood oppressed with their variety and inutility; the approaches to the heart are blocked up with solemn lumber.' His conviction that the preaching of a 'pure and genuine Christianity' would have produced a change for the better in the behaviour of Irish Catholics is perhaps open to question. But he was at least correct in suggesting that a religious authority which was not supported by internalised constraints as well as external sanctions was unlikely to prove a very effective form of social control.[71]

Finally, it must be recognised that — whether the methods used by the Catholic clergy of this period in dealing with delinquents are seen as simple coercion or from the point of view of more subtle techniques of management — their effectiveness in all cases depended very largely on the attitudes of the ordinary congregation. Public penance, for example, presupposed that the Church's condemnation of the offence concerned was shared by the people before whom the sinner confessed his guilt and displayed his repentance. Where this did in fact happen — for example, where a woman had given birth to an illegitimate child — the ritual was probably a very effective one. The offender was made to feel the disapproval and hostility of the local community, and at the same time public rejection of the offence was confirmed and reinforced. Where this disapproval and rejection did not exist, however, the ritual of public penance could have little meaning. Thus in the case of couples who had eloped in order to force priests or parents to consent to their marriage, a tactic frowned on by the church authorities but not condemned by the community as a whole, the performance was said to be looked on 'more as fun than punishment'. 'Who cares a pin about standing, when three-halves of the parish are married in the same way?'[72] Denunciation from the altar, similarly, would have had most effect when the priest merely articulated popular hostility towards the offender, and least where the behaviour being condemned was something which was generally tolerated or approved. Excommunication too could have serious social consequences only if people were in fact prepared to ostracise the person concerned. Even in the exercise of what seemed to be their greatest power, then, the Catholic clergy remained circumscribed by the attitudes and values of the society in which they operated. This limitation, as will be seen in the chapters that follow, does much to explain both the successes and the failures of their attempts to control and shape the behaviour of their congregations.

4

Wakes and Patterns

1. 'Unbecoming, Disorderly and Irreligious Assemblages'

In 1814 the Rector of Kilberry, Co. Kildare, prepared a report on his parish for William Shaw Mason's *Statistical Account or Parochial Survey of Ireland*. He noted, among other things, that the parish contained a well where, on 24 June each year, 'people came from far and near to drink the water, pray and dance'.[1] The combination of activities was not as incongruous as might at first sight appear. The pattern, a combination of ritual observance and boisterous celebration, was one of the most prominent — and most often criticised — features of the social life of pre-famine Ireland.

'Pattern' is a corruption of the word 'patron'. It was the name given to certain assemblies which took place on fixed days at sites which were believed to be of a sacred character, in some cases a ruined church or monastery, but most commonly a well which was regarded as holy. Places of this kind were common throughout Ireland. 'Nearly every district of the country', Mr and Mrs Hall reported in 1841, 'contains some object of peculiar sanctity to which ignorance attributes the power of curing diseases and, frequently, of remitting sins.'[2] Many of these sites could be visited at any time in the year, and in some cases there was no date that had any special significance in relation to them. Most commonly, however, it was believed that visits to a site of this kind were particularly effective on what was known as the patron day, which was generally the festival of the saint to whom the well or shrine was dedicated. It was on this day that people gathered there in large numbers and that the pattern, a major social event as well as a religious pilgrimage, took place.

The ceremonies performed by those who visited these sites on patron day were in most cases broadly similar. The most important part of the procedure was normally for the visitor to make a prescribed number of circuits round the well or some other landmark, in some cases barefoot or on his bare knees, reciting certain prayers as he did so. In many cases there was a stone or rock adjacent to the site on which pilgrims scratched a cross or some other mark. It was normally the custom for visitors to leave behind them a token of their visit, in some cases a coin, a pin or some other small object, but most frequently a piece of cloth tied to a nearby bush or tree. Pilgrims also drank some of the water from the well, and sick persons sometimes bathed the part of their body affected by the illness. In addition to these standard features, individual sites had their own peculiar observances. At St Declan's well in Ardmore, Co. Waterford, pilgrims paid their respects not only to a well and a ruined chapel but also to a large stone on which the saint's bell was believed to have been miraculously borne across the seas from Rome, and earth from the saint's grave was carried away as a protection against sickness and misfortune. In Kilcummin, Co. Kerry, cattle were brought on May Eve to drink the water from a holy well at which stations were performed on that day, in the belief that this would preserve them from contagious diseases in the ensuing year.[3]

These observances constituted the religious, or at least the ceremonial, side of the pattern. At the same time such gatherings were also important as an occasion on which people could meet to socialise and amuse themselves. They were encouraged and facilitated in this by tradesmen, hawkers and entertainers of various kinds, who set up stalls near the site of a pattern, providing food, drink, music for dancing and other forms of entertainment. The result was something resembling a fair or carnival. Thus in 1748 two English visitors described the scene they had witnessed at a well in Co. Cork: 'When their devotions were over they retired to several sutlers' tents erected for that purpose, some to eat and drink, others to wrestling and yelling, dancing, noise and merriment, which brought on several boxing bouts while we stood there.' Similar descriptions were offered by a variety of travellers and observers over the following century or so, while an insider's view of the same events may be found in the diary of the Co. Kilkenny schoolmaster, Humphrey O'Sullivan, for the year 1829:

> The twenty-sixth day, Sunday. Feast-day of St James, that is, patron day at St James's well, close to Callan. . . . My three youngest children and myself went to the patron. There were gooseberries and currants and cherries for children; gingerbread for grown girls; strong beer and maddening whiskey for wranglers and busybodies; open-doored booths filled with lovers; bagpipers and fiddlers making music there for young folks; and pious pilgrims making their stations round the well. My children and myself left the well at six o'clock. Well-dressed respectable people were moving about in crowds everywhere.[4]

Patterns were known in all parts of the country during this period. Well-attended gatherings took place not only in remote parts of Munster and Connacht but also on the outskirts of the cities of Dublin and Cork. When a pattern was held at Kilmurry, two miles outside Waterford, in 1822, a local newspaper observed that 'several thousands of the peasantry intermingled with crowds of the inhabitants of this city, of various ages and conditions'. The numbers reported as assembling at other gatherings of this kind varied. Police attending a pattern at Croom, Co. Limerick, in 1838 recorded that 'thousands of the peasantry attended from miles adjacent'; a magistrate in Co. Monaghan noted 'an assemblage of nearly a thousand people' at a pattern in 1807. The pattern held at Clonmacnoise on 9 September was estimated in 1816 to attract between three and four thousand people, while a visitor to St Declan's well at Ardmore around 1840 calculated that a total of twelve to fifteen thousand persons attended, and counted sixty-four tents erected for their entertainment.[5]

The origin of these popular festivals, with their mixture of Christian devotion and traditional magic, ritual observance and festive celebration, is not altogether clear. Some at least of these gatherings represented the continuation under Christian labels of assemblies and practices which had been part of an older tradition. It is significant that some of the most popular patterns of early nineteenth-century Ireland — for example, the gatherings at Lough Gougaun in Co. Cork, at Kilmainham outside Dublin, and at St John's well in Co. Meath — centred around wells supposed to be dedicated to St John and were held on St John's Eve, the great midsummer festival. In the same way a number of patterns held at the end of July or the beginning of August have been identified as survivals of the Celtic festival of Lughnasa. In other cases, it has been suggested, patterns began as celebrations of the feast-day of the saint to whom an early parish chapel was dedicated, acquiring their less orthodox features only with the passage of time. It would be a mistake, however, to assume that all the patterns celebrated in rural Ireland in the late eighteenth and early nineteenth centuries were assemblies of great antiquity, Christian or otherwise. The body of custom and belief which surrounded the pattern was a living tradition, not an inflexible inheritance from the distant past. Even in the early nineteenth century it was possible for a spring to acquire the status of a holy well and to become the object of the usual devotions. The ability of popular tradition to fuse long-established custom and recent happenings, as well as Christian and non-Christian elements, is well illustrated in an episode from Rosscarbery, Co. Cork. Until at least the year 1858 large numbers of people in this district assembled at the tomb of a priest named John Power, who had died in 1831, making rounds as they would at a holy well and praying for relief from illnesses. The day on which they assembled for this purpose was St John's Eve.[6]

Contemporaries were sometimes sceptical of the motives of persons who attended these pattern-day gatherings. 'The far greater number of attendants', the Rev. Horatio Townsend maintained in 1810, 'are influenced by considerations in which sanctity has very little concern. They meet to make merry, which in frequent interpretation is to drink and fight.' No doubt there were many pilgrims whose main reasons for attending patterns were social ones — who came, as one visitor to a holy well told the French traveller Latocnaye, 'to do what the others do and to see the women'. But other gatherings, like May Eve and St John's Eve, were also widely enjoyed as social occasions, while at the same time retaining an important place as ritual observances marking stages in the yearly round. The majority of accounts of patterns in this period do not suggest any sharp distinction between those who participated in the ceremonies at the holy well and those who took part in the entertainments. At gatherings of this kind, Carleton observed in 1854,

> It is quite usual to see young men and women devoutly circumambulating the well or lake on their bare knees, with all the marks of penitence and contrition strongly impressed upon their faces; whilst again, after an hour or two, the same individuals may be found in a tent dancing with ecstatic vehemence to the music of the bagpipe or fiddle.

Neither were these performances, involving as they did such features as a circuit barefoot or on bare knees over sharp stones or up a steep rough slope, something which might be undertaken lightheartedly, as a formal observance or to provide a pretext for the revels that followed.[7]

In spite of the scepticism of some observers, therefore, there are reasons for thinking that the ritual as well as the social side of the pattern continued to be of importance to those who gathered at these sites. Many of those who attended came in search of cures for some illness, and different wells were credited with particular efficacy in healing certain ailments. Others attended and performed the prescribed ceremonies with no such specific end in mind, as a general act of penance and devotion. If it is not always possible to determine the relative importance in those ceremonies of Christian and non-Christian elements, this is largely because no conflict between these elements existed in the minds of the participants themselves. Whether seen as devotions at the shrine of a Christian saint or as ritual practices at a well or other site believed to have magical powers, the ceremonies of the pattern fulfilled much the same function. They enabled men to feel that customary observances had been made at the correct time, and thus that something had been done to invoke supernatural protection and assistance for themselves and their concerns.

Contemporary observers were in general very critical of these pattern-day gatherings. A pattern, the Rector of St Peter's, Athlone, maintained in 1819, 'seems more like the celebration of the orgies of Bacchus than the memory of a pious saint, from the drunken quarrels and obscenities practised on these occasions'. Such gatherings, a colleague in Co. Kilkenny agreed, seemed 'now wholly set apart to celebrate the orgies of the Prince of Darkness'. Isaac Weld, describing the pattern at Kilronan, Co. Roscommon, referred darkly to 'scenes of licentiousness . . . over which it will be best to drop a veil'. The Halls, while believing that behaviour at these gatherings had greatly improved by the 1840s, recalled with distaste the pattern at St Ronogue's well in Cork, where 'to the superstitious rites of the morning succeeded the saturnalia of the evening, the having drunk of the holy water being considered as a licence for every sort of debauchery'. Comments of this kind must, of course, be treated with a certain caution. A practice which could provide such illustrations both of the irresponsibility of the Irish peasant and of the crudity of his religious ideas was clearly ideal ammunition for denominational and political polemic. But not all such comment can be attributed simply to ethnic or religious prejudice. By the 1820s even a sympathetic observer of Irish tradition and folk custom like Thomas Crofton Croker could complain of 'the disgraceful riot of the patron, a meeting that seems established only to profane all that is impressive, simple and pious'.[8] By the same time, furthermore, similar criticisms were being heard with increasing frequency from the one group who could not be accused of even the slightest denominational prejudice in this matter — the clergy of the Catholic Church.

Instances of opposition to patterns and similar assemblies on the part of the Catholic clergy can be discovered from at least the middle decades of the eighteenth century. In 1754 priests on the outskirts of Dublin attempted to prevent the celebration of the annual pattern at Mulhuddart by persuading landholders in the vicinity to forbid the erection of tents or booths on their land. In 1771 Bishop Sweetman of Ferns urged the priests of his diocese 'to put back and discourage as much as ye can patrons or pilgrimages, or meetings of pretended devotion, or rather of real dissipation and dissoluteness'. The bishops of the province of Cashel agreed in 1777 that patterns, along with wakes and night-time dances, were 'to be hindered by exemplary punishments and exhortations'. Four years later their colleagues in Armagh announced that all the pilgrimages in that province – with the exception of that to Lough Derg – were 'the occasions of various evil consequences' and should be suppressed. In Ossory Bishop Troy ordered in 1782 that persons who let their ground for the erection of tents or booths on a pattern day should be excluded from the sacraments until they promised amendment. And in 1797 Archbishop Bray of Cashel prohibited 'all unbecoming, disorderly and irreligious assemblages of people at *Patrons*, wheresoever held in our diocese of Cashel and Emly'. He ordered that a solemn sentence of excommunication should be pronounced in the parish chapels against all those who attended one particularly disorderly pattern, that at Doneskeagh, and also against those who provided persons attending that pattern with either food or drink. Priests in other parts of the diocese were authorised where necessary to pronounce a similar sentence of excommunication against those attending patterns in their areas.[9]

Already by 1800, therefore, there was substantial opposition among at least the upper levels of the Catholic clergy to assemblies at holy wells and other sites of that kind. But this opposition was not unanimous. The pattern, whatever its other features, was nominally a celebration of the feast-day of a Christian saint, and some at least among the lower clergy were prepared to join in its observance as such. In Clonmany, Co. Donegal, for example, mass was at one time celebrated on the same day that rounds were performed at a local holy well dedicated to St Colmcille. This was, of course, a perfectly orthodox means of recognising a feast-day of particular local significance; the same thing is done in some Irish rural areas up to the present day. But there were other cases in which priests appear to have gone further and to have lent the sanction of their presence to gatherings little different to those which colleagues elsewhere were attempting to suppress. The Parish Priest of Kilbride,

Co. Mayo, at one time attended the annual prilgrimage to Downpatrick Head and said mass for the people assembled there. Up to 1804, similarly, a priest is reported to have attended at the gatherings which took place on St John's Eve at St Patrick's wells, Struell, Co. Down.[10] Some senior churchmen were clearly unhappy about the encouragement given by certain of the lower clergy to what they saw as an undesirable practice. Both Sweetman in 1771 and Troy in 1782 thought it necessary, when denouncing patterns, to forbid their clergy to celebrate mass on the site of any of these assemblies; Troy in fact prohibited the celebration of any public mass at all on the day of a pattern, unless this happened also to be a holiday of obligation.

Up to the early years of the nineteenth century, then, despite clear indications of a growing uneasiness among senior churchmen, popular veneration of holy wells continued to receive the sanction and encouragement of at least a section of the lower clergy. As in the case of other traditional observances, however, there are signs that in the decades before the famine this tolerance was giving way to a more critical, if not positively hostile, outlook. One notable example concerns St Patrick's wells in Struell, Co. Down. In 1752 the bishop of the diocese had approved of pilgrimages to these wells sufficiently to suggest that certain indulgences should be extended to persons who visited them on a particular day. Up to the year 1804, as already mentioned, a priest from Downpatrick attended at the gatherings which took place there on St John's Eve. By 1836, however, attendance at the well had been forbidden by the Catholic clergy. At about the same time priests ceased to attend the stations performed at a well in Co. Cavan and to say mass at a ruined church near Kilkenny on the day on which stations were performed at an adjacent well. In Lackan, Co. Westmeath, a former parish priest had himself performed stations at a holy well and encouraged his parishioners to do the same. By 1837, however, his successor had put a stop to the ceremonies performed there, 'by telling the people that they might as well fill an old pot with water and pray around it as around the holy well to which the saint gave his blessing'. The Halls, writing in 1841, summed up what seemed to them a general change in clerical attitudes: 'The Roman Catholic clergy now "set their faces" directly against practices which, for ages, they tolerated generally and encouraged partially.'[11]

Increasing clerical opposition to the celebration of patterns can in part be attributed to the same more 'Protestant' attitude to traditional religious practices already noted in the preceding chapter. In the eighteenth century patterns had been condemned as occasions of drunkenness, violence and general misconduct. 'Our deluded people', Troy complained in 1782,

> assemble on these days for wicked purposes. Instead of praying they wish damnation to themselves and acquaintances with most horrid and deliberate imprecations. They profane the name of God and everything else that is sacred by most execrable oaths and finish the day by the perpetration of the grossest impurities, by shedding their neighbour's blood, by murder, and the transgression of every law.

By the early nineteenth century, on the other hand, there are also indications, as in the case of the Parish Priest of Lackan, of scepticism or hostility directed against the ceremonial side of the pattern. But the change of emphasis was only a minor one. When, a few decades later, a new generation of priests looked back, as antiquarians or local historians, to the suppression of patterns by their early nineteenth-century predecessors, they spoke of them as having been put down as occasions of fighting, drinking and other forms of 'immorality'.[12] Contemporary accounts also agree in suggesting that it was against the social aspect of these gatherings that the main thrust of clerical disapproval continued to be directed, and the same view is confirmed by the fact that patterns attracted a degree of opposition not seen in the case of any other aspect of popular magic. If a greater hostility to patterns was partly the result of a more critical attitude to manifestations of non-Christian supernaturalism, therefore, it also, and to a much greater extent, reflected a tightening of the broader social discipline which the Catholic clergy sought to impose on their congregations.

This clerical opposition to patterns did not, initially at

least, have very much success. From time to time during the
late eighteenth century individual patterns were abolished
or fell into disuse,[13] but there is nothing to suggest a general
decline in the popularity of the custom. Furthermore, in
those cases where it is possible to trace the outcome of
clerical efforts to suppress specific assemblies, these appear
to have had little result. When the bishops of the province
of Armagh resolved in 1781 to suppress all pilgrimages in
their dioceses, for example, they singled out the gatherings
at St John's well in Co. Meath for special mention as being
'attended with such scandalous enormities as to require
immediate redress'. Within the next two years both the
Bishop of Meath and the Archbishop of Dublin had prohibited attendance at this well on pain of incurring the most
severe ecclesiastical penalties. But when Edward Wakefield
visited the spot in 1810, the same Bishop of Meath was still
attempting to suppress the assembly there, and the well, in
spite of thirty years of sustained clerical opposition, remained
'an annual scene of confusion, drunkenness and debauchery,
bearing a greater resemblance to a fair than an assembly for
the purpose of devotion'. Meanwhile, in 1786 and again in
1787, Archbishop Carpenter of Dublin prohibited attendance
at another St John's well, that at Kilmainham on the outskirts of the city. In spite of this and later attempts to
suppress the gatherings at this site, however, it remained
the scene of an important pattern up to the mid-1830s.
Bishop Troy of Ossory appears to have met with equally
little success. Later accounts make clear that patterns continued to be celebrated in the diocese of Ossory forty years
or more after he introduced measures in 1782 to suppress
all gatherings of this kind.[14]

In the eighteenth century, then, and perhaps in the early
years of the nineteenth, clerical opposition to the celebration of pattern-day gatherings appears to have been
largely ineffective. By the 1830s and 1840s, however, there
were indications that the more widespread and determined
efforts now being made to suppress these assemblies were
beginning to affect their popularity. Thus in 1836 attendance
at Struell wells was reported to be rapidly declining, 'it
having been forbidden by the clergy of the Roman Catholic

Church'. As early as 1812 the Parish Priest of Leighlin, Co. Carlow, had successfully prohibited a pattern held at a well dedicated to St Laserian, after a man had been killed in a fight at one of these gatherings. Other accounts from the 1830s and 1840s also speak of wells which over the previous thirty years or so had been suppressed or greatly diminished in popularity through the influence of the Catholic clergy. Isaac Weld, writing in 1832, described how attendance at a well in Brideswell, Co. Roscommon, had been prohibited by the Catholic clergy:

> Their mandates had been implicitly obeyed during the two years which preceded my visit. Nothing can more decidedly show the great influence of the priesthood than the ready compliance of the people with their orders to abandon festivities which, during a long series of years, had been hailed both by old and young as a source of annual delight and enjoyment.[15]

Even where patterns were not suppressed entirely, there were reports that the Catholic clergy had succeeded in exercising a more effective supervision over the conduct of those who attended. Thus the newspaper report of a pattern near Waterford city in 1822, already quoted, recorded approvingly that 'At the seasonable hour of eight o'clock in the evening, at the request of the respectable Catholic clergymen of the parish, the numerous tents, standings, etc. were promptly and willingly removed by the proprietors, and the neighbouring public houses closed.' The *Parliamentary Gazetteer of Ireland* reported in 1845 that 'strenuous and laudable efforts' had recently been made by the Catholic clergy to put an end to disorderly scenes at patterns and pilgrimages, and that 'even previous to the singularly successful career of Father Mathew in the cause of temperance, these efforts were very largely effective'.[16]

This is not to suggest, however, that clerical efforts to suppress or modify the customary practices of the pattern were now completely successful. Contemporaries may have credited the exertions of the priests with having brought about an improvement in popular behaviour, but they gave no sign of believing that the problem of disorderly patterns had been eliminated. And in fact it is clear from later accounts that in the second half of the nineteenth century, and in some cases even later, the church authorities continued to find the celebration of these festivals a cause for concern. 'Within the last fifty years or so', a Co. Kildare antiquary observed in 1908, 'the clergy have had to suppress patterns, owing to the bad characters that were drawn to the locality and also on account of the drinking and faction-fighting that followed.' Other accounts from the counties of Louth, Meath, Fermanagh, Waterford and Limerick also tell of patterns being suppressed by the Catholic clergy in the 1860s or later. In 1922 the annual pilgrimage to Downpatrick Head was condemned by the local priest, while at about the same time the annual pattern on one of the Aran Islands was suppressed by the clergy there. Whatever successes had been achieved in the decades before the famine, it is clear that patterns continued for a considerable time afterwards to attract the disapproval of concerned clergymen.[17]

A similar mixed result can be seen in the case of clerical opposition to the ceremonial side of the pattern. The practice of venerating holy wells, Eugene O'Curry reported from Co. Dublin in 1837, 'is now almost done away with throughout the county, through the interference of the Catholic priests', and a similar suppression of traditional observances was reported in other areas. In a parish in Co. Galway, on the other hand, people continued to visit a well in spite of the condemnations of the local priests, 'being convinced that the blessings of St Greallain [the patron saint of the well] cannot be rendered null and void by a man who only studied a few years at Maynooth and who never was able to perform one miracle', and there were also other cases in which clerical condemnations were ignored or defied. It is possible, in fact, that private observances at holy wells proved even harder to do away with than the more conspicuous gatherings for amusement which accompanied a full-scale pattern. In the diocese of Derry, it was reported in the mid-1830s, pilgrimages to wells had been forbidden by the priests, but the practice 'is still continued secretly'. Bishop Doyle of Kildare and Leighlin assured a parliamentary committee in 1825 that the clergy of his province did all they could to restrain the practice of making such pilgrimages, but added regretfully: 'It is hard, however, to root out prejudices.'[18]

Finally, even in those cases where clerical opposition to patterns did appear to achieve a measure of success, this cannot always be taken at face value. By the 1830s and 1840s, as was seen in the preceding chapter, observers were beginning to comment on a general decline in traditional beliefs and practices among the Irish poor; the people, as John O'Donovan observed on one occasion, were becoming 'too sensible etc.' for pilgrimages to holy wells and similar observances. If the Catholic clergy of these decades appeared to be having more success than their predecessors in their efforts to discourage patterns, therefore, this must have been at least partly because their parishioners were themselves beginning to lose interest in the custom.

A similar point can be made about the much more rapid decline in popular enthusiasm for pattern-day assemblies which took place in the two or three decades following the famine. In the 1840s patterns, even if somewhat diminished in popularity, remained a familiar part of Irish life. By 1873, on the other hand, the antiquary John Hogan could write of them as something which the majority of adults would remember but which by his time had largely fallen into disuse. Their disappearance, in Hogan's view, could be attributed on the one hand to the disruption and demoralisation caused by the famine, and on the other to broader processes of social change: 'the unsparing hand of social progress and the stern utilitarianism of modern times'.[19] Today one might prefer a more precise definition of 'social progress', and in addition a shift in emphasis from the immediate disruption caused by the famine to the long-term changes which it brought to the social structure of rural Ireland. But the basic point remains clear — that the final disappearance of the pattern, like that of other traditional beliefs and practices, came about only as part of a much wider transformation in the character of Irish society.

To sum up, then, it can be suggested that the opposition of the Catholic clergy to patterns and similar assemblies achieved a real but limited success. The already widespread condemnation and opposition of the second half of the eighteenth century, it seems clear, was largely ineffective. By the 1830s and 1840s, on the other hand, the clergy had succeeded in suppressing a number of these gatherings altogether and in imposing some degree of control on the behaviour seen at others. But even by the 1840s they had not managed to eliminate those practices, either social or ritual, of which they disapproved. The successes which were achieved, furthermore, must be seen in the context of broader changes which were taking place in popular attitudes and behaviour as a whole range of traditional beliefs and practices began to be abandoned. And it was not until the famine and its aftermath, with the far-reaching changes which these brought to the structure and character of Irish society, that the real decline of pattern-day gatherings as a major social event took place.

2.   *Wakes and Keening*

The practice of holding wakes, vigils of friends and neighbours over the body of a recently dead person, survives in some parts of Ireland up to the present day. Over the past one hundred years or less, however, the character of these gatherings has altered radically. In its modern form the wake is a subdued and decorous occasion, where prayers are said for the soul of the dead person, and the visitors, having been given something to eat and drink, sit talking quietly among themselves until it is time for them to leave. The purpose of such gatherings is seen as being 'to pray for the dead and to sympathise with the relatives of the dead person'. In the period before the famine, on the other hand — and indeed for some time after it — wakes had a very different character. 'These wakes', Thomas Campbell observed in 1778,

> are meetings of merriment and festivity, to which they resort from far and near. The old people amuse themselves in smoking tobacco, drinking whiskey and telling stories in the room with the corpse; whilst the young men, in the barn or some separate apartment, exhibit

feats of activity; or, inspired by their sweethearts, dance away the night to the melodious *pleasing* of a bagpipe.

Later accounts presented a similar picture. In Donegal, it was reported in 1816, wakes 'are often attended with unbounded mirth and festivity, which are not restrained by the presence of the nearest relatives of the deceased'. In Galway 'they are places where the young of both sexes meet, and the night is generally consumed in drinking whiskey, smoking tobacco and playing different games of romps etc.'. In Armagh, similarly, John Donaldson complained in 1838 that wakes were the scene of 'different kinds of diversions, tricks and pastimes quite unbecoming in such a place'.[20]

These 'diversions, tricks and pastimes' have been catalogued and reconstructed in some detail in Seán Ó Súilleabháin's classic account of the traditional Irish wake. For the most part they consisted of party games of a fairly familiar and predictable type. There were competitions involving riddles, tongue-twisters and extempore versifying, games in which men competed with each other in performing feats of strength, agility or endurance, and elaborate practical jokes which could end with the victim being drenched with water, tossed onto a dunghill or otherwise maltreated. Other games took the form of a mime, in which everyday activities like an appearance in court or the buying and selling of an animal were imitated and parodied. In addition to organised games of this kind, visitors to a wake-house could engage in all the normal amusements of an Irish social gathering — dancing, story-telling, singing, and what contemporaries frequently complained of as excessive drinking. All in all, as one disapproving observer put it, the customary pastimes of a wake 'seem to say, that they are come to the house of feasting and not of mourning'.[21]

These festive activities — laughter, music, singing, dancing, practical joking and the playing of various games — went on in the same house as was occupied by the mourning relatives and the corpse itself. In some cases, it appears, the older people attending the wake remained in one part of the house with the corpse, while the younger members of the group retired to the barn or to another room to engage in

the dancing and other amusements of the wake. Where
this was done, however, it seems to have been for convenience
rather than out of any unwillingness to go on with the traditional festivities in the presence of the corpse.[22] In other
cases, meanwhile, the entire wake took place in the same
room as the body, which was laid out either underneath a
table and concealed by a sheet or on top of the table and
in full view, the custom varying from one area to the next.
There are reports of practical jokes involving the corpse
itself, and of cases in which the deceased was dealt a hand
of cards, had a pipe inserted in his mouth, or was taken onto
the floor for a dance. While such accounts are naturally
difficult to verify, it does seem clear that boisterous celebration was something that was not only tolerated on these
occasions, but actually expected. Contemporaries commented
on the willingness of the Irish poor to endure hardship and
deprivation in order to leave sufficient money for a good
wake, and a well-known anecdote described how a son was
heard to complain indignantly that not a single man had been
knocked down at his mother's funeral.[23]

Festive wakes of this kind existed throughout practically
the whole of Ireland in the late eighteenth and early nineteenth centuries. The only exception appears to have been
south-west Cork and south-west Kerry, where the only
entertainment known to have existed at such gatherings
is story-telling. Elsewhere the custom was a general one,
existing not only in rural districts but even in the cities
of Belfast, Cork and Dublin. Nor was it confined to the
Catholic population. Reports to the Ordnance Survey from
different parts of Co. Antrim show that there wakes had at
one time been attended for amusement by Presbyterians
and others. By the 1830s, however, this was no longer the
case. In Ahoghill the Presbyterian clergy had successfully
prohibited the offering of whiskey as a refreshment at
wakes. In Ballynure, similarly, class leaders of the Methodist
society 'have succeeded in great measure in abolishing the old
system of drinking at wakes and playing'. Elsewhere too it
was reported that wakes were now observed with proper
solemnity, although it was still customary to hand round
whiskey once or twice during the evening and one report

from Co. Tyrone complained of the expense to which the dead man's family were put by the necessity of providing liquor.[24]

How is this apparently incongruous practice of marking the death of a relative or neighbour with a festive social gathering to be understood? One possible explanation would be to see it as reflecting nothing more than a callous or at best fatalistic attitude to death, attributable perhaps to a combination of high mortality with ignorance of many of its principal causes. But this is hardly satisfactory, and it becomes even less so when it is realised that the practice of the festive wake existed not only among all denominations in Ireland but also in a wide range of other societies, being recorded, at one time or another, in Mexico, in the Pacific Islands and among the American Indians, as well as in the greater part of Europe.[25] A practice established in so many separate cultures, it seems clear, embodied a basic means by which certain types of community sought to deal with the emotional and psychological stress occasioned by the death of one of their number. An explanation in these terms is a somewhat risky venture. Apart from the difficulty of discussing a topic like human responses to death without sounding unbearably pretentious, there is the fact that this type of analysis, in which attention is focused on the function of popular customs and traditions rather than on the way in which they are understood by those involved, has begun to fall out of favour – first with anthropologists and then (after the usual time-lag) with those historians who aspire to imitate their methods. And there can be no doubt that a reflexive and undiscriminating functionalism can lead to absurd results: an example has already been discussed in the section on popular magic. At the same time the point should not be overstated. To say that a belief or practice can be better understood by an appreciation of the emotional or psychological needs it helps to satisfy is not to claim that the content of that belief or custom is entirely determined by those needs. And in the case of the wake, as already mentioned, the appearance of the same basic response in very different societies suggests that, in this particular instance, an interpretation which centres on social needs rather than on the autonomous development of a culture's mental universe is perhaps more relevant than usual.

One explanation of the function of the festive wake, in Ireland and elsewhere, has been suggested by Seán Ó Súilleabháin. The wake, Ó Súilleabháin argues, was primarily intended to comfort and placate the spirit of the deceased person by means of a last great feast at which he was present as the guest of honour. 'It was an attempt to heal the wound of death, and to do final justice to the deceased while he was still physically present. . . . He had to be assured of his popularity and of his continuing presence as one of the company.' The main force behind the liveliness of the wake, according to this interpretation, was a fear of the dead person himself, who was conceived of as still present in the company and still possessed of power to harm the living.[26]

Ó Súilleabháin's theory, backed up by findings on attitudes to death and the dead in traditional European cultures generally, is a plausible one. At the same time it can be supplemented by the suggestion that the celebrations of the festive wake also derived part of their vigour from the fact that they were an assertion of continued vitality in the face of a sudden reminder of universal mortality, and of continuity in the face of the abrupt removal from a close-knit community of one of its members. The first of these two points is particularly well illustrated by what is in many ways the most surprising aspect of the Irish wake: an explicit assertion of sexuality quite at variance with the attitudes which appear generally to have prevailed in Irish society at this period.

This sexual expression took two main forms. The first of these was represented by a number of games whose main function appears to have been to pair off the young people present into mutually acceptable couples. One such game, known as 'Frimsy Framsy', is described in some detail by William Carleton:

A chair or stool is placed in the middle of the flure, and the man who manages the play sits down upon it, and calls his sweetheart, or the prettiest girl in the house. She, accordingly, comes forward and must kiss him. He then rises up and she sits down. 'Come now,' he says, 'fair maid — *frimsy framsy*, who's your fancy?' She then calls them she likes best, and when the young man she calls comes over and kisses her, he then takes her place, and calls another girl — and so on, smacking away for a couple of hours. Well, throth, it's no wonder that Ireland's full of people; for I believe they do nothing but coort from the time they're the hoith of my leg.

In another game a man dressed in a dark coat and wig went through a parody of the marriage ceremony with each couple in turn. After each pair had been married the man 'places his wife upon his knee; for fraid of taking up too much room, *you persave*; then they court away again, and why shouldn't they?' In a third game, 'The White Cockade', each man in turn was led round the circle until he had picked out the girl he wanted by placing a hat on her head. 'When it's all over, that is, when every young man has picked upon the girl that he wishes to be his sweetheart, they sit down and sing songs and coort, just as they did at the marrying.'[27]

Carleton's account of these games, it is true, is presented within the framework of a short story. Most of its features, however, are confirmed by other sources. 'Frimsy Framsy', for example, was singled out for special mention in clerical condemnations of wakes on at least three occasions during the eighteenth century, being denounced as a 'most disgraceful ceremony', 'the cause of a multitude of sins'. On other occasions also the church authorities complained of lewd and indecent games being played at wakes, and of parodies of the sacrament of marriage. Mary Fogarty, growing up in Co. Limerick in the 1870s, heard accounts from her elder sister of various games played at wakes, 'including a very wicked one called the mock marriage'.[28]

The second way in which the customary amusements of the Irish wake became a vehicle for sexual expression was in the symbolism of some of the mimes and dances performed on these occasions. The antiquarian J. G. A. Prim, writing in 1853, provided a brief account of what he described as 'the gross obscenity' of Irish wake-games as they had been played up to a short time before. Prim, unfortunately, was torn between conflicting instincts of scholarship and propriety, believing that some account of such practices should be preserved, but also feeling obliged, in order to spare the feelings of his readers, to confine his own account to the most general terms. Of the game called 'Bout', for example, he is prepared to say only that it 'was joined in by men and women who all acted a very obscene part which cannot be described'. Another game, 'Making the Ship', was apparently an elaborate mime of the process of construction, 'with its several parts of "laying the keel", forming the "stem and stern", and erecting "the mast", the latter of which was done by a female using a gesture and expression proving beyond doubt that it was a relic of Pagan rites'. In the game 'Drawing the Ship out of the Mud' 'the men engaged actually presented themselves before the rest of the assembly, females as well as males, in a state of nudity', while in another unnamed game 'the female performers attired themselves in men's clothing and conducted themselves in a very strange manner'. 'Brief as are these particulars,' Prim concludes, 'they will give sufficient idea of the obscene and demoralising tendency of the wake orgies, and show the necessity which existed for their total suppression.'

Prim's reticence is frustrating, but the broad outlines of what he is suggesting are clear enough. His account, furthermore, is confirmed and to some extent amplified by other sources. W. G. Wood-Martin, writing half a century later, presented a very similar description of wake-games, drawing heavily on Prim's article but supplementing it with additional material collected by himself. William Carleton, meanwhile, describes in one of his stories what appears to have been a fairly explicit piece of phallic miming, which the context suggests was performed at wakes: '[It] could not be danced without the emblematic aids of a stick and handkerchief. It was addressed to an individual passion and was unquestionably one of those symbolic dances that were used in pagan rites.'[29]

The traditional amusements of the Irish wake, then, appear to have involved both the symbolic representation of sexuality through mime and ritual and its more concrete expression in games like 'Frimsy Framsy'. Regular condemnations by the church authorities of obscene songs and of what they described as shameful or scurrilous talk at wakes also contribute to the picture of a general atmosphere of ribaldry and heightened sexual awareness.[30] The original place of all this in the wake-house celebrations is clear enough: the relationship between sexuality and death is a familiar one both in literature and in anthropology. A more difficult problem is to determine how important these elements remained in the wakes of the late eighteenth and early nineteenth centuries. The character of a game like 'Mock Marriages', for example, depended entirely on those who took part. Thus in Lady Wilde's account of the game, written in 1890, the procedure remains the same as that described by Carleton but the main point of the proceedings is no longer sexual play but rather practical joking. The most incongruous partners are said to have been chosen for each other, and the high point of the game occurs when the 'priest' delivers a homily on the defects of the different couples he has just married and the miserable lives they are sure to live together.[31] But Lady Wilde was writing fifty years after Carleton, and her own sensibilities may have led her to interpret the game in this light. Carleton's own account, certainly, seems to leave little doubt that the main function of the games he described was to divide up those present into mutually agreeable couples who would go on to enjoy the evening in each other's company. In the case of mimes such as 'Making the Ship' it is necessary to ask to what extent those who took part in these games were aware of the sexual symbolism that lay behind them. Long-standing tradition no doubt gave the practices of the wake-house a special status, allowing them to retain features which in other contexts would have been regarded as unacceptable. The people who took part in these games, Prim assured his readers, 'had no idea of outraging propriety or religion in their performance, holding an unquestioning faith in the old traditions that such observances were right and proper at wakes, whilst under any other circumstances they would shrink with horror from such indelicate exhibitions'. But this does not necessarily mean that the original sexual content of games like 'Making the Ship' was forgotten or suppressed.

A strict code of sexual behaviour, as will be seen in a later chapter, should not be confused with innocence or sexual naïevty. If the symbolism of these mimes was sufficiently explicit for Prim, Carleton and others to be left in no doubt about what they represented, it is unlikely that their meaning was lost on those who acted them out.

One further aspect of Irish wake amusements requires some comment here. This is the element of anti-religious, or at least anticlerical, satire which can be observed in a number of the games played on these occasions. Prim regarded this aspect of the wake as a further indication of its pagan origins:

> The game called 'Hold the Light', in which a man is blindfolded and flogged, has been looked upon as a profane travesty of the passion of our Lord; and religion might also be considered as brought into contempt by another of the series, in which a person caricaturing a priest, and wearing a rosary composed of small potatoes strung together, enters into conflict with the 'Borekeen' [the person in charge of the games] and is put down and expelled from the room by direction of the latter. If the former games be deemed remnants of Pagan rites and of ante-Christian origin, these latter may be looked upon as anti-Christian, and devised with a view of making religion ridiculous, at a time when the masses had a lingering predilection for Paganism.

Wood-Martin, similarly, describes a play called 'The Building of the Fort', which in his view was 'filled with sarcasms on various Christian rites and customs'. To these might be added the parodies of the marriage ceremony already mentioned, and also mock confessions in which penitents confessed to a man representing the priest, the latter listening in caricatured shock and horror and imposing a ludicrous penance. It is hardly necessary, however, to see these games as remnants of anti-Christian propaganda surviving from a far-off pagan era. The popular culture of the pre-famine period, as was noted in an earlier chapter, contained a considerable body of satire directed at the Catholic clergy and at aspects of Catholic teaching and religious practice, and games of this type are merely a further illustration of this general lack of reverence.[32]

While celebration and festivity were the aspects of the wake which attracted most attention from contemporary observers, the practices customary on these occasions did also involve a recognition that the occasion was one of mourning. Successive observers of Irish society in this period described what they referred to as the 'Irish cry' or 'keen', the latter term being derived from the Irish *caoineadh*. This was a eulogy in verse on the qualities of the dead person and a lament for his passing, interspersed with loud wailings and cries of grief, which was pronounced at intervals over the corpse, first at the wake and later at the funeral procession and during the burial itself. The keen could be performed by the friends and relatives of the deceased, but even in the nineteenth century it appears to have been a frequent practice to hire specialist keeners who would do full justice to the occasion. The qualities of the resulting lament must have varied considerably with the abilities of the individual performer, but keening appears to have been a highly developed art. The Rev. James Hall, an unsympathetic observer, conceded that 'Some of the women rhyme extempore and offhand with wonderful facility, particularly when they have got a little (but not too much) whiskey.' The cries and wailings that accompanied such performances were even less popular than the verbal lament; but here too the Protestant curate of Dungiven, Co. Londonderry, could write in 1814 that 'However it may offend the judgment or shock our present refinement, its affecting cadences will continue to find admirers wherever what is truly sad and plaintive can be relished or understood.' A colleague in Co. Antrim also commented on the 'melancholy sweetness' of the keen as practised in his neighbourhood.[33]

A more important question, for our present purposes, than the musical qualities of the keen, is the function which it fulfilled for those who took part or listened. One possible interpretation would be to see the keen as something fairly impersonal, another part of the tribute which custom demanded should be paid to the dead. This would accord fairly well with the formal nature of the lament and the fact that it might be pronounced by those who had no personal connection with the deceased. At the same time it can also be suggested that the keen provided those for whom the death was experienced as a personal loss with a controlled outlet for their emotions, encouraging them to express in a structured and manageable form feelings which might otherwise have remained partly suppressed. This could be the case whether they pronounced the keen themselves or merely acted as chorus to a lament given out by a specialist performer.[34] Examples of the keen described by J. M. Synge on the island of Inismaan about the turn of the twentieth century suggest that it was in fact capable of performing both these functions. At the funeral of an elderly woman who had died of natural causes the keen was pronounced, not as an expression of personal loss, but rather as a lament for human mortality in general — although the feeling behind it, if Synge is to be believed, was not any less real or passionate for that. 'In this cry of pain', he writes, 'the inner consciousness of the people seems to lay itself bare for an instant, and to reveal the mood of beings who feel their isolation in the face of a universe that wars on them with winds and seas.' At the funeral of a young man who had been drowned at sea, on the other hand, the keen took on a more personal character. It 'lost a part of its formal nature, and was recited as the expression of intense personal grief by the young men and women of the man's own family'.[35]

The festive wake, then, was a body of procedures which enabled the community to come to terms with the death of one of its members. These procedures were not always considered appropriate: at the death of a young person, or where the circumstances were regarded as particularly tragic, the wake was generally a quiet and mournful affair.[36] On other occasions, however, where the death could be regarded as more or less in the natural order of things, the traditional practices offered a variety of consolations. The company as a whole could feel that due respect had been paid to the deceased person and could overcome any uneasiness which they might feel concerning his continued and potentially dangerous presence among them. They were also permitted to respond to a reminder of general mortality, and to the abrupt disappearance of a member of a tightly knit community, by a compensatory display of vitality and gaiety, and in particular through an assertion of potency and sexuality. The more immediately bereaved, meanwhile, found in the rituals of the wake, and particularly in the keen, a means of expressing their feelings in a controlled and manageable form. There were other incidental benefits: the family of the dead person were provided with company and a certain amount of distraction in the period immediately after the death. The principal importance of the wake, however, was that it ensured that both the fact of an individual death and its more general implications were openly and fully recognised, with rituals that encouraged and structured the appropriate responses from all concerned. To outsiders the results may have appeared incongruous and shocking; but they may also have relieved those who took part from some of the burdens of anxiety and guilt with which more modern modes of reacting to death have made us familiar.

These, of course, were the functions of the wake at its most developed. By the late eighteenth and early nineteenth centuries it is likely that many of the distinctive features of the original custom had become blurred or altogether forgotten. Even the elaborate mimes described by Prim were probably watered-down versions of the original practice. Nevertheless, it is still in these terms that the practice of the festive wake must be understood. The passage of time may have modified the beliefs and attitudes which had given rise to the custom; men may no longer have been capable of explaining (if, indeed, they had ever been) why they acted as they did. But those who took part in the games and practices of the wake behaved in a manner that in any other context could only appear grotesque and barbarous. That they continued to do so for so long, and in the face of so much condemnation and disapproval, can only suggest that the wake continued to perform important psychological functions for those who participated in it.

* * *

Already by the end of the eighteenth century the opposition

of the Catholic Church to the practices of the festive wake had a long history. On several occasions during the seventeenth century, beginning with the legislation of the Synod of Armagh in 1614, regulations had been introduced condemning and prohibiting excessive drinking, unseemly amusements, sexual misbehaviour and keening at wakes and funerals. Such prohibitions were repeated in the first half of the eighteenth century. The statutes of the diocese of Dublin, introduced in 1730, ordered that all persons having the cure of souls should make efforts to prevent abuses at wakes by imposing public penances on anyone who engaged in lewd games or sang obscene songs on these occasions. In the diocese of Leighlin it was ordered in 1748 that no clergyman was to say mass 'over the corpse of a defunct at whose wake such immodest songs, profane tricks or immoderate crowds are permitted'. Priests were also ordered to take measures both against professional keeners and against ordinary men and women who cried or howled at funerals.[37]

Further legislation of the same type was introduced in different dioceses during the decades that followed. Regulations for the diocese of Armagh published in 1761 forbade the provision of drink at wakes or funerals. In 1777 the bishops of the province of Cashel named 'profanations at wakes', along with patterns and night-time dances, as practices that were 'to be hindered by exemplary punishments and exhortations'. Regulations introduced in the archdiocese of Cashel in 1782 threatened persons who took part in lewd games at wakes with excommunication. The statutes of the diocese of Clogher in 1789 ordered that abuses and scandals at wakes were to be 'vigorously restricted by pastors and eventually abolished'. Any priest who knowingly celebrated mass at a funeral where drink had been distributed was suspended, while any person who distributed drink in this way was to be excluded from the sacraments until he made a public retraction of his error and paid a fine.[38]

By the beginning of the nineteenth century, then, the practices of the festive wake had long been an object of ecclesiastical condemnation and prohibition. In the decades that followed, however, continued legislation on the same issues made clear that wakes continued to be a source of serious concern to the church authorities. The visitation book of Bishop Plunkett of Meath indicates that over a period of more than twenty years, from the 1780s up to 1810, he preached repeatedly against attendance at these gatherings and against the custom of distributing drink at funerals. In Cashel around 1806 Archbishop Bray devoted a whole pastoral letter to the subject, condemning 'all sorts of plays and amusements at wakes, those especially against decency and modesty, and which are in mock imitation of the sacred rites of the Church, particularly in the celebration of marriage'. Persons who encouraged or took part in indecent or irreverent games of this kind were declared to be excommunicated. Heads of families who permitted such performances in their houses were to be publicly reprimanded and excluded from the sacraments until they had promised before the congregation not to permit such abuses in their houses again. The same penalty was imposed on heads of households who permitted or caused whiskey to be distributed at wakes and funerals, and priests were forbidden to officiate in any way at a funeral where drink had been given out or games played at the wake. Statutes for the diocese of Dublin, introduced in 1831, also recognised that the practice of the festive wake was still carried on there: 'Disorderly vigils for the dead are forbidden; they are to be gradually abolished and those who favour them rebuked.' Here as elsewhere, furthermore, there were special provisions against attendance at wakes by young persons and by those who were not married. Such prohibitions make clear that the church authorities were particularly conscious of the threat which certain aspects of the festive wake presented to the sexual morality they were attempting to maintain. They also imply a recognition that prohibitions directed at the practice as a whole were proving ineffective.[39]

Clerical opposition to the festive wake, in both the eighteenth and nineteenth centuries, was caused principally by the disorderly conduct for which these gatherings provided the occasion. The church authorities, it is true, were aware of the mockery of their teachings and rituals which took place on these occasions. Archbishop Butler's catechism, published in 1775, demanded:

Q.   What do you think of Theatrical Representations, and of other amusements, *particularly* at *Wakes*, in which Religion, its Ministers, and Sacred Ceremonies are ridiculed?

A.   They are impious and highly criminal, and strictly forbidden by the first commandment.

Bishop Plunkett of Meath, similarly, preached during his visitation of 1809 against 'mimickry of the sacraments at wakes', and other prelates also condemned parodies of marriage and of other sacraments on these occasions. But there is little to indicate that the church authorities objected to the wake as a survival of pre-Christian practices or as a ritual response to death whose premises differed radically from their own. Archbishop Butler began his denunciation of wake abuses in 1782 with the statement that these vigils had originally been instituted chiefly in order that the souls of the faithful should be helped by the prayers of pious persons, and went on to condemn the indecent games by which this function was frustrated.[40]

The main reasons for clerical opposition to wakes and wake-games, then, were practical rather than ideological. Wakes were condemned because they were seen as occasions of undesirable behaviour, with repeated allusions to drinking and sexual misdemeanours indicating that it was these offences in particular which gave rise to concern. At the same time the attitude of the Catholic clergy was also influenced by ideas of religious propriety. This can be seen in particular in their marked hostility to the practice of keening, a custom which — unlike other aspects of the wake — did not appear to constitute a direct threat to the morals of their flocks. Keening, the bishop and clergy of Leighlin agreed in 1748, was a 'heathenish' and 'anti-Christian' practice, reflecting a deplorable vanity on the part of persons visited by God with the loss of a friend, and contrary to the express commands of St Paul, who had forbidden displays of immoderate grief for the dead. Archbishop Bray of Cashel in 1806 condemned 'all unnatural screams and shrieks and fictitious tuneful cries and elegies at wakes, together with the savage custom of howling and bawling at funerals', activities which he described as 'pagan practices, so unmeaning and so unbecoming Christians'. Elsewhere too there were reports in the early nineteenth century that the Catholic clergy were suppressing the practice of keening at funerals and replacing it with prayers and the singing of hymns. The same desire to impose their own formulae and what they regarded as a suitable atmosphere on the traditional practices of the wake and funeral can also be seen in other regulations drawn up by the church authorities. The rules for the parish of Tydavenet, Co. Monaghan, introduced in 1832, laid down that no funeral service would be celebrated for any parishioner 'until some responsible person engage that there shall be no pipes or tobacco brought for the purpose of smoking in the grave-yard on the day of interment'. There was also an injunction that 'some good book, on death, hell, judgment or heaven' should be read at wakes. The priests of the dioceses of Dublin and Ardagh and Clonmacnoise, similarly, were instructed to ensure that prayers for the soul of the dead person were recited at wakes and that spiritual books were read.[41]

Repeated condemnations of the festive wake by the church authorities in the years after 1800 indicate, as already mentioned, that earlier prohibitions of the practice had been unsuccessful. This is not to say that such efforts were entirely ineffective. By the early decades of the nineteenth century there are indications that clerical prohibitions were having some effect on popular attitudes and behaviour. Thus the Protestant curate of Maghera, Co. Londonderry, reported in 1814 that the Irish cry had recently been replaced, through the influence of the Catholic clergy, by 'solemn hymns in the Latin language, set to the Gregorian music'. Other reports from Antrim and Londonderry also noted the decline of the keen and its replacement by hymns and attributed the change to the influence of the Catholic clergy. Clerical opposition to drinking at wakes and funerals also met with at least occasional success. The same curate of Maghera reported that the use of whiskey, which had previously been drunk in large quantities on these occasions, had been success-fully prohibited by the Catholic clergy. In Magilligan, Co.

Londonderry, similarly, drunkenness at wakes was said to have been 'greatly diminished through the influence of the priesthood'. Such successes were not confined to the north of Ireland. The Parish Priest of Dromahair, Co. Leitrim, informed the Poor Inquiry commissioners that at funerals 'we have succeeded in putting a stop to whiskey-drinking in a great measure'; and according to the Parish Priest of Galmoy, Co. Kilkenny, 'The extravagance formerly indulged in at the funerals of the poor has been materially checked by the prohibition issued to the Roman Catholic clergy to officiate in any house where whiskey is introduced.'[42]

Successes of this kind, however, were limited in extent. The practice of keening may have been suppressed before the famine in parts of Ulster, but in most areas it continued a good deal longer, and even at the very end of the nineteenth century it was still being opposed by the Catholic clergy. Similarly, drunkenness and other forms of misbehaviour at wakes continued to attract regular clerical condemnation throughout the second half of the nineteenth century and even later. Among the topics listed for discussion at a synod of the diocese of Clogher in 1861 was 'revival of funeral whiskey', and a decree of the synod reiterated that this practice was strictly forbidden. A national synod of bishops, meeting at Maynooth in 1875, declared: 'Parish priests must put an end to unchristian wakes, where the corpse is present and where games, dances, singing and drinking are carried on — these abuses are a shame and a disgrace to the house of the dead.' A similar prohibition was repeated by the national synod of 1927. Wake-games were still being forbidden in the statutes of the diocese of Ferns, introduced in 1898, while as late as 1903 the Bishop of Ardagh and Clonmacnoise forbade unmarried men and women to attend wakes between sunset and sunrise.[43]

The opposition of the Catholic clergy of the pre-famine period to the custom of the festive wake, therefore, was not a very effective one. Temporary or local successes may have been achieved, but it is clear that throughout most of the country these practices were to remain a serious problem for a considerable time to come. In the longer term, also, the importance of clerical opposition in bringing about the decline of the traditional wake is open to question. Ó Súilleabháin suggests that the practice died out in most areas towards the end of the nineteenth century, although wake-games were still being played after 1900 in the counties of Monaghan, Cavan, Louth and Armagh, while Ó Súilleabháin himself witnessed a lively wake of the traditional type in Mayo in 1921.[44] Some observers attributed the eventual decline of the practice to the continued opposition of the Catholic clergy. Other important developments, however, contributed to the same process. This is well illustrated in Henry Morris's account of the decline of the festive wake in his part of Co. Monaghan during the early years of the twentieth century. Here, according to Morris, the more blatantly pagan elements of the practice had been eliminated at some earlier stage, so that clerical opposition to what remained of the lively wake was never heard of in that county. What brought about the decline of the practice was rather the abandonment of the custom of laying out the corpse in the barn for a night before removing it for burial. 'This was due less to religious considerations than to the general spirit of anglicisation and snobbery, which caused the people to ape the manners and customs of those above them, and these were always non-Gaelic.'[45] A change in attitudes of the type referred to by Morris must have taken place in many other areas at this time or somewhat earlier. Morris's choice of wording is obviously coloured by strong personal prejudices, but he may well have been correct in suggesting that it was this, rather than the continued opposition of the Catholic clergy, which brought about the eventual abandonment of the traditional wake.

3. *'The Tribute of Idleness'*
This chapter has been concerned with the opposition of the Catholic clergy of the late eighteenth and early nineteenth centuries to the traditional practices of the pattern and the festive wake. Both these episodes can be seen as casting further light on the relationship between official and popular Catholicism in this period. The issues involved in the two cases, however, were not identical. Patterns provide further examples both of the ability of popular

tradition to combine Christian and non-Christian elements in a single body of ideas and observances, and of the change in clerical attitudes which took place in this period as practices which had previously been tolerated or even encouraged began to encounter a new suspicion and hostility. The custom of waking the dead had not taken on the same veneer of Christian symbolism and practice. Hence clerical opposition began earlier than in the case of the pattern and had none of the ambivalence which a section at least of the lower clergy showed towards assemblies at holy wells and the practices customary there. At the same time wakes, whatever the ideas concerning the dead and their continued presence among the living that had given rise to the custom, retained little in their outward character to indicate an origin in doctrines radically different to those of the Catholic Church. The comforts which they offered to those who took part were functional rather than ritual. For this reason clerical opposition remained almost exclusively concerned with the different types of misconduct for which the wake provided an occasion, without even the limited conflict between rival supernaturalisms which can be seen in the case of the pattern.

Neither wakes nor patterns, however, were opposed primarily on account of their non-Christian features. The comments of the church authorities make clear that in both cases their main concern was with the various forms of misconduct — principally drunkenness, sexual immorality and brawling — for which these two customs provided the occasion. For the same reason the degree of opposition offered to both practices went far beyond that encountered by other manifestations of popular magic in this period. The main issue, then, was one of standards of behaviour rather than of religious orthodoxy. But in order to understand fully what the church authorities were attempting to achieve in their campaign against wakes and patterns, and the difficulties which confronted them, it is necessary to set their efforts in a broader context.

Wakes and patterns, in the first place, were not the only occasions on which the Irish lower orders of this period abandoned themselves to enjoyment and celebration. At christenings and weddings, as well as at wakes and funerals, relatives, friends and neighbours might be brought together for drinking and festivity. In addition to the patterns held at different dates in each locality, there were other festivals scattered throughout the year, notably St John's Eve, May Eve, Christmas and Easter Monday, on which men ceased work, drank and amused themselves. To these occasions were added the amusements of the Irish Sunday and the holydays or saints' days on which the faithful were required by the law of their church to attend mass and to abstain from servile work. The afternoons of Sundays and holydays, a Co. Cork rector complained in 1819, 'are invariably consumed in discussions at the ale-house, accompanied by the bagpipe and the fiddle; or in goaling parties by the young men in the fields, and the evenings regularly terminate in dancing and debauchery'. A colleague in Co. Sligo, writing three years earlier, lamented in similar tones that, although his Catholic parishioners scrupulously abstained from working on saints' days, 'Their sanctity does not operate on their minds so as to induce them to refrain from sports and pastimes, cursing or swearing, and frequenting tippling houses and drinking to excess.'[46] A further occasion for regular amusement and relaxation, finally, was provided by the fairs which took place at centres throughout Ireland and which, it was generally agreed, were attended as much for pleasure as for the transaction of business.

If wakes and patterns were not the only occasions for amusement and festivity available to the people of pre-famine Ireland, neither were they the only occasions to meet with condemnation and hostility from the authorities of the Catholic Church. Reports from different parts of Ulster in the 1820s and 1830s show that the Catholic clergy of that province were exerting their influence not only against wakes and patterns but also against other popular amusements. 'Crowded meetings for the purpose of amusement', it was reported in Rostrevor, Co. Down, 'do not now take place as formerly, such meetings being opposed by the Roman Catholic clergy.' In Ballinascreen, Co. Londonderry, priests had prohibited the gatherings for dancing and other amusements which had accompanied the lighting of the midsummer bonfire on St John's Eve. Such gatherings were also being discouraged by the priests of Errigle, Co. Londonderry, on account of the drinking and fighting which took place at them. In Cushendall, Co. Antrim, it had been customary for each public house to hire two pipers or fiddlers on fair days, so that their customers would have music to dance by, 'but their priest within the last year put a total stop to it'. In Duneane, Co. Antrim, similarly, dancing and cockfighting had been the favourite amusements of the inhabitants, 'but they are denounced by their clergy and partially given up.'[47]

All these examples come from the same source, the detailed reports on social conditions in different parts of Ulster compiled by investigators for the Ordnance Survey. The evidence from other parts of the country is less complete, but here too there are indications that the Catholic clergy sought to use their influence to suppress or modify a whole range of popular amusements. William Farrell of Carlow records in his autobiography how a new parish priest, appointed around 1780, 'set about reforming every abuse that came within his reach (and they were many,) such as bull-beating [sic], cockfighting, manfighting, gambling and everything of that description'. Opposition to dancing, as will be seen in a later chapter, appears to have been widespread during this period. Attempts were also made in a number of cases to restrict Sunday recreation, whether out of a desire to see the sabbath observed in a decorous manner or out of disapproval of the amusements to which it was commonly devoted. Bishop Troy of Ossory lamented in 1778 that many of the Catholics of his diocese were guilty of riot, injury to private property and other crimes. 'As these and other grievous excesses are frequently the consequence of intemperate drinking on the Lord's day,' he instructed his clergy, 'it is requisite that you should inculcate the necessity of sanctifying it with prayer and good works.' Bishop Caulfield of Ferns ordered his clergy in 1798 to preach against gatherings for ball-playing and other amusements on Sundays and festivals. Bishop Plunkett of Meath preached regularly against Sunday amusements, singling out what he described as 'promiscuous assemblies of both sexes', 'dancing at improper hours' and 'dangerous amusements, intoxication etc.' as offences frequently committed on that day. Archbishop Everard of Cashel, as well as preaching against violations of the sabbath by unnecessary servile work, forbade games of hurling on that day. The church authorities also shared in the general concern over the manner in which Catholic holidays were observed in Ireland. The observance of these days, Bishop Doyle maintained in 1830, 'is injurious to good morals and to all the interests of the people'. An appeal to Rome, in which Doyle took the leading part, led to the abrogation of two feast-days, Easter Monday and Whit Monday, in 1829, and of the feast of St John the Baptist in 1831. A proposal that they go on to seek the abrogation of most of the remaining ten festivals was supported by a majority of the Irish bishops, although it was not proceeded with since unanimity could not be obtained.[48]

In addition to prohibitions of patterns, wakes, dances, Sunday amusements and other customs, the church authorities took various measures against excessive drinking. In the diocese of Clogher in 1789 Catholics were forbidden on pain of mortal sin to drink any intoxicating liquor in taverns on Sundays or feast-days, exceptions being made for persons eating or lodging in such houses and for those on a journey of more than ten miles. Priests in Co. Kilkenny in the 1830s denounced from the altar the practice of giving drink on credit or in exchange for work to be done. In some cases Catholic clergymen established or encouraged local temperance societies, such as that established by the Rev. James Maher in Carlow around 1830.[49] Efforts of the latter kind, however, do not appear to have been very common. It was only with the total abstinence crusade launched by Father Theobald Mathew in 1838 that a major attempt was made to act against drinking itself, rather than against the social occasions which gave rise to drunkenness.

The wide range of popular festivals and amusements which continued to flourish in Ireland in the late eighteenth and early nineteenth centuries gave rise to frequent complaints concerning the idle and feckless disposition of the lower orders. 'The peasant who pays the tribute of idleness and drunkenness to half the saints in the calendar,' John

O'Driscol pointed out in 1823, 'and thinks himself also bound to visit all the fairs within seven miles of him, has great deductions to make from the time which ought to be devoted to industry.' Allegations of moral deficiency or of a national propensity to idleness, however, are not convincing. To see this it is only necessary to look at the record of Irish workers in England, whether as seasonal migrants or as permanent settlers. Instead popular recreation must be seen in the context of social conditions, and also of a society at a particular stage of economic development. The standard of living and general prospects of a large section of the Irish population, as many of their more sympathetic contemporaries recognised, provided little incentive to either thrift or industry. 'Their utmost exertions', a Co. Tyrone rector observed of the cottiers of his parish in 1819, '...produce them so little, that by a perversion of argument not uncommon in every line of life when great exertions fail, they seem to think that little the less worth taking care of.'

More important still was the fact that the type of work on which the majority of the poorer classes of pre-famine Ireland depended for their support encouraged an irregular alternation of work and leisure, in which bouts of intense labour were punctuated by periods of idleness, rather than the consistent, methodical industry favoured by contemporary moralists. This can be seen most clearly in the case of the agricultural labourer and small farmer, whose work was concentrated at certain times of the year and, even in the busiest seasons, might have to be postponed or hurried as the weather demanded. But the same was true of other occupational groups. The most important non-agricultural occupation in the pre-famine countryside was the weaving of cotton or linen, done on a handloom in the weaver's own home, with a middleman supplying the raw material and paying the weaver for the finished cloth. And here too it was found that workers, even in Protestant Ulster, used the freedom conferred by piece-work to make their own hours, relieving the monotony of work with a wide range of sports and pastimes and in addition, when rates of payment rose beyond a certain level, opting for more leisure rather than higher earnings. A similar freedom existed in many areas of urban industry, organised as it was around small groups of skilled workmen rather than large factories with a timetable dominated by the need to run expensive machinery. In both Dublin and Belfast during this period there were complaints that tradesmen frequently chose to spend their Mondays, and on some occasions their Tuesdays also, drinking and amusing themselves, relying for their support on what work they could cram into the remaining days of the week.[50]

None of these circumstances was peculiar to Ireland in the pre-famine period. In the present day industrialists attempting to establish enterprises in developing countries have found themselves in conflict with an attitude to work radically different to that with which they are familiar, manifesting itself in high rates of absenteeism, indifference to conventional wage incentives, and a general reluctance to accept regular hours. Similar attitudes, and the same irregular patterns of work, remained common in Europe up to the coming of large-scale factory-based industry. Thus many of the complaints which were directed at the Irish farmers, tradesmen and labourers of the late eighteenth and early nineteenth centuries were also being levelled at their English counterparts. The idleness of the lower orders, their irregular habits of work and the undesirable nature of their sports and recreations were all common themes among the writers of this period. Much energy was devoted to attempts to instil in the labouring poor the classic virtues of industry, self-discipline and time-thrift, while the same period witnessed vigorous attacks by social reformers, religious and secular, on fairs, festivals and popular amusements of all kinds.

In the case of England these efforts to alter the character of popular leisure were to a large extent successful. By the 1830s and 1840s, it was generally agreed, there had been a general decline in the popularity of traditional amusements. Accompanying this there had been a change in the character of the English poor. In the words of E. P. Thompson, 'The "average" working man became more disciplined, more subject to the productive tempo of "the clock", more reserved and methodical, less violent and less spontaneous.' Various explanations can be offered for this change in popular manners: the disruption of established customs and social relationships brought about by the transition from a rural society to an urban and industrial one, the erosion of leisure by falling returns for labour, reforming efforts from above, and the influence of evangelical religion. But at the centre of the transformation, underlying all other developments, was a change in the nature of work itself. The irregular habits of the eighteenth century could be accommodated in a small workshop or in a system of domestic industry, where the individual craftsman or artisan could be left to work at his own pace and paid according to what he produced. Factory-based industry, on the other hand, involved the division of tasks among large numbers of workers, whose efforts had thus to be co-ordinated with each other, and the subordination of all of these to the operation of complex machinery. It was this which ultimately made necessary the cultivation of a new work discipline, with consequences which affected the whole pattern of popular leisure.[51]

This is the context in which one must set the efforts of the Irish Catholic clergy to suppress or modify wakes, patterns and other popular amusements. Like the political economists and moral reformers of the same period in England, they were attempting to impose orderly habits on a population whose living conditions and whose work itself encouraged irregularity and disorder, but their efforts were not supplemented by the massive economic and social changes which were taking place in Britain. Their efforts, it is true, were not entirely without effect. If the opposition of the clergy to the festive wake had only a marginal impact on popular attitudes and behaviour, their opposition to patterns does appear to have had some results. A number of reasons can be suggested for the difference in the degree of success achieved in these two cases. Large public assemblies were easier to oppose successfully than what went on in private houses. More important, perhaps, the customary practices of the wake catered for psychological needs that were more acute than any met by the pattern-day celebrations. For this reason they proved more resistant both to clerical opposition and condemnation and to the changes in popular attitudes and behaviour which by the 1830s and 1840s had already begun to undermine the popularity of patterns. In neither of these two cases, however, did the Catholic clergy succeed in eliminating the forms of behaviour to which they were opposed. Nor is this very surprising. As long as pre-famine Ireland remained the society it was there was probably little that any authority could do to reshape the pattern of work and leisure that prevailed there.

This is not to say that Irish social life, deprived of the side-effects of large-scale industrialisation, remained unchanged throughout the nineteenth century. The decades after the famine, as was seen in an earlier chapter, brought important changes to the social structure of rural Ireland, along with a general improvement in standards of living and exposure to new cultural influences and new models of behaviour. The result was the adoption of new standards of respectability and decorum, and these inevitably brought with them the decline of many of the less inhibited amusements of the Irish countryside and the modification of others. But the difference between English and Irish society remained noticeable. By the end of the nineteenth century the stereotyped image of the Irishman, eternally ready for either brawling or drinking, more violent and spontaneous and less disciplined than his English counterpart, was well established in English popular mythology. More careful observers, however, noted that it was not only the extent but also the character of Irish drunkenness which was different. The Irish, Sir Horace Plunkett maintained in 1904, were actually less physiologically dependent on drink than the English. 'By far the greater proportion of the drinking which retards our progress', he pointed out, 'is of a festive character. It takes place at fairs and markets, sometimes, even yet, at "wakes", those ghastly parodies on the blessed consolation of religion in bereavment.'[52] The passing of the irregular rhythms which had characterised the social life of pre-famine Ireland was a long, slow process. And it is significant that excessive drinking, both in the second half of the nineteenth century and after, remained the area of behaviour in which the Irish Catholic clergy — no matter how great their apparent authority in other spheres — most conspicuously failed to exercise an effective influence over their congregations.

Marriage and Sexual Behaviour

For anyone interested in the way in which the Catholic
Church and its clergy have influenced the character of
modern Irish society, the question of sexual behaviour
must be a particularly important one. From the later nineteenth century onwards observers have commented frequently on the strictness of the sexual attitudes that have
prevailed throughout the greater part of Ireland, and the
same observers have often seen in the Catholic clergy the
principal custodians – if not the actual creators – of this
stern morality.[1] The sexual puritanism of modern Irish
Catholicism has in fact been for many people its most
prominent characteristic, and the apparent success of the
Catholic clergy in transmitting this puritanism to their
congregations has frequently been seen as the most striking
indication of the influence which that body are capable
of exerting.

Historians who have attempted to discuss this aspect of
modern Irish Catholicism have sometimes been blamed for
their uncritical acceptance of the vivid picture presented
in the writings of Irish novelists and playwrights and in
other accounts and comments of a blatantly polemical
character. There are, of course, obvious dangers in relying
too heavily on material of these kinds. But the idea of
Ireland, and particularly Catholic Ireland, as a puritanical
and sexually repressive society does not depend solely on
the evidence of alienated artists and disgruntled intellectuals.
One must also take into account the testimony of twentieth-
century social scientists reporting from first-hand observation
of particular Irish communities: the American anthropologists
Arensberg and Kimball in Co. Clare in the 1930s, the so-

ciologist Alexander Humphreys among first-generation
Dubliners in 1949–51, and the more recent and more con-
troversial work of J. C. Messenger on one of the Aran Islands.
And to these academic outsiders may be added the evidence
of witnesses who were part of the society they described but
basically friendly to it – for example, the predominantly
Catholic and conservative contributors to the well-known
collection of essays, *The Vanishing Irish* (1954), on the
subject of Ireland's declining population, or the woman
teacher from Co. Cork who at about the same time described her youth in the years before the First World War
for the benefit of the Irish Folklore Commission:

> We wouldn't face in home to our parents with a boy-
> friend, or we would not dare walk with him in public.
> If we met our father or mother when walking or talking
> to one, we'd sink through the ground with the fright of
> it. . . . Then the evils of company-keeping were stormed
> at from the pulpit in the old days. It was a constant
> subject for censure from those in authority. It is no
> wonder we have a legacy of bachelors and spinsters.

For an earlier period, similarly there is the testimony of
Mary Fogarty's affectionate but revealing memoir of her
childhood in Co. Limerick in the 1860s and 1870s. Crossroads dancing, even then, 'was strictly forbidden by priests
and parents', while the maids and farm-boys employed on
her father's farm were kept strictly apart from each other
at all times. When one of the maids scandalised the household by allowing a young man to walk her home after mass,
authority in both its major forms was invoked against her:
'My mother was shocked by their effrontery in appearing at
the door together, for "keeping company" was strictly
forbidden. She reprimanded Rosie, who sulked for a week;
the priest spoke to her as well and made her cry.'[2]
   Strict attitudes to sexual behaviour have not, of course,
been unique to Irish Catholicism over the past one hundred
years or so. The prudery of Victorian England is well known.
Even in the twentieth century Anglican clergymen continued
to denounce the use of artificial methods of birth control,
and it was not until the Lambeth Conference of 1958 that

such methods were unequivocally accepted as legitimate. Indeed, J. H. Whyte, pointing to a number of early twentieth-century parallels, has suggested that the campaign waged by Irish Catholic churchmen in the 1920s against dances, pornography and other threats to sexual morality was 'only an extreme example of a trend to be found among the more traditionally minded people all over the world'. But in Ireland puritanism appears both to have been more widely accepted and to have lasted longer than in most comparable societies. It is difficult, furthermore, not to conclude that this puritanism had its roots in something more complex than a simple desire to preserve traditional values. Thus Humphreys, in his study of Dublin families, discovered not only a strict code of sexual behaviour but also prevalent and very strong feelings of sexual guilt and anxiety. 'I think there is something wrong with sex', one married woman confessed,

> and nothing will ever change me.... And I think that is the general attitude. One woman friend of mine who is married told me once that she felt after she was married that the loss of her virginity was the greatest loss of her life. And I felt the same way about it.

The private attitudes of Catholic clergymen have not been probed in the same way. But here too the general reaction to what were perceived as threats to sexual morality appears often to have been out of all proportion to the situation which produced it. It is unlikely, for example, that the crossroads dances of the 1920s were really sufficiently orgiastic to merit the campaign mounted against them. 'Wooden road-side platforms were set on fire by curates; surer still, the priests drove their motor-cars backward and forward over the timber platforms; concertinas were sent flying into hill streams and those who played music at dances were branded as outcasts.' It takes an effort of the imagination to join with the Dean of All Hallows College in discovering even among the best of the films 'dumped on the shores of holy Ireland' in the year 1923 'sudden intrusions, highly erotic scenes, for instance, which are prolonged'. And it is equally difficult to recognise the Ireland of 1924 in the comments of Cardinal Logue in his Lenten pastoral for that year: 'The dress, or rather the want of dress, of women at the present day is a crying scandal. There seems to be a rivalry among them as to how little dress they can wear without incurring universal reprobation.'[3]

The sexual attitudes, both lay and clerical, of twentieth-century Ireland have been the subject of much discussion. Yet surprisingly little effort has been made to examine the origins of this strict morality by comparing the attitudes and behaviour of the late nineteenth century and after with those of earlier decades. This chapter begins by looking at the regulations which the Catholic clergy of the late eighteenth and early nineteenth centuries attempted to impose on the sexual behaviour of their congregations, and at the actual character of Irish sexual attitudes and behaviour in the decades before the famine. From this it goes on to examine the way in which the church authorities of this period attempted to impose a measure of control on the marriages of Irish Catholics, and the extent to which their efforts in that area were successful. An inquiry of this kind should be of interest for what it can reveal of relations between priests and people in pre-famine Ireland. It might also be of value in providing a longer perspective on the problem of the sexual puritanism of Irish society in more recent decades, and on the precise part played by the Catholic clergy in the development of that puritanism.

1.   *Sexual Morality: Clerical Attitudes and Policies*

The broad outlines of the discipline which the Irish Catholic clergy of the late eighteenth and early nineteenth centuries would have been attempting to impose on the sexual behaviour of their congregations are not really in much doubt. The principal prohibitions of the sixth and ninth commandments* were summed up in Andrew Donlevy's catechism, first published in 1742. These two commandments

---

*Readers more familiar with the Anglican catechism should perhaps be reminded that this is the numbering of the commandments favoured by the Catholic Church, in which the prohibition of graven images is reduced to the status of an addendum to the prohibition of false gods contained in the first commandment, while the offence of coveting a neighbour's wife is separated, as the ninth commandment, from that of coveting his house, servants or oxen.

forbid a man to have any carnal communication with any other woman than his own wife; and a woman with any other man than her own husband; and even to covet or desire any such sinful commerce.

Are immodest looks or unchaste kisses a breach of this commandment?

They are, as also unchaste touches of ourselves or others, wilfull pollution, lewd discourses, filthy songs, reading of love-books, and every other impudent or shameless action.

Are unchaste thoughts, without any design of coming to action, a breach of this commandment?

Yes, if entertained with delight and pleasure.[4]

Few clergymen of any denomination at that time or even today, would have been able to disagree with this formulation. The real issue, if we are to talk in terms of a church or its clergy being puritanical or otherwise, is one of emphasis. Did the Catholic clergy of this period place an exceptionally heavy stress on the sins of the flesh, their dangers and the need to avoid them? Unfortunately there is no satisfactory means of quantifying the strictness or otherwise of a given attitude to sexual behaviour. And even if such a measurement could be devised, there would still be the problem of determining, for each individual place and time, what is to be regarded as 'exceptional' and what as 'normal'. It is better to begin with more concrete issues. Given that the prohibitions of the sixth and ninth commandments were part of the morality which the Catholic clergy were attempting to communicate and enforce, what steps did they take to see that these prohibitions were observed, and in particular how did they deal with those who offended against them?

The most obvious, and in many cases also the most vulnerable, offender against the principles of sexual morality put forward by the church authorities was the woman who gave birth to a child outside lawful marriage. The statutes and regulations laid down for the government of different dioceses make clear that such women were in fact regarded as offenders to be punished. The common penalty was to withhold either temporarily or altogether the ceremony of churching, the thanksgiving or purification carried out after the birth of a child. In the diocese of Dublin it was ordered in 1730 that unmarried mothers were not to be churched until an interval of ten days had elapsed; later statutes in the dioceses of Cork and Cashel laid down intervals of one month for a first offence and two months for a second. In 1831 clergy in the diocese of Dublin were ordered not to church unmarried women at all, and this also seems to have been the policy in Co. Clare at about the same time. In the eighteenth century at least such women could also be subjected to more positive penalties. The same regulations for the diocese of Dublin in 1730 ordered that as well as the withholding of churching a woman whose behaviour had given rise to major scandal was to be required to do penance by acknowledging her guilt in the chapel before the congregation. Regulations introduced in the diocese of Limerick in 1752 laid down that a woman giving birth to an illegitimate child in a parish other than her own 'is to be remitted to her ordinary pastor to receive condign punishment', while in Achonry in 1759 it was ruled that no unmarried woman was to be churched until after she had been punished publicly in such a way that her disgrace would deter others from the same offence.[5]

A second type of offender against the rules of sexual conduct prescribed by the church authorities were those couples who either lived together or conducted open liaisons without having been lawfully married. The policy of the Catholic clergy in such cases was summed up by Archbishop Carpenter of Dublin in a visitation sermon preached in 1775:

> It is [the priest's] duty to remove as much as in him lies all scandals, to dissolve all infamous connections and to refuse the sacraments to those who in spite of the censures of the Church and the heavy curse of God himself
> · will not separate, but live together in a criminal intercourse, to the crying disedification of the faithful and to their own eternal damnation. And it is yours [i.e. the congregation's] to second him in those pious undertakings and to shun like a leper all those who obstinately stop their ears against the voice of God and his holy Church.

Similar sanctions were employed in other dioceses. In 1780 a parish priest in Co. Cork excommunicated a man who had been living openly with another man's wife. Bishop Plunkett of Meath in 1801 authorised one of his priests to excommunicate a man who was living in adultery, while in Kildare and Leighlin in 1829 Doyle gave orders for the excommunication of a cohabiting couple. Nor was it only open cohabitation by unmarried persons which attracted such penalties. In Co. Meath around 1838 a man who had married a woman with whom he was supposed to have had a relationship while his previous wife was still alive — going outside his own parish for the ceremony — was denounced from the altar and excluded from the chapel. And in Co. Cork as late as 1857 W. J. O'Neill Daunt recorded in his diary that the local priest had announced after mass 'that if a certain person who has been too attentive to the wife of a man now absent in America did not, on or before next Sunday, cut the connection and make a solemn promise to live morally henceforth, he and his frail friend should be publicly excommunicated'.[6]

One aspect of the policy adopted by the church authorities in cases of this kind has already been discussed. This was their concern, not only with the individual sinner, but also with the effect of his offence on others. Couples who openly flouted the Church's rules on sexual behaviour, as Carpenter noted in his sermon, threatened to bring about not just their own damnation but also 'the crying disedification of the faithful'. For this reason, as he made clear on another occasion, such couples, if they repented, could not be reconciled to the Church until they had made reparation 'for the detestable and horrid scandal they have given'. In the same way Doyle ordered that the cohabiting couple whose excommunication he ordered in 1829 were not to be received back into the Church until they had undergone 'some ignominious or painful humiliation'. From this point of view excommunication can be seen not merely as a penalty imposed on the offender but also (as the wording of Carpenter's sermon again makes clear) as a means of involving the whole congregation in a complete rejection of both the individual and his crime.[7]

The same awareness of the damage done by open breaches of the official sexual code can be seen in the policy adopted towards couples who were known to have engaged in sexual intercourse outside marriage or who were suspected of having done so. Here the main concern of the church authorities appears to have been to induce such couples to marry in order to undo the damage they had caused. In cases of this kind, the Parish Priest of Skibbereen, Co. Cork, agreed in 1825, it was the priest's duty to recommend that the couple should be married. Other accounts confirmed that wherever the woman's character was otherwise good, and where the social status of the parties was roughly equal, efforts were generally made to bring about such marriages. One senior police officer had heard reports of priests announcing publicly in the chapels the names of young people whom they had heard had been intimate together — presumably either to increase the social pressures on such couples to marry or to punish them for having resisted clerical efforts to make them do so.[8]

The efforts of the Catholic clergy to bring about marriages in such cases appear to have met with mixed success. A magistrate in Co. Galway was confident that 'by the influence of a magistrate and a clergyman, any man might be forced into marriage', and a parish priest in the same county believed that the influence of the Catholic clergy had done much to ensure that the fathers of twelve of the fourteen bastards born in his area over the previous eight years had subsequently married the mothers. In Cork, on the other hand, it was said to be rare for the father of an illegitimate child to marry the mother on account of the influence of the priest. The comments of two Carlow priests also suggest that their efforts in this matter were not generally successful. The first reported that his efforts 'have not succeeded in bringing about such a reparation in more than two or three instances'. The other 'has three cases at this moment who refuse marriage; one of them notwithstanding promises and the consent of parents, and even the banns being published'.[9]

These were the policies adopted towards actual offenders. The Catholic clergy of the eighteenth and early nineteenth centuries also showed themselves to be concerned with discouraging or suppressing practices which might have provided the occasion for sexual irregularity. Opposition to dancing, in particular, was not merely a feature of the later nineteenth century and after. 'Dancing schools and balls at night', the bishops of the province of Cashel resolved in 1777, were to be 'hindered by exemplary punishments and exhortations'. Twelve years later the statutes of the diocese of Clogher demanded that night-time dances 'should be vigorously restricted by pastors and eventually abolished'. The schedule to be completed by each priest in the diocese of Dublin on the occasion of an episcopal visitation included 'public dances' among the 'abuses' of which the archbishop would expect to be informed. The same hostility and suspicion towards dances and similar amusements can be seen in the activities of individual priests. One elderly priest serving in the diocese of Kildare and Leighlin in the early nineteenth century is reported to have 'endeavoured with a firm hand to put down dances and . . . waged war inextinguishable against all itinerant musicians'. John Casey, Parish Priest of Ballyferriter, Co. Kerry, from 1819 to 1844, was remembered as 'a deadly enemy of pipers and card-players'. The diary of a fellow-priest describes how he happened to visit a house where a dance was being held in secret, with a piper from a neighbouring parish supplying the music: 'His anger knew no bounds, he rushed over, laid hold of the innocent but unfortunate piper, kicked, cuffed and beat him unmercifully, broke his pipes and completely dispersed the whole assembly.' The regulations laid down for the government of one Co. Monaghan parish in 1832 warned that persons who attended night-time dances would be excluded from the sacraments until they performed public penance in the parish chapel. Bishop Plunkett of Meath complained in 1803 that 'the morals of young persons' were endangered by dances on Sundays and holydays, and condemned the practice as 'too often dangerous and criminal' — not, apparently, because it constituted a breach of the sabbath, but 'on account of the circumstances that accompany it'.[10]

A survey of the policies adopted by the authorities of the Catholic Church in the late eighteenth and early nineteenth centuries, therefore, suggests that their attitudes to sexual morality were in no way lax or even lenient. Instead they can be seen attempting to maintain strict standards of behaviour, both directly — through the punishment of offenders — and indirectly, by their opposition to forms of amusement which might have led to breaches of the moral code they propagated. Explicit statements on the general subject of sexual morality and its enforcement are more difficult to find, but the comments of at least two bishops confirm the impression that clerical attitudes were generally strict. Archbishop MacHale of Tuam, in written evidence to the Poor Inquiry commissioners in 1835, endorsed as a 'correct and Christian feeling' the popular prejudice against persons of illegitimate birth and complained of the danger that such 'virtuous impressions' would be weakened by the bad example of persons in higher social classes, 'many of whom have often no delicacy in forming matrimonial alliances with persons of illegitimate birth'. He also defended the otherwise almost universally lamented practice of early marriage as a safeguard against sexual immorality. 'The sorrows of this world', he wrote in 1831, 'are but little in the eyes of our flocks in comparison with their virtue. That virtue they guard against danger by flying at an early age into the sanctuary of marriage.' Bishop Plunkett of Meath, whose specific condemnations of dancing have already been mentioned, on other occasions preached in more general terms: 'impurity' appears repeatedly as a theme in his sermons, while one of his subjects in 1801 was 'lewdness held up to the detestation of the flock', and in 1811 'the crime of those who harboured lewd women'.[11]

The teaching of the Catholic clergy of this period on matters of sexual morality cannot, of course, be seen in isolation from their broader religious outlook. Where more recent decades are concerned, the sexual puritanism of Irish Catholicism has frequently been seen as part of a general tendency towards severity in religious and moral matters. Thus Humphreys has linked the rigid sexual attitudes he discusses with the dominance within Irish Catholicism of what he describes as 'Augustinianism', a religious outlook laying heavy stress on such themes as the sinfulness of man and the innate corruption of human nature. And in the late eighteenth and early nineteenth centuries a similar strain can be detected in the religious attitudes of both clergy and laity. Brady and Corish, discussing the nature of the Irish Catholic spirituality which emerged in the course of the eighteenth century, have seen as one of its features what they describe as an 'anxious morality' and 'a tendency to take the stern view in moral matters'. The official historian of Maynooth, writing in 1895, noted a similar emphasis in the teaching given in the early years of that college, although this — as was suggested in an earlier chapter — was probably no more than a continuation of influences to which some at least among earlier generations of priests had been exposed in continental seminaries. Other pieces of evidence point in the same direction. The regulations on fasting imposed by the Irish church authorities in the century before the famine appear to have been strict even by the far from lax standards of the later nineteenth century. For L. F. Renehan, writing in 1861, the Lenten regulations introduced by Archbishop Christopher Butler in 1741 showed 'how much we have degenerated, in little more than a century, from the strict discipline of our fathers', while W. J. Fitzpatrick in 1880 suggested that the regulations introduced in Kildare and Leighlin in 1820 'would nowadays be regarded as exceedingly rigid'. As late as the time of James Warren Doyle penance by the use of a hair shirt and by self-flagellation (the 'discipline') was still being practised by some members of the Irish regular clergy — including, apparently, Doyle himself.[12]

Various explanations have been offered for the presence of this element in the religious outlook of Irish Catholics of the eighteenth and early nineteenth centuries. One popular theory, that Irish Catholicism had come under the influence of the Jansenist movement on the continent, has been shown to be without foundation. But there is evidence, as already mentioned, that the teaching given in the continental seminaries attended by Irish priests, and later by the emigré professors who dominated Maynooth in its early years, inclined towards rigorism. An alternative theory, put forward by Brady and Corish, is that Irish Catholics were influenced by

an English Catholic spirituality marked by what they describe as a 'streak of sadness verging on severity'. What all
explanations along these lines overlook, however, is the
prominence of this same penitential tradition among sections
of the Catholic population which were largely or entirely
beyond the reach of all such intellectual influences. The
best-known example of this element in popular Catholicism
was, of course, the island of Lough Derg, where estimates
from the 1830s and 1840s suggest that between ten and
fifteen thousand pilgrims attended every year, to spend three
or more days in a rigorous programme of fasting, prayer
and penance. But similar practices were common at other
sites throughout the country, where pilgrims performed a
circuit barefoot or on bare knees round a holy well, a stone
or some other landmark. Thackeray, writing in 1843, quoted
distastefully from an account of people coming away from
the annual pilgrimage to Croagh Patrick, 'wounded and
bleeding in the knees and feet, and some of the women
shrieking with the pain of their wounds', while the French
traveller Latocnaye, a more sympathetic observer, also
recorded having seen 'many a scarred and bloody knee' at
a holy well in Munster in 1796 or 1797. If Irish priests of
the eighteenth and early nineteenth centuries proved particularly receptive to rigorist influences from England or the
continent, this popular tradition of extreme asceticism
does much to explain why. And the severe religious outlook
which resulted from this meeting of influences provides a
background against which strict attitudes to sexual misbehaviour are scarcely to be wondered at.[13]

2.   *Sexual Behaviour: Popular Attitudes and Practice*
Contemporary observers in the decades preceding the
famine had in general a high opinion of the sexual morals
of the Irish lower orders. The modesty of Irish women, Sir
John Carr maintained in 1806, 'must be the subject of
remark and eulogy with every stranger. I have been speaking
of the respectable class of female society, but the same virtue
is to be found in the wretched mud cabin.' 'The chastity of
the Irish female in every class of life', another account
agreed, 'has long been the subject of merited eulogy.' Thirty

years later the French traveller Gustave de Beaumont found the Irish 'remarkable for chastity', while his travelling companion de Tocqueville confirmed that their morals were 'very chaste'. A parliamentary committee inquiring in 1830 into the state of the Irish poor was told that the moral character of the poorer females in Ireland was 'very respectable' and 'much superior to the English'. One witness had been informed — somewhat ambiguously — that the 800 men employed by the Ordnance Survey in Ireland, most of whom were soldiers, 'had almost all married there, in consequence of the chastity of the women'.[14]

It was, of course, recognised that not all sections of Irish society lived up to these glowing descriptions. It had to be admitted, in the first place, that Irish towns had a certain amount of prostitution. In Athlone, for example, the Protestant rector complained in 1819 of the 'multitudes of common prostitutes who, in the face of the sun, infest the streets as well as the hedges and ditches about the town', and prostitutes were also reported in other urban centres. It was generally agreed, however, that prostitution was a good deal less extensive in Irish than in English towns, and that where it did exist it was largely confined to the specialised clientele provided by large military establishments. As far as the majority of ordinary urban dwellers were concerned, contemporaries do not appear to have felt that their conduct differed very greatly from that of their rural counterparts. In Derry city, the Catholic bishop of that area reported, 'concubinage before marriage is not common, [and] marriage does not often take place to save the mother from disgrace'. In the town of Drogheda, similarly, 'there are comparatively few cases of bastardy, and in general it may be said that pregnancy is the consequence and not the cause of marriage'. Among the poor of the city of Dublin illegitimacy was said to be 'of rare occurrence', in spite of the appallingly overcrowded conditions in which this section of the population lived.[15]

A more important exception to contemporary generalisations regarding the chastity and high moral character of the Irish population concerned the inhabitants of certain parts of the province of Ulster. 'Illicit intercourse', Edward

Wakefield concluded in 1812, 'is more prevalent among the uneducated order of females in the north than among the Roman Catholic women of the same rank in any other part of the kingdom.'[9] His comment was borne out by the memoirs compiled for different parishes in Co. Antrim by employees of the Ordnance Survey in the 1830s. In Island Magee, for example, 'conjugal fidelity is among any class a virtue but little practised on the part of either husband or wife', while girls were stated to be more frequently than otherwise either pregnant or already mothers when they came to the altar. In Carrickfergus, similarly, 'the observance of conjugal fidelity is by no means strict', and 'illegitimacy is of rather frequent occurrence', while in Raloo the inhabitants were 'not proverbial for chastity'. These remarks came from persons who had no vested interest in producing unfavourable comparisons between the moral characters of Catholic and Protestant females. And the suggestion that attitudes to sexual misbehaviour were more lax in parts of Ulster than elsewhere in the country was to be fully borne out by the regional pattern revealed when official statistics on the incidence of illegitimacy became available for the first time in 1864.[16]

With these two exceptions the general opinion of contemporaries was that Irish standards of sexual behaviour were strict and that instances of sexual irregularity were rare. This was further confirmed when the commissioners appointed in 1835 to inquire into the form of Poor Law most suitable for Ireland turned their attention to the question of bastardy. A few respondents — most of them once again from different parts of Ulster — indicated that illegitimacy in their areas was more frequent than they would have wished. The great majority of those who gave evidence to the commissioners, however, reported that illegitimacy was not common. Witnesses agreed, furthermore, that an unmarried woman who became pregnant incurred the most severe social sanctions. In some cases she might find herself thrown out by her family, refused employment on account of her bad character, and possibly driven to beggary or prostitution in order to support herself. Even if not completely ostracised, she was regarded as a person who had incurred the greatest possible disgrace. Reports from different areas spoke of the unmarried mother as being 'cast off from society', 'held in very low estimation' and 'slighted and shunned by all her former acquaintances'. Women in this position, it was reported, were 'looked on as degraded persons and scarcely associated with', and even witnesses who expressed sympathy for their situation admitted that they would be sorry to have their daughters seen talking to them. It was generally agreed, furthermore, that women who had had an illegitimate child experienced great difficulty in finding anyone willing to marry them, unless at a social level well below their own, and that many never married at all on account of the strength of the feeling against them. This hostility and rejection extended not only to the mother of an illegitimate child but also to the bastard himself. In Tipperary, for example, 'a bastard is thought nothing of; it sticks to him through life and to his children and grand-children for five or six generations'. In Longford, similarly, 'the stigma on the bastard is indelible', while in Donegal 'the stain', as it was described, would be 'cast up to their children's children'. The bastard, like his mother, found it difficult to procure a partner in marriage, and while in his case it appears that possession of sufficient land or property could normally compensate for the stigma of his birth, illegitimacy was nevertheless a serious disadvantage in the making of a good match.[17]

Contemporary generalisations concerning sexual beha-viour and attitudes can be tested against the available sta-tistical evidence on the incidence of illegitimacy and pre-nuptial pregnancy.[18] In 1864, the first year in which official statistics were collected, the proportion of illegitimate to total births was 3·8 per cent; in the first seven years of civil registration, 1864—70, it was 3·2 per cent. This was a considerably lower proportion than that recorded in most other parts of Europe at the same time. In 1876—80, for example, the illegitimacy ratio in both Italy and France was 7·2 per cent, in Germany 8·7 per cent, and in Austria 13·8 per cent. In England and Wales the ratio was 6·1 per cent in 1861—70 and 5·0 per cent in 1871—80. These sta-tistics, of course, relate to a period more than two decades after the famine. However, the more limited information available for earlier decades – the statistical data collected by the Poor Inquiry commissioners in the mid-1830s and an analysis of a small number of Catholic parish registers – suggests that the proportion of illegitimate births in the first half of the nineteenth century was not significantly higher than that recorded in 1864. Nor can the relative infrequency of illegitimate births be attributed to a greater willingness to enter into marriage after children had been conceived. Analysis of a sample of marriages recorded in six Irish parishes at different times between 1759 and 1860 suggests that the proportion of Irish brides pregnant at the time of their marriage was on average about one in ten. In rural England in the eighteenth and early nineteenth centuries the proportion was two out of every five.

The statistical evidence so far available, then, largely bears out the comments of contemporaries on the strict code of conduct which governed sexual behaviour in Ireland in the late eighteenth and early nineteenth centuries. At the same time this evidence also makes clear that such comments applied more strongly to some parts of the country than to others. Contemporaries themselves, as already mentioned, were aware that in parts of Ulster sexual attitudes were less restrictive than in other regions, and their comments on this point are supported by the figures collected in the early years of civil registration. In 1864, for example, illegitimate births in the north-east registration division amounted to 6·2 per cent of the total, roughly the same as the ratio recorded in England and Wales at this period and almost twice that recorded in Ireland as a whole. More surprisingly, the figures for the same year reveal that there were also three counties outside Ulster, Waterford, Carlow and Queen's County, in which illegitimate births amounted to more than 5 per cent of the total. Once again this evidence relates to a later period than that being discussed here. But once again, also, the limited statistical evidence available for earlier decades suggests that a broadly similar regional pattern existed in the first half of the nineteenth century, with illegitimacy ratios in the west and north midlands being generally under 3 per cent, while in parts of the south and south-east ratios could amount to 5 per cent or more. Even the latter ratios, of course, remained low by the standards of many European countries. But at the same time it seems clear that, even apart from eastern and central Ulster, the constraints on sexual behaviour did not operate with equal effectiveness in all parts of pre-famine Ireland.

One potentially misleading feature of Irish sexual attitudes in this period is that the culture of the majority of the population appears to have been one which placed relatively little emphasis on reticence in sexual matters. The Gaelic literature of the period, in particular, had a distinctly earthy and ribald strain. The embarrassment which this was to cause to the publicists of that literature in later decades is illustrated in the letter which An tAthair Peader Ó Laoghaire wrote to a friend in 1895, complaining of a lecture which Pádraig Ó Laoghaire, another figure in the Gaelic revival, had recently given in Cork on the subject of Irish love songs. 'Can we not find enough good, clean, healthy Irish,' the priest inquired, 'without putting filthy things like this before the public?' 'These love songs', he continued,

are doing great damage to the Irish language. I believe that the Craoibhín [i.e. Douglas Hyde] put into print words and passages that he himself did not properly understand, and that he would not have printed if he did understand. But I think Pádraig should have had more sense than he showed in Cork.

No doubt he meant no harm, but if his lecture were read to anyone in English they would say to him, as was said to the Craoibhín in my presence: 'If that is the sort of thing we are to get in Irish the sooner it is dead the better!!!'

Enough of that!! I have written to Pádraig. I told him we should adopt the following rule — not to put anything into print in Irish that we would not be perfectly happy to put into print in English.

I would like to have your opinion on this rule, to know whether it is too harsh or too weak.

Other editors of the later nineteenth century and after shared Peadar Ó Laoghaire's opinion and carefully bowdlerised the texts they offered to their public.[19]

This ribald and uninhibited strain which can be detected in the Gaelic literature of the pre-famine period has some-times led to the suggestion that the society which produced it must have been more liberal in its sexual attitudes than that which was to follow. But it would be wrong to assume that tolerance for a degree of ribaldry in conversation will necessarily imply an equally permissive approach to sexual behaviour, or that strict attitudes to behaviour must be accompanied by a cult of exceptional physical and verbal modesty. Extreme reticence of the kind now regarded as typical of Victorian sexual attitudes was obviously an ideal more suited to the lifestyle of an urban middle class than to that of rural dwellers anywhere, and the way of life of at least a large section of the Irish population in the decades before the famine was even less likely than most to encourage the cultivation of such refinements. Visitors to the Irish countryside in the early nineteenth century reported that it was common to find whole families, and in some cases non-relatives also, sleeping together in a single room.[20] Accom-modation in the houses of the larger farmers was, of course, better than that provided in the cabins of labourers and cottiers, but even there the opportunities for personal privacy were often very limited.

It is not surprising, under these circumstances, that Irish rural society in the early nineteenth century appears to have placed so little emphasis either on physical modesty or on verbal reticence. 'In Ireland,' de Tocqueville noted in 1835, 'where there are hardly any illegitimate children and where, therefore, morals are very chaste, women take less trouble to hide themselves than in any other country in the world, and men seem to have no repugnance to showing themselves almost naked. I have seen young girls bathing in the sea at a short distance from young men.' Edward Wakefield, similarly, observed that the women of Sligo and Mayo, while strict in their sexual conduct, were 'easy and unreserved in their manners', willing to 'converse freely and sometimes indulge in double entendre which would call a blush to the cheeks of our town-bred ladies'. This lack of inhibition remained a feature of Irish rural society, in some parts of the country

at least, up to the present century. The American anthropologists Arensberg and Kimball, working in Co. Clare in
the 1930s, found that attitudes to sexual conduct were
exceptionally strict, with any manifestation of sexual interest
among the young and unmarried regarded as something to be
censured and suppressed, and with any lapse from virtue
being severely punished. In other contexts, however, sex
could become a matter for casual and sometimes ribald
comment, with frequent banter and repartee on the age-old
themes of individual prowess (or lack of it) and individual
sexual appetites.[21]

Another aspect of this tolerance, in certain situations,
of overt sexual expression has been discussed in an earlier
chapter. This was the body of practices customary at the
festive wake, which included both party games designed to
facilitate the pairing off of mutually agreeable couples and
a variety of mimes which incorporated a fairly unambiguous
sexual symbolism. Activities of this kind were not confined
to wakes, as John Donaldson's account of the May Day
practices current in Co. Louth around 1838 makes clear:

> The figure of a female is made up, fixed upon a short
> pole and dressed in a fantastic manner, with flowers,
> ribbons, etc. This figure they call 'The May Baby'. . . .
> Around this figure a man and woman (generally his wife)
> of the humble class, dressed also fantastically with straw
> etc. dance to the sound of a fiddle, and entertain the
> people with indecent shows and postures, the figure at
> the same time being kept moving by the rustic maiden
> that supports it. These exhibitions cause great merriment
> among the assembled populace; women who have had no
> children to their husbands also attend (some of them from
> a considerable distance) to see this figure and exhibition,
> which they imagine will promote fruitfulness in them
> and cause them to have children.[22]

The precise significance of customs of this kind, and the
extent to which their full meaning continued to be recognised
by those who perpetuated them into the nineteenth century,
must await fuller investigation. But if the sexual attitudes of
the Irish lower orders in the decades before the famine lived up

in many ways to contemporary comment on their exceptional strictness, they nevertheless continued to incorporate elements which few of the same contemporaries would have recognised as part of the chastity they praised so highly.

3.   *The Regulation of Marriage*

Marriage in Ireland in the decades before the famine was subject to two kinds of control or attempted control. Parents attempted to direct the marriages of their sons and daughters in the interest of forming advantageous alliances which would either preserve or increase the status and resources of the family. The authorities of the Catholic Church, meanwhile, tried to enforce regulations governing both the choice of partner and the formal procedures to be followed in a marriage. It was the efforts of many couples to evade this dual control of priests and parents, rather than any indulgence in extra-marital sexual activity, which were to present the Catholic clergy of this period with their greatest problems.

It is well known that marriage in rural Ireland in the second half of the nineteenth century, and indeed for many years afterwards, was frequently the outcome of the bargain known as a 'match'. Representatives of an eligible couple would conduct detailed negotiations, in which the fortune or dowry which the girl could expect was set against the farm which the man occupied or would inherit, and the success or failure of these negotiations determined whether or not the couple would marry. In this process of bargaining the couple concerned had often little say. Fathers intending to make over the family farm to a son, or to provide a respectable dowry for a daughter, could and did claim a decisive voice in the selection of a marriage partner for that son or daughter. The extent to which the wishes of the parties themselves were taken into account varied with the personalities and the circumstances. Some sons or daughters were permitted to reject an otherwise acceptable match. Others, like Peig Sayers, born in Co. Kerry in 1873, did not even meet their future partners until the day of the wedding.[23]

Matchmaking was not a new development of the later nineteenth century. Already in the decades before the famine considerations of property, and bargaining over dowries and inheritance, played an important part in the marriages of substantial and not-so-substantial farmers. 'The small farmer's son who has a little money', it was reported, 'expects and seeks for as much at least in a wife, and the negotiations on this score with the girl's parents become a complete "Smithfield bargain"; every shilling in money or stock, on either side, being carefully brought into the account and set against the other party's means.' The amounts given as dowries varied with the status of the families concerned. Small farmers in the neighbourhood of Roscrea, Co. Tipperary, were said to deposit sums of twenty and thirty pounds in the local savings bank as marriage portions for their daughters. Large farmers in Co. Cork, on the other hand, were reported to provide dowries of one, two and three hundred pounds, while in Co. Kilkenny in 1819 it was reported that middling farmers — men occupying holdings of between ten and thirty acres — were able to give their daughters marriage portions of from fifty to a hundred pounds. It is hardly surprising, in this situation, that parents claimed a substantial voice both in the timing of their children's marriages and in the choice of partner. 'From all that I could learn,' Henry Inglis reported in 1834, 'marriage in this country is a very commercial concern, arranged by parents and respecting which there is as much higgling as about any other bargain. Girls are extremely obedient and sometimes never see the bridegroom until the moment of the marriage.' 'The power assumed in this case by parents in Ireland', Edward Wakefield observed, 'seems to be as great as is given to them by the laws and customs in some of the oriental nations.'[24]

Observers of Irish society in this period were, of course, deeply concerned over what they described as improvident marriages, arguing that lack of foresight and the absence of any prospect of bettering their condition led the Irish lower orders to marry early and without concern for their ability to support a family. As with other issues, however, it becomes clear on closer inspection that generalisations of this kind applied overwhelmingly to one particular sector of the community: the labourer and cottier classes among whom the most serious social problems of rural Ireland in the decades before the famine were concentrated. Contemporaries were themselves aware of the contrast in the behaviour of different sectors of rural society. 'The labourer', a Longford parish priest reported, 'is more precipitate, he is readily matched, as he seeks no fortune, and his parent has less power to enforce providence, as he can hold out no expectations.' In Co. Limerick, similarly, 'the farmers' marriages are marriages of interest, arranged by the parents, but among the labourers they choose their own wives'. If the average age at marriage rose in post-famine Ireland, it was not because a new spirit of calculation had entered into a hitherto feckless peasantry, but rather — as Professor Joseph Lee has pointed out — because the rural families that remained after the famine were drawn disproportionately from social groups which were already well accustomed to the mercenary practices of the match.[25]

The regulations on marriage imposed by the Catholic Church involved a variety of restrictions and prohibitions. Both parties to an intended marriage, in the first place, had to be free of any impediment such as a previous marriage or a previous contract to marry someone else. Couples were normally required to have the consent of their parents, although this requirement could be dispensed with if such consent were being unreasonably withheld. In addition, there was the prohibition on marriage within certain degrees of consanguinity, which at this period extended as far as what was known as the fourth degree of affinity, the relationship between third cousins. Dispensations to permit the marriage of persons related in the third and fourth degrees (that is, second and third cousins) appear to have been fairly easily obtainable, but they could on occasion be refused by the church authorities. Dispensations for marriage between first cousins, on the other hand, were granted only rarely, in cases where there were special grounds for permitting the marriage.[26]

Where mixed marriages, between Catholics and members of other denominations, were concerned, the policy of the church authorities was to discourage such unions wherever possible and, where not, to ensure that the claims of their church were fully asserted. Marriages between Catholics and Protestants, Archbishop Troy wrote to a colleague in 1780, were 'unlawful, wicked and dangerous', and he admitted elsewhere that he did not wish to see the civil laws against marriages of this kind repealed, because they deterred Catholics from entering such unions. Archbishop Murray of Dublin, who on most issues was one of the most moderate members of the Irish hierarchy, admitted in 1825 that the Catholic clergy 'do not recommend Roman Catholics marrying with Protestants', since 'frequently the children of such marriages grow up without an attachment, perhaps, to either religion'. Such marriages, he added, were generally permitted only on condition that any children would be educated as Catholics. The bishops of the province of Cashel ordered in 1808 that any Catholic who married a Protestant in the latter's church was to be required to repeat the ceremony before a Catholic priest, and that in cases where the Protestant party refused to comply his or her partner was to be excluded from the sacraments until it was shown that they had made every possible effort to procure the celebration of the marriage in a Catholic chapel.[27]

Quite apart from the clear hostility of the church authorities to intermarriage between members of their own and other denominations, the laws in force during the greater part of the pre-famine period made the celebration of such unions something to be approached with a good deal of caution. Legislation introduced in the first half of the eighteenth century had made it a capital offence for a Catholic clergyman to officiate at the marriage of a Catholic and a Protestant, and a suspended priest had in fact been executed under this statute in 1726. An act of 1793, while not repealing the earlier capital statute, substituted a fine of £500, and this in turn was commuted in practice into a short term of imprisonment. Nevertheless, a return drawn up in 1832, the year before the legislation was repealed, showed that over the previous twelve years a total of six men in Catholic orders had been convicted and imprisoned for celebrating mixed marriages. All these, it is true, were probably degraded clergymen making a living as 'couple-beggars', but the same legislation could have been invoked against parish clergy who officiated at mixed marriages. Where priests did officiate illegally at marriages of this kind they were clearly very aware of the risks they were running. In 1835, after the legal penalties had been removed, a curate in the parish of Slieverue, Co. Kilkenny, added this note to the parish register:

> Rev. John Fitzpatrick told me that he married Thomas Kehal and Frances Fitzgerald in presence of Major Thomas Fitzgerald and Sara Fitzgerald on the 15 of Novr 1807 — but that fearing the penalty of the law, the bride being a Protestant, he did not register the marriage in the parish book. This memorandum is therefore to supply the place of said register.

A Protestant labourer and his Catholic wife revealed in 1831 that they had been married some years before in the chapel at Athlone by a priest who had remained hidden from them throughout the ceremony so that they were unable to see his face.[28]

A third possible way in which the Catholic clergy of this period attempted to impose restrictions on the marriages of their congregations was in discouraging the marriages of couples who in their opinion did not possess the means to support a family. There were, it is true, frequent allegations that the Catholic clergy, depending for a large part of their support on the fees which they received for celebrating marriages, encouraged early and improvident unions among their congregations. It was also reported — perhaps more credibly — that priests were reluctant to oppose such marriages on account of the damage which that opposition might do to the sexual morals of their flocks. At the same time priests in Cork, Sligo and Longford maintained that they attempted to discourage such unions, while a retired shopkeeper in Co. Clare confirmed that he had known his parish priest demand a higher fee than usual from indigent couples in order to deter them from going ahead with their planned marriage.[29]

In order to ensure that these different regulations and prohibitions were observed, two main rules were laid down governing the celebration of marriages. All marriages, in the first place, were to be performed by the parish priest of the couple involved, or else by a clergyman authorised either by him or by the bishop of the diocese. If a person wished to be married in a parish other than their own, then he or she was required to obtain a certificate from their parish priest testifying to their freedom to marry. Even in cases where the strict discipline of the Council of Trent, under which marriages performed in any circumstances other than these were rendered null and void, had not yet been introduced, priests were strictly forbidden to marry persons other than their own parishioners without proper authorisation, the penalty for disobeying this rule being either suspension or excommunication. Diocesan statutes also included regular warnings that priests should exercise special caution when called on to celebrate the marriages of servants, vagrants and other persons who moved from place to place. Soldiers, for example, might be required to have their freedom to marry certified by their commanding officer.[30]

The second main precaution which could be taken against breaches of the Church's regulations on marriage was the publication of banns. The Council of Trent had laid down that the names of all persons intending to marry should be read to the congregations to which they belonged on three successive Sundays or holydays before the wedding so that any objections or impediments could be made known. In the south of Ireland, however, it had become customary for the publication of banns to be dispensed with by the purchase of a licence from the bishop of the diocese — indeed, according to Edward Wakefield, publication of banns was regarded as a disgraceful admission of poverty which couples were prepared to go to almost any length to avoid. Elsewhere the practice could be either more or less strict. The Bishop of Clogher reported in 1801 that he had, 'with much trouble and perseverance', largely succeeded in restoring the publication of banns in his diocese. In Kildare and Leighlin, on the other hand, Bishop Doyle reported in 1825 that neither banns nor a licence were required for the celebration of a marriage to which there was no impediment.[31]

Marriage in Ireland in the decades before the famine, therefore, contained within it the seeds of a whole variety of disputes and conflicts. The attitudes and aspirations of parents led many of them to demand a considerable

measure of control over the marriages of their children.
The authorities of the Catholic Church had both to deal
with the clashes that inevitably resulted and to seek to
impose their own regulations on such matters as consanguinity, mixed marriage and the calling of banns. All
this, furthermore, had to be done in an area in which there
was unique scope for embarrassing and potentially damaging
scandal. It is not surprising, therefore, that two sets of
diocesan statutes from this period should have included
the observation that of all the sacraments that had to be
administered to the faithful marriage was the one which
presented the greatest and most frequent difficulties.[32]

* * *

There were a number of ways in which couples attempted
to evade the restrictions which were thus imposed on their
marriages by priests and parents. The first of these, clandestine marriage, involved resorting to what were generally
known as 'couple-beggars', suspended clergymen and others
who had taken up the business of celebrating marriages as
a means of earning a living. The majority of these couple-
beggars were clergymen of either the Catholic Church or the
Established Church. Some had been deprived of their offices
on account of a breach of ecclesiastical discipline and had
turned to clandestine marriages as an alternative source of
income. Others were Catholic priests who had conformed to
the Established Church but had not been offered livings
there. Others again may simply have been attracted by the
money. Certainly the £1,000 reported to have been left on
his death in 1737 by Samuel D'Assigny, 'the famous couple-
beggar', would have compared very favourably with what
the great majority of Catholic clergymen in this period —
and many of their Protestant counterparts also — could
have hoped to end their lives with. D'Assigny, however,
while regularly officiating in clerical dress, had never been
in orders of any kind, and he was not the only layman to
set himself up as a couple-beggar in this period.[33]

To contract or officiate at a clandestine marriage was
a serious offence against the discipline of the Catholic Church.
Regulations introduced for the diocese of Leighlin in 1748

laid down that any priest who knowingly married a couple who were not his parishioners should be suspended for each of the first two offences and excommunicated for a third. The couple who contracted a clandestine marriage, meanwhile, were to be excluded from mass and the sacraments until they gave public satisfaction for the scandal they had given and revealed the name of the priest who had married them. Very similar regulations were introduced at about the same time in the neighbouring diocese of Ossory, while in Dublin and Limerick in the same year sentences of excommunication were pronounced against clergymen who had celebrated clandestine marriages. Other couple-beggars were publicly denounced and excommunicated in Limerick in 1761 and in Ferns ten years later. Regulations introduced by the bishops of the province of Cashel in 1777, the statutes of the diocese of Clogher in 1789, and a pastoral by Archbishop Troy of Dublin in the same year all extended the penalty of excommunication not only to the celebrant of a clandestine marriage and the contracting couple but also to the witnesses, the latter two including in addition any other persons who co-operated in the performance of the marriage.[34]

While clandestine marriages were condemned and penalised by the church authorities, however, they were not necessarily held to be invalid. A decree of the Council of Trent had ruled that marriages which were not celebrated by the parish priest of one of the parties (or by a clergyman authorised by the parish priest) in the presence of two witnesses were null and void. This regulation, however, did not come into force in any diocese until it had been formally published there. The decree was published in some parts of the province of Tuam before 1685 and in the remainder in 1745, and it was published around 1680 in the whole of the province of Armagh. Elsewhere, however, the disorganised state of the Church, and possibly a reluctance to be seen by the authorities to be implementing fresh papal legislation, prevented the publication of the decree. The result was an embarrassing anomaly in the marriage laws of the Church. While clandestine marriages were invalid from before 1700 in the province of Armagh and part of the province of Tuam, they remained valid, although strictly forbidden, in other parts of the country. The situation was considerably improved when the Tridentine decree was published in the whole of the province of Cashel in 1775. Even then, however, three areas remained in which the legislation was not yet in force: the wardenship of Galway, which at this time was an independent unit of ecclesiastical government; the diocese of Meath, where the legislation had been introduced in 1680 but was subsequently permitted to fall into disuse; and, most important of all, the entire ecclesiastical province of Dublin.[35]

The church authorities were aware of this inconsistency in their legislation and were anxious to see it removed. But proposals that the Tridentine decree should come into force in Dublin and the other outstanding areas met with strong objections. One problem was that publication of the decree might be interpreted as declaring invalid the marriages of Protestants celebrated by Protestant clergymen – on the grounds that the real parish priest even of a Protestant, and therefore the only person empowered to celebrate his marriage, was the local Catholic incumbent. This objection was removed in 1785, when Rome ruled that this particular decree did not apply to persons of other denominations. However, other difficulties remained. Since the civil law recognised as valid all marriages between Catholics celebrated by a Catholic priest, irrespective of whether the latter was a couple-beggar or a properly authorised clergyman, the annulling of clandestine marriages would have given rise to awkward disputes over the inheritance of property. In addition, any party to a clandestine marriage who later married another person according to the rites of the Catholic Church might expose himself to the charge of bigamy and the celebrant of the second marriage to the charge of being an accessory to the crime.[36] For these reasons it was not until 1827 that the decree relating to clandestine marriage was published simultaneously in every diocese of the country and came into force throughout Ireland.

The concern of the church authorities over the practice of clandestine marriage is easy to understand. Archbishop Troy, in his pastoral of 1789, presented a vivid picture of the abuses which the practice could permit. In some cases ungrateful sons and daughters sought to defy the reasonable and legitimate wishes of their parents. In others couples who had been turned away by their parish priest when they presented themselves for marriage, totally unprepared and often insensible from drink, 'fly immediately to a profligate, excommunicated priest, generally as intoxicated as themselves, who runs over the marriage ceremony without the smallest inquiry about kindred, consent of parents, difference of religion, a former contract of marriage, or other impediments'. In other cases again 'the artful libertine or insidious man of intrigue too often avails himself of such wicked means and opportunities to deceive an unguarded female and destroy the peace of the family', frequently abandoning his victim after a short period and leaving her to become 'an outcast of society, reduced to the sad necessity of prolonging a wretched existence by the wages of prostitution'.[37] No doubt it was true that a couple-beggar, depending for his livelihood on the fees received from couples who preferred to come to him rather than to their officially recognised pastor, would not normally have been disposed to inquire very closely into the circumstances of his customers. At the same time there are a number of reasons for thinking that Troy's account of the circumstances in which clandestine marriages were generally contracted was an unduly lurid one.

There were, to begin with, a whole variety of reasons why a couple should wish to contract a clandestine marriage, and not all of these had to do with bigamy, seduction or the entrapment of heiresses. Couples might resort to a couple-beggar in cases where their parents refused to give their consent to the marriage, or where they had been unable to obtain a dispensation permitting them to marry within the prohibited degrees of kindred. Others may have done so because they were unable to find a priest willing to celebrate a mixed marriage; certainly it is noticeable that many of the couple-beggars who appear in the records of the period do so because they had fallen foul of the civil law by celebrating marriages of this kind.[38] Others among a couple-beggar's clients may simply have been unwilling to go through the delays and procedures required by church legislation, especially if they had no fixed place of residence and would be required to await the result of special inquiries into their freedom to marry. In other cases, as has already been mentioned, the opposition of the Catholic clergy to certain marriages was on prudential rather than on moral grounds. A Sligo priest informed the Poor Inquiry commissioners in 1835 that parishioners whom he had tried to deflect from improvident marriages 'say they cannot be worse than they are, and threaten to go to a "tackem"; when it comes to that, nothing will deter them'. A final, and possibly very important, consideration was that clandestine marriages were considerably cheaper than those celebrated by the Catholic parish clergy. The fees charged by couple-beggars in Dublin city in the early nineteenth century were generally under ten shillings, and sometimes as low as half a crown or less. The fees given to the Catholic parish clergy for marriages, on the other hand, were generally between half a guinea and a guinea, and the couple opting for a clandestine marriage could also avoid the expensive celebration they might otherwise be expected to provide.[39]

Two other considerations support the view that clandestine marriage should not be thought of solely in terms of the type of abuses described by Archbishop Troy. In the first place it must be remembered that clandestine marriages, though unlawful, were in some areas still recognised as valid by the Church. This is important because it is noticeable that the great majority of the instances of clandestine marriage mentioned in the sources drawn on here occurred in areas in which the decree of the Council of Trent had not yet been published at the time: in the city of Dublin and in the dioceses of Ferns and Ossory in Dublin province; in Limerick city before the publication of the Tridentine decree in the province of Cashel; in Galway city, where the decree did not come into force until 1827; and in the diocese of Meath, where the decree had been published but then allowed to fall into disuse. The practice, furthermore, does not appear to have survived on any significant scale after the publication of the decree throughout the country in 1827. A couple who contracted a clandestine marriage, therefore, were in many cases entering a union which their church would recognise as valid, and they may well have regarded their breach of ecclesiastical regulations, and any penalties they incurred because of it, as a small price to pay for achieving that result. The register of the parish of St Canice's in Kilkenny city noted in 1779 that two parishioners had been clandestinely married, 'but having afterwards given signs of repentance they were publicly of a Sunday in presence of the congregation absolved from their censure by his lordship Doctor Troy'. Since the Tridentine decree had not yet been published in the province of Dublin, their marriage was, of course, a valid one. Similar cases of persons who had been clandestinely married and later reconciled occur in the registers of Nobber, Co. Meath, and of Slieverue, Co. Kilkenny, both of which were also within the area in which such marriages were recognised as valid. Even where clandestine marriages were no longer recognised, furthermore, they did not necessarily involve placing oneself permanently outside the law of the Church. Instead both priests and parents were given strong reasons for seeking to minimise the scandal by agreeing wherever possible to a legitimate marriage between the parties. The section of the Cashel diocesan statutes dealing with the question of persons who had contracted clandestine marriages certainly seems to have envisaged such a solution, laying down detailed regulations on how it was to be achieved with the minimum of damage to the prestige and authority of the Church.[40]

In discussing the significance of clandestine marriage, secondly, it is necessary to allow for the peculiar attitude of Irish Catholics to the suspended priest. 'The belief of the lower classes', Carleton explained,

> is that after having once received full ordination, neither bishop, primate nor Pope himself can deprive a priest of his of the spiritual authority. The only length to which ecclesiastical authority is supposed to be capable to going is to deprive him of the official authority of exercising it. As to anything else the people say that he possesses the full right of conferring the sacraments.

In fact, as already mentioned, popular tradition presented the suspended priest not merely as still deserving of respect but as possessed of special powers which other priests did not have.[41] Seen in this light, the practice of clandestine marriage, while still a major breach of the Church's regulations, once again appears a good deal less sinister than in Archbishop Troy's denunciation.

Facilities for clandestine marriage appear to have been pretty generally available, at least in those areas where such marriages were recognised as valid. Dublin, with the anonymity it offered, clearly had special attractions for the couple-beggar and his clients alike. Troy reported to Rome in 1802 that many of the couple-beggars operating in the city were degraded priests from other dioceses, and that they married people who came to them from all parts of the kingdom for that purpose. At the same time instances have been noted here of couple-beggars operating in the towns of Kilkenny, Limerick and Galway. When William Carleton was imprisoned for debt in Mullingar, Co. Westmeath, in the early 1820s, he found himself sharing a cell with a suspended priest of alcoholic tendencies, jailed for having celebrated a marriage between a Catholic and a Protestant, who carried on a lively trade in clandestine marriages even from within the prison. Couple-beggars were also reported in the 1830s in Bushmills, Co. Antrim, and in the town of Belfast. A couple-beggar operating in an urban centre could draw his clientele from a large area of the surrounding countryside. Thus Bishop Plunkett of Meath preached regularly against clandestine marriage on his visits to parishes that were either wholly rural or contained no more than a small town or village. His warnings and denunciations were presumably directed at persons who might contemplate seeking the services of a couple-beggar in Dublin, Mullingar or some other sizeable centre. An entry in the parish register for Nobber, naming two parishioners 'clandestinely married in Dublin and reconciled by authority', indicates that his concern on this point was justified.[42]

There are no sources from which the precise number of clandestine marriages which took place in Ireland in the decades before the famine could be calculated. However, the trade in clandestine marriages was clearly an extensive one. The registers kept by eleven clergymen who celebrated marriages at two addresses in Dublin between 1799 and 1844 were estimated to contain records of some 30,000 marriages. Some couple-beggars found it worth their while to insert advertisements in the newspapers, announcing their presence as clergymen, qualified but without provision, who could be found at a particular address by all who required their services.[43] These circumstances, along with the evident concern which clandestine marriage caused to the church authorities, suggest that the number of persons who chose, for whatever reason, to be married in this way was quite considerable.

A second means by which couples sought to evade the control exercised over their marriages by priests and parents was the practice known as the runaway match. A couple whose marriage was opposed by either authority would meet secretly and go to the house of a sympathetic relative or neighbour, having previously arranged with a group of their friends to meet them there. The entire company then settled down to a night of celebration. The following day word was sent to the girl's parents to inform them of where she was. The parents were allowed to come and take her away, but the girl was now regarded as compromised, and her parents almost invariably gave their consent to a marriage between the couple.

The runaway match was not a simple act of rebellion by young couples against the restrictions imposed on them by their society. It was conducted, in the first place, according to a well-defined and recognised procedure — so well defined, in fact, that almost identical descriptions of it can be found in William Carleton's reminiscences of his life in Co. Tyrone in the first two decades of the nineteenth century and in accounts relating to the counties of Longford, Leitrim and Roscommon in the decades after the famine collected within the last twenty-five years by the Irish Folklore Commission. It was also a commitment from which neither party could easily withdraw. Different accounts agree that it was practically unheard of for a couple who had run away together not to marry. In the rare cases where a marriage was not permitted to follow, the popular attitude to the girl concerned revealed both the strictness of the conventions surrounding the practice and the extent to which the elopment itself was regarded as a legitimate tactic. The girl was not seen as having done anything shameful or morally wrong. According to Carleton, there was 'neither scandal nor impropriety' connected with the act of running away, and a girl in this position was 'received in society like any other young female of her class' — an attitude which can be contrasted with the widespread condemnation and rejection which an un-married mother experienced in the same communities. At the same time 'no Irishman living', in Carleton's words, would consider marrying a woman in this position; the fact of having run away with a man who had failed to marry her was 'a verdict of celibacy for life'. The involvement in the runaway match of the couple's friends and neigh-bours also suggests that their action, while presumably disapproved of by their parents and possibly by others also, was not generally regarded as a serious breach of funda-mental rules or values.[44]

Runaway matches were a subject of considerable concern to the clergy of the Catholic Church. Some priests, the Rev. James Hall reported in 1813, fined couples who had run away together sums of five and six pounds, while others 'make such pay all the marriage money, perform many pilgrimages, and beg pardon of the congregation' on pain of incurring a sentence of excommunication. In Kilmactige, Co. Sligo, similarly, couples who ran away or married clandes-tinely 'are charged a certain sum in proportion to the nature of the offence, by way of punishment'. Carleton reported that eloping couples were sometimes punished by being made to 'stand' or do public penance in the chapel. This sanction, however, was not very effective; in general 'it is looked upon more as fun than punishment', and it did not succeed in deterring couples from resorting to this tactic. Instead runaway matches continued to be a cause of con-cern to the church authorities both of Clogher and of the north midlands. The issue of 'runaways' was among the items to be discussed at a synod of the diocese of Clogher in 1861. In Errigal Kiernan, a parish in the same diocese, the Catholic clergy were still attempting to eliminate the practice in the second half of the nineteenth century, again levying fines on eloping couples in an effort to deter other offenders. In the diocese of Elphin also the runaway match survived into the second half of the nineteenth century, the bishop attempting to put an end to the practice by requiring couples to perform a public penance and — when this proved ineffective — pronouncing a sentence of excommunication against runaways and all who harboured them.[45]

These accounts of the runaway match come from the north midlands counties of Longford, Roscommon and Leitrim and from the diocese of Clogher. Other descriptions of what appears to be the same practice relate to Co. Londonderry and to south Armagh.[46] In other areas the runaway match, conducted according to the well-defined procedure outlined here, does not appear to have been known. Elopement as a means of securing the consent of priests or parents to a marriage to which they were opposed, however, did occur. In Co. Limerick, for example, 'it is a frequent practice for a man to elope with a farmer's daughter and not to marry her until he forces her parents to give a larger fortune than their means would justify, in order to save her character'. The comments of the Catholic clergy also indicate that it was not only in areas like Longford and Tyrone that elopement presented them with problems of discipline. Bishop Plunkett of Meath several times denounced the practice in visitation sermons. The statutes of the diocese of Cashel in 1813 condemned 'those who elope together, in order to extract the consent of parents for immediate marriage'. Such couples were not to be married until they had separated and spent a week apart from each other 'in spiritual retreat, imploring God's mercy and preparing for a good confession'. Those who encouraged or assisted at elopements, meanwhile, were to be severely reprimanded from the altar. In spite of these regulations, however, elopements were still complained of in a visitation of the diocese fifteen years later. The Parish Priest of Moyferta, Co. Clare, adopted a more stern policy. Young people of the lower class, he reported in 1825, eloped together 'when they see no prospect of a future fortune from the parent', but in such cases he frequently refused to marry them, in order 'that they may not entail misery on their offspring, and to prevent an additional burden on the parish'.[47]

In addition to these cases of open elopement, there were other occasions on which women anxious for a marriage to which their families would not agree allowed themselves to be carried off, with an appropriate show of reluctance on their part, by the men concerned. Many of the incidents reported to the police as abductions, it was claimed, were in fact cases of this type. But there were also frequent reports of genuine abductions, where a woman was carried away against her will by a man anxious either for her hand in marriage or for the dowry which would come with her. Some observers went so far as to suggest that farmers — particularly in Co. Clare, where abductions were especially common — were induced to arrange marriages for their daughters at the earliest possible moment in order to remove the risk of their being abducted for the sake of their fortunes. What made abduction so much feared was the fact that the man who carried away a woman was subsequently able to take advantage of the same strict conventions which made the runaway match so effective a tactic. According to the Parish Priest of Moyferta,

> The common practice was not to force them by night, but to meet them in the day-time, and turn them into a house, and there keep them two or three hours; and such is the delicacy of the Irish people, that no man would marry her after; thus he was sure of her being his future wife.

When sixteen-year-old Bridget Burns of Easky, Co. Sligo, was taken from her parents' home by a rejected suitor in 1838, her mother explained that it would now be necessary to permit the man to marry her daughter. 'She never would have consented to give her daughter to said Burke, but now since this has happened and that no Christian will ever marry her daughter after being carried away she would give her consent.'[48]

Even apart from the specific problems of clandestine marriage, elopement and abduction, the church authorities of both the eighteenth and early nineteenth centuries appear to have recognised that the control they could exercise over their congregations in the matter of marriage was at best a

limited one. Bishop Moylan of Kerry reported to Rome in
1785 that he was sometimes compelled to give dispensations
for marriage even in the case of first cousins 'because of
their hardness of heart, and in order to prevent the spiritual
ruin of the parties'. His colleague, Bishop Young of Limerick,
was more explicit. 'I find by experience', he explained in
1799,

> [that] the good of religion in this diocese requires that
> dispensations in 2 & 2 should not be refused when there
> is a colour for granting them, for I have found the per-
> verseness of the parties to be such that if I object against
> gratifying them they go off together and get themselves
> married in [the Protestant] church, and obtain the sanction
> of the civil law for what they do, and cause us nothing
> but trouble to rectify matters afterwards, which after
> all ends in getting them married over again, and often
> [we] are disappointed in the little dues on such occasions.

In the following year he wrote again to complain of the
problems caused by the difference between the civil law
and the law of the Catholic Church on this and other issues,
and of 'the advantage that is taken in consequence of that
difference by many licentious people among us, who get
themselves married by the established clergy in many cases
which it is impossible for us to give a sanction to'.[49]

Tactics of the kind complained of by Bishop Young
continued to be resorted to in the early decades of the
nineteenth century, apparently with equal success. Michael
Collins, Parish Priest of Skibbereen, Co. Cork, reported to
a parliamentary committee in 1825 that couples who had
been refused marriage on account of consanguinity, withholding of their parents' consent or other reasons 'sometimes resort to the Protestant clergy and are married as a
matter of right'. Such couples, he added, were invariably
reconciled to the Church at a later date and were married
by the priest after performing a suitable penance. Bishop
Doyle of Kildare and Leighlin and Archbishop Kelly of
Tuam confirmed that they too had known of instances of
such couples resorting to the Protestant clergy. A more
surprising expedient was reported by John O'Driscol, a

barrister from Co. Cork, who had known of cases in which priests had refused to marry persons 'and there afterwards has been cohabitation, or threatened cohabitation, without marriage. In those cases the priests have considered themselves as bound to marry them.' Even the Parish Priest of Moyferta, whose refusal to marry couples who had eloped together has already been mentioned, was powerless before this challenge. 'The poor', he acknowledged, 'frequently have had recourse to this stratagem to induce me to marry them; and where I find the matter to be founded in fact I recommend marriage to obviate immorality and bad example.'[50]

Gestures of this kind, however startling they might at first sight appear, were not intended to entail a permanent break with the discipline of the Catholic Church. Both Young and Collins suggested that couples who applied to be married by the clergy of other denominations were generally reconciled to their own church at a later date and had their marriage solemnised according to its rites. The cohabitation or illicit intercourse reported by two other observers, meanwhile, was a form of moral blackmail designed to overcome objections to the marriage of the parties. In this respect such tactics were similar in character to both clandestine marriage and the runaway match. Clandestine marriage, it was suggested earlier, was for many couples a convenient loophole in the law of the Church, retaining the validity of an authorised marriage while enabling them to evade regulations which would otherwise have stood in their way. The practice of the runaway match was distinguished by the strictness of the conventions which surrounded it, and it too was intended to bring about the eventual marriage of the parties. The couples who sought in these different ways to evade the control which priests and parents claimed to exercise over their marriages, therefore, cannot be seen as casting off the discipline of the Catholic Church. What they were seeking was rather to bend the rules of that discipline, or at most to step temporarily outside them, as a short-term means to the end of a legitimate marriage.

In spite of the limited nature of the disobedience which they involved, however, the practices discussed in this section remain of considerable significance. The willingness of these couples to manipulate or ignore the marriage regulations of their church can be set against the extensive evidence collected by the Poor Inquiry commissioners regarding the extreme intolerance generally shown to sexual misdemeanours. The tactics adopted by these couples, furthermore, appear to have enjoyed a large measure of success. Whether faced with a clandestine marriage, an elopement or a couple married by the clergy of the Established Church, the policy of the Catholic clergy appears to have been to minimise the scandal by arranging wherever possible for the marriage to be solemnised according to their own rites. In this situation, it is clear, the influence which they could hope to exercise over the marriages of their congregations was at best a limited one.

4. *Conclusion*

Having looked at the sexual attitudes and behaviour of the pre-famine population and at the policies adopted by the church authorities, it is time to return to the questions with which this chapter began: To what extent did the Catholic clergy of the late eighteenth and early nineteenth centuries succeed in influencing the sexual attitudes of their congregations? And what light, if any, does the situation in this period throw on the origins of the sexual puritanism which was to be such a prominent feature of Catholic Ireland in the later nineteenth century and after?

Whatever may be said about the success of clerical efforts to influence the character of sexual behaviour in pre-famine Ireland, there can at least be little doubt about the purpose of those efforts. From at least the middle of the eighteenth century there are indications that priests and bishops were attempting to impose what even by the standards of the time was probably a fairly strict discipline, extending not only to the punishment of actual offenders but also to attempts to eliminate what were regarded as possible occasions of sin. And at first sight it might seem that, in this area at least, the social control exercised by the Catholic clergy proved highly effective. Visitors to Ireland in the first half of the nineteenth century were almost unanimous in their praise of the chastity of the Catholic Irish, and the statistical evidence so far available suggests that both illegitimacy and pre-nuptial pregnancy were considerably less common in Ireland than in most other parts of Europe at this time. But on closer examination it becomes clear that the efforts of the Catholic clergy to impose their standards of behaviour were not as successful as might at first be imagined. Pre-famine Ireland was a society in which sexual relations outside marriage took place relatively rarely and to general disapproval. But it was also a society in which little value was placed on reticence in sexual matters, in which wake-games involving a strong element of overt sexual expression continued to be common, and where the authorities of the Catholic Church experienced grave difficulties in imposing their regulations concerning consanguinity and other matters relating to marriage.

The failure of the Catholic clergy to suppress what they regarded as obscene games at wakes, or to prevent such practices as clandestine marriage and the runaway match, suggests that their apparent success in instilling strict standards of sexual morality was largely fortuitous, depending less on the influence of the preacher than on the general acceptability of his message. Clerical denunciation of sexual immorality was powerfully reinforced by the hostility and rejection which offenders in this area of behaviour could expect to encounter from the great majority of those around them. The judgment of the laity could in fact be harsher than that of the clergy. Bishop Kinsella of Ossory remarked to de Tocqueville in 1835: 'Public opinion, one might almost say, has gone too far in this direction. A woman suspected is lost for her whole life.'[51] Where the conduct condemned by the Catholic clergy did not conflict in the same way with popular norms and values, as in the case of clandestine marriage or the licensed sexual play-acting at wakes, the results of that condemnation proved to be much less impressive.

A second reason for questioning the apparent success of the Catholic clergy in imposing a strict sexual morality on their congregations is provided by the regional variations which can be observed in the incidence of extra-marital fertility. Both the official statistics collected in 1864 and subsequent years and the more limited statistical information available for earlier years suggest the same broad geographical pattern, in which the lowest illegitimacy ratios are found in the west, north-west and south-west, and significantly higher incidences are recorded not only in the eastern half of Ulster but also in parts of the south and south-east. But these western regions are also the ones in which the resources of the Catholic Church were at their weakest in this period, and in which Catholic religious practice was most neglected. The pattern of Irish chastity, in other words, appears to have run quite counter to that of Irish Catholic piety.

To suggest that the strictness of Irish sexual attitudes in the decades before the famine cannot be attributed to the influence of the Catholic clergy inevitably raises the question of what alternative explanations can be offered. The possibilities are numerous, and the issues involved are too complex to be gone into in any detail here. Of the different lines of explanation which might be offered, the most promising – at least where the rural majority of the population is concerned – is probably that which centres on the part played in economic and social life by the family and by family relationships. Such an explanation would stress the extent to which the lives of a large section of the pre-famine population – whether these were farmers proper or smallholders partly dependent on the labour they performed for others – centred round the working of a family holding. This had two main implications. In the first place it provided the means for a strict control of the sexual behaviour of the unmarried young, making possible a greater degree of parental authority over children of both sexes than could exist in cases where the latter were economically independent. Equally important, it provided the motives for such control. The economy of the smallholders may have provided more generously than that of the larger occupiers for the marriage of its members, through the subdivision of holdings. But even here some restrictions were essential. Coming at the wrong time, an unplanned marriage or the pregnancy of an unmarried daughter could prove disastrous for a delicately balanced family economy. For the farming class, meanwhile, the preservation of the family holding and its orderly transfer from one generation to the next depended on a system of arranged marriage, for which strict control of the sexual behaviour of those whose marriages these would be was clearly essential. To 'destroy a girl's character' by involving her in sexual scandal, as Arensberg and Kimball observed in their study of Co. Clare, would be 'to upset the pattern of family and community life by over-throwing the possibility of an orderly change in farm succession. Much more than a shooting or a fight, a sexual irregularity which cannot be righted in a match is capable of destroying the intricate mutual obligations and expectancies of rural familism.' To these points might be added the broader significance of the family, even apart from its function as a unit of production, in the social life of rural Ireland. Then as later a person's ancestry and the status of their family were a vital part of their social identity, and family relationships were the most important of the bonds of co-operation and mutual obligation which linked the members of rural Irish society. And here too sexual irregularity, damaging both the reputation of the family and the quality of the line, was inevitably regarded as a major offence. 'There is a great feeling against bastards,' it was explained in Co. Limerick. ' . . . They think much of the clan or family of the party married, and of making numerous connections by marriage.'[52]

An interpretation along these lines, emphasising the social and economic importance of the family in pre-famine Ireland, helps to account not only for the relatively low level of extra-marital sexual activity in the country as a whole but also for what appear to have been clear regional variations in attitudes and behaviour. Illegitimate births were least common in the west, where the largest proportion of the population were occupiers of family holdings and where traditional ideas of family might be expected to have been at their strongest. They were more common in the south and south-east, where there was a higher proportion of landless labourers, farm servants and other persons for whom the family was of less importance, whether as an economic or as a social unit. (A broadly similar explanation, it may be noted, has recently been offered for the contrast between the relatively low incidence of illegitimacy in the highlands of nineteenth-century Scotland and the much higher incidence in other districts.) In addition, of course, it can be suggested that in western districts the constraints imposed by the family system were rendered easier to bear by a lower average age of marriage than was normal in other regions.

This is not to suggest that the Catholic clergy played no part whatever in shaping Irish sexual attitudes during this period. The Church's teaching may well have helped to confirm and reinforce popular disapproval of extra-marital sexual relations and the general rejection of offenders against this strict morality. But it seems unlikely, given the limited extent of clerical influence in other, closely related areas, that this teaching can have had more than a subsidiary role. That the chastity so much admired by contemporary observers had its roots more in Irish ideas of family than in any variety of Christian moral teaching may also be seen from the way in which popular hostility extended not only to the unmarried mother but also to her offspring and beyond. Some churchmen, like Archbishop MacHale, may have shared and endorsed this prejudice against the illegitimate, but in doing so they merely illustrated the extent to which they were themselves part of the society in which they operated.

This conclusion is of relevance not only to the period before the famine but also to any consideration of later decades. There are some indications that sexual attitudes in the post-famine period became even more restrictive than they had earlier been, as farmers, the class with most incentive to regulate the sexual behaviour of the unmarried young, became increasingly the dominant group in rural society, and as rising standards of living permitted the adoption of new models of behaviour through which something of the genteel sexual puritanism of the Victorian middle classes was grafted onto more traditional attitudes. The incidence of illegitimacy, already low in 1864, fell to still lower levels in the years that followed, and ratios of 5 per cent or over became unknown outside Ulster. At the same time, although over a much longer period, extending almost to the present day, the ribald strain in Irish traditional culture was replaced by an extreme reticence in sexual matters. But any such developments can at most have modified what even in the first half of the nineteenth century had been an exceptionally strict code of sexual conduct. And where discussions centred on the twentieth century have frequently seen the priest as the principal force behind the obsessive chastity of the Irish Catholic, a longer perspective suggests that his true role was rather to articulate and reinforce an outlook whose roots lay far deeper in the structure and assumptions of the society of which he was himself a product.

6

'Vile and Wicked Conspiracies'

Pre-famine Ireland was a violent society in which public order was often precarious and sometimes non-existent. This violence was of several different kinds. In the countryside agrarian agitation began with the first phase of the Whiteboy movement in Munster and south Leinster in the 1760s and recurred in every subsequent decade up to and including the 1840s. In the cities food riots and similar disturbances were regular occurrences. In the 1790s the efforts of the United Irishmen to harness popular discontents in the service of a programme of radical political reform resulted in a cycle of outrage and repression culminating in the rebellion of 1798, in which an estimated 30,000 persons lost their lives. Sectarian animosities were a source of recurrent fighting throughout this period, principally though not exclusively in Ulster. There was also the random violence of brawls and assaults, which could take place on any occasion but which were particularly common at fairs, patterns and similar social gatherings. Such gatherings also provided a regular battleground for local factions, formidable alliances, capable in some cases of mustering armies several hundred strong, yet apparently bound together by nothing more than their common animosity to the opposing party. At times the clashes between these factions may have been little more than a pastime, governed by their own rituals and conventions. In other cases, however, they developed into what was all too clearly a murderous feud.[1]

To all of these forms of violence the authorities of the Catholic Church were strongly and consistently opposed. This chapter will look at their opposition under three headings. Firstly, it will discuss the preaching of the church authorities on the topic of public order and obedience to established authority, and attempt to define more precisely the attitudes which lay behind their opposition to popular disturbances. Secondly, it will consider the other means which were used by the Catholic clergy to suppress or discourage such activities. Finally, it will examine a different aspect of the relationship between the Catholic clergy and those engaged in disturbances — the way in which the clergy themselves more than once became the targets for violence and intimidation.

1.   *Doctrines of Subordination*

Throughout the eighteenth century the Catholic clergy preached regularly to their congregations on the subject of public order, condemning every form of disturbance or agitation and emphasising the duty of all men to show obedience to their temporal rulers. In the city of Dublin riots of every kind, from demonstrations over the hoarding of corn in times of shortage or over the sale of imported goods, to ordinary brawls such as those arising out of the long-standing hostility between civilians and soldiers quartered in the capital, were denounced vehemently and those involved excommunicated or excluded from the sacraments. More organised agitations in the country at large, the Whiteboys, the Defenders, the United Irishmen, as well as combinations among the workers of the capital, were similarly condemned and offenders penalised in the same way. Other occasions permitted a more positive expression of loyalty. Public prayers were offered at different times for the health and happiness of the royal family, while in 1795 and again in 1800 there were similar prayers in thanksgiving for the failure of attempts to assassinate the king. In times of war prayers were ordered for the success of His Majesty's arms by land and sea, and the public fasts ordered by the government on those occasions when such success did not appear to be readily forthcoming were announced by the Catholic clergy to their congregations with instructions that they were to be regarded as carrying the force of a religious obligation.[2]

These constant exhortations to loyal and peaceful behaviour were supported by two main arguments. In the first place Catholics were reminded of the toleration which had been granted to them by the government, and at the same time were warned that any misbehaviour could result in a stricter enforcement of the laws against their religion. 'A regular, prudent and Christian deportment', the Archbishop of Dublin advised in 1749, 'will justly entitle us to the favour of our superiors, whereas a contrary behaviour will involve the innocent in a punishment due only to the guilty.' As the century progressed this point could be made in increasingly positive terms, with the threat of a new phase of repression giving way to the prospect of further measures of Catholic relief as the reward for good behaviour. Tributes to the benevolence of the monarch and his government, meanwhile, became increasingly flowery. 'Our gracious king,' one pastoral letter announced after the Relief Act of 1793,

> the common father of all his people, has with peculiar energy recommended his faithful Roman Catholic subjects of this kingdom to the wisdom and liberality of our enlightened parliament. How can we, dear Christians, express our heartfelt acknowledgments for this signal and unprecedented instance of royal benevolence and condescension? Words are insufficient. . . . [3]

The second main argument to which the church authorities appealed was the religious obligation of obedience to temporal rulers. Riots and other forms of disorderly behaviour, the Catholics of Dublin were warned in 1771, 'must not only draw on the offenders the just and severe frowns of government, but also the indignation and chastisement of angry heaven'. Particular emphasis was given to the fact that the obligations of subjects were in no way affected by the religion of their superiors. Christ, the Apostles, and the early Christians were all cited as examples of unquestioning obedience to one's earthly rulers, regardless of differences of religion. Archbishop Carpenter summed up the teachings of his church in the 'clear, explicit and absolute' precepts of St Paul: 'Let everyone be subject to higher powers, for there is no power but from God. The powers that are God has ordained. Whoever resists the power resists the ordinance of God.'[4]

It was these two arguments, the prospect of continued and greater toleration and the sinfulness of resistance to temporal superiors, which constituted between them the main basis for clerical denunciations of all forms of popular disturbance. Specifically political doctrines about the nature of civil society and the place of the citizen within it are conspicuous by their absence. In the 1790s, it is true, the church authorities were inevitably led to condemn the principles associated with the French Revolution – 'the rotten tree of French liberty', as Archbishop Troy described it, whose fruit was 'fair to the eye but deadly to those who taste it'. Even here, however, the pastorals of the Irish bishops dwelt less on political doctrines than on the misery which the revolution had brought to those countries it had already affected and on the hostility of the revolutionaries to religion.[5]

In spite of the many pronouncements of the authorities of the Catholic Church in this period on the theme of political obedience, therefore, their actual political ideas must be deduced from occasional references and asides scattered throughout their statements. Where this can be done, however, what emerges are fairly conventional views concerning the inevitability of social inequality and the necessary sub-ordination of man to man. Archbishop Butler of Cashel condemned the Whiteboys 'who, it seems, would fain bring down to their own level all superior ranks of people, would crush them if they could, and give the Law to those whom the Almighty has thought proper to put above them'. Bishop Coppinger of Cloyne and Ross, writing in 1798, ridiculed the whole idea of social equality. 'How can there be cultivation where there are no tillers?' he asked. 'And where shall you find tillers if all become gentlemen?' 'Rank and property', he continued,

> must go hand in hand, the inequality of both in every civilised country must be as various as the talents of men. Were every individual in the land possessed at this day of an equal share of property, a lapse of twelve months would exhibit innumerable gradations. The industrious,

the thrifty, the honest, the temperate would soon surpass the idle, the profligate, the squanderers and the licentious. In the general scale of human depravity the latter description will be always the more numerous; the poor will still be the poor under every form of government.

Bishop Moylan of Cork provided the theological counterpart to his colleague's social theory, reminding his hearers that this life was a state of trial preparing them for entry into a better world.

Instead, then, of indulging in fruitless and unseemly murmurs, or seeking by unlawful methods to soften the hardships of your condition, console yourselves, my dear brethren, with the assurance which religion holds out to you that for whatever you suffer in this world you shall, if it be not your own fault, be amply rewarded in the next.

Both Coppinger and Moylan explicitly declined to discuss the political origins of the crisis on the grounds that these were matters which their hearers could not be expected to understand.[6]

The Irish hierarchy of this period produced one more detailed treatment of political principles. This was Archbishop Troy of Dublin's pamphlet *On the Duties of Christian Citizens*, published in 1793. Here too social inequality was presented as an inevitable part of human society. Temporal authority, Troy maintained, had been instituted by God because absolute freedom – owing to the corruption of human nature in its fallen state – could not exist without anarchy. 'Society implies different classes and orders of men, necessarily subordinate and dependent.' Troy, it is true, went on to deny that Catholicism favoured despotic government, pointing to various examples from history of Catholic resistance to tyranny. When he turned back to his own place and time, however, he became more circumspect. Abuses, he admitted, could exist under any system of government, but on the question of how these should be remedied he noted only that 'Our remonstrances against abuses should be always loyal and decorous.' In a second edition of his pamphlet

Troy added a specific endorsement of the British constitution as in his view particularly calculated to avoid the two extremes of despotism and anarchy.[7]

The terms in which the authorities of the Catholic Church in the eighteenth century preached the duty of loyalty and obedience to temporal authority enable us to define more clearly the thinking which lay behind that preaching. In particular they reveal how simple ideological labels like 'conservative' or 'reactionary' can prove misleading in this case. The majority of senior churchmen do appear to have subscribed to fairly conservative doctrines concerning the inevitability of hierarchy and inequality in human society. But such ideas were clearly less important in their minds than the religious obligation of obedience to temporal superiors and the still precarious degree of toleration enjoyed by the Irish Catholic Church in this period.

It is, of course, possible that the church authorities recognised that their view of civil society was not the part of their thinking most likely to win the hearts of their congregations, and that they constructed their public statements accordingly. But the superficial nature of their attachment to hierarchical principles of the kind discussed above can also be seen in the speed with which these were abandoned. In 1822, when Bishop Doyle of Kildare and Leighlin issued a pastoral letter denouncing the 'vile and wicked conspiracy' of the Ribbonmen, he was still finding metaphors for the necessary subordination of some members of society to others:

> The body of a nation is like, in some degree, to our own. The different ranks and orders which compose it are ordained of God, that the whole may be preserved entire. If any of them should seek to usurp the place of the other, discord would ensue. If your feet, seeing your hands are idle, would refuse to walk — if your hands would undertake to do the duties of the head, how monstrous and absurd would it not appear? So in the State, if those whom God has appointed to labour, should abandon their station, and seek to govern — if the ignorant would take the place of the wise — the soldier the place of the

peasant — the tradesman that of the Magistrate — the schoolmaster that of the bishop or judge, how could society exist?

The argument could have come from Troy or one of his colleagues in the 1790s. Yet within a few years of this pastoral letter the Catholic hierarchy and clergy — not least among them Doyle himself — had emerged as the leaders of a series of popular agitations, first for the removal of the remaining legal restrictions on Irish Catholics, then for the abolition of tithes paid to the Established Church, and finally for the repeal of the Act of Union. Individual churchmen differed in the degree to which they were prepared to commit themselves, but by the end of the 1820s the doctrine of total passivity in the face of temporal authority had clearly been left behind.[8]

Just as the hierarchical social thinking which can be detected in the statements of eighteenth-century bishops does not appear to have played a very prominent part in their opposition to popular disturbances, so the abandonment of those principles in the 1820s and after did not bring with it any slackening of such opposition. The response of the church authorities of the early nineteenth century to agrarian and other secret societies was in fact very similar to that of their eighteenth-century predecessors. Their pastoral letters on the subject dwelt at length on the sinfulness of unlawful oaths, destruction of property and other forms of violence or outrage, and at the same time put forward utilitarian arguments about the damage which such disturbances did to the true interests of those involved, and the severe punishment which they invited from government. There were, of course, certain changes of emphasis: the sinfulness of particular crimes had replaced the duty of unqualified obedience to temporal authority; the alternative to violent action was no longer either passive resignation or reliance on the benevolence of social superiors, but legal and constitutional agitation. But abstract political doctrine continued to take second place to arguments derived from religious obligation on the one hand and to pragmatic considerations on the other.[9]

The discussion so far has been concerned with the official political attitudes of the Irish Catholic Church, as reflected in the pastoral letters and other statements of a number of prominent bishops. It would be a mistake to assume that such statements were always representative. At least one bishop was prepared to adopt a considerably less submissive tone in his comments on the government and its policy. This was Thomas Hussey, Bishop of Waterford and Lismore, who in 1797 caused consternation among his episcopal colleagues and outrage in official circles with a pastoral letter in which he urged his clergy not to permit themselves to be used by the rich as instruments against the poor, and went on to order them to oppose all forms of proselytism, particularly as it affected Catholic soldiers.[10] Hussey may have been an exception; certainly no other bishop dissented so clearly in a public statement from the docile approach favoured by Troy and other spokesmen. At the same time the episode is a warning against assuming too great a degree of unanimity among the Catholic bishops of this period.

Dissent from the official policy of uncritical obedience may also have existed among the lower clergy. Accusations that priests were involved in the Whiteboy movement of the 1760s are unlikely to have had any real foundation, but there are indications that some priests might have involved themselves in milder forms of agitation. It appears to have been his involvement in local resistance to the payment of tithes which first brought the ill-fated Nicholas Sheehy to the attention of the authorities. A report in 1778 that the Parish Priest of Shinrone, King's County, had marched into the town at the head of more than two hundred supporters intending to murder a local gentleman with whom he had had a dispute may be a distorted account of a similar local conflict. Certainly there is evidence twenty years later that the same priest was the object of considerable hostility on the part of the local gentry.[11]

Whatever had been the political attitudes and behaviour of the lower clergy in earlier decades, it became clear in the 1790s that not all of them shared the hostility of their ecclesiastical superiors to the United Irishmen. Richard Hayes has assembled information on the activities of 58 priests during this period. Three of these were killed fighting on the rebel side in 1798, eight were executed by the government, 11 became fugitives after the collapse of the rebellion, and a further 26 were arrested, of whom at least 15 were convicted and sentenced to imprisonment or transportation. The remaining ten were men who were accused by informers or others of having been involved in treasonable activities during this period, but against whom no action was taken.[12] While the involvement of Catholic priests in the events of 1798 is undeniable, however, its significance must be interpreted with care.

In the first place, how widespread was that involvement? Hayes argues that clerical support for the United Irishmen went far beyond the relatively small number of priests whose activities he is able to document, and that a majority of the Catholic clergy were in fact sympathetic to the aims of the movement. The main evidence for widespread disaffection in the ranks of the lower clergy, however, is supplied by the reports of various informers to their employers in Dublin Castle. These were notoriously unreliable: at one point, for example, it was claimed that no less a person than Archbishop Troy of Dublin had taken the oath of the United Irishmen.[13] Other evidence, meanwhile, makes clear that there were active loyalists among the lower clergy as well as among the hierarchy. 'The priests in this neighbourhood', a correspondent in Westmeath reported in May 1798, 'have for some time past lectured their congregations every Sunday and preached up the support of the king and constitution.' In Tipperary a local military commander praised 'the zealous exertions and pathetic eloquence' of a Catholic curate who had been largely responsible for persuading a particularly disturbed parish to give up its arms.[14] In other cases, as will be seen later in this chapter, priests were reported to have made themselves unpopular, and even to have endangered their lives, by their opposition to the United Irishmen. The correspondence of the church authorities suggests that they regarded those priests who took part in the rebellion as a deviant minority rather than as the tip of an iceberg of widespread disloyalty. The bishops, of course, had good reason to minimise the extent of disaffection among their subordinates. But they were not the only ones to take this view. 'The priests saved the infamous English government in Ireland from destruction,' wrote the United Irish leader Miles Byrne many years later, adding that 'For their pious assiduity and earnest endeavours on this occasion, to keep the people in thraldom, they were but poorly recompensed.'[15]

To appreciate the significance of clerical involvement in the events of 1798 it is also necessary to define more clearly the character of that involvement. Some of the priests concerned, like James Quigley, had been supporters of the United Irishmen before the outbreak of rebellion. These can be seen as dissidents on ideological grounds from the official political stance of their church, comparable to the clerical supporters of the Fenian movement in the 1860s and of other extreme nationalist groups after that date. Other priests, however, appear to have become involved in the rebellion only after it was irreversibly under way. Father John Murphy of Boulevogue, perhaps the best-known clerical leader of the Wexford rebellion, had earlier been active in persuading his congregation to surrender their arms to the authorities. Other priests who supported the rebellion, both in Wexford and in Mayo, appear to have undergone a similar change of heart.[16] In these cases what we see is not dissent on grounds of principle from the loyalism preached by the church authorities, but rather a demonstration of the limitations of that loyalism. In spite of the elaborate rhetoric devoted to its expression, it was suggested earlier in this section, the political submissiveness of the Catholic hierarchy of the late eighteenth century did not have deep ideological roots. The considerations uppermost in the minds of its most energetic exponents appear to have been, firstly, the teachings of their church on the subject of obedience to temporal rulers, and secondly, a pragmatic concern for the position of the Catholic Church in Irish society. In ordinary circumstances these may have been sufficient to keep the majority of Catholic clergymen in the loyalist camp. But the theological requirements for legitimate resistance to authority, like those for a just war, have always been notoriously flexible. And as for pragmatism, the course of action which it seemed to suggest to the ordinary priest in his parish might sometimes be very different to that which it dictated to a senior member of the hierarchy, concerned with the interests of the national Church.

2. Policing the Countryside

Clerical denunciations of agrarian outrage and other forms of disturbance were backed up by a variety of positive sanctions. The penalty of excommunication was regularly applied in the eighteenth century. It was used both against rioters in the capital and against the Whiteboys in several dioceses, while in the 1790s Archbishop Troy excommunicated both the Defenders and the United Irishmen.[17] By the early nineteenth century, however, formal sentences of excommunication had become markedly less common. In some dioceses excommunication remained the automatic consequence of membership of an oath-bound secret society,[18] but the penalty figured much less prominently in the warnings and exhortations of the church authorities than it had done in earlier decades. Bishop Doyle, one of his clergy explained in 1831, had not excommunicated the societies known as Whitefeet and Blackfeet, although he had threatened to do so; excommunication was 'a power looked upon as very odious', and the witness had never known Doyle use it against an offender of any kind.[19] This may have reflected a general trend towards a more cautious and more discriminating use of what was intended to be the ultimate sanction provided by the machinery of church discipline. But agrarian agitation was a case in which the use of excommunication as a blanket sentence imposed on whole categories of offenders was particularly likely to have no effect other than to weaken the impact of the whole procedure.

In place of excommunication Doyle introduced a strict set of rules for all confessors in his diocese. Priests were required to ask all suspected persons who came to them for confession whether they were connected with any illegal association. If he admitted that he was so connected, a penitent was not to be absolved until he had withdrawn from the society and performed a penance (either the stations of the cross or the seven penitential psalms) in a chapel of the diocese every Sunday for a year. He was also to bε required to make reparation for any damage or injurie for which he or his confederates had been responsible, 'at the expense of all his wordly goods, which he now has or may hereafter acquire, at the expense also of his feelings and character, and at the risk, if necessary, even of his life'. It is difficult to believe that the last requirement was successfully enforced in many cases. Priests in other dioceses also refused to grant absolution to members of secret societies. Both in Kildare and Leighlin and elsewhere, however, the effectiveness of such refusal was limited by the willingness of those involved with secret societies to stay away from confession during the period that disturbances were in progress.[20]

In their efforts to deal with the somewhat different disturbances arising out of faction-fighting the church authorities again reinforced their denunciations with more concrete penalties. Under regulations agreed on by the bishops of the province of Cashel in 1777,

> All riots and quarrels are to be punished with the utmost rigour, part of which punishment is that they shall come barefooted to the ordinary or vicar general, there to be ordered proper penance. A general penance is that they shall stand *in albis* three Sundays at the church door of the parish where they gave scandal.

Regulations introduced in the diocese of Ossory five years later provided that any person who struck another at a fair or other public place, unless in self-defence, was to be excluded from the sacraments until he had come before the congregation on a Sunday to make a public acknowledgment of his crime and solemnly promise amendment. In 1808 the Bishop of Ferns was reported to have made some of the persons concerned in a fight between two townlands in his diocese do penance by going twice round the outside of the parish chapel on their bare knees.[21] The use of public penances in cases like these may have been inspired largely by the belief that brawling could be most effectively suppressed by hitting at the pride and public respect the participants were defending. At the same time it emphasised that fighting was being penalised as an antisocial offence, a breach of the public peace and of communal harmony which had to be repaired by an act of public reparation.

There were also occasions on which priests intervened personally to break up faction-fights or similar disturbances. In the first half of the eighteenth century at least this could be a hazardous undertaking. In 1732 a Co. Meath priest was killed by a stone while trying to break up a fight at a hurling match, while one of the four priests who tried to quell a riot at Kilcock, Co. Kildare, in 1753 was seriously injured in the attempt.[22] By the early nineteenth century clerical crowd control may have become more effective. John Burke, Parish Priest of Castlepollard, Co. Westmeath, and himself a prominent figure in the agitation against tithes, described in 1831 how he had tackled one man during a riot in the town:

> I went up to him and caught him by the collar; he seemed in a violent state, partly through drink and partly through passion. I told him to go out of the fair, or I would make him. He said he would, and I made the people round promise to put him out of the fair.

At Mallow in 1821 the Catholic curate appeared when two opposing factions had already assembled and were shouting the preliminary battle-cries. Accompanied by a Protestant clergyman, he 'entered at considerable risk into the midst of the combatants [and] had a conversation with one of the parties, the O'Mahonys. . . . He reasoned with, and eventually succeeded in inducing them to return home, which they did in a body of about 500.' In Errigle, Co. Londonderry, around 1830 two factions, the O'Mullans and the O'Hagans, numbering several hundred between them, assembled for a battle but were dispersed by the Catholic clergyman. At the fair in Ballydehob, Co. Cork, in 1838 two priests were able to pacify a crowd who were stoning the police.[23]

This type of personal intervention by the local clergy at scenes of open disturbance was backed up by a more general supervision of the activities of their parishioners. In at least one Limerick parish during the disturbances of 1821 the parish priest and his curate patrolled the area at night, giving 'great assistance' to the local magistrate in his efforts to put down disturbances. The activities of other priests reveal the use which they were able to make of a detailed personal knowledge of what was going on in their parishes. When the Parish Priest of Maryborough, Queen's County, learned in 1822 that about twenty individuals had been sworn in as Ribbonmen in his parish, he was able to visit each of the men concerned and extract promises from all but two of them that they would give up the society immediately. (The two who refused were strangers to the parish, the men who had originally introduced the system there, and these he denounced from his altar the following Sunday.) In the same way five years later another Queen's County parish priest got rid of two travelling masons who were said to be administering oaths to inhabitants of his parish by denouncing them from the altar. This priest, according to his own account, had 'prevented a great deal of outrage on personal property' by acting on information which he had received about intended crimes. 'It is a matter of notoriety', he explained,

> that the perpetrators of crime generally come from a distance. When information of such intended crime comes to my knowledge from my intercourse with the people, I lose no time in writing to the parish priest in whose district the agents reside, and by our mutual co-operation and interference we have in most cases frustrated their intentions.[24]

The laws of the Church forbade priests to make use of information they had received in the confessional, but even without this their knowledge of their parishioners gave them an advantage shared by few other opponents of popular conspiracy and disturbance.

Priests active against agrarian and other forms of agitation did not rely solely on their own efforts, but also worked closely with the civil authorities. The Parish Priest of Abington, Co. Limerick, described in 1825 how, accompanied by a magistrate, he had visited the houses of persons known to be administering secret oaths and persuaded them to give up their arms and make promises of good behaviour for the future. On other occasions priests invited magistrates to come to their chapels so that they could unite in exhorting the congregations against illegal associations. Priests in a disturbed area of Galway in 1819 added their names to resolutions drawn up by the local magistrates calling for a detachment of soldiers to be sent to the area. Three years later the Parish Priest of Ballingarry, Co. Tipperary, went a step further, instituting a subscription to pay for the rent of a barracks so that soldiers could be stationed there. The collection, he reported, was made with the assistance of 'four very respectable magistrates'.[25]

In other cases priests passed on to magistrates and others the information they possessed concerning the progress of disturbances in their parishes. An officer stationed in Kerry reported in 1805 that he had received information of this kind from confidential conversations with the Parish Priest of Ballylongford, 'a man of great zeal and known loyalty'. In 1822 an army officer stationed in Mohill, Co. Leitrim, was warned by 'a most zealous and loyal Catholic priest' that in spite of the apparent tranquillity of the area, illegal oaths were being administered. The priest recommended a general search for arms, and also that all schoolmasters — a class frequently credited with a leading role in organising disturbances — should be called in and made to take the oath of allegiance. In the same way chief constables stationed in Mayo and Roscommon in 1836 were warned by Catholic clergymen that disturbances were beginning in their areas.[26]

Some priests were prepared not merely to give general information of this kind but to point out individuals known to be involved in illegal activities, particularly when the latter were not members of their congregations. In 1823 the Parish Priest of Arklow, Co. Wicklow, learning that a blacksmith had come to the area to swear in recruits for a secret society, informed the local magistrates, who had the man arrested. In 1831 the Catholic Curate of Oranmore, near Galway, had two men who were swearing in his parishioners arrested in the same way, while a few years later the Parish Priest of Navan, Co. Meath, gave information which led to the arrest of several members of a Ribbon society. Other priests carried out their own arrests. In 1821 the Parish Priest of Castleisland, Co. Kerry, assisted by a dozen of his parishioners, seized and handed over to the authorities a man who had come to the parish to administer oaths. In Limerick in the following year the Parish Priest of Rathcahill led part of his congregation out of the parish chapel, armed with sticks and stones, to assist four local gentlemen in seizing a band of seven armed men and holding them prisoner until a party of soldiers arrived to take them into custody.[27]

While Catholic clergymen were sometimes prepared to identify themselves openly with the repressive and even the punitive measures of the civil authorities, they also had an important role as intermediaries between the authorities and their congregations. In 1822 the Parish Priest of Kilmoremoy, Co. Mayo, was able to arrange with local magistrates for his parishioners to assemble in the local chapel and take the oath of allegiance, on the understanding that the fact of their having earlier taken the oath of the Ribbonmen would not be held against them. In other cases priests arranged for the surrender of illegally held arms, either to themselves or directly to the authorities.[28]

In other ways too the Catholic clergy of this period took an active part in the preservation of public order. When a man was murdered in Newcastle, Co. Limerick, in 1822, the parish priest, 'with his usual activity and exertion in preserving the public peace and in support of the laws, assembled his parishioners early on the morning of Friday and after some hours diligent search found the body in the River Deel'.[29] In Co. Clare during 1831, when the agrarian society known as the Terry Alts had adopted the tactic of digging up pasture land so that its owners would have no alternative but to let it out for tillage, several parish priests persuaded their congregations to turn out in force and replace the grass that had been turned up in this way, and at least one of them personally led his parishioners in the operation.[30] At Carigeen, Co. Kilkenny, after a threatening notice had been posted on the chapel door, a meeting was convened in the chapel, with the parish priest as chairman. Those present passed resolutions expressing 'our abhorrence at this first attempt to disturb and stigmatise our tranquil and peaceable parish', pledged themselves to resist any attempt to involve them in disturbances, and instituted a subscription so that a reward could be offered for the capture of the person responsible for the notice. In a number of parishes in Cork and Kerry during 1821 and 1822 the parish priests organised similar public meetings at which the inhabitants passed resolutions expressing their opposition to all forms of illegal agitation and their determination to resist any attempt to extend the disturbances to their area.[31]

In all these cases Catholic clergymen were attempting to mobilise the well-disposed members of their congregations in defence of law and order. On several occasions they attempted to extend this mobilisation to the recruitment either of local vigilante groups or of special constables to assist the authorities in suppressing disturbances. During his visitation of 1818 and 1819 Archbishop Everard of Cashel gave instructions in each parish he inspected for the formation of what he described as an 'association for the preservation of lives and property'. In the parish of Cloneen and Killusty, which he visited on 24 July 1820, he noted

An improvement in this congregation since the last visitation. The respectable persons of this parish assembled at the chapel and formed an association against some bad and wicked intruders who disturbed the neighbourhood: by their exertions they completely put down the disturbers of the public peace.[32]

Clergymen elsewhere followed, or attempted to follow, Everard's example. A Co. Kildare gentleman, writing in 1821, attributed the tranquillity of his area to 'the spirited conduct of the gentry and Catholic clergy who, on the appearance of danger, had all the respectable landholders sworn in as special constables, to the amount of 700 men'. Ten years later Bishop Doyle advised the clergy of his diocese to exhort the owners of property in their parishes and 'the well disposed of every class' 'to form themselves, in concert with the constitutional authorities, into armed associations for the protection of lives and property, to patrol the country by day and night whilst necessary'. Several of the clergy of his diocese attempted to follow this advice and applied to the civil authorities for permission to form such associations, but they appear to have met with little encouragement. The official view, as one magistrate explained, was that such bodies 'would manifestly be an increase rather than the contrary of dangerous confederacies in the country'. These suspicions were not shared by Joseph Greene, a Co. Kilkenny magistrate who reported to Dublin that he had agreed to a proposal by the Parish Priest of Clara that some of 'the most respectable farmers' of that area should be sworn in as special constables, who would patrol along with the police at night, and asking for permission to provide some arms for their use.[33]

* * *

This section has looked at some of the practical ways in which the Catholic clergy demonstrated their opposition to agrarian and other forms of disturbance: through the penalising of offenders, through a close personal supervision of their parishioners, through co-operation with the civil authorities, and through the mobilisation of their parishioners in support of law and order. Taken together, these different activities add up to a substantial involvement on the part of the parish clergy in the formal and informal policing of their districts. All the examples of such involvement given here, however, have come from the early nineteenth century, the great majority of them from the 1820s and 1830s. This may in part reflect the fact that sources of information on the conduct of the Catholic clergy in the period after 1800 are more detailed and more sympathetic than those which exist for earlier decades. At the same time it is difficult to avoid the conclusion that active law-enforcement of the kind discussed in this section was more common in the 1820s and 1830s than had previously been the case.

An increase in clerical involvement in the maintenance of law and order is unlikely to have been the result of any change in attitude on the part of Catholic priests. Whatever the degree of dissent from official policies which existed in the case of the United Irishmen, there is nothing to indicate that clerical opposition to agrarian violence was less wholehearted in the late eighteenth century than it was to be in the early nineteenth. The anticlericalism of the Whiteboys is evidence of how seriously that opposition was taken by those at whom it was directed, and it also makes the existence of any sympathy for their activities among Catholic churchmen even more unlikely. A more plausible explanation for the apparent growth of clerical involvement in law-enforcement is provided by the changing social position of the Catholic priest. During the 1820s and 1830s the Catholic clergy took on a new role as political agitators, and with it a new prominence in public affairs. The change in their status is summarised in the comments of a dissident Cork priest, David Croly, in 1834:

> The humility or the obscurity of former times has entirely disappeared and is forgotten. The country priest now copes with the country squire, keeps sporting dogs, controls elections, presides at political clubs and sits 'cheek by jowl' at public dinners and public assemblies with peers of the land and members of parliament.[34]

It is the same more confident and assertive approach to public affairs which can be seen in clerical responses to crime and outrage. The priest who assembled his parishioners at dawn to search for a missing body, or who arranged for members of his congregation to declare their loyalty at a public meeting or to volunteer for service as special constables, was acting essentially as a local leader, organising and co-ordinating the activities of his parishioners in much the same way as he had begun to do in the political sphere. The emergence of the Catholic clergy as local agents in O'Connell's political machine and their new prominence in the maintenance of law and order, in other words, can be seen as two aspects of the same general process, whereby the local priest assumed a new and more prominent place in the structure of power and influence within his community.

One further point requires discussion here. The recurrent agrarian disturbances of the pre-famine period, as Professor Lee has pointed out, cannot be seen solely in terms of conflict between tenant farmers and their landlords over rent, eviction and similar issues. Two other forms of conflict also played a major part. The first of these concerned the employment of agricultural labourers. Different agrarian societies attempted to regulate the wages paid to such workers, to protect them from dismissal, and to prevent the employment of outsiders in work which might otherwise have gone to inhabitants of the area. A report on disturbances in Co. Limerick in 1800, for example, summarised their objects as being 'to raise the present price of labour, to reduce the price of food, to prevent the farmers from hiring the Kerrymen, and to abolish tithes'. The other major cause of disturbance was the cost and availability of conacre. Conacre, the letting of a piece of ground for a single season, generally for the raising of a crop of potatoes, was the principal means by which the landless labourer in many areas fed himself and his family. Conflict arose not merely out of the rents charged for conacre but also out of disputes over the amount of land which should be let in this way. The availability of conacre became a particularly serious issue after 1815, when changes in market conditions made it increasingly less attractive for farmers to let their land on such terms. However, the tactic of digging up meadowland so that it became useless for grazing and its owner had no option but to let it for tillage was already being used by the Whiteboys in 1762 and by agrarian societies in Limerick in 1800.[35]

The importance of this for the activities of the Catholic clergy is that agrarian violence was not simply a conflict between members of the Catholic community on the one hand and persons outside that community — such as landlords, tithe-owners and their agents — on the other. It was also a conflict within the Catholic population. The persons involved in disturbances, different observers agreed, were predominantly labourers, farm servants and the smallest occupiers of land. Substantial farmers were more likely to appear as the victims of agrarian agitation than as its supporters. In Westmeath, according to a local magistrate and land agent, the respectable Catholic farmers were 'much aggrieved' at the activities of the Ribbon society 'in regulating their servants, in regulating the mode of letting their land, those particularly who set what is termed conacre in Ireland, and in various ways'. The German traveller Johann Kohl observed in 1844 that most of the farmers he visited had guns in their houses and insisted that they could not do without them. 'These rich farmers', he explained, 'express the same opinions as their landlords, and to a man stand on their side; for since, as middlemen, they often have their under-tenants, so also they have as much to apprehend from the peasantry as their landlords.'[36]

It was not mere rhetoric, then, which led Catholic churchmen of the pre-famine period to distinguish between their 'respectable' parishioners on the one hand and the persons involved in agrarian disturbances on the other. Instead such statements acknowledged a real distinction between different sections of the rural Catholic population — the farmers, who were frequently the victims of agrarian violence, and the labourers, cottiers and other small occupiers of land, who were its main perpetrators. Seen in this context, some of the activities of the Catholic clergy take on a new significance — especially, perhaps, their willingness to organise vigilante groups among the farmers of their parishes 'to detect and apprehend or to terrify into better habits the evildoers', as Doyle put it, 'who could then safely be dismissed should they fail in the duties they owe to God and to their employers'.[37] The point should not be exaggerated. There is little to indicate that either the Catholic clergy or the persons engaged in agrarian disturbances saw themselves as taking part in a class war. Neither were the activities of the Catholic clergy entirely one-sided. In Co. Limerick in 1821, for example, one parish priest arranged a meeting of the principal farmers of his district, at which they agreed to reduce the rents they charged for conacre by more than one-third.[38] At the same time it is important, whether considering the opposition of the Catholic clergy to agrarian disturbances or the popular response to that opposition, to remember that the priest who opposed such disturbances was not merely enforcing the law of church and state. He was also taking sides in a conflict within his congregation.

3. *Anticlerical Agitation*

A willingness to retaliate violently against what were

regarded as excessive clerical denunciations appears to have been a feature of agrarian agitation from its earliest stages. In 1762 the Limerick priest John White was already observing that the Whiteboys 'damage indiscriminately both Catholics and Protestants, and even punish the priests who exert themselves against them'. In 1775 a group of Whiteboys visited Johnstown in Co. Kildare:

> Besides breaking the windows of the inhabitants and other similar outrages, [they] buried a priest to the neck, first enclosing him naked in brambles and thorns, and threatened the like usage to every priest they could lay hands on, on account of their endeavours to dissuade them from these wicked practices.

In King's County in the following year Whiteboys attacked the house of the Coadjutor Bishop of Meath in reprisal for his having preached against their activities. Three years later the Parish Priest of Philipstown, in the same county, announced a sentence of excommunication to be incurred by anyone who maliciously maimed another's livestock, and was punished by having his own horse and cow houghed soon afterwards.[39]

In the third phase of the Whiteboy movement, between 1785 and 1787, hostility towards the Catholic clergy and the use of violence against them appears to have reached new levels. In different parts of Cork and Kerry priests were abused or physically assaulted, and the doors of Catholic chapels were nailed up by their congregations. Some of these incidents arose out of the campaign being conducted by the Whiteboys against the financial demands of the Catholic clergy, but others were clearly reprisals for clerical denunciations of the movement. At Clonakilty in May 1786 the parish priest was reported to have been insulted in his chapel while preaching against disturbances, while another priest was knocked off his horse by the same 'ungovernable mob'. In Bantry a month later the Parish Priest of Creagh and Tullagh, 'a very worthy man who had been very zealous to keep his flock from entering into those combinations' was seized by Whiteboys who broke into his house early one morning. 'They brought him out naked in the midst of wind and rain, and after using him very ill they made him swear [i.e. to abide by the rules of the Whiteboys].' When he preached against them again, he was forced to seek refuge in the house of a Protestant clergyman, where an armed party was ready to fight off any attack. In Tralee a month later a priest who had been active against the White-boys had several shots fired into his bedroom.[40]

In the 1790s there were further incidents which de-monstrated the dangers to which a priest was exposed if he condemned agitation or advocated an uncongenial sub-mission to the government. In 1793 a priest in the neigh-bourhood of Athlone 'was strung up by his own flock and nearly hung to death for preaching to them the necessity of submission to the militia act'. In Co. Kerry several priests who had made returns to the government of the number of persons fit for service in the militia were reported to have had the doors of their chapels nailed up or to have been driven out of their parishes as a result. The Defenders of Co. Meath, a Catholic pamphleteer reported in the following year, exhibited a 'contempt and hatred' towards the Catholic clergy, and 'talked of massacring their priests according to the French fashion'.[41] In 1796 a priest in Co. Tyrone who had preached against Defenderism had his life threatened, and a threatening letter was also sent to the man in whose house he lodged. Similar threats were directed at other priests who opposed the United Irishmen and their allies. The Parish Priest of Emly, Co. Tipperary, who had followed his archbishop's instructions in offering prayers of thanks-giving for the preservation of the kingdom from French invasion and in denouncing disturbances in his area, was visited at night by a group of armed men who presented him with a threatening letter and fired a shot through his door before departing. In the city of Limerick a priest who had been active against local 'agitators' had a narrow escape when two shots were fired into his bedroom. Tactics of this kind appear to have had some effect: Bishop Lanigan of Ossory reported to Troy in 1798 that priests in his diocese had told him that fear of assassination prevented them from de-nouncing the United Irishmen as vigorously as they would otherwise have been disposed to do.[42]

The pastorals issued by a number of Irish bishops during this period reveal that the United Irishmen, in their efforts to counter opposition to their movement, did not rely solely on force, but also made use of anticlerical propaganda. Archbishop Troy referred in three separate letters to charges that the Catholic clergy were insensible to the sufferings of the poor and anxious to ingratiate themselves with the civil authorities. They were represented, he wrote, 'as so many mercenaries prostituting their venal pens and exhortations for pensions and bribes'. Bishop Caulfield of Ferns concluded one of his pastorals by solemnly denying a charge which was being 'industriously propagated' in his diocese 'that I am fee'd, bribed, or pensioned by government, and that to a considerable amount; of course, that, as a mercenary, I censure and condemn the measures of United Irishmen and revolutionists'. Bishop Moylan of Cork made a similar denial, explaining that the charge was one he had always despised 'and should still continue to consider as unworthy of notice were it not for the impression that I hear this and similar falsehoods have made on the minds of some of the lower order of my flock'.[43] The willingness of bishops to issue these public denials suggests that the United Irishmen had had some success in questioning the motives of churchmen who opposed them.

As agrarian agitation continued into the 1820s and 1830s there were further instances of priests who opposed popular disturbances being threatened with punishment for their activities. One Tipperary priest in 1821 was visited at night 'by a party of these armed ruffians, who cautioned him to be silent and to make no comment whatsoever at his chapel on their proceedings'. Other priests active against disturbances received letters conveying similar warnings. Threats of this kind were taken seriously by the recipients. Bishop MacMahon of Killaloe moved his residence to the town of Ennis in 1831 as a result of some threatening letters he had received and did not return to his own house until after the agitation had begun to die down. In Kildare and Leighlin Bishop Doyle transferred a priest who had been active against the Ribbonmen to a different parish because they both feared that he was in danger of assassination if he remained where he was.[44]

The continued caution of these churchmen is understandable. By the 1820s and 1830s, however, deliberate acts of violence directed at the Catholic clergy had become unusual. Many priests, no doubt, were alarmed by the murder in November 1819 of a Limerick parish priest, John Mulqueen. However, this was not the dire warning it appeared to be. Mulqueen was killed because he challenged a group of men whom he met on the road at night. Three of the party fled when he accosted them, but the fourth, having failed to clear a ditch and make his escape with the rest, turned and shot his pursuer. The men were not aware that Mulqueen was a priest, and, according to one of their number, they 'regretted exceedingly' when they found out whom they had killed.[45] There were some other instances of violence directed at Catholic clergymen in this period. In 1821 a Limerick priest was attacked in the grounds of his chapel by a group of men, some of whom wanted to kill him but were dissuaded by the rest. Another priest in the same county was attacked at the altar by members of his congregation while preaching against disturbances.[46] Such incidents, however, appear to have been both less frequent and less serious than had been the case in the 1780s and 1790s. While the threat of reprisal for clerical denunciation continued to be freely used, in other words, its execution had become comparatively rare.

* * *

The second type of agitation directed against the Catholic clergy during this period arose out of economic grievances. There were occasional instances of priests being ordered to give up land or houses which they had rented, presumably because by doing so they had replaced an evicted tenant or otherwise violated the code of behaviour prescribed by some agrarian society.[47] The main focus of anticlerical agitation, however, was the fees which the parish clergy expected for their services and on which they depended for their support.

In the absence of any legally established system of tithes, the Catholic clergy depended for their support on a variety of payments, regulated by custom and, to some extent, by ecclesiastical legislation. The main outlines of the system were the same throughout the country, although the details varied considerably from one area to the next. The incomes of the parish clergy were derived from two sources: from the dues paid twice a year, at Christmas and Easter, by the heads of families in the parish, and from the fees which they received for specific services — marriages, baptisms and churching, private masses, sick calls and attendance at funerals. Of the latter the fees for marriage were by far the most important, both because the sums paid were larger than those which were customary on other occasions and because it was the usual practice in some parts of the country to hold a collection among the assembled wedding guests for the benefit of the priest who had officiated. In northern dioceses a collection of the same kind was held for the priest who had officiated at a funeral. In some cases also the priest received payments in kind of corn, hay or other goods, or had work done for him free of charge, either in addition to his pecuniary dues or as a substitute for cash payments. In addition, as was seen earlier, priests were entitled by custom to receive a meal — sometimes a very elaborate one — when they held a station in a private house.[48]

The first major demonstration of popular hostility to this system of formal and informal levies came during the third phase of the Whiteboy movement in the counties of Cork and Kerry in 1785—87. The movement began as a campaign for the reduction of tithes, but by 1786 this had been extended to an attempt to regulate the fees paid to the Catholic clergy. On 1 July 1786 a meeting in Cork of what were described as delegates of the Munster peasantry drew up a table setting out the amounts that were to be paid for baptisms, confessions, marriages, extreme unction and funeral masses. Similar regulations were laid down in notices posted up on chapel doors and elsewhere and in the oaths administered by the Whiteboys. The campaign extended not merely to dues and fees but also to other customary prerogatives of the Catholic clergy. 'No entertainment for them in future,' one version of the Whiteboy regulations ran, 'neither are they to be assisted in drawing or cutting their turf, but must pay like any other man.'[49]

These rules were supported by violence or the threat of violence, directed against clergy and laity alike. In December 1785 Whiteboys in Ballyshoneen, Co. Cork, came to the house where the parish priest was spending the night and warned him 'on pain of death' not to charge more than certain sums for marriages and christenings. In August 1786 a priest from Tralee, Co. Kerry, was accosted on the road by three men who demanded the five shillings which he had accepted, 'contrary to Captain Right's rules', for a licence to marry without banns, and fired three shots at him as he fled. In the same month a farmer near Killarney who had invited a priest to have dinner in his house after a station was made to do penance by walking though the streets of the town without hat, waistcoat, shoes or stockings. In other cases people who had paid more than the prescribed fees to Catholic priests were beaten by the Whiteboys. In several Cork parishes, meanwhile, the inhabitants demonstrated their alienation from the Catholic clergy by deserting their chapels and attending the local Protestant churches instead. Such tactics caused great alarm. 'The great barriers that heretofore secured the religion of the common people', one priest wrote to Archbishop Butler, 'are now broken down. Their abhorrence of the Protestant churches and their respect for their own clergy have vanished. All confidence in their p[arish] priests is lost.'[50]

The concern which this display of popular hostility to the Catholic clergy aroused in the minds of the church authorities can be seen in the way they responded to the agitation. On 26 June 1786 Archbishop Butler of Cashel summoned a meeting of the bishops of his province in Cork. In a joint pastoral issued after the meeting the bishops promised to inquire as soon as they returned to their dioceses into any financial abuses of which their clergy might have been guilty. In the meantime they issued a general instruction that their clergy should never 'bargain mercenarily' for their dues, warned that priests who extorted even the customary sums from those who were not well able to pay them would be severely dealt with, and forbade the clergy to impose on the hospitality of their parishioners at stations, weddings or similar occasions. If they could not decline an invitation without giving offence, priests were told, they were to discourage their hosts from going to unnecessary expense, and they should 'always content themselves with such frugal fare as their parishioners will cheerfully and can without burden to themselves provide'. The conciliatory tone of the pastoral did not reflect the private opinions of all the bishops. Bishop Conway of Limerick, writing to Butler a month later, demanded to know what had been achieved by 'our condescensions and attention to their real or imaginary grievances'. Bishop MacKenna of Cloyne and Ross also continued to see rigorous extortion of dues as 'a pretended cause of complaint . . . which to our knowledge scarcely existed anywhere'. But the bishops as a body had clearly been convinced of the necessity of immediate steps to deal with the grievances expressed by the Whiteboys. Their opinion was shared by Bishop Troy of Ossory, where the Whiteboys had also been active. In September 1786 Troy issued his own set of regulations setting out the fees that were to be paid for marriage, baptism and other services, and forbidding the exaction of entertainment and the refusal of sacraments on account of fees not having been paid.[51]

The Whiteboys accused the Catholic clergy of demanding unreasonable fees for their services. 'Our grievances', the delegates of the Munster peasantry declared in July 1786, 'are daily accumulating, through the avarice of the priest-hood and intolerable exactions of the tithe-farmers.' Arch-bishop Butler later maintained that objections to the fees of the Catholic clergy began only after they had begun to oppose the Whiteboys. Gerard Teahan, Butler's informant in the diocese of Cloyne and Ross, also blamed the rift between priests and people on the manner in which the former had opposed the Whiteboys. The priests, he wrote, had imprudently joined hands with the Protestant clergy against their own congregations and against the faction among the Cork gentry who supported or connived at the Whiteboy campaign against tithes.

For support and protection against their own flocks they have relied on the notorious tools of Ld Sh[anno]n. By the terror of fire arms in aid of the Church's artillery they have strove to intimidate their parishioners, and kept on boasting what a triumph they would obtain over their enemies at the assizes. The assizes are ended, and the triumph is against them.[52]

At the same time the bishops who assembled at Cork city in June 1786 clearly regarded the outcry against clerical exactions as genuine, and not merely as a tactical device designed to silence criticism of the Whiteboys. While they never admitted it in so many words, furthermore, their conciliatory response and their public warnings to their clergy seemed to concede that charges of clerical avarice and extortion had some foundation in fact.

It is difficult, in the absence of precise information on the actual fees charged by the Catholic clergy of Cork and Kerry in this period, to say how great a gap existed between the amounts which the Whiteboys were prepared to allow for these fees and the amounts which the clergy themselves demanded. The most serious cause of discontent, the bishops maintained in their joint pastoral, was the fee charged for marriages. The highest fee charged anywhere in the province, they reported, was 7s 6d, 'which we are convinced cannot in reason at this day be complained of'. It was also their 'fixed resolution' that not more than 5s was in future to be charged for a licence permitting a couple to marry without banns. The Whiteboys, however, fixed a maximum fee for marriage of 5s and appear to have prohibited any payment at all for permission to marry without banns. In this area at least there was a substantial gap between what the church authorities regarded as a reasonable fee and what the Whiteboys were prepared to allow. At the same the fees prescribed by the Whiteboys — 5s for a marriage, 1s 6d for baptism, and 1s twice yearly in dues — were substantial enough: the minimum wage demanded for labourers at the same period was only 6½d a day. The Whiteboys, then, were not seeking to abolish fees paid to the Catholic clergy or to reduce them to purely nominal sums. Here, as in other matters, their approach was a pragmatic one, concerned with bargaining for more favourable terms rather than attempting to change the basis structure of relationships and obligations under which they lived.[53]

Further demonstrations of hostility to the financial demands of the Catholic clergy occurred from time to time during the 1790s. In 1793 it was reported that the oath of the Defenders in Co. Wexford bound them 'to cut down their own clergy to a certain rate of parish dues'. In 1799 three men who broke into the house of the Parish Priest of Abbyfeale, Co. Limerick, and burned him with a hot iron to make him reveal the whereabouts of his money, also forced him to swear not to accept more than 5s for performing marriages.[54] There was no major agitation on the issue of clerical dues, however, until the campaign conducted by the Threshers, a secret society which first appeared in Sligo and Mayo in the autumn of 1806 and had spread by the end of that year into Roscommon, Leitrim, Longford and Cavan. While the Threshers in different areas concerned themselves with wages, the price of provisions and the letting of land, their main objects in all cases were to reduce both tithes and the fees paid to the Catholic clergy. In Roscommon at least agitation on the subject of priests' fees continued until 1812, and the following year saw a further outbreak of agitation on the same issue in Westmeath.[55]

The Threshers publicised their demands in a number of ways — by visiting houses at night and administering oaths to the inmates, by putting up written notices, and by having messages delivered to the congregations assembled in the chapels. One parish priest was told in front of his congregation to charge no more than certain fees for his services, and if he disobeyed, 'to have his coffin convenient'. Another was similarly warned to limit his demands and was told that he would suffer if he disobeyed. In Roscommon in 1809 Edward Wakefield came across a newly married couple whom the Threshers had carded* because they had paid more than the prescribed amount to the priest who officiated at their wedding. Reprisals directed against the Catholic clergy were also reported, although here the level of violence appears to have been much less than in earlier decades. Archbishop Kelly of Tuam later recalled that in 1807 and

---

*'Carding' was a form of torture in which a board studded with nails, normally used for carding wool, was used to lacerate the victim's back.

1808 there had been cases of corn belonging to Catholic priests being set on fire. In 1811 a priest near Roscommon was said to have been turned out of his chapel by the congregation. In Westmeath people who paid more than the prescribed sums to the Catholic clergy were also punished by being carded. The priests of the county at first rejected demands that they should lower their fees. However, 'they were compelled to comply; they were threatened themselves with destruction if they did not'.[56]

This outbreak of anticlerical hostility appears to have been provoked by the Catholic clergy themselves. 'In fact', Lord Hartland wrote from Co. Longford in 1808, after reporting that a man in his district had been carded by the Threshers, 'this business is a quarrel between the priests and their flocks about clerical duties, viz. christenings, marriages etc., for which they have lately considerably raised their fees and against which these Thrashers complain much and swear every one not to comply with them nor give more than what was usual.' In Co. Mayo the fee for baptisms had been increased from 1s 6d to 5s, and the fee for private masses from 1s to 2s 6d, while the fee for marriages, previously 10s 6d, had also been increased. The period of the Napoleonic Wars was a time of rising prices and general prosperity. Nevertheless, it is hardly surprising that increases in fees of this magnitude should have given rise to resentment and protest. The Threshers, like the Whiteboys twenty years before, were not concerned solely with cash payments. The Parish Priest of Minola, Co. Mayo, was warned in 1806 that 'at any house to which he came to confession [i.e. to hold a station], if he got hay and oats for his horse to take it, but if not to go away, on pain of suffering for it'. This would suggest that payments in kind were not treated by the Catholic clergy as a voluntary matter, and that they were substantial enough to be a cause of grievance.[57]

Agitation on the subject of clerical fees reappeared, although this time only as a subsidiary theme, in the disturbances of the early 1820s. In Aglish, Co. Kerry, in January 1822 a group of men broke into the house of the parish priest, seized a gun that he owned, and forced him to promise that he would reduce his dues. Elsewhere in Cork and Kerry there were reports at about this time of demands for a lowering of clerical fees. In Kilkenny a notice signed by 'Sir Simon Straight, commander-in-chief of the county' and posted up in the chapel at Callan, set out the amount that was to be paid in rents and tithes and ordered that only half of the existing dues were in future to be paid to Catholic priests. In Mayo in the same year an anonymous notice demanded that both Protestant and Catholic clergy 'dispense with the one-half of their charge on us poor worms and footstools'. The Ribbonmen of Galway, meanwhile, were reported to have laid down that no more than half a guinea was to be paid for marriages, instead of the usual charge of one guinea. On this occasion, however, little seems to have been done to compel the Catholic clergy to abide by regulations of this kind. Archbishop Kelly of Tuam confirmed in 1825 that the Ribbonmen of his diocese had complained about the level of fees, but reported that — in contrast to events in 1807–8 — there had been no personal insult or injury offered to the Catholic clergy.[58]

The last major outbreak of agitation on the subject of clerical fees was in the winter of 1842–43. It was more localised than earlier agitations of this kind, being largely confined to the baronies of Gallen and Costello in the eastern part of Co. Mayo and to the adjoining baronies of Leyny and Tireragh in Co. Sligo. It also differed from earlier movements in being confined almost entirely to the issue of clerical fees, rather than combining agitation on this point with the expression of other grievances, and in the tactics it employed. Where the Whiteboys and the Threshers had made use of the methods of agrarian terrorism, this movement relied mainly on peaceful demonstrations and the voluntary taking of oaths. The procedure adopted was for a large party of men, sometimes several hundred strong, to come to a parish and administer an oath to the inhabitants. This oath bound those who took it not only to pay no more than certain sums to the Catholic clergy but also to go in their turn to the next parish and administer a similar oath there. A magistrate in Co. Sligo described how he had encountered 'the entire of the male Roman Catholic population' of the parish of Kilglass proceeding in a body to the neighbouring parish of Easkey.

The main party amounted to more than a thousand men, 'whilst as far as the eye could reach parties of five and six were seen going from house to house, collecting the men and by throwing a book on the ground swearing them to abide their regulations, to accompany them that day to the chapel, and to travel [to] the next parish the following day'. They insisted to him that they intended to do nothing illegal, and he discovered that they were under orders not to take any drink and to be back in their houses by six o'clock. In the same way a party of four to five hundred men who assembled in Coolcarney, Co. Sligo, informed a constable 'that they did not come to do any thing contrary to the Queen nor the laws of the land, but if possible to acquit themselves of some of the enormous charge which their priest was imposing on them'. Similar protestations were made in other cases, and for the most part these appear to have been genuine. There were some instances of violence or damage to property: men who had refused to abide by the regulations concerning clerical fees had their turf stacks set on fire, one man's house was burned, and another had a shot fired into his house. Such episodes, however, appear to have been incidental to the main campaign, where the emphasis was clearly on voluntary compacts and mass demonstrations of popular disapproval rather than on threats or intimidation.[59]

The demands of this agitation were similar to those made during earlier attempts to limit clerical fees. The charge for marriages was fixed at 10s, and one man in Co. Mayo had his turf stack burned for paying a guinea to the priest who officiated at his wedding. Baptisms and masses for the dead were to be 1s each, while dues were fixed at 2s annually. No oats, money or potatoes were to be given to curates, and priests who employed servants were to pay them themselves. Confessions and baptisms were to take place in the chapel — an indication that the practice of entertaining priests after stations and other services in private houses continued in this area and was sufficiently burdensome to cause resentment. Support for these demands appears to have been widespread. 'The most respectable Roman Catholics in these parishes', one magistrate reported from Co. Sligo, 'attended these meetings and the feeling appears very general that the priests' dues are excessive and that they spend nothing in the country for what they receive. . . . The Kilglass people told me the Protestant curate on £75 was living more respectably and doing more good in the parish than Father Lavelle with ten times as much.' There had, it is true, been one parish in which, 'the priest being more popular, he had a party ready to oppose the movement', and a breach of the peace had been threatened. In most cases, however, the oath regarding priests' fees appears to have been willingly taken and enthusiastically carried from one district to the next.[60]

* * *

From the 1760s to the 1840s, then, the Catholic laity repeatedly proved themselves willing to resort to open protest, threats and even violence in order to express their dissatisfaction with the conduct of their clergy. Such episodes contrast sharply with the pious picture sometimes presented of a clergy and laity united by common social origins and shared grievances. While the peculiar social position of the Irish Catholic clergy may help to explain some aspects of their relationship to their congregations, it clearly did not prevent them becoming objects of popular resentment on occasions when either their support of law and order or their financial demands gave offence.

At the same time the significance of this kind of anticlerical agitation should not be overstated. In the case of reprisals for clerical opposition to popular disturbances, to begin with, the level of anticlerical violence is insignificant when set beside the full extent of clerical involvement in the maintenance of law and order. There is little to indicate, furthermore, that resentment of this kind was translated into hostility against the Catholic clergy as a whole. The United Irishmen, it is true, went some way in this direction. Their charges that churchmen who opposed them did so for financial gain or in order to curry favour with the authorities have already been mentioned, while the basis for a generalised anticlericalism is even more apparent in the remarkable document sent to the Catholic clergy of Lazer's Hill chapel in Dublin in protest at their having excommunicated members of the society:

> We never before thought any of our clergy false or ill heard. We thought they ware men of piaty, men of love, men of God, untill last sunday. We often heard their admonitions which we aprehended was to keep themselves from the cinsure of government, but how great was our astonishment on last sunday when we could hear ourselves cursed and excommunicated like by the ministers of that very church we are suffering for. We are sure ye heard the effects of such conduct in France, a place that now over flows with milk and honey as god promised. . . . We find there is treachery in spiritual life as well as in layaty. But still that won't forc hus to deny the true church of christ, thoug some of the ministers of it has shewn ingratitude and scandal. We will revive it shortly with the assistance of almighty in this country, when we will cleanse the church as well as the state of some of its unworthy members, which untill now we intended to leave to its presint directors, but bad men will be found out by good informations.[61]

However, there is little either in the contemporary evidence or in the subsequent history of relations between priests and people to indicate that ideas of this kind were shared by many ordinary United Irishmen, still less by many members of agrarian secret societies. In many cases, indeed, it is possible that anticlerical activities were not so much an expression of resentment as a utilitarian tactic intended to neutralise an inconvenient opposition.

Caution is also required in the case of agitation on the subject of clerical fees. Here there can be no question that strong popular resentment did exist. Even outside the periods of major agitation on this subject a variety of minor incidents testify to the friction and ill-feeling aroused by the financial demands of the clergy. Clerical avarice is also a common and obviously popular theme in the Gaelic poetry of the period.[62] At the same time it is necessary to keep the issue in perspective. Various proposals were made in the late

eighteenth and early nineteenth centuries for a state provision for the Catholic clergy which would do away with
their dependence on allegedly voluntary contributions.
The church authorities were prepared to negotiate on the
matter as part of a deal on Catholic Emancipation, but
they did not welcome the idea. A state provision, they
argued, would damage the influence of the Catholic clergy
over their congregations. In addition, there was the danger
that it would attract a less desirable type of person into the
priesthood and diminish the attention which priests paid
to their clerical duties.[63] In spite of the alarming events
of the 1780s and after, then, leading churchmen continued
to believe that the advantages of the voluntary system
outweighed its disadvantages – a belief which suggests
that the importance of popular resentment at the financial
demands of the Catholic clergy should not be exaggerated.

In considering the anticlerical agitations of the pre-famine
decades, finally, it is important not to present too static a
picture. While demonstrations of popular disapproval both
of the financial demands of the Catholic clergy and of their
support for law and order continued throughout this period,
the character of such demonstrations underwent an important change. The Whiteboys and other groups in the
late eighteenth century appear to have been ready to direct
against their own clergy the same techniques of intimidation
and reprisal which they employed against land agents, tithe
proctors or other persons who offended against the code of
behaviour they prescribed. In the 1820s and 1830s, on the
other hand, direct assault on the Catholic clergy or even on
their property appears to have been rare. Anticlerical agitation was largely confined to threatening letters or to the
sort of mass protest employed in Mayo and Sligo in 1842–43.
In the case of agitation on the subject of clerical fees this
may have been partly the result of the general reform of
internal discipline which was taking place in these years
and which may have done something to restrain the more
exorbitant financial demands of the lower clergy. It is possibly significant that it was in Connacht, where reform of
this kind was slowest to take effect, that agitation over
clerical fees continued longest. At the same time there is

evidence in folklore and popular literature to suggest that resentment at what was seen as clerical avarice continued into the second half of the nineteenth century and after.[64] In the case of reprisals for clerical condemnation of popular combinations or disturbances all the indications are that the Catholic clergy of the 1820s and 1830s were more actively involved than their predecessors in the preservation of law and order. The provocation, in other words, had become greater, not less. Yet here too the measures taken against offending priests were far milder than those which had been employed thirty or forty years before.

The falling off in anticlerical violence, then, cannot be attributed to changes in the behaviour of the Catholic clergy. Instead it would seem to reflect a change in the status of the priest which made congregations less willing than they had been in earlier decades to resort to tactics of this kind. A priest in the diocese of Cork, writing in 1806, believed that confidence in the Catholic clergy, which in his view had 'ceased in a great measure to exist among the people' after the Whiteboy disturbances of 1786, had recently begun to revive.[65] His explanation of that revival – that the events of 1798 had proved the wisdom of clerical admonitions against disloyalty – may be questioned. But he was correct in suggesting that the 1780s and 1790s had been the high point of popular anticlericalism. The causes which had given rise to friction between priests and people continued long after that date, but the Catholic laity would never again be as ready to translate their grievances into action.

4. Conclusion

In conclusion two questions can be asked: How successful was clerical opposition to the popular disturbances of the pre-famine decades? And what, if any, were the long-term effects of this divergence between the loyalism of the Catholic clergy and the disaffection of a section of their congregations?

At the most basic level the efforts of the Catholic clergy of the late eighteenth and early nineteenth centuries to discourage popular disturbances can be seen as revealing the ineffectiveness of their influence. In spite of their efforts, agrarian agitation, faction-fighting and other forms of disorder continued throughout this period. But this is hardly a complete answer. The fact that the Catholic clergy did not succeed in preventing all forms of disturbance does not necessarily mean that their efforts did not have some effect. 'Harmony with the Catholic titular bishop and the priest in the neighbourhood of Carrick', the agent of the Shirley estates in Co. Monaghan was advised in 1778, '[is] of use in quelling disorder and riot, by private application to them.' In 1825 James Lawler, a Co. Kerry magistrate, after mentioning several examples of priests being defied by their parishioners in times of disturbance, was still able to maintain that 'You would have had all the peasantry in Munster up, but for the priests, in the winters of 1821—22.' 'Their efforts', the Anglican Bishop of Limerick commented in 1823, 'have been most praiseworthy, and, all things considered, in no small degree successful.' A Limerick magistrate attributed the peacefulness of his area 'in a great measure to the good conduct of the Catholic clergy', although adding that their ability to keep their congregations quiet depended on their influence being supplemented by that of resident gentry and magistrates. A colleague in Queen's County agreed that the presence of the Catholic clergy could be 'very highly useful' in preventing outrage.[66]

At the same time neither contemporary observers nor the Catholic clergy themselves were in any doubt about the limited nature of clerical influence in times of disturbance. 'In cases of popular disturbances', John O'Driscol maintained, 'clergymen generally lose all power and authority over the people.' A magistrate in Queen's County reported in 1831 that the Whitefeet there paid little attention to their clergy and that exhortations from the latter for the surrender of arms to the authorities had been largely ignored. Major Warburton, who believed that the Catholic clergy had great influence over the minds of their people, had nevertheless

known instances in cases of disturbances where the priests are set at defiance by the people and not allowed to interfere at all, and I know at those periods I have heard from

the priests themselves that, except through the instrument-
ality of the females, they could know nothing at all; that
the men totally abstained from all communication with
them at times when they felt they were acting contrary
to the law and creating disturbances.

Such assessments were confirmed by the Catholic clergy
themselves. When the people were excited, the Parish Priest
of Kilcummin, Co. Kerry, reported in 1836, 'the clergyman
loses his influence over them'. Around the year 1820, according to Archbishop Kelly of Tuam, the influence of the
Catholic clergy in his diocese had been 'very much impaired.
... Those who, on all former occasions, paid very great
attention to my advice, disregarded it upon that occasion.'[67]
  If the influence of the Catholic clergy over persons involved
in disturbances was as limited as these comments suggest, in
what sense can they be said to have contributed to the
maintenance of public order? One answer is that there was
more than one kind of involvement in disturbances. As
well as those who actually became members of an agrarian
or other secret society, there would have been others who
sympathised in varying degrees with their proceedings and
who lent them either passive or active assistance. Even among
actual members, furthermore, there must have been different
levels of commitment. When the Parish Priest of Maryborough,
Queen's County, succeeded in 1822 in persuading about
twenty of his own parishioners to withdraw from a secret
society they had been sworn into, but was defied by the two
men who had come into the parish from outside to recruit
them, this may have reflected the difference between a
priest's authority over members of his own congregation and
his authority over other persons. However, it is likely that
there was also a distinction between the two committed
activists and the less wholehearted recruits they had just
acquired. Francis Blackburne in 1825 described the successful efforts of the Catholic clergy in the northern part of
Co. Limerick, an area 'where the spirit of insurrection never
had established itself', to preserve that district from 'the con-
tagion' of the disturbances which affected other areas.[68] If
the Catholic clergy had little or no influence over those most

deeply involved in the popular disturbances of this period, they may nevertheless have had a crucial role in tilting the balance in innumerable borderline cases, whether these concerned individuals or whole districts.

The character and limitations of the contribution which the Catholic clergy could make to the containment of popular disturbances is illustrated by an area in which they were particularly active, the surrender of illegally held arms. Many accounts were received during this period of Catholic priests being instrumental in bringing about the surrender of such arms to the authorities. The matter, however, was more complex than it appeared at first sight. The surrender of arms was the centre of a bargaining process by which those who had been engaged in disturbances signalled to the authorities that they were ready to suspend their activities. In many cases what the Catholic clergy communicated was an offer that arms would be surrendered on condition that an amnesty was granted to all persons who had not been guilty of murder or other serious offences. The authorities, furthermore, soon learned to treat the giving up of arms with some suspicion. When arms were handed in, they were frequently found to be damaged or unserviceable; the real weapons remained hidden. Major Willcocks, writing from Limerick in April 1822, calculated that of 529 weapons which he knew to have been stolen in the county since the previous October only 30 were among those that had recently been given up to the authorities. It was true that they had received some weapons through the priests, he added shrewdly, 'but if we did, the law was close at the heels of those who surrendered them'. Willcocks and others also suspected that the sudden willingness of the people of Limerick to give up their arms at this time arose from the hope that certain prisoners then awaiting trial might be treated with greater leniency if they did so.[69]

In this situation the sincerity of the Catholic clergy who came to the authorities with offers to have arms surrendered in return for amnesties was sometimes questioned. 'Many of the priests', one correspondent reported in April 1822, 'are bringing in arms that must have been buried for years, they are perfectly rotten, and they present them as a peace offering. Now as they so well know where to find one they certainly could get the other if they wished it.' 'As to the priests,' Major Willcocks observed, 'I wish to stand upon fair grounds with them, but I by no means place implicit confidence in the sincerity of their intention or exertions.' These correspondents may well have been correct in believing that the parish clergy did not always share their priorities and that some at least among them were more concerned with protecting their parishioners from the rigours of the law than with the quantity or quality of the weapons surrendered. At the same time the suggestion that the Catholic clergy could just as easily have brought about a genuine surrender of arms was incorrect. In this matter the priest was essentially an intermediary, with little power to change the terms set by either side. In April 1831 the Bishop and Dean of Killaloe were asked by the Lord Lieutenant, then on a visit to Co. Clare, to use their influence to persuade the people to surrender their arms. The dean inquired whether in return for such a surrender an amnesty would be offered for all crimes other than murder. When the Attorney-General refused to commit himself on that point, the dean 'declared his belief that the efforts of the clergy could, under such circumstances, be of little use'.[70]

This episode and others like it suggest that it is misleading to see the contribution of the Catholic clergy to the maintenance of law and order solely or even principally in terms of hardened Ribbonmen or Terry Alts being persuaded or coerced into renouncing their conspiritorial activities. While such conversions may have occurred from time to time, the recurrence throughout this period of agrarian violence and other forms of disturbance, as well as the testimony of the Catholic clergy themselves, suggest that the majority of those deeply involved in such activities successfully resisted whatever pressure their clergy attempted to bring to bear. Where the influence of the Catholic clergy operated most effectively was rather at the boundaries of popular disturbance — in dissuading waverers on the brink of involvement, in detaching others who had been drawn in at the periphery, and in preventing the spread of agitation into marginal areas balanced between disturbances and tranquillity. To influence of this kind must be added another important role — that of organisers, co-ordinating and giving direction to the activities of those who shared their opposition to agrarian and other disturbances. The priests who in 1821—22 arranged for meetings of their parishioners to draw up resolutions proclaiming their opposition to agrarian disturbances hardly expected that their efforts would make much difference to the persons actually engaged in such disturbances. The purpose of these meetings was rather to strengthen the resolve of that section of their congregations which was not disposed to join in agrarian violence, and to make them commit themselves publicly to a continued opposition to such activities. In the same way those priests who sought to have parishioners sworn in as special constables or issued with arms to enable them to assist the authorities in keeping the peace were merely harnessing and directing an existing opposition to disturbances. The point which has often been made of the political role of the Catholic clergy of this period can be applied with equal truth to this aspect of their activities — that their main function was not to impose a course of action contrary to people's inclinations, but rather to lead all or part of their congregations in the direction in which they wanted to go.

Whatever its exact character, however, the ability of the Catholic clergy to contain agrarian and other disturbances was definitely a limited one. Throughout this period agrarian outrage, popular conspiracy, faction-fighting and other forms of disorder continued, in spite of all the exhortations, warnings and censures of the Catholic clergy. It might be expected that this constant conflict between the Catholic clergy and a section of their congregations would eventually have formed the basis for the development of some element of popular anticlericalism. The evidence for any such development, however, is slight. While the loyalist activities of individual priests undoubtedly provoked reprisals, there is little to indicate that the resentment they created was very often translated into antipathy towards the Catholic clergy as a whole. Instead the expression of such anticlerical sentiment as existed appears to have become more rather than less inhibited as time went on. In the period after the famine there were to be further collisions between the Catholic clergy and agitations enjoying a substantial degree of popular support, but once again conflict does not appear to have given rise to any significant degree of anticlerical sentiment.

The explanation which is usually offered for the absence of any significant tradition of anticlericalism among Irish Catholics is that the Catholic clergy were not identified with the social and political establishment in the way that their Protestant counterparts were. It was argued earlier that this point should not be idealised: Irish rural society had its own clearly defined distinctions of status, within which the Catholic clergy occupied a particular place. At the same time the fact that the Catholic Church was not the esablished one, nor the church of the gentry, must have made it that much less likely that it would injure its popularity by its support of law and order. The political leadership assumed by the Catholic clergy from the 1820s, further-more, meant that their opposition to one set of popular agitations was balanced by their support for another. The part played by the Catholic clergy of the 1820s and 1830s in the campaigns for Catholic Emancipation, tithe abolition and Repeal probably does much to explain why in this period instances of direct reprisals against priests became so much less common than they had previously been, in spite of the increasing prominence of the Catholic clergy in the maintenance of law and order.

The non-established status of the Irish Catholic Church and the peculiar social position of its clergy, however, do not tell the whole story. In considering the failure of a tradition of anticlericalism to develop out of political con-flict between priests and their congregations it is also neces-sary to recognise that while conflict of this kind continued into the second half of the nineteenth century and beyond, it took a much milder form than it had done in the decades before the famine. In the 1860s, it is true, the Church's con-demnation of the Fenian movement was strong enough to provoke a hostile popular reaction. Even here, however,

clerical opposition was confined to verbal denunciation
and the withholding of sacraments: there appears to have
been no question of priests acting as an ancillary arm of the
civil law in the way they had done in the 1820s and 1830s.
The activities of the Land League in 1879 and after actually
attracted a substantial measure of clerical support, and even
those churchmen who disapproved of the movement maintained a discreet silence or condemned it only in fairly muted
terms. Finally, when political violence reappeared on a large
scale in 1916—21, the response of the church authorities was
not merely cautious but positively equivocal. Condemnations
of ambushes and assassinations were tempered by the suggestion that the blame for such episodes lay mainly with the
government whose actions had provoked them, and every
effort was made to distinguish between the principles of the
Sinn Féin leaders and the actions of their supporters. As in
earlier periods, furthermore, the caution of the majority of
churchmen was balanced by the less reserved support given
to Sinn Féin by a minority of bishops and by many of the
lower clergy.[71]

The changing response of the church authorities to popular
agitations and political movements can be attributed partly
to prudence. If opposition to the Fenians had resulted in a
certain amount of friction between priests and people,
opposition to the more broadly based agitation of the Land
League or to the ultimately victorious progress of Sinn Féin
might have had much more serious consequences. A second
explanation is that the character of Irish popular agitations
also changed with time. The tactics adopted by the Land
League, boycotting and the withholding of rents, were very
different to those which had been employed by the Ribbonmen or the Rockites. Whereas the Fenians had seemed to
Cardinal Cullen and his colleagues to be infidels as well as
revolutionaries, the parliamentary allies of the Land League
demonstrated their acceptability by voting for the exclusion
of the atheist Bradlaugh from the House of Commons and by
supporting the demands of the Catholic Church on educational
matters. Sinn Féin was to show an equal anxiety to demonstrate its soundness on education and social policy.
Conflict between the Catholic Church and popular agita-

tions, then, was modified not only by the growing circumspection of the former but also by the social conservatism of the latter.

The different causes which might have contributed to the development of this social conservatism are too numerous and complex to be gone into here. One point, however, can be briefly mentioned. Professor Lee has drawn attention to the crucial difference between the agrarian agitations of the early nineteenth century and the land war of the 1880s. The former involved not merely conflict between landlord and tenant but also conflict between farmers on the one hand and cottiers and labourers on the other over employment, wages and the letting of land in conacre. The latter was to a much larger extent straightforward confrontation between tenant farmers and their landlords over the amount of rent to be paid. It would be unrealistic to interpret the activities of the Catholic clergy solely in terms of social class. At the same time it is easy to see how priests — themselves predominantly the products of farming backgrounds — were able to support the Land League in a way they could hardly have supported the Ribbonmen or the Terry Alts, even if the methods of the latter had been less violent. Behind this change in the social composition of agrarian unrest lay the changes which the famine and its aftermath had brought to the structure of rural Ireland. In the 1840s the cottier and labourer classes had outnumbered the tenant farmers. By the 1880s cottiers had almost disappeared from the Irish countryside, while the agricultural labourers were a depressed minority whose continued grievances no longer played a central part in agrarian unrest. No doubt it is correct to stress the positive side of the relationship between the Catholic clergy and the popular political movements of the later nineteenth century and after. But it would be wise to bear in mind also the possibility that if the famine had not so drastically altered the balance of classes in rural Ireland, then the Catholic Church might have found itself confronted by movements with which it could not so easily come to terms, and the subsequent history of relations between priests and people might well have been very different.

Priests, Church and People — Pre-Famine and Post-Famine

' ... ignorant, violent, intemperate, and as incapable of resisting the first impulse as savages.' The comments of Bishop Kinsella of Ossory, with which this book began, may also serve to introduce its conclusions. One might continue to quarrel with the bishop's choice of words, but the tone of his remarks need no longer cause surprise. From the point of view of the standards of decorum and morality which the church authorities were committed to upholding, as the three preceding chapters have made clear, the behaviour of large sections of the Catholic population of pre-famine Ireland left much to be desired. The practices of the pattern and the wake — even allowing for the exaggerations of contemporary observers — provided the occasion for what churchmen could only regard as dangerously uninhibited festivity, as well as for what they came increasingly to see as an equally unacceptable perpetuation of non-Christian supernaturalism; these practices, furthermore, were only part of a much broader range of popular amusement and tradition which attracted such disapproval. Public order was at all times precarious, menaced both by a widespread willingness to resort to violence and intimidation as a means of settling disputes or seeking redress of grievances, and by the equally bloody and even less comprehensible feuding of rival factions. Where sexual morality is concerned, it is true that Irish attitudes to extra-marital indulgence managed largely (although not entirely) to live up to the high claims made for them by contemporaries. But even this had to be set against other, less acceptable features of popular attitudes — notably the survival, in wake-games and elsewhere, of an older and much more open attitude to sexual expression, as well as a distinctly cavalier approach to the finer points of Catholic marriage law.

Against this lack of 'the civil virtues' the bishop had set the religious qualities of the people: 'There is no better Christian than the Irishman.' And there was undoubtedly some basis for this view. The absence of any significant tradition of popular irreligion among Irish Catholics, their deep attachment to basic Catholic rites of passage, their strong resistance in the first half of the nineteenth century to the missionary efforts of evangelical Protestants, must all have seemed in healthy contrast to the increasingly unsettling prospects faced by most churchmen in Britain and on the continent. As early as 1825 Bishop Doyle of Kildare and Leighlin could put forward a claim which was to become a favourite with later generations of churchmen, that the Irish were a people especially suited to religion:

> The Irish are, morally speaking, not only religious, like other nations, but entirely devoted to religion. The geographical position of the country, its soil and climate, as well as the state of society, have a strong influence in forming the natural temperament of the people; they are more sanguine than the English, less mercurial than the French; they seem to be compounded of both these nations, and more suited than either to seek after and indulge in spiritual affections. When it pleased God to have an Island of Saints upon the earth, he prepared Ireland from afar for this high destiny.[1]

On close examination, however, the superior religious character of the Catholic Irish turns out to have been very much a relative matter. The Catholic clergy may have succeeded in impressing on their congregations a strong sense of the importance of baptism and extreme unction. But with other supposedly compulsory aspects of Catholic religious practice they had been much less successful. Attendance at Sunday mass, confession and communion all frequently fell well below the canonical minimum; indeed, Sunday mass attendance in the mid-1830s appears to have been no higher than the attendance at churches of all denominations recorded in England and Wales in 1851.[2] And even more important than such quantitative failings is the evidence of a qualitative weakness in religious attitudes and practice. Orthodox Catholic doctrines shared their place in the lives of large sections of the Catholic population with magical beliefs of varying origins. Ideas of religious obligation appear to have been often crude and legalistic, with external deterrents being freely used by the church authorities to supplement internal constraints and imperatives. If popular custom and social attitudes diverged at many points from the model favoured by the Catholic clergy, the same was true of popular religion.

When these points are considered, it is not after all so surprising that the bishop should not have baulked at the term 'savage' in the way that his questioner obviously expected. But this is not to say that the question was well phrased. The word 'savage', apart from its pejorative overtones, carries with it the suggestion that what the church authorities confronted was an undisciplined society, where the problem was the lack of rules governing men's conduct. In fact, as should be clear from the foregoing chapters, the most serious problems encountered by the Catholic clergy were of precisely the opposite kind. To condemn or prohibit wakes or patterns, for example, was not just to regulate disorderly gatherings for amusement, but also to oppose the manifestations of an alternative supernaturalism which continued to play an important part in the lives of large sections of the Catholic population. It was also to set oneself up against a whole rhythm of work and leisure, extravagance and deprivation which, however at variance with the standards and outlook of Catholic churchmen, remained intimately related to the conditions of rural Irish society and to its level of economic development. To oppose faction-fighting, equally, was not just to prohibit random brawling, but to seek to discourage behaviour legitimised and even encouraged by a strong popular ethic of group loyalty and mutual obligation. Opposition to the activities of agrarian secret societies must have involved a similar conflict with popular traditions of solidarity, together with whatever political or subpolitical notions of rights and grievances justified these activities in the eyes of those involved. Most striking of all, the problem presented by clandestine marriage and the runaway match arose not from popular tolerance of sexual licence, but rather from the existence of an alternative set of rules and conventions, whose very strictness made it possible for them to be used to circumvent the Church's regulations.

In all the major areas of behaviour discussed in this book, then, the conduct which gave rise to most concern among Catholic churchmen turns out to have arisen less out of a simple lack of social discipline among their congregations than out of a conflict between the code of conduct which they were attempting to prescribe and other, equally well-defined standards of behaviour. To some extent one can talk of a popular culture, diverging in important respects from that represented by the Catholic Church and its clergy. This idea, it is true, should not be interpreted too literally. The Catholic population of pre-famine Ireland, as this study has more than once tried to emphasise, contained within it wide variations in social position, attitudes and behaviour. If one talks of a 'popular culture', therefore, it would be wrong to conceive of this as a body of beliefs, attitudes and customs actually coexisting in a clearly defined social group; the most one can hope to do is to abstract certain more or less distinctive characteristics which can then be said to have been present in differing degrees among different sections of the population. But the important point, however it is expressed, is that the disciplinary problems encountered by the church authorities of late eighteenth- and early nineteenth-century Ireland did not begin and end with the particular issues discussed in this book — with wakes, with patterns or with runaway matches and clandestine marriage — but involved a much broader divergence in social attitudes and standards of behaviour.

The first result of our explorations, then, has been to provide a somewhat clearer definition of the 'savagery' described by Bishop Kinsella. But what of the other side of the picture? If large sections of the Catholic population in this period went some way towards fitting a nineteenth-century definition of 'savages', to what extent did their clergy take on the corresponding role of missionaries, attempting to impose on that population what they regarded as more civilised attitudes and standards of behaviour? And, to the extent that they did take on such a role, how successful were their efforts?

Where the first of these questions is concerned, it would certainly be wrong to assume that all sections of the Catholic clergy were equally opposed to popular beliefs and practices of the kind discussed above. Studies of pre-famine Catholicism must of necessity rely heavily on official church sources – on pastoral letters, diocesan statutes, the correspondence found in episcopal archives. In doing so they run an obvious risk of mistaking the views of senior churchmen for those of the clergy as a whole. And in fact, where it has been possible to go beyond these sources to the attitudes and policies of the rank and file – most notably in the case of non-Christian supernaturalism, but also to some extent with matters of law and order – it has been clear that the outlook of the lower clergy was not always as far removed from that of their congregations as the tone of official pronouncements would suggest. Yet this point should not be exaggerated. Already by the second half of the eighteenth century, whatever the reservations of individual priests, a quite sharp conflict existed between church teaching, as transmitted from the bishops through the parish clergy, and popular attitudes and standards of behaviour. By the 1830s, furthermore, there were indications that changes in the training and social position of the lower clergy, and in the discipline to which they were subjected, had begun to bring their attitudes more closely into line with those of their ecclesiastical superiors, and in doing so to broaden the gap which separated the local pastor from large sections of his congregation.

Secondly, there is the question of the degree of success achieved by this mounting attack on unacceptable aspects of popular custom and tradition. Contemporary observers, as was seen in an earlier chapter, frequently maintained that the Catholic clergy of this period exercised an exceptional degree of influence over their congregations, and much of the evidence presented in this study would seem – at first sight at least – to bear this out. Thus there have been cases in which priests have appeared to demonstrate a remarkable degree of personal authority, single-handedly breaking up faction-fights, dispersing or pacifying unruly crowds, or scattering the revellers gathered at patterns, dances or other forbidden occasions. There have also been more general testimonials to the effectiveness of clerical action: the many tributes paid to the role of the Catholic clergy in preventing or minimising agrarian disturbances, for example, and the comments, from both approving and disapproving observers, on their part in bringing about the decline of wakes, patterns and other popular customs. But other evidence has not fitted in so well with the contemporary picture of a dominant priest-hood and a submissive flock. If there were cases where the Catholic clergy could command a remarkable obedience, there were others in which their prohibitions were ignored or evaded. The crowd assembled for a faction-fight did not always scatter at the appearance of a priest; men resisted clerical efforts to force them to marry women they had seduced; and couples refused marriage by their local priest turned instead to couple-beggars or to the clergy of the Established Church. More striking still are those cases in which congregations openly resisted clergymen appointed against their wishes, or in which the financial demands of Catholic priests and their opposition to popular agitations gave rise to demonstrations of hostility and sometimes to direct retaliation. Faced with such apparently irreconcilable opposites, it becomes easy to sympathise with the rather lame conclusion to which Edward Wakefield was driven in his account of 1812: 'In the course of my tour I remarked several instances of the unbounded influence which the priests have over the people; but I have also observed cases where they did not possess any.'[3]

The apparent contradictions in the evidence, however, should not in fact surprise. The relationship between priests and people in this period, it was suggested earlier, was the product not only of the peculiar social position of the Catholic clergy but also, and more important, of an au-thoritarian and deferential culture. From the outside such cultures will, by their very nature, appear to be ones in which social control, and the subordination of some men to others, is absolute and unchallengeable. That is the basis on which authority of this kind rests. But this does not mean that one should take such societies entirely at their own valuation by assuming that a genuine deference is in any way incompatible with the existence of conflict and even of periodic rebellion. Indeed, it might be suggested that the very nature of authority in societies of this kind, where social inequality is experienced essentially as a personal relationship, is particularly likely to give rise to a mixture of genuine submissiveness and of equally genuine resentment. In a society whose model of authority is derived from the patriarchal family it is hardly surprising that social conflict should have some of the characteristics of a family row. Thus a recent study of the use of anonymous letters as a form of social protest in eighteenth-century England has emphasised how, side by side with the ubiquitous expressions of consensus and deference normally taken as characteristic of this age, one must set evidence of a massive sense of grievance and a hatred of the rich and powerful.[4] In the same way one need see no necessary contradiction between examples of a total obedience to clerical authority and examples of rebellion against that authority, or between a genuine deference to the local priest and an equally genuine resentment of certain of his actions or privileges. No doubt detailed case studies would do much to demonstrate the precise combinations of circumstances — the personalities of both priest and laymen, the type of issue involved, differences in regional character and in the social structure of congregations — which contributed at different times to demonstrations of complete submission to the Catholic clergy and to instances of open defiance.

The outcome of efforts by clergymen to impose new attitudes and standards of behaviour on their congregations, however, cannot be discussed solely in terms of individual successes and failures. Some attempt must also be made to assess the long-term effects of these efforts, to ask how the sum total of such successes and failures affected the character of Irish society as a whole. And here it seems clear that, however spectacular the success achieved by isolated interventions, the overall influence exerted by the Catholic clergy was a very limited one. Clerical opposition to the pattern-day gatherings at holy wells, whose popularity had already begun to decline before 1845, had at best a partial success; clerical opposition to the waking of the dead, where signs of decline had yet to appear, remained largely ineffective. Agrarian violence, in spite of consistent condemnations, the application of major ecclesiastical censures and, from the 1820s, the active involvement of the local clergy in the maintenance of law and order, remained a major problem throughout this period. The other main source of rural violence, faction-fighting, also continued unabated up to the mid-1830s, and it owed its eventual decline not to the opposition of the Catholic clergy but to the determined campaign mounted against it by the newly formed Irish Constabulary after 1836.[5] Even the relative infrequence of extra-marital sexual relations in pre-famine Ireland, it was suggested in Chapter 5, was the result less of clerical influence than of other social pressures, while in the equally important area of marriage law the efforts of Catholic churchmen to apply their regulations once again met with only indifferent success.

This is not to suggest that clerical teaching and exhortation, combined with other efforts to impose a measure of discipline, were entirely without effect. In the case of agrarian violence, it was suggested earlier, the influence of the Catholic clergy, while apparently making little impression on those most deeply involved, may well have been a deciding factor in the case of individuals or districts poised on the borderline between quiescence and participation. In other areas too there can be little doubt that pre-famine Ireland, without the influence of the Catholic clergy, would have been a somewhat different society — more violent, less restricted in its sexual behaviour, exhibiting more vigorous traditions of popular magic and customary celebration. At the same time the most important single point to emerge from a consideration of the different areas of social life discussed in this study is the limited nature of the influence exercised by Catholic churchmen and the apparent absence of any significant progress in the task of bringing the behaviour of their congregations under tighter control. If the disciplinary problems encountered by the church authorities in the decades before the famine can indeed be described as resulting from the existence of a rival popular culture, then the inroads which they succeeded in making on that culture, over several decades of mounting effort, were remarkably unimpressive.

* * *

All this, of course, is in sharp contrast to the picture of the character and social influence of Irish Catholicism which is familiar to us from more recent times. The precise degree of influence wielded by the Catholic Church in contemporary Ireland remains the subject of much debate. At the very least, however, it would be difficult to deny that Ireland stands out among Western European societies for the exceptionally high levels of religious belief and practice observed among its population and for the prominent place which the Catholic Church and its clergy continue to occupy in most areas of social life. No doubt it is always dangerous to move from a detailed analysis of one period to what will inevitably be less well-founded generalisations about another. In this case, however, it would hardly be possible to conclude without some attempt to discuss the links between the Catholicism of pre-famine Ireland and that of the present day. This may be done by looking briefly at three developments of the period after the famine.

The first of these is a change in the tone of relations between individual priests and their congregations. Neither the lively tradition of anticlerical satire nor the willingness to resort to open demonstrations of hostility against offending clergymen noted in earlier chapters of this study appear to have had a parallel in later nineteenth-century Ireland. Professor John A. Murphy, surveying the development of relations between priests and people since the Reformation, suggests that an earlier relationship based on 'give and take' and a 'native independence of attitude' was replaced in the later nineteenth century by a new form of deference in which 'robust criticism of the clergy was replaced by private grumblings, respect became confused with obsequiousness'.[6] This is to state the contrast too starkly. Even in the early nineteenth century, as was seen earlier, relations between priests and people bore the marks of a strongly authoritarian culture. At the same time it can be agreed that the second half of the nineteenth century appears to have seen a strengthening of what had earlier been a real, but far from absolute, personal authority.

A growth in the personal authority of the individual priest, however, is a symptom rather than a cause. A second, and more important, development of the decades after the famine is in the area of popular religious behaviour. The background to this has already been outlined. Before the famine the Irish Catholic Church had operated under two serious disadvantages. The first was a general weakness of ecclesiastical discipline, reflecting both the results of prolonged disruption and of a semi-legal status and a certain lack of zeal on the part of its servants. The second was a constant shortage of manpower and material resources, reflecting the inability of large sections of the Catholic population to support a church establishment adequate to their needs. The results of these disadvantages were seen, among other places, in the nature of popular religious practice and in the restricted range of pastoral services provided by churchmen to the laity. In the second half of the nineteenth century both of these circumstances changed. Internal discipline, already greatly improved by the 1840s, was further tightened in the two or three decades that followed, while the drastic changes which the famine and its aftermath brought to the social structure of rural Ireland, along with the general prosperity of the succeeding period, left the Irish Church dependent for its support on a laity which was at the same time smaller in number and considerably more affluent. The result was to make possible the transformation of popular religious practice which Professor Larkin has labelled 'the devotional revolution'.

To put the matter in this way, of course, is to evade the most important question of all: Why was it, given this improvement in the general prosperity of the Catholic laity, that such a high proportion of its increased resources were devoted to the Catholic Church rather than to other purposes? Consideration of this issue clearly lies outside the scope of the present study. A partial explanation might be sought in the links which by this time had been quite firmly established between religious and political loyalties. Alternatively one might look, as in the case of Professor Larkin and Professor Miller, to the part played by Catholicism in resolving a 'crisis of identity' precipitated by the decline of traditional language and culture.[7] More prosaically it might be suggested that the Catholic Church, by virtue of its position in this newly emerging society, and in particular of its near-complete control of the educational system, was simply well placed to ensure that a substantial proportion of any increased resources would be directed towards itself. But whatever the precise reason — and the issues raised are in most cases of the broad and abstract kind which are unlikely ever to be open to proof or disproof — it is clear that the opportunity was seized. In the second half of the nineteenth century, at a time when churchmen elsewhere were coming to terms with falling church attendances and a growth in popular indifference, Irish Catholics moved in the opposite direction, developing the remarkably high levels of religious practice which continue to distinguish them today.

The implications of all this for the degree of influence which the Catholic clergy could hope to exercise over their congregations are obvious. In purely practical terms the continued tightening of ecclesiastical discipline, ensuring that regulations and policies would be more consistently and conscientiously put into operation, and the fact that a larger number of priests was now available to supervise a smaller Catholic population, would between them have made possible a more effective regulation of personal behaviour. More important, however, these developments affected the place which the Catholic Church and its doctrines occupied in the lives and minds of its adherents. In the new conditions of post-famine Ireland the claims of religion were presented to individuals more forcefully and from more directions than ever before as Irish Catholics came to participate in a remarkable variety of devotional practices, both public and private, and as they became exposed to an increasingly formidable display of external magnificence and grandeur from their church. More important still, it was during this period that the Catholic laity came for the first time to be thoroughly instructed in the doctrines of their church. The limited influence of the Catholic clergy in pre-famine Ireland, it was suggested earlier, was in part a result of the crude and narrow terms in which many Irish Catholics conceived of the obligations imposed by religion. In the later nineteenth century the way was clear for this outlook to be replaced by a receptiveness to forms of influence which were at once more subtle and more penetrating.

It is necessary to emphasise this point, because discussions of the role of Catholicism in modern Ireland have tended to pass directly from a consideration of the underlying social causes supposed to account for that role to the ultimate social effects, without pausing to consider what lies between. Various explanations, as already mentioned, can be offered for the continued vigour of Catholicism in modern Irish society, and there can be no doubt that that dominance has had effects which have extended far beyond the realm of religious belief and practice. But this should not be allowed to obscure the fact that Catholicism, as it presented itself both to its adherents and to its full-time servants, was first and foremost a religion, and that its influence can be fully understood only in terms of religious belief and emotion. Any analysis of the place and influence of the Catholic Church in modern Irish society will have to take account of such factors as the peculiar social position of the Catholic clergy and the links which had been established between religious and political allegiance. But when individual Irish Catholics responded to the influence of their church and its clergy, they did not do so just, or even mainly, because the priest was the best-educated man in the locality, or because religious and nationalist sentiments overlapped and reinforced one another. These things, after all, had been true even before 1845, without permitting the establishment of a particularly effective social discipline. Instead they responded as they did because they were people to whom the mental world of Catholic religious doctrine, with all the internal constraints and imperatives it embodied, had been communicated with exceptional thoroughness and power. The conventional stereotype of the Irish Catholic, we should remember, involves not only a willingness to cringe at a priestly frown but also a highly developed sense of personal guilt.

Side by side with this increase in the potential influence of the Catholic Church and its clergy must be set another, even more important development. The drastic changes which the famine and its aftermath had brought to the social structure and material circumstances of the Catholic population were reflected not only in the ability of Irish Catholics to support a much larger church establishment but also in their attitudes, customs and standards of behaviour. The extent to which this was so may be seen in the case of each of the areas of Irish social life examined in this book. On the eve of the famine the practice of celebrating patterns, along with other elements of non-Christian supernaturalism, while already showing the first signs of decline, remained a prominent part of Irish culture. In the two or three decades following, on the other hand, traditional beliefs and practices of this kind underwent a rapid decline, to be followed a little later by the abandonment of the festive wake. The virtual disappearance of such customs, it was suggested earlier, owed less to the continued opposition of the authorities of the Catholic Church than to changes in the outlook and aspirations of the Catholic laity as greater prosperity brought with it an increased openness to outside influences and new standards of propriety and respectability. In the same way it can be suggested that the regulation of marriage became significantly easier in the decades after the famine as the matchmaking system, already common among the farming classes, became both more rigid and more widespread. In addition, the famine brought a brutal end to the desperate struggles of the cottier, the landless labourer and the small occupier to maintain their posiion in an increasingly hostile world, and thus to the recurrent agrarian violence of the early nineteenth century. When agrarian discontent reappeared in the 1880s it was to be of a very different character, and the response of the church authorities, apart from some initial qualms, was to be correspondingly different.

What all three of these examples suggest is that the effect of the famine was not just to increase the resources available to the Irish Catholic Church, but also to leave it with a population which was from the start more docile and more manageable than that of pre-famine Ireland had been. The extent to which it was this development which lay behind the greater degree of influence apparently enjoyed by the Catholic clergy of the later nineteenth century and after is suggested by those cases where social change did not have the effect of bringing popular attitudes and standards so comfortably into line with those of the Catholic clergy. Thus the success enjoyed by Irish priests in their war against sexual immorality may be contrasted with the continued ineffectiveness of their opposition to drunkenness, where lay attitudes remained tolerant and where – as was argued earlier – something of the pre-famine pattern of social life continued into the later nineteenth century and beyond. The changing social basis of Irish discontent, similarly, may have made it easier for churchmen to reach an accommodation with popular agitation; but where areas of conflict remained, the authority of the Catholic clergy was repeatedly shown to be a limited one. However, these were the exceptions. If the main problems of social discipline encountered by the church authorities in pre-famine Ireland can be said to have arisen from the existence of a rival popular culture, then the famine and its aftermath largely destroyed that rival. In post-famine Ireland, more affluent, more prudent, and aspiring to new models of propriety, the Catholic clergy were to find a population far more amenable to the discipline they sought to impose.

The extent of the social changes brought by the famine should not, of course, be exaggerated. Landless labourers, though greatly reduced in number and as a proportion of the population, remained a significant minority within rural society. Along the congested districts of the west coast, equally, there were still large numbers of impoverished smallholders whose way of life remained in many ways reminiscent of that described by pre-famine observers. The social and cultural history of both these groups in later nineteenth-century Ireland remains to be properly explored. For the moment, however, it seems reasonable to suggest that the labourers, an impoverished and socially inferior minority, would not have been disposed to offer much resistance to penetration by the standards of their betters, and that the assimilation of both groups into what was now the majority culture was significantly accelerated by the steady extension of elementary education in the course of the nineteenth century.

In the period after the famine, then, two main developments combined to give the Catholic Church and its clergy the dominant position within Irish society which they have retained, to a large extent, down to the present day. The first was the growing effectiveness of Catholicism itself — Catholicism considered not just as a part of the structures of local power and influence, or as an auxiliary to nationalist politics, but as a religion, a system of beliefs, values and rules of behaviour supported by an appeal to supernatural realities. The second was social change, decimating those sections of the population whose behaviour had been the source of greatest concern to pre-famine churchmen, and bringing into being a new and more respectable society in which the Church's discipline was from the start more readily accepted. To the official representatives of Catholicism the resulting advances in the power and glory of their church could hardly appear as other than an unqualified triumph. But there was also another side of the picture. For the triumph of the post-famine Church was also the victory of one culture over another, and when modern Irish Catholicism came into its inheritance it did so only by means of the destruction of a rival world.

Appendices

APPENDIX A

The Social Structure of Rural Ireland

The figures in Table 1 are derived from three sources:

(1) The account of the number of persons occupying holdings of different sizes drawn up in 1845 from returns made by the Poor Law commissioners and printed in that year by the Devon Commission. The return gives a total of 935,000 holdings, of which Table 1 excludes 4,000 holdings which the commissioners failed to classify, and 70,000 holdings of one acre or less which were used as gardens rather than for general tillage.[1]

(2) The occupational data in the census of 1841, which included, under the heading of persons 'ministering to food', 453,000 farmers and a total of 1,128,000 labourers, servants, herdsmen, ploughmen and dairy-keepers.[2]

(3) The census of 1831, which returned a total of 567,000 labourers employed in agriculture, and 99,000 male servants, as well as 95,000 occupiers employing labourers and 564,000 occupiers not employing labourers.[3]

The figure for 'smallholders' used in Table 1 was obtained by subtracting the 453,000 farmers returned in (2) above from the 861,000 occupiers of land returned in (1). This left a total of 408,000 occupiers of holdings who were not of sufficient status to classify themselves, or to be classified by the census enumerators, as farmers.

Calculation of the number of labourers presents greater difficulties. The figure of 1,105,000 labourers (plus 23,000 herdsmen, ploughmen and dairy-keepers) given in the census of 1841 is unrealistically high. Two main reasons may be suggested for this: firstly, the inclusion as labourers of many — perhaps the great majority — of the 408,000 small occupiers just referred to, and secondly, the inclusion under the same heading of the adult sons and other male relatives of farmers. Some attempt might be made to estimate the number of male relatives returned as farmers, on the basis of the proportions returned in 1881, when such relatives were classified separately.[4] But there is no way of knowing what proportion of smallholders were weavers or tradesmen of other kinds, and what proportion were engaged solely in agriculture, and thus likely to be returned as labourers. For these reasons it was decided to go instead to the census of 1831, increasing the figures in (3) above by 5 per cent to allow for the growth of population between 1831 and 1841.

APPENDIX B

Statistics of Religious Affiliation
in Ireland in the
Eighteenth and Nineteenth Centuries

The first census of religious affiliation in Ireland was not taken until 1861. However, two earlier surveys provide some indication of the relative size of the different denominations.

(1) In 1732–33 the agents employed in the collection of the hearth tax were instructed to make a report of the religion of the families listed in their returns. They returned a total of 386,902 families, of which 105,501 were Protestant and 281,401 Catholic. On the basis of this return it was estimated that the Catholic population in that year amounted to 1,417,005, or 72 per cent of a total population of 1,979,810. The hearth-tax returns of this period were, however, seriously deficient and substantially understate the true number of houses in the country. K. H. Connell's estimate of total population in 1732–33, based on a revision of the hearth-tax figures to take account of their deficiencies, is 3,018,000. It is likely that the understatement affects the Catholic population more than other groups, since Catholics were more likely to live either in houses too poor for the collectors to concern themselves with or in areas too inaccessible or too inhospitable for accurate returns to be made. However, an upper limit on the degree to which the figures understate the relative as well as the absolute size of the Catholic population can be fixed by assuming that all the houses omitted from the return were Catholic ones. This would mean that the entire Protestant population was included in the 105,501 Protestant families returned by the collectors, so that Protestants – taking Connell's estimate of 5·2 persons per house in the mid-1730s – numbered 548,605, or 18 per cent of a total population of 3,018,000. Consequently it seems safe to assume that the Catholic share of total popula-

tion was somewhere between 72 and 82 per cent, and it is likely that it was at least two or three percentage points removed from either extreme.[5]

(2) In 1834 the Commissioners of Public Instruction attempted a survey of religious affiliations. Copies of the returns which had been made for the census of 1831 were sent back to the enumerators who had been employed on that census, with the request that they would fill in the religion of each person listed there. The enumerators were required to verify their returns on oath, but were not bound to visit each house in person as they had been in the taking of the original census. Instead, it appears, they were expected to list religious affiliations on the basis of their local knowledge, supplemented by any necessary inquiries. A public hearing was then held in each parish, at which the enumerator's return could be corrected or challenged by anyone who wished to do so. In some cases the local clergy, especially those of the Established Church, had prepared an original census of all or part of their parish, and where this was found on inquiry to be an accurate one it was adopted in place of the enumerator's return. Where no such census was forthcoming, the commissioners adjusted the figures supplied by the census enumerators to bring them up to date to 1834, using as a guide the changes in population recorded in the county concerned between 1821 and 1831, with allowances for any special local circumstances. The procedure adopted, and in particular the last-mentioned adjustments, make the resulting data inferior to a true census of religious affiliations. At the same time comparison of the proportion of Catholics and others returned in individual dioceses in 1834 and 1861 do not reveal any glaring discrepancies, suggesting that the commissioners' figures can be accepted as a reasonably accurate return.[6]

The estimates of total Catholic population used in Table 2 were obtained in the following ways:

1732–33 By taking the Catholic population as 76 per cent of a total population of 3,018,000, 76 per cent being chosen as a mid-point between the upper and lower levels of 72 and 82 per cent suggested above.

1800 By taking the Catholic population at 80 per cent of 5,400,000, the latter figure being arrived at by increasing Connell's estimate of 4,753,000 in 1791 by one-third of the difference between it and the total of 6,800,000 recorded in the census of 1821.

1834 Catholic population as estimated by the Commissioners of Public Instruction.

1840 By taking the Catholic population at 80 per cent of the 8,175,000 recorded in the census of the following year.

The figure for 1871 is the number of Catholics recorded in the census for that year.

APPENDIX C

The Number of Catholic Priests
1731–1871

The figures for the number of Catholic priests officiating in Ireland in 1731, 1800, 1835, 1840 and 1871 set out in Tables 2 and 3 were obtained in the following ways:

(1) The figure for 1731 is derived from a report on the state of popery in Ireland prepared in that year by a committee of the Irish House of Lords.[7] The report was based on returns made by the high sheriffs of counties, the principal magistrates in the towns, and the archbishops and bishops of the Established Church. The committee concluded 'that the number of mass houses in this kingdom (besides huts, sheds and moveable altars, of which above one hundred are returned) is 892; the number of private chapels is 54; the number of priests officiating in them and in private houses is 1,445; the number of friaries is 51; friars 254; nunneries 9; and the number of popish schools is 549'.

These figures are clearly less precise than those for later periods. Thus they do not state whether all of the 1,445 priests referred to were engaged in regular pastoral duties, or if any of the 254 friars were engaged in that capacity. The accuracy of the returns is also open to question. No figures were received from the diocese of Kerry or from various parishes in other dioceses, and even where returns were received it is likely that substantial numbers of clergymen were overlooked. In the case of friars it has been estimated that the number returned amounts to little more than one-third of the real figure. The part of the return relating to the secular clergy is probably more accurate, since the authorities were in general less hostile to that body, but it is likely that it too contains omissions. Consequently the total of 1,445 priests should be treated as a minimum figure rather than as an accurate count.

(2) Figures on the number of priests in Ireland in 1800 are provided in the return submitted to the government by the Catholic bishops at the beginning of 1801 in connection with proposals for a state provision for the Catholic clergy. When these returns were printed in 1849, in the fourth volume of the *Memoirs and Correspondence of Viscount Castlereagh*, they were accompanied by a short summary of the data they contained.[8] According to this summary, the number of parish priests returned by the Catholic bishops was 1,026, and the number of curates nearly 800, giving a total of 'upwards of 1,800 Roman Catholic clergymen in this kingdom, of whom 1,400 are seculars and 400 are regulars'. This version of the figures has been the one generally quoted by historians. Elsewhere in the summary, however, we are told that of the 400 regular clergy in Ireland 150 are employed as parish priests and curates, 187 are in religious houses, and about 60 are attached neither to parishes nor to religious communities. It follows that, if the figure of 1,800 Catholic clergymen includes all 400 regulars, the total number of parish priests and curates can be only in the region of 1,550. It should also be noted that the figure of 1,026 parish priests is improbably high by comparison with later figures. The compiler of the summary seems to have taken the total number of Catholic parishes, forgetting that there were 34 parishes held *in commendam* by the bishops of different dioceses and that there would always have been a few others temporarily vacant in the interval between the death or transfer of an incumbent and the appointment of a successor.

The task of deriving more accurate figures from the bishops' returns is complicated by the fact that there is no return for the diocese of Cork and that the return for Killaloe omits to specify the number of curates serving there. In the other five dioceses of the province of Cashel the number of curates increased from 136 in 1800 to 278 in 1835. The number of parish priests changed only slightly, from 221 in 1800 to 215 in 1835. Consequently it seems reasonable to assume that the number of parish priests in Cork in 1800 would have been roughly the same as that in 1835 and that the number of curates in Cork and Killaloe would have been roughly half the number there in 1835. On this basis the strength of the Catholic Church establishment in 1800 can be estimated at:

Archbishops and bishops	26
Parish priests	986
Curates	628
Regular clergy not employed in parishes	247
Total	1,887

(3) The figures for the number of Catholic parish priests and curates in 1835 are taken from a return furnished to the Commissioners of Public Instruction by the Catholic bishops in May 1835.[9] They exclude four regulars and two other clergymen in the diocese of Ossory and two priests in the diocese of Limerick, all of whom were returned as performing parochial work but who were not parish priests or curates.

(4) The figures for 1840 were obtained by counting the priests listed in the *Catholic Directory* of that year, and those for 1871 from a table printed in the same periodical.[10] Again the figures relate only to persons serving as parish priests or curates.

Notes

A Note on References

Full details of the primary and secondary sources cited in these notes appear in the bibliography. Wherever possible, books and articles have been cited simply by the author's name and the date of publication; where this might lead to ambiguity, further details have been added. References where the author's name is followed by 'ed.' are to edited and calendared documents, which are listed separately in Section B2 of the bibliography. References beginning *LC* (Lords' Committee) and *SC* (Select Committee) are to parliamentary papers. Other abbreviations which might not be easily identifiable are listed below.

Anal. Hib.	*Analecta Hibernica*
Arch. Hib.	*Archivium Hibernicum*
Cashel P	Cashel Diocesan Papers
Cath. Dir.	*Catholic Directory*
Clogher P	Clogher Diocesan Papers
Collect. Hib.	*Collectanea Hibernica*
DEP	*Dublin Evening Post*
HMC	Historical Manuscripts Commission
IFC	Irish Folklore Commission
IHS	*Irish Historical Studies*
JBI, JBII	James Butler I Papers, James Butler II Papers (subdivisions of Cashel Diocesan Papers)
JRSAI	*Journal of the Royal Society of Antiquaries of Ireland*
NLI	National Library of Ireland
OSL	Ordnance Survey Letters
OSM	Ordnance Survey Memoirs
Outrage P	Outrage Papers
PROI	Public Record Office of Ireland
PRONI	Public Record Office of Northern Ireland
Rep. Nov.	*Reportorium Novum*
RP	Rebellion Papers
SOC	State of the Country Papers
SPO	State Paper Office

Introduction
(pp. 1–5)
1. De Tocqueville (1958 trans.), 140–2.
2. Ibid., 136.

Chapter 1
PRE-FAMINE IRELAND: RELIGION AND SOCIETY
(pp. 6–23)
1. For a summary of the legislation and a discussion of its enforcement see Lecky (1892 ed.), I, 145–63. Wall (1961) confines itself almost entirely to the laws relating to the Catholic clergy. For a review of nineteenth- and twentieth-century writing on the subject see Burns (1959).
2. Lecky (1892 ed.), I, 255–65; MacGrath (1949); 'Report on the State of Popery', *Arch. Hib.* I–IV (1912–15); Giblin ed. (1966), 27, 37–8; Renehan ed. (1861–74), I, 102, 311–12; NLI, White MS, 113–14.
3. Wall (1961), 44–5, 67; Flood ed. (1913), 101; NLI, White MS, 153; Brady ed. (1965), 105, 108, 128; NLI, White MS, 184; O'Connell (1967).
4. Curran ed. (1956), 383; Thomas Hearn to Bray, 5 Nov. 1800 (Cashel P, Bray 1800/30); Coppinger to Bray, 3 Nov. 1800 (ibid., Bray 1800/28); Coppinger to Florence MacCarthy, Coadj. Bp Cork, 29 Dec. 1806 (Newenham MSS).
5. Butler (1787); Moylan to Bray, 28 Jul. 1796 (Cashel P, Bray 1796/21) – cf. Egan's own letter to Abp Butler of Cashel, n.d. [1784] (ibid., JBII 1784/2), and the account of the funeral of Bp Power of the same diocese in *DEP*, 6 Feb. 1816.
6. Meagher (1853), 63–4; Corish ed. (1972), 54, 62–3; (1974), 13.
7. Fenning ed., 'Two Diocesan Reports' (1972), 27; cf. MacMahon to Bray, 15 Nov. 1792 (Cashel P, 1792/22). For the origins of sectarian conflict in Ulster see Senior (1966), 1–38; Crawford & Trainor ed. (1969), 171–6.
8. Information of Daniel McCarthy, 5 May 1798 (RP 620/37/27); court martial of John Begley, 6 Sep. 1799 (ibid. 620/5/59/9); notes marked 'Michael Edwards, 28 Jan. 1798' (ibid. 620/35/71); court martial of John Kelly (ibid. 620/5/61/12); Pakenham (1972 ed.), 226–7, 290–3, 145–6, 153–4, 367–8; Thomas Shea, Mullingar, 6 Sep. 1798 (RP 620/40/24); statement of Michael Burke (ibid. 620/52/123) – cf. Teeling (1876), 315–16.
9. Resolutions passed at a meeting of the inhabitants of Belfast, 18 Aug. 1813 (SPO, OPMA 106/2/17); Baker (1973), 789–814.
10. Outrage P (1836) 27/402; ibid. (1837) 21/189; Zimmermann (1966), 44–5; pp. 109–10 below; Lewis (1836), 129ff.
11. Reynolds (1954); O'Donoghue (1966); Broderick (1951), 109–62 (quotation on p. 149); ballad impounded at Killimore market, Co. Galway, 12 Jul. 1843 (Outrage P (1843) 11/14217). This is not, of course, to suggest that politicisation was a uniform process, affect-

ing the entire Catholic population at the same time. For some discussion of class and regional variations see Hoppen (1977), 63—6, and, for the case of Ulster, Connolly (1981).

12. De Tocqueville (1958 trans.), 134, 151; Inglis (1834), I, 40—1; Hall (1841—43), II, 313; *SC Crime* (1839), 522, T. F. Uniacke; Corish ed. (1972), 48.
13. Shanin ed. (1971), 14—16, 239—45.
14. Carbery (1973 ed.), 8—10, 20; Cullen (1972), 112; Ó Laoghaire (1973 ed.), 1, 8; *Railway Commissioners, Second Report* (1837—38), 80—cf. pp. 18—19 below.
15. Murray (1971—72 ed.), 470.
16. *Railway Commissioners, Second Report* (1837—38), 80; table of wages in *Poor Inquiry* (1835—37), App. H, 12; ibid., App. H, Pt 2, 4—6.
17. Lee (1971), 191—5; *Poor Inquiry* (1835—37), App. H, Pt 2, 3, Bicheno.
18. Connell (1950); Crotty (1966), 12—65; Cullen (1972), 100—34.
19. *Poor Inquiry* (1835—37), App. H, 12; pp. 237—9 below.
20. *Railway Commissioners, Second Report* (1837—38), 5—6; Cullen (1972), 111—12, 130—1.
21. This estimate is based on the fact that the total number of persons returned in the census as labourers — a figure which, as is argued below (pp. 279—80), includes a considerable number of small occupiers as well as landless labourers — declined from 1,105,000 in 1841 to 718,000 in 1851.

Chapter 2
THE CATHOLIC CHURCH
(pp. 24—73)
1. William O'Brien, PP Clonakilty, to Florence MacCarthy, Coadj. Bp Cork, 24 May 1807 (Newenham MSS); *LC State of Ire.* (1825), 498—504. For a review of censuses of religion before 1861 see *Cen. 1861, Pt IV*, 1—5.
2. See Appendix B.
3. Simms (1956), 158—62; resolutions of the Catholic Committee, 5 Jul. 1809 (Cashel P, Bray 1809/6); *Burke's Peerage and Baronetage* (105th ed., London 1975), 1005, 2502; list of annual incomes of leading Irish Roman Catholics, *c.* 1780 (PRONI, D1514/1/5/40); Wakefield (1812), I, 276; II, 592—632; MacLysaght ed. (1942), viii—xii, 262.
4. Wakefield (1812), II, 630—2.
5. Wall (1958—59); Wall (1960); *LC State of Ire.* (1825), 136—7, 253; *Cen. 1861, Pt IV*, 715—25. For figures on the proportion of Catholics in trade in different towns I am indebted to Dr David Dickson, who allowed me to read his unpublished O'Donnell Lecture, 'Catholics and Trade in Eighteenth-Century Ireland'.
6. *Cen. 1861, Pt IV*, 701, 708, 715, 724; ibid., 10—12, 39, 41. For the social status of Ulster Catholics see Connolly (1981), and for

a more detailed description of social structure in general see pp. 15–20 above.

7. Pp. 20–1 above.

8. Wakefield (1812), II, 544–5; Outrage P (1835) 27/233; pp. 237–9 below. For tensions within the Catholic Committee see *Rep. Nov.* II, 1 (1958), 212–13; Lecky (1892 ed.), III, 23. The social composition of the campaigns for Emancipation and Repeal await detailed investigation, but see Hoppen (1977), 63–6.

9. Campbell (1778), 129–30; NLI, White MS, 121; D. McEniry, PP Borrisoleigh, to Bray, 17 Mar. 1796 (Cashel P, Bray 1796/6); E. Marnane to Bray, 13 Mar. 1808 (ibid., Bray 1808/3); Carbery (1973 ed.), 25.

10. Blake to Rev. William O'Brien, 19 Sep. 1833 (PRONI, T3371, p. 20); Power (1937), 206–7. For other disputes over pews see Carrigan (1905), I, 170; NLI, White MS, 121; Cashel P, Bray 1796/6–12, 14, 15; Crolly (1851), xxxviii–xxxix.

11. For comments on the number of priests in the first half of the eighteenth century see 'Report on the State of Popery', *Arch. Hib.* III (1914), 141; Fenning ed., 'Clerical Recruitment' (1972); Giblin ed. (1967), 90. For the complaints of Irish bishops in 1801 see *Castlereagh Corr.*, IV, 99, 123, 131, 136, 159, 160. For the number of regulars in the first half of the eighteenth century see Brady & Corish (1971), 40, and in 1800 p. 285 below. In 1836 the *Catholic Directory* estimated the number of regulars at about 500, but this was probably a considerable exaggeration.

12. John Power, Bp Waterford and Lismore, to Sir John Newport, 18 Apr. 1808, in *HMC Dropmore*, IX, 196.

13. *Castlereagh Corr.*, IV, 136. A detailed return compiled by the trustees of Maynooth in 1808 suggested a total of 476 students ('State of the Establishment on the Continent for the Education of the Irish Secular Roman Catholic Clergymen previous to the French Revolution', PRONI, D207/5/39 – cf. Healy (1895), 76–7, 696–7).

14. In Cloyne and Ross there were 77 parish priests and curates in 1771, compared with 83 in 1800; in Kerry 64 in 1785, compared with 75 in 1800; and in Cashel and Emly 71 in 1792, compared with 81 in 1800 (Moran ed. (1874–84), III, 339; O'Shea ed. (1974), 28–9; Cashel P, Bray 1792/21; *Castlereagh Corr.*, IV, 129, 122–3, 126). These figures – all admittedly for dioceses in Cashel province – suggest that clerical numbers around 1780 were no higher than in 1800. This would mean that clerical numbers had increased by 12 per cent or less in the fifty years since 1731, while population had grown by over 40 per cent.

15. Andrew Dunn to Sir John Newport, 8 Dec. 1806 (PROI, M483/12); *Maynooth Inquiry* (1826–27), 8–9. In 1853 the president of the college estimated that the number of students in Maynooth was twice that being educated in other institutions, while ten years before the same number of students had been educated outside

Maynooth as within it. Since there were 519 students on the books of the college in 1853, and 438 in 1844, this would suggest a total number of 780 students in the former year and 876 in the latter (*Maynooth Inquiry* (1854—55), Evidence, 223, App., 50). But the president was probably exaggerating the extent to which the number of clerical students in rival institutions had declined.

16. *Castlereagh Corr.*, IV, 123, 131.
17. *Irish Priests* (1821), 9; *SC Disturbances* (1825), 150, Maj. G. Warburton; *LC State of Ire.* (1825), 569, Rev. M. O'Sullivan; Wakefield (1812), II, 559; Croker (1824), 327—8; *SC Disturbances* (1825), 194, W. H. Newenham; Inglis (1834), II, 341—2. See also the letter from a priest of the diocese of Cork — identified elsewhere (see Murphy (1965), 120) as a Dr Walsh — printed in Townsend (1810), App., 90.
18. *Maynooth Inquiry* (1826—27), 433; *Maynooth Inquiry* (1854—55), Evidence, 42; *Maynooth Inquiry* (1826—27), 58; Power to Newport, 18 Apr. 1808, in *HMC Dropmore*, IX, 196; de Tocqueville (1958 trans.), 174.
19. Dunn to Newport, 8 Dec. 1806 (PROI, M483/12); *Maynooth Inquiry* (1826—27), 56—8; Ó Laoghaire (1973 ed.), 24, 28—30.
20. *Maynooth Inquiry* (1826—27), 8, 56; Michael Blake, Bp Dromore, to Michael Montague, President of Maynooth College, 10 Sep. 1834 (PRONI, T3371, p. 79).
21. *Papers relating to Maynooth* (1812—13), 6—27.
22. *Cath. Dir.* (1841), 393; Giblin (1971), 9—14; *Hibernian Journal*, 4 Nov. 1774, in Brady ed. (1965), 168; Michael Daly, President of St Patrick's College, Lisbon, to Bray, 1 Apr. 1795, 27 Jun. 1795 (Cashel P, Bray 1795/11, 23); 'State of the Establishment on the Continent . . .' (PRONI, D207/5/39); petition of Edmund Derry, PP Rathfriland, Co. Down, in favour of Rev. Bernard Magennis, 6 Jun. 1800 (RP 620/9/100/6).
23. *DEP*, 15 Nov. 1788, in Brady ed. (1965), 262; for the trade of couple-beggar followed by Fay and others see pp. 200—7 below. Townsend (1810), App., 90; Joseph King, Cork, to —, Mar. 1809 (PRONI, D207/5/20); *LC State of Ire.* (1825), 155. For the number of priests ordained from Maynooth in the first years of its existence see *Papers relating to Maynooth* (1812—13), 6—27.
24. See Murphy (1969), 251.
25. Hall (1841—43), II, 279—80; *LC State of Ire.* (1825), 482, C. of I. Abp Dublin; Inglis (1834), II, 339—40; *LC Disturbances* (1825), 86, Maj. G. Warburton; *SC Disturbances* (1825), 100, Maj. Richard Willcocks. For an observer who was less likely than most to speak from simple prejudice see the comments of John O'Donovan in OSL Down, 6—7.
26. *Maynooth Inquiry* (1826—27), 127, Rev. P. J. Carew, Professor of Latin and Greek; *SC State of Ire.* (1825), 128—9, O'Connell; *Maynooth Inquiry* (1826—27), 60—2; Corish ed. (1973), 2.

27. Healy (1895), 283—7; *SC State of Ire.* (1825), 129; Hall (1841—43), II, 285n; *Maynooth Inquiry* (1826—27), 14; Maguire (1898 ed.), 13—14.

28. *Maynooth Inquiry* (1826—27), 13, 119; Healy (1895), 286; Noonan (1967), 477; Fitzpatrick (1880 ed.), I, 142.

29. *Maynooth Inquiry* (1826—27), 8—9, 51—2; *Maynooth Inquiry* (1854—55), Report, 34, App., 132.

30. Printed in *Castlereagh Corr.*, IV, 97—173. The return was requested from Troy in Oct. 1800 and seems to have been passed on by him to his fellow-archbishops, who then communicated it to their suffragans: see Cashel P, Bray 1800/25, 26, 28, 29, 30.

31. *Castlereagh Corr.*, IV, 138, 153, 157; OSM 21/II/1 (1835), 39; Clogher P, 1/9A.

32. Townsend (1810), App., 86; see also Wakefield (1812), II, 561; *Poor Inquiry* (1835—37), App. D, 96, 97, 108—10. For priests with agricultural holdings see Moran ed. (1874—84), III, 598; Cashel P, Everard Visitation Book, 24; Whyte (1962), 20.

33. *Castlereagh Corr.*, IV, 99, 154; *LC State of Ire.* (1825), 369, John Keily, PP Mitchelstown, Co. Cork. For evidence that dues made up half of total parochial revenues see *Castlereagh Corr.*, IV, 124 (diocese of Cashel); *LC Disturbances* (1825), 128, Malachi Duggan, PP Moyferta, Co. Clare.

34. *LC State of Ire.* (1825), 369; ibid., 256; *SC State of Ire.* (1831—32), 197; *LC State of Ire.* (1825), 66; *SC State of Ire.* (1825), 82; Larkin (1967), 859; Larkin (1972), 634.

35. *Castlereagh Corr.*, IV, 123, 131, 137, 157; ibid., IV, 99, 121; *SC State of Ire.* (1825), 83; *LC State of Ire.* (1825), 67. See also *SC State of Ire.* (1825), 169; *SC Disturbances* (1825), 118.

36. *Castlereagh Corr.*, IV, 97—8; James Browne to Christopher Boylan, 10 Mar. 1828 (Clogher P, 1/5C/2); Moylan to Bray, 16 Aug. 1793 (Cashel P, Bray 1793/28); Nihill to Bray, 29 Jul. 1793, 6 Oct. 1794 (ibid., Bray 1793/27, 1794/15); Dillon to Bray, 7 Dec. 1799 (ibid., Bray 1799/15); *LC State of Ire.* (1825), 255, 231; *SC State of Ire.* (1825), 185; de Tocqueville (1958 trans.), 133, 145.

37. Akenson (1971), 87, 94; *SC State of Ire.* (1825), 344—7, Rev. Henry Cooke.

38. *SC Disturbances* (1825), 112; *LC Disturbances* (1825), 194, W. H. Newenham; de Tocqueville (1958 trans.), 162—3.

39. De Beaumont (1839), II, 89; *SC Disturbances* (1825), 161; Connell (1968), 86.

40. Townsend (1810), App., 88; *LC State of Ire.* (1825), 369, John Keily, PP Mitchelstown, Co. Cork. It is perhaps significant that around this time Keily found himself under attack for refusing to take part in the collecting of the 'Catholic rent' (ibid., 368).

41. Pp. 42—3 above.

42. Pp. 243—51 below.

43. *SC Crime* (1839), 837, John Cahill, Crown Prosecutor, Co. Tip-

perary. For examples of this role see O'Neill (1973), 135—6; petition by farmers of Ballynoe, Co. Kerry, to their landlord, William Stoughton, 11 Jan. 1846 (PROI, Relief Commission Papers, Co. Kerry II/1/407).

44. Bicheno (1830), 184 — cf. Wakefield (1812), II, 565. For the purely practical reasons for the political prominence of the Catholic clergy see Whyte (1960), 248—51.

45. Young (1892 ed.), II, 53—6; Wakefield (1812), II, 773; Arensberg & Kimball (1968 ed.), 55—6; Whyte (1971), 21—3. For the reality which lay behind Young and Wakefield's comparisons with contemporary England see Thompson (1968 ed.), chap. 4; Thompson (1978), 165 and passim.

46. Guinan (1906 ed.), 66; de Tocqueville (1958 trans.), 163; *SC State of Ire.* (1825), 459, O'Sullivan; *LC State of Ire.* (1825), 570, idem; *SC State of Ire.* (1825), 702, Col. John Irwin, magistrate, Co. Sligo; Outrage P (1838) 11/156, 21/115. Wakefield observed in his journal for 1808 that the Parish Priest of Castlepollard, Co. Westmeath, 'beats his parishioners into respect for their clergy when they displease him, and they submit to this treatment without the least grumbling' (1812, II, 626 — cf. II, 610, 612, 555). O'Donovan, writing from Inishmore, Aran Islands, Co. Galway, in August 1839, recorded that because the owner of the inn in which he was staying had been drunk and quarrelsome the night before, 'he was after getting a beating from the priest, who deemed it his duty to beat him into something like rationality' (OSL Galway, III, 248).

47. Visitation diary (1753) in Flood ed. (1913), 101—5.

48. Visitation records (1780) in Cogan (1862—70), III, 27—44.

49. Bossy (1971); Millett (1968).

50. Wall (1961), 15—19, 36—7; Brady & Corish (1971), 7—8.

51. Giblin ed. (1966), 14—15, 35—7, 46—7.

52. Presentation of Charles Sughrue to the parish of Killarney, 4 Sep. 1797 (Cashel P, Bray 1797/19); Lord Kenmare to Bray, 22 Feb. 1793 (ibid., Bray 1793/6). For cases of a disputed right of presentation see Nihill to Bray, 6 Oct. 1794 (ibid., Bray 1794/15); Carrigan (1905), I, 167—8; Faulkner (1977). For the consideration shown to the wishes of a local magnate see Lord Donoughmore to Bray, 20 Aug. 1796 (Cashel P, Bray 1796/24); same to same, 18 Sep. 1796 (ibid., Bray 1796/28); see also ibid., Bray 1796/26, 34. Sheil's comment in *SC State of Ire.* (1825), 102.

53. NLI, White MS, 143—8; 'A Statement of the Facts Connected with the Rebellion of East Aughnamullen', 31 Dec. 1844 (Clogher P, 1/10B/3); Patrick Bellew to Charles McNally, 21 Jul. 1836 (ibid., 1/10A/9); Cogan (1862—70), III, 148—76; P. J. Murphy (1973), 127—8. For other examples see 'Report on the State of Popery', *Arch. Hib.* II (1913), 112; Cashel P, Bray 1795/12, 1796/35, 1800/2 (cf. de Latocnaye (1917 ed.), 128); O'Rorke (1878), 492—4; O'Laverty (1878—95), III, 328—9; IV, 500; Begley (1938),

468; William Byrne to Laffan, 23 Mar. 1832 (Cashel P, Laffan 1832/3).

54. For non-residence in the 1730s see Giblin ed. (1962), 123–4; (1966), 30–2, 49–59. For complaints at other times see letter of Benedict XIV (1746) in Brenan (1864 ed.), 557–60; Giblin (1971), 43–6; Brady & Corish (1971), 31; Wall (1961), 41; Curran ed. (1955), 155; Fenning ed. (1966), 59–62, 65. For O'Shaughnessy see Carrigan (1905), I, 155, and for Blake see Whelan (1970).

55. For Bellew see Troy to Bray, 19 Sep. 1809 (Cashel P, Bray 1809/23); Moylan to Bray, n.d. [1809] (ibid., Bray 1802/16); Hoban (1972). For Dunboyne see Kingston (1961–62), 62–82. For Delany see Fitzpatrick (1880 ed.), I, 126–7. Fitzpatrick notes that readers of the first edition of his biography objected to these comments on Delany, but quotes in his own defence a letter from a priest, a relative of the bishop, who tells him that there is nothing in his account 'that could offend the most fastidious admirer of Doctor Delany' (ibid., I, 128–9n).

56. Pastoral letter [*c.* 1770] in Curran ed. (1958), 151–2; pp. 70–1 below.

57. Bicheno (1830), 180. For examples of priests accused of sexual immorality see P. J. Murphy (1973), 129–30; Larkin (1972), 627–8; and the case of Patrick Scanlan (p. 62 above).

58. Bicheno (1830), 190–1; Wakefield (1812), II, 555; J. Carroll to Troy, 11 Aug. 1788, in Moran ed. (1874–84), III, 505. See also Carleton (1968 ed.), 235; Cogan (1862–70), III, 52–3, 248–9; Curran ed. (1955), 160; O'Dwyer ed. (1976–77), 64.

59. Croly (1834), 30; Fitzpatrick (1880 ed.), I, 104, 286. For another hunting priest see O'Laverty (1878–95), I, 376. McGrath ed. (1928–31), II, 363, 361; ibid., I, 279–81. See also ibid., I, 287, 311; II, 27, 125, 299, 349, 367; III, 9.

60. Carleton (1852 ed.), II, 139, 'Denis O'Shaughnessy Going to Maynooth'; minutes of diocesan synod, 23 May 1861 (Clogher P, 1/12/3); *LC State of Ire.* (1825), 369, John Keily, PP Mitchelstown, Co. Cork; regulations of the bishops of Cashel province (1808) in *Cashel Statutes* (1813), 130; *Ardagh Statutes* (1834), 56; *SC Disturbances* (1825), 291, John Dunn, Queen's Co.

61. Giblin ed. (1966), 8–11; (1962), 16–17; (1967), 99–101; Whelan (1970); Ó Dufaigh (1968); Bowen (1970), 54–65; Cashel P, Bray 1809/23, 30, 37.

62. Young to Bray, 5 Nov. 1796 (Cashel P, Bray 1796/34). See also Moylan to Bray, 28 Jul. 1796 (ibid., Bray 1796/21); same to same, 4 Aug. 1796 (ibid., Bray 1796/22); Moylan's comments on the next occasion on which this diocese became vacant (Moylan to Bray, 15 Feb. 1804, ibid., Bray 1804/2); Coppinger to Laffan, 3 Jan. 1827 (ibid., Laffan 1827/1).

63. For reform in the Church of Ireland see Akenson (1971), chaps 1–2.

64. Fitzpatrick (1880 ed.), I, 104–15, 126–9, 138–43, 283–91, 463.

65. Plunket's letter in Larkin (1962), 298—300; Ó Dufaigh (1968);
    Meagher (1853), esp. 32—50; Dillon to Bray, 6 Aug. 1799 (Cashel
    P, Bray 1799/9); Troy to Bray, 19 Sep. 1809 (ibid., Bray 1809/
    23).
66. Meagher (1853), 127*—30*; Ahern (1952), 3—4; Cunningham
    (1970), 1 n. 3.
67. Ahern (1951), (1952); Barry (1959).
68. Cullen to Fransoni, 17 Jan. 1853, in Mac Suibhne ed. (1961—77),
    III, 157; see also Cullen's comments on the bishops of Tuam
    province in 1851 (ibid., II, 107—8; III, 99—100). For the state of
    Tuam in MacHale's last years see Corish ed. (1972), 31, 80—93.
    For brief but useful accounts of Cullen's role in introducing
    stricter standards of internal discipline see Norman (1965), 4—12;
    Lee, *Modernisation* (1973), 42—9; Larkin (1972).

Chapter 3
POPULAR AND OFFICIAL RELIGION
(pp. 74—134)

1. Troy to J. Joyce, 3 Oct. 1792, in MacLysaght ed. (1944), 65—6;
   Cen. 1861, Pt IV, 7.
2. Report of Bp of Elphin (1753) in Fenning ed., 'Two Diocesan
   Reports' (1972), 24; O'Dwyer ed. (1976—77), 3—40; Wakefield
   (1812), II, 617, 626; Mason (1814—19), I, 458; III, 631; Doyle
   (1825), 73—4; *LC State of Ire.* (1825), 285, Sir John Newport.
3. For a full account see Bowen (1970); Bowen (1978).
4. Text of 'An Sotach 's a Mháthair' in *Béaloideas* VI, 2 (1936),
   316—26; Mercier (1962), 176—81; pp. 156—7 below. See also,
   for more recent evidence of what appears to be a survival of the
   same tradition in a particularly isolated community, Messenger
   (1969), 90—1.
5. Thomas (1973 ed.), 189—206; OSL Fermanagh, 51.
6. *Cen. 1861, Pt IV*, 38—41; *Cen. 1841*, xxxii—xxxvi, 438—9.
7. Wall (1958), 109—11.
8. Cashel statutes (1782) in Renehan ed. (1861—74), I, 478; Ó
   Maolagáin ed. (1946), 63; *Dublin Statutes* (1831), 119—22; *SC
   State of Ire.* (1825), 198—9, Doyle; P. Ó Súilleabháin (1963),
   31—6; O'Dwyer ed. (1975), 60—73; Bicheno (1830), 173; p. 59
   above; Meagher (1853), 33—4; Fitzpatrick (1880 ed.), I, 109; Larkin
   (1962), 299.
9. *Cen. 1851*, xlvi—xlviii; Mason (1814—19), I, 198; II, 113 and
   passim.
10. Jones (1952), 32; Kernan to McDermott, 4 Nov. 1828 (Clogher P,
    1/5A/26); Dillon to Bray, 7 Dec. 1799 (Cashel P, Bray 1799/15);
    Bray to Moylan, 26 Oct. 1802, in Bolster ed. (1971), 125. See also
    the complaints of Bp MacDonough of Killaloe (1748) in Moran
    ed. (1874—84), III, 162—4.
11. MacMahon to Charles O'Kelly, 5 Jun. 1792, in Fenning ed., 'Two
    Diocesan Reports' (1972), 26—7; Ó Súilleabháin (1959), I, 145—50,

189–247. For the Ursuline convent, Cork, see Milner (1808), 176, and for St Finian's see Bp Plunkett's letter to the Catholic Association, 27 May 1824, in Brady ed. (1941), 235.

12. *Education Inquiry, Second Report* (1826–27), 17–18, 46–7; *Cen. 1861, Pt IV*, 50–3. The Education Inquiry printed two sets of returns, received from the Catholic and the Anglican clergy. However, they amended each set by adding schools omitted there but included in the returns of the other denomination, and the two sets of figures differ only slightly. The figures cited here are in all cases those of the Catholic clergy.

13. The total number of Catholic children returned as attending day schools in 1824 was 397,212. From this must be deducted 29,964 children attending schools of the Kildare Place Society, 17,656 attending schools of the London Hibernian Society, and 33,847 attending Catholic day schools, as well as smaller numbers attending other schools run by societies or boards.

14. O'Dwyer ed. (1975), 68, 69, 73; (1976–77), 5, 31, 39; *Education Inquiry, First Report* (1825), 810–13, Cooke; Fitzpatrick (1880 ed.), I, 176; Ó Súilleabháin (1959), I, 310.

15. Dublin statutes (1730) in Moran ed. (1874–84), III, 147; *Cork Statutes* (1768), 20; *Ardagh Statutes* (1834), App., i–ii, *Education Inquiry, First Report* (1825), 88; Hall (1813), II, 107–8.

16. *SC State of Ire.* (1825), 198; Ó Súilleabháin (1959), I, 312–14; resolutions of the bishops of Cashel province, Oct. 1789 (Cashel P. JBII 1789/6); Cogan (1862–70), III, 276; *Education Inquiry, First Report* (1825), 88.

17. Butler to Plunkett, 18 Jun. 1780, in Cogan (1862–70), III, 24; OSL Mayo, I, 201; Carleton (1862 ed.), I, 167, 'The Station'.

18. Akenson (1970), chap. 5; Murphy (1971), 12ff; Cullen to Fransoni, Sep. 1851, in Mac Suibhne ed. (1961–77), III, 90; *Comm. Nat. Ed. Report 37* (1871), 12–17; Moriarty to Kirby, 1 Sep. 1859, quoted in O'Shea (1971), 113.

19. Paul-Dubois (1908), 492–3; figures for Austria, France, Italy and other European countries in Mol (1972), 52, 179, 313 and passim; Irish figures in Nic Giolla Phádraig (1976).

20. Milner (1808), 57–8; Mason (1814–19), I, 456. See also *SC State of Ire.* (1825), 441, Col. J. S. Rochford.

21. Miller (1975).

22. This figure is inevitably a somewhat arbitrary one. Children too young to attend mass would have included all those under 5 (15 per cent of total population in 1841) and perhaps half those aged between 6 and 16 (25 per cent of total population in 1841). Some of these children would in fact have attended mass, but against them can be set adults who were unable to attend owing to illness, old age or unavoidable domestic chores.

23. *Poor Inquiry* (1835–37), App. A, 357, 380, 434, 436n, 440, 669. See also *SC Disturbances* (1825), 207, Malachi Duggan, PP Moyferta, Co. Clare; OSM 21/II/2 (1825) (Clonavaddogue, Co.

Donegal). For compulsory church collections see *SC Disturbances* (1825), 359, Michael Collins, PP Skibbereen, Co. Cork; Kohl (1844), 184—5.

24. Meagher (1853), 107. For further comment on Professor Miller's argument see pp. 119—20 below.

25. Cogan (1862—70), III, 37; Troy to his clergy, 15 Jan. 1780, in Moran ed. (1874—84), III, 373—4; Cashel P, Everard Visitation Book, 10, 13—15, 25, 32, 33, 35; ibid., Laffan Visitation Book, 3, 7, 14, and 20, 21, 29, 31 Jul., 10, 18 Aug. 1828.

26. For baptism see Connolly (1979), 10 n. 17. For extreme unction see Bicheno (1830), 183; Hall (1841—43), I, 221—2. For marriage see pp. 200—13 below. For confirmation see Fitzpatrick (1880 ed.), I, 127—8; *Cath. Dir.* (1841), 387, 264; Mark Tierney, *Croke of Cashel: The Life of Archbishop Thomas William Croke, 1823— 1902*, Dublin 1976, 83 (I am indebted for this reference to Mr Colm Croker); Corish ed. (1973), 47; Cullen to Fransoni, 28 Sep. 1851, in Mac Suibhne ed. (1961—77), III, 99.

27. Ó Súilleabháin (1966), 74—5; *Cath. Dir.* (1847), 344; *Cashel Statutes* (1813), 284ff; *Cath. Dir.* (1841), 278. For other examples see *Cath. Dir.* (1836), 37—8; ibid. (1847), 261—3; PRONI, T3371, pp. 32, 51, 55, 60.

28. Hosp (1975), 269; Ahern (1952), 5; P. F. Moran to Rev. James Taylor, 19 Jan. 1853 (reporting the comments of a former president of a Catholic seminary in Philadelphia), in Mac Suibhne ed. (1961—77), III, 160.

29. *Comm. Public Instruction, First Report* (1835), App. II, 66; OSM 35/II/2 (1835), 77; *Comm. Public Instruction, First Report* (1835), 129a—155a, 261a; see also Carleton (1968 ed.), 43. For church-building in the early nineteenth century see Kennedy (1970), 1—15, and (for Carlow cathedral) de Tocqueville (1958 trans.), 134. For the state of Catholic chapels see *SC State of Ire.* (1825), 255—6, Oliver Kelly; *LC State of Ire* (1825), 453, T. Browne; *SC State of Ire* (1825), 288, James Magauran; ibid. 299, Col. W. S. Currey; *SC Disturbances* (1825), 359, Rev. Michael Collins; *LC State of Ire.* (1825), 429, Earl of Kingston.

30. See pp. 58—9, 70 above; Fahey (1893), 416—17; Dillon to Bray 17 Apr. 1799 (Cashel P, Bray 1799/3); de Tocqueville (1958 trans.), 168—9; Carbery (1973 ed.), 25—6.

31. For baptism and marriage in private houses see Croly (1834), 36; Rev. Richard Wright to Bray, 23 Mar. 1811 (Cashel P, Bray 1811/8). Stations were opposed both because of objections to the socialising for which they provided the opportunity, and because it was considered undesirable that the sacraments should be administered in such a setting. For the former objection see p. 67 above, and for the latter see Larkin (1972), 636—7. See also Ahern (1952), 4—6; Barry (1959), 138—44; *SC Births, Deaths and Marriages Bill* (1861), 32, P. D. O'Regan, PP Kanturk, Co. Cork; Mac Suibhne ed. (1961—77), III, 152; Corish ed. (1972),

78; (1973), 14—15, 51; (1974), 59.

32. Croke quoted in Tierney (1966), 45; Comerford (1883—86), II, 235. For chapels used as schoolhouses see *SC State of Ire.* (1825), 258, 289, Abp Kelly, James Magauran, Bp Ardagh and Clonmacnoise; Mason (1814—19), III, 291—2, 391—2. Carleton (1862 ed.), I, 121, 'The Battle of the Factions'; Cogan (1862—70), III, 27—44; Joyce (1910), 196.

33. Larkin (1972); Paul-Dubois (1908), 477—8. For church-building see also Larkin (1967), 864—5.

34. Campbell (1778), 281; Croker (1824), 78ff; Donaldson (1923 ed.), 72—3; Carr (1806), 264—5; OSM 10/IV/3 (1837), 26 (Duneane, Co. Antrim); ibid., 29/II/6 (1835) (Aghanboo, Co. Londonderry); Kohl (1844), 38—9; Danaher (1972), 123—4 (quoting *Morning Post,* Jul. 1826); Outrage P (1837) 3/87; Hall (1841—43), III, 248—9n (citing *Tipperary Constitution,* 10 Apr. 1840). For the case of Bridget Cleary see *Irish Times,* 26, 27, 28 Mar., 2 Apr. 1895; Byrne (1967), 56—67.

35. Ó Súilleabháin (n.d.), 18, 24, 65—7; Danaher (1972), 109—15; Wilde (1852), 54—9; Carbery (1973 ed.), 158—9; Croker (1824), 93—4; Donaldson (1923 ed.), 74; Ó Coindealbháin (1946), 158; OSL Mayo, I, 98; Lewis (1837), II, 24—5.

36. For the continental stereotype of witchcraft see Cohn (1975), esp. 99—102. For witchcraft in Tudor and Stuart England see Macfarlane (1970), chap. 15; Thomas (1973 ed.), chap. 17.

37. Ó Súilleabháin (n.d.), 8—9; Croker (1824), 82—3; Outrage P (1836) 14/195; ibid. (1842), 21/20467, J. MacDonnell, 28 Oct. 1842; Donaldson (1923 ed.), 75—6; Evans (1957), 304. The statutes of the diocese of Cloyne and Ross in 1755 condemned 'the curing of alleged strokes and arrows by the spirits of the air or ghosts or certain fairies which our country people imagine' (quoted in Manning (1976), 79n).

38. OSL Kilkenny, II, 11; ibid. Roscommon I, 25; II, 173; ibid. Monaghan, 34—5; ibid. Mayo, I, 173; ibid. Galway, I, 52—3; Mason (1814—19), III, 163—4. See also Smith (1815 ed.), I, 185—6; Edward Willes to Sally Wise [*c.*1759] (PRONI, Mic. 148); Armstrong *et al.* (1922); Carrigan (1905), III, 440—1; IV, 38.

39. Danaher (1972), passim. The relationship between the major festivals and the cycle of the agricultural year is stressed in Miller (1975). For a discussion of his views see pp. 119—20 below. For other useful accounts of Irish calendar custom see Ó Súilleabháin (n.d.), 61—73; Wilde (1852), 36—67; 'Omurethi' (1906—8); as well as MacNeill's massive study of the festival of Lughnasa (1962).

40. Lewis (1837), II, 310; Townsend (1810), 91; OSL Galway, III, 69—70; Carbery (1973 ed.), 158.

41. Wilde (1852), 28; McGrath ed. (1928—31), II, 133—5; III, 5—7, 155; Carbery (1973 ed.), 158.

42. OSL Roscommon, I, 97; ibid. Offaly, I, 28; Hall (1841—43), III, 237; Introduction (written in 1849) to Wilde (1852), 10—11.

43. Danaher (1972), 13–37, 230–2 and passim; MacNeill (1962).
44. 'Pastorini' (1820 ed.); *St Columbkille's Sayings* (1844). For the widespread circulation of prophecies see, e.g., *SC Disturbances* (1825), 65, 93, 143–5, 311; *LC Disturbances* (1825), 7, 82. See also Carleton (1862 ed.), I, 16, 'Ned M'Keown'; *Trial of Edward Browne and Others* (1822), 80–1. For prophecy in England and among Ulster Presbyterians see Thompson (1968 ed.), 127–30, 420–6, 878–82; Miller (1978).
45. Danaher (1972), 19, 22, 139; Ó Súilleabháin (n.d.), 82–3; Synge (1962 ed.), 164–5.
46. Synod of Drogheda (1614) in Renehan ed. (1861–74), I, 433; Synod of Kilkenny (1614) in Comerford (1883–86), I, 248; Limerick statutes (1721) in NLI, White MS, 91; Dublin statutes (1730) in Moran ed. (1874–84), III, 144; Kerry (1747) and Cloyne and Ross (1755) quoted in Manning (1976), 78–9n; *Cork Statutes* (1768), 4; *Cashel Statutes* (1813), 89; Marley quoted in Brady & Corish (1971), 79–80; Butler (1814 ed.), 27.
47. O'Dwyer ed. (1975), 49; (1976–77), 23, 24, 27, 40; Cashel P, Everard Visitation Book, 15, 29; ibid., Laffan Visitation Book, 10 Aug. 1828.
48. Manning (1976), 78; Flood ed. (1914), 117; *Cork Statutes* (1768), 10.
49. Danaher (1972), 135; IFC, MS 1399, p. 538; OSL Galway, I, 52–3.
50. Wilde (1852), 17n; OSL Roscommon, I, 64; OSM 21/IV/1 (1834), 21 (Clonmany, Co. Donegal); OSL Mayo, II, 142–3; ibid. I, 98; *LC State of Ire.* (1825), 245–6, Doyle.
51. Gamble (1819), 397.
52. Manning (1976), 77–8; Butler to Plunkett, 18 Feb. 1791, in Cogan (1862–70), III, 182.
53. *DEP*, 26 Jun., 19 Aug. 1823; Fitzpatrick (1880 ed.), I, 245–51; Meagher (1853), 144–8.
54. *LC State of Ire.* (1825), 504, Rev. T. W. Dixon; Croly (1834), 67; Croker (1824), 170; MacEvoy (1954), 131; Hartnett (1941), 104, 112–13; *Trans. Ossory Hist. Soc.* I (1874–79), 206; Bowen (1978), 54; Maguire (1898 ed.), 525–34; letter from Mathew quoted in Hall (1841–43), I, 43 and n; Kohl (1844), 66–7; *Particulars of the Horrible Murder of Catherine Sinnott* (n.d.); *Report of the Trial of the Rev. John Carroll* (1824); *Annual Register* (1824), 40*–44*; *DEP*, 17 Jul., 7 Aug. 1824.
55. Ó Súilleabháin (n.d.), 38; *SC State of Ire.* (1831–32), 199, Col. Sir John Harvey.
56. Miller (1975).
57. Carbery (1973 ed.), 157–8.
58. Enclosure in Outrage P (1838) 21/109; Wakefield (1812), II, 609, 746–7; Thackeray (1879 ed.), 122; p. 91 above; *SC State of Ire.* (1825), 196–7, 258–9, 594, Doyle, Abp Kelly, Rev. William O'Brien, PP Doneraile, Co. Cork; *SC Disturbances* (1825), 364, Rev. Michael Collins.

59. Wakefield (1812), II, 628 (journal for 19 Dec. 1808); Hall (1813), I, 60—2; Mason (1814—19), II, 369; *LC State of Ire*. (1825), 442, Archdeacon Trench (C. of I.); Hall (1841—43), I, 279; Manning (1976), 89; *Cashel Statutes* (1813), 203; *SC State of Ire*. (1825), 242, Kelly.

60. 'Articles of General Discipline', 15—16 Oct. 1777 (Cashel P, JBII 1777/6); *Dublin Chronicle*, 17 Sep. 1791, in Brady ed. (1965), 278; Troy to his clergy, 12 Dec. 1782 (Cashel P, JBII 1782/8); Fitzpatrick (1880 ed.), I, 512—13; regulations for the parish of Tydavnet, Co. Monaghan, in *Arch. Hib*. XII (1946), 69; IFC, MS 1461, p. 369—cf. recollections of Michael Gaynor (b. Elphin 1845) in *Béaloideas* IV (1934), 179.

61. *Cashel Statutes* (1813), 203; *Dublin Statutes* (1831), 108—9; *Ardagh Statutes* (1834), 76.

62. *Cashel Statutes* (1813), 37—8, 106, 219; Cogan (1862—70), III, 32; *Dublin Statutes* (1831), 108—9; *Ardagh Statutes* (1834), 76; pastoral of the bishops of Cashel province, 26 Jun. 1787, in Butler (1787), App., 6 (see p. 245 below); Coppinger to Bray, 28 Jul. 1804 (Cashel P, Bray 1804/6); Outrage P (1837) 6/152, A. Woodhouse, Mitchelstown, 13 Jun.; for other examples of offenders being named from the altar see pp. 181—2, 232 below.

63. Troy to his clergy, 12 Dec. 1782 (Cashel P, JBII 1782/8); Clogher statutes (1789) in Ó Dufaigh (1968), 469; *Cashel Statutes* (1813), 12.

64. *LC State of Ire*. (1825), 312—13, Doyle; *Maynooth Inquiry* (1826—27), 80—2, Bartholemew Crotty, President; *Maynooth Inquiry* (1854—55), Evidence, 342—4, 349, Henry Neville, Professor of Theology.

65. Pastoral, 17 May 1797, in *Cashel Statutes* (1813), 234; Troy to his clergy, 11 Oct. 1779, in Moran ed. (1874—84), III, 372—3.

66. Curran ed. (1958), 164; *DEP*, 30 Jul. 1831, supplement; Begley (1938), 496—7.

67. *LC State of Ire*. (1825), 312—13, Doyle; Fitzpatrick (1880 ed.), I, 379—80, 521—2.

68. Kernan (1810), 57—8, 67—70; *DEP*, 30 Jul. 1831, supplement. For the case of Peter Boyle see also McLaughlin's circular letter to the Irish prelates, May 1809 (Cashel P, Bray 1809/20).

69. Chadwick (1966—70), I, 489.

70. Hall (1841—43), I, 35; Croker (1824), 228; Kohl (1833), 107; Carleton (1862 ed.), II, 1—74, 'The Geography of an Irish Oath'.

71. Information of Mary Scanlon, 7 Dec. 1842 (Outrage P (1842) 26/22409); O'Driscol (1823), I, 143—6.

72. Carleton (1862 ed.), I, 57—8 and n, 'Shane Fadh's Wedding'. For popular attitudes to elopement, and to sexual behaviour in general, see pp. 188—9, 207—8 below.

Chapter 4
WAKES AND PATTERNS
(pp. 135—174)

1. Mason (1814—19), I, 450.
2. Hall (1841—43), I, 279.
3. Ibid., I, 283—4 and n — see also Lewis (1837), I, 54; OSL Kerry, 92. See also Mason (1814—19), I, 185.
4. Quoted in Ó Coindealbháin (1946), 162; McGrath ed. (1928—31), II, 183. For other contemporary accounts see Carr (1806), 255—6; Hall (1813), II, 216; Croker (1824), 277—82; Inglis (1834), II, 46—52.
5. For wells at Mulhuddart and Kilmainham, both on the outskirts of Dublin, see pp. 140, 144 below, and for St Bartholomew's well near Cork city see Smith (1815 ed.), I, 359—60. *Waterford Chronicle*, repr. *DEP*, 3 Sep. 1822; Outrage P (1838) 17/206; SOC 1120/59, James Daniell, Carrickmacross, 4 Aug. 1807; Mason (1814—19), II, 146; Hall (1841—43), I, 284.
6. Croker (1824), 276—82; p. 144 below; MacNeill (1962), 106—37, 260—85 and App. III; *Béaloideas* XII (1942), 128—9; O'Donovan's comments in OSL Wexford, I, 144; O'Donovan Rossa (1898), 5—8.
7. Townsend (1810), 91n; de Latocnaye (1917 ed.), 110; Introduction (1854) to Carleton (1862 ed.), I, xxiv. For penitential practices at holy wells see p. 186 below.
8. Mason (1814—19), III, 72—3; ibid., I, 368; Weld (1832), 269; Hall (1841—43), I, 280—1; Croker (1824), 283.
9. Brady ed. (1965), 85; regulations for the diocese of Ferns (1771) in Flood ed. (1914), 118; 'Articles of General Discipline', 15—16 Oct. 1777 (Cashel P, JBII 1777/6); resolutions of the bishops of Armagh province, Aug. 1781, in Moran ed. (1874—84), III, 393; pastoral to the clergy of Ossory, 12 Dec. 1782 (copy in Cashel P, JBII 1782/8); instructions on patterns, 12 May 1797, in *Cashel Statutes* (1813), 230—6.
10. Mason (1814—19), I, 185; OSL Mayo, I, 146; Lewis (1837), 491. See also MacNeill (1962), 126, 158; Comerford (1883—86), III, 163; Carr (1806), 255.
11. O'Laverty (1878—95), I, 49; OSM 23/XXVIII/1 (1836), 43; OSL Cavan, 64; ibid. Kilkenny, I, 91; ibid. Westmeath, II, 119—20; Hall (1841—43), I, 282.
12. Pastoral to the clergy of Ossory, 12 Dec. 1782 (copy in Cashel P, JBII 1782/8). For the views of clerical historians later in the century see *Trans. Ossory Arch. Soc.* I (1874—79), 28, 65, 81; O'Rorke (1878), 259—63.
13. For examples see O'Toole (1934), 4; OSL Kilkenny, I, 19, 103.
14. For St John's well in Co. Meath see Moran ed. (1874—84), III, 393; notice read from the altars in Dublin diocese, 15 Jun. 1783, in Curran ed. (1958), 168—9; Wakefield (1812), II, 605. For Kilmainham see Curran ed. (1958), 171; Brady ed. (1965), 256;

Warburton *et al.* (1818), II, 1175; Lewis (1837), II, 27; Danaher (1972), 150. For Ossory see numerous accounts in OSL Kilkenny and in *Trans. Ossory Arch. Soc.* I (1874—79).

15. OSM 23/XXVIII/1 (1836), 43; OSL Carlow, 71; ibid. Donegal, 39, 111; ibid. Kilkenny, II, 26—7; ibid. Louth, 25; ibid. Offaly, I, 22—3; ibid. Waterford, 15, 50; ibid. Wexford, I, 98; OSM 51/XI/1 (1834), 11 (Clogherny, Co. Tyrone); Hall (1841—43), I, 417; *Trans. Ossory Arch. Soc.* I (1874—79), 28, 65, 81; Weld (1832), 515—16.

16. *Waterford Chronicle*, repr. *DEP*, 3 Sep. 1822; *Parl. Gazetteer*, I (1845), 449n.

17. 'Omurethi' (1906—8), 453; Coyle (1956), 200—1; MacNeill (1962), 606; Power (1912), 75—6, 184; Power (1937), 138; Danaher (1966—67), 50; Curry (1968), 140; Messenger (1969), 92.

18. OSL Dublin, 32; ibid. Galway, I, 205—6; OSM 33/I/15 (n.d.), 6; *LC State of Ire.* (1825), 246.

19. Hogan (1873), 261—7. See also Shearman (1879), iv—vi.

20. Ó Súilleabháin (1967), 13; Campbell (1778), 210—11; Mason (1814—19), II, 160; Dutton (1824), 521; Donaldson (1923 ed.), 67.

21. Ó Súilleabháin (1967), 26—129 — see also Morris (1938); Rawson (1807), 25.

22. Thus in Carleton's account 'the songs and divarsion and divilment' had begun well before the young people retired to the barn, and their reason for doing so was to leave more room for the old people who remained with the corpse.

23. Ó Súilleabháin (1967), 31—2, 67, 172—3; Campbell (1778), 211; Hall (1841—43), I, 221; Croker (1824), 166—7; Daunt (1896), 20—1; Ó Súilleabháin (1967), 72.

24. OSM 1/IV/6 (1834), 34 (Ahoghill); ibid. 4/II/2 (1837), 5—6 (Ballynure); ibid. 9/IV/4 (1838), 37 (Donegore); ibid. 11/IV/1 (1840), 97 (Island Magee); ibid. 16/IV/2 (1840), 64 (Templecorran); ibid. 16/VIII/1 (1836) (Tullyrush); OSM 52/XX/1 (n.d.) (Muff, Co. Tyrone). For wakes in Belfast, Cork and Dublin see Hall (1813), I, 36, 187; *Poor Inquiry* (1835—37), App.C, Pt 1, 21.

25. Ó Súilleabháin (1967), 159—65.

26. Ibid., 166—74.

27. Carleton (1862 ed.), I, 107—11, 'Larry M'Farland's Wake'.

28. Martin Marley, *The Good Confessor* (1743), quoted in Ó Súilleabháin (1967), 95; regulations for the diocese of Leighlin (1748) in Comerford (1883—86), I, 81; *Cashel Statutes* (1813), 72; Butler (1814 ed.), 31; pastoral to the clergy and laity of Cashel and Emly (Cashel P, Bray 1806/13); *Ardagh Statutes* (1834), 98—9; Carbery (1973 ed.), 169.

29. Prim (1852—53), 333—4n; Wood-Martin (1902), I, 314—16; Carleton, 'The Country Dancing Master' (1840), quoted in Mercier (1962), 51—2.

30. Regulations for the diocese of Dublin (1730) in Moran ed. (1874—84), III, 142—3; regulations for the diocese of Leighlin (1748) in Comerford (1883—86), I, 81; *Cashel Statutes* (1813), 72. See

also Mercier (1962), 52.

31. Wilde (1890), 131–2.
32. Prim (1852–53), 334n; Wood-Martin (1902), I, 315–16; Ó Súilleabháin (1967), 96–9; pp. 76–7 above.
33. Young (1892 ed.), I, 249; Campbell (1778), 206–8; Carr (1806), 257, 352; Hall (1813), II, 282; Croker (1824), 172–3; Mason (1814–19), I, 319; II, 160, 460, 510.
34. See Donaldson's account (1923 ed., 67), where at intervals in the verbal lament the person performing the keen 'raises the keenagh or cry and is joined by the whole party'.
35. Synge (1962 ed.), 192, 297.
36. Ó Súilleabháin (1967), 26, 28; Wilde (1890), 134; Prim (1852–53), 334n; *Béaloideas* X (1940), 285.
37. Ó Súilleabháin (1967), 19–20, 138–9, 146–8; Bossy (1971), 164–5; Dublin statutes (1730) in Moran ed. (1874–84), II, 143–4; regulations for the diocese of Leighlin (1748) in Comerford (1883–86), I, 81–2.
38. Regulations for the diocese of Armagh (1761) in Renehan ed. (1861–74), I, 105; 'Articles of General Discipline', 15–16 Oct. 1777 (Cashel P, JBII 1777/6); Cashel statutes (1782) in Renehan (1861–74), I, 479; Clogher statutes (1789) in Ó Dufaigh (1968), 469–70.
39. Plunkett's visitation diary in Cogan (1862–70), II, 205, 206; III, 258, 284, 296, 316, 330, 380n, 387n; pastoral, n.d. (Cashel P, Bray 1806/13 – also printed in *Cashel Statutes* (1813), 105–8); *Dublin Statutes* (1831), 138. For other instances of the banning of young and unmarried persons from wakes see McGrath ed. (1928–31), III, 37–9; regulations for Tydavnet, Co. Monaghan (1832) in *Arch. Hib.* XII (1946), 69; *Ardagh Statutes* (1834), 99.
40. Butler (1814 ed.), 28; Cogan (1862–70), III, 380n; pastoral, n.d. (Cashel P, Bray 1806/13); *Ardagh Statutes* (1834), 98–9; Cashel statutes (1782) in Renehan (1861–74), I, 479.
41. Comerford (1883–86), I, 81–2; pastoral, n.d. (Cashel P, Bray 1806/13); Hall (1813), II, 282; Mason (1814–19), I, 597; Gamble (1819), 397; regulations for Tydavnet in *Arch. Hib.* XII (1946), 69; *Dublin Statutes* (1831), 138–9; *Ardagh Statutes* (1834), 99.
42. Mason (1814–19), I, 597; OSM 10/IV/4 (1836) (Duneane, Co. Antrim); ibid. 42/III/2 (1836), 13 (Killelagh, Co. Londonderry); ibid. 29/V/2 (n.d.), 49–50 (Artrea, Co. Londonderry); ibid. 45/II/2 (n.d.), 27 (Magilligan); *Poor Inquiry* (1835–37), App. D, 93–4, 97.
43. Ó Súilleabháin (1967), 141–3, 153–4; Morris (1938), 128; minutes of Clogher diocesan chapter, 30 Apr. 1861 (Clogher P, 1/12/1); minutes of Clogher diocesan synod, 23 May 1861 (ibid., 1/12/3).
44. Ó Súilleabháin (1967), 9–11, 26, 29, 143, 164–5; Morris (1938), 124–7.
45. Morris (1938), 140–1.
46. Mason (1814–19), III, 471; ibid., II, 364.

47. OSM 24/VI/1 (1836), 15, 59; ibid. 48/I/2 (1821), sect. vi; ibid. 40/I/4 (1836), 32; ibid. 14/III/3 (1835); ibid. 10/IV/4 (1836).
48. Farrell (1949) 39; p. 183 below; Troy to his clergy, 10 Sep. 1778, in Moran ed. (1874–84), III, 367; Caulfield to his clergy (1798) ibid., III, 563; Plunkett's visitation diary in Cogan (1862–70), II, 221; III, 318, 324; Cashel P, Everard Visitation Book (1815–21), 6, 16, 23, 30, 33; *SC Poor* (1830), 453, Doyle.
49. Clogher statutes (1789) in Ó Dufaigh (1968), 470; *Poor Inquiry* (1835–37), App. E, 103; *SC Drunkenness* (1834), 260.
50. O'Driscol (1823), II, 426; Mason (1814–19), III, 174. For the working habits of Ulster weavers see Young (1892 ed.), I, 127, 132. For 'Saint Monday' in Dublin and Belfast see Archer (1801), 221; *SC Drunkenness* (1834), 71, Rev. John Edgar.
51. Thompson (1967); Thompson (1968 ed.), 440–51; Pollard (1963); Reid (1976); Malcolmson (1973).
52. Plunkett (1904), 113.

Chapter 5
MARRIAGE AND SEXUAL BEHAVIOUR
(pp. 175–218)

1. For a wide selection of contemporary comment see Connell (1968), 113–62.
2. Arensberg & Kimball (1968 ed.), chap. 11; Humphreys (1966), 37–8, 116–20, 138–40, 232; Messenger (1969), 68–9, 107–10; Messenger (1971); O'Brien (1954), 12, 39, 80, 155–6, 188, 209–13; IFC, MS 1459, pp. 292–5; Carbery (1973 ed.), 22, 46–7, 62.
3. Campbell (1960), 131–47; Whyte (1971), 34; Humphreys (1966), 139; Bryan MacMahon in O'Brien (1954), 212; *Cath. Dir.* (1924), 548, 559.
4. Donlevy (1848 ed.), 101–3.
5. Dublin statutes (1730) in Moran ed. (1874–84), III, 144; *Cork Statutes* (1768), 27; Cashel statutes (1782) in Renehan ed. (1861–74), I, 475; *Dublin Statutes* (1831), 97; *Poor Inquiry* (1835–37), App. A, 83; Limerick statutes (1752) in NLI, White MS, 128; Achonry statutes (1759) in Moran ed. (1874–84), III, 273.
6. Curran ed. (1958), 158; Brady ed. (1965), 210; Plunkett's visitation diary in Cogan (1862–70), III, 320; Fitzpatrick (1880 ed.), I, 521–2; Outrage P (1838) 22/139; Daunt (1896), 140.
7. Curran ed. (1958), 164; p. 124 above.
8. *SC Disturbances* (1825), 150, 358, Maj. G. Warburton, Rev. Michael Collins; *Poor Inquiry* (1835–37), App. A, 397–425, 461–5.
9. *Poor Inquiry* (1835–37), App. A, 49–50, 86, 60–1.
10. 'Articles of General Discipline', 15–16 Oct. 1777 (Cashel P, JBII 1777/6); Clogher statutes (1789) in Ó Dufaigh (1968), 469; *Dublin Statutes* (1831), 147; Fitzpatrick (1880 ed.), I, 298; diary of Archdeacon Sullivan (1850), quoted in de Brún (1974), 83–4; regulations for Tydavnet (1832) in *Arch. Hib.* XII (1946),

69; Plunkett's visitation diary in Cogan (1862–70), III, 321, 334.

11. *Poor Inquiry* (1835–37), Addenda to App. A, 5; O'Reilly (1890), I, 155; Cogan (1862–70), II, 196, 201, 212, 223; III, 271, 322, 325, 326, 332.

12. Humphreys (1966), 25–7; Brady & Corish (1971), 84–8; Healy (1895), 283–7; pp. 44–6 above; Renehan ed. (1861–74), I, 310; Fitzpatrick (1880 ed.), I, 125.

13. The question of Jansenism is comprehensively dealt with in Clark (1932). For Lough Derg see OSM 22/IX/1 (1835); Lewis (1837), II, 603; *Parl. Gazetteer*, II (1846), 10. For penitential practice at other sites see Thackeray (1879 ed.), 224–5; de Latocnaye (1917 ed.), 136; OSM 51/XI/1 (1834), 10–11 (Clogherny, Co. Tyrone); ibid. 23/XXVIII/1 (1836), 42 (Struell, Co. Down); Mason (1814–19), II, 459; III, 322; *Béaloideas* IV (1934), 115.

14. Carr (1806), 236, 281; Warburton, Whitelaw & Walsh (1818), II, 698; de Beaumont (1839), II, 35; de Tocqueville (1958 trans.), 131, 142, 191; *SC Poor* (1830), 241, 483, 65.

15. Mason (1814–19), III, 79; Thackeray (1879 ed.), 122; Wakefield (1812), II, 767; Warburton, Whitelaw & Walsh (1818), II, 1169; Weld (1832), 407–8; *Poor Inquiry* (1835–37), App. C, Pt 1, 51, 65; ibid., App. C, Pt 2, 3, 4, 42, 116.

16. Wakefield (1812), II, 746–7; OSM 11/VI/1 (1840), 86; OSM 7/7–8/II (1839), 256; OSM 7/7–8/III (1839), 49; OSM 15/VI/1 (1840); p. 190 below.

17. *Poor Inquiry* (1835–37), App. A. & Supp., passim.

18. For a detailed account of the statistics on illegitimacy and pre-nuptial pregnancy referred to in this and the following paragraph see Connolly (1979).

19. Ó Laoghaire to Seosamh Laoide, 7 Sep. 1895, in *Éigse* XI, 4 (1966), 252 (my translation). For bowdlerisation of Irish texts see Mercier (1962), 66.

20. Bicheno (1830), 33; *SC Disturbances* (1825), 10, 99–100; *Poor Inquiry* (1835–37), App. A, 383, 442.

21. De Tocqueville (1958 trans.), 191; Wakefield (1812), II, 749; Arensberg & Kimball (1968 ed.), 197–201.

22. Pp. 152–6 above; Donaldson (1923 ed.), 69–70.

23. Sayers (1962 ed.), x. For general accounts of matchmaking in post-famine Ireland see Connell (1957); Connell (1962).

24. *Poor Inquiry* (1835–37), App. F, 59; ibid., App. A, 454; *LC State of Ire.* (1825), 369, John Keily, PP Mitchelstown; Mason (1814–19), III, 243; Inglis (1834), I, 129; Wakefield (1812), II, 764.

25. *Poor Inquiry* (1835–37), App. A, 404, 450, 451; ibid., App. F, 71; Lee (1968).

26. For impediments arising out of a previous contract to marry see Cashel P, Bray 1795/8; *LC State of Ire.* (1825), 266. For consent of parents see *Cork Statutes* (1768), 28; Brady ed. (1956),

484; memorandum of Irish bishops (1801) in *Castlereagh Corr.*, IV, 100, 129; *Cashel Statutes* (1813), 213. For consanguinity see *SC State of Ire*. (1825), 427.

27. Troy quoted in Renehan ed. (1861–74), I, 448, 450; *LC State of Ire*. (1825), 265; regulations for Cashel province (1808) in *Cashel Statutes* (1813), 125.

28. Faloon (1881), 9–22; NLI, White MS, 80; H.C. 1831–32 (589) XXX; marriage register, Slieverue, 1806; *DEP*, 23 Jun. 1831.

29. *LC Disturbances* (1825), 18–19; *LC State of Ire*. (1825), 66; Inglis (1834), I, 247; *Poor Inquiry* (1835–37), App. A, 407. For the priests' side of the case see *SC State of Ire*. (1825), 395; *Poor Inquiry* (1835–37), App. A, 392, 406, 416, 442.

30. Limerick statutes (1752) in NLI, White MS, 128; Dublin statutes (1730) in Moran ed. (1874–84), III, 145; *Cork Statutes* (1768), 28; regulations for the clergy of Dublin (1791) in Moran ed. (1874–84), III, 438; *Cashel Statutes* (1813), 61, 211–18, 220–1. For an example of a certificate of freedom, granted in Co. Galway in 1821, see PROI, M6935/73(21).

31. Dr Walsh's letter in Townsend (1810), App., 83; *SC State of Ire*. (1825), 394, John Keily, PP Mitchelstown; ibid, 425–6, Thomas Costello, PP Abington, Co. Limerick; Wakefield (1812), II, 611; Hugh O'Reilly to Troy, 2 Jan. 1801, in *Castlereagh Corr.*, IV, 111; *LC State of Ire*. (1825), 231, Doyle.

32. *Cork Statutes* (1768), 27, repeated verbatim in *Cashel Statutes* (1813), 58–9.

33. For a conforming priest turned couple-beggar see de Latocnaye (1917 ed.), 100. For D'Assigny see Brady ed. (1965), 62n, and for another lay couple-beggar see NLI, White MS, 172.

34. Leighlin regulations (1748) in Comerford ed. (1883–86), I, 79–80; Ossory regulations (1748) in Carrigan (1905), I, 152–3; Brady ed. (1965), 76; NLI, White MS, 120, 172; Ferns regulations (1771) in Flood ed. (1913), 118–19; 'Articles of General Discipline', 15–16 Oct. 1777 (Cashel P, JBII 1777/6); Clogher statutes (1789) in Ó Dufaigh (1968), 469; Brady ed. (1956), 484–5.

35. Renehan ed. (1861–74), I, 437–53.

36. 'Reasons for Receiving the Decree of the Council of Trent Relative to Clandestine Marriage', n.d. (Cashel P, JBII 1790/10); report to Rome by Bp of Cloyne and Ross (1775) in Moran ed. (1874–84), III, 340–1; Plunkett to Troy, 16 Feb. 1821, in Brady ed. (1941), 233.

37. Brady ed. (1956), 481–5.

38. Brady ed. (1965), 62, 81–2, 141–2; Carleton (1968 ed.), 234–6; *DEP*, 2 Apr. 1831, 5 Aug. 1823; p. 197 above.

39. *Poor Inquiry* (1835–37), App. A, 392. For the fees charged by couple-beggars see Wood (1902), 23, and for the fees charged by the Catholic clergy see pp. 247–51 below. See also Wakefield (1812), II, 626.

40. Marriage registers, St Canice's, 21 Feb. 1779; Nobber, 20 Jul. 1769; baptismal register, Slieverue, 24 Sep. 1807; *Cashel Statutes* (1813), 216—18.
41. Carleton (1968 ed.), 235; p. 118 above.
42. Troy's report to Rome (1802) in Moran ed. (1874—84), III, 639—40; Carleton (1968 ed.), 234—6; OSM 42/IV/1 (n.d.), 37—8; *Poor Inquiry* (1835—37), App. A, Supp., 276; Biggar (1908), 140; Plunkett's visitation diary in Cogan (1862—70), II, 182—227; III, 249—443; marriage register, Nobber, 20 Jul. 1769.
43. *PROI, Rep. Dep. Keeper* 33 (1901), 7 — these registers have not survived; Brady ed. (1965), 62 n. 1; Brady ed. (1956), 482—3.
44. Carleton (1968 ed.), 85—7; Carleton (1862 ed.), I, 51—83, 'Shane Fadh's Wedding'; IFC, MS 1457, pp. 88—90 (Co. Longford); ibid., MS 1460, pp. 151—2 (Co. Longford), 193—4 (Co. Leitrim); ibid., MS 1461, pp. 368—9 (Co. Roscommon).
45. Hall (1813), I, 151; Mason (1814—19), II, 379; Carleton (1862 ed.), I, 57—8n, 'Shane Fadh's Wedding'; minutes of a meeting of Clogher diocesan chapter, 30 Apr. 1861 (Clogher P, 1/12/1); MacEvoy (1954), 124; IFC, MS 1461, p. 369; recollections of Michael Gaynor (b. Elphin 1845) in *Béaloideas* IV (1934), 179.
46. OSM 36/I/2 (n.d.) (Cumber, Co. Londonderry); Donaldson (1923 ed.), 64.
47. *Poor Inquiry* (1835—37), App. A, 451, 692; Cogan (1862—70), III, 327, 336, 318—19; *Cashel Statutes* (1813), 218—19; Cashel P, Laffan Visitation Book, 29 Jul. 1828; *SC Disturbances* (1825), 211, Rev. Malachi Duggan.
48. *LC Disturbances* (1825), 123, Rev. Malachi Duggan; information of Mary Burns, 19 Feb. 1838 (Outrage P (1838) 26/32). For sham 'uctions see Inglis (1834), I, 289; *SC Crime* (1839), 1044—5, T. Brew, Stip. Magistrate, Co. Clare. For the real thing see *SC Disturbances* (1825), 151, 386; *Poor Inquiry* (1835—37), App. A, 416—20.
49. O'Shea ed. (1974), 33—4; Young to Bray, 22 Feb. 1799, 5 Nov. 1800 (Cashel P, Bray 1799/1, 1800/29).
50. *SC Disturbances* (1825), 358, Rev. Michael Collins; *SC Poor* (1830), 423, Doyle; *SC State of Ire.* (1825), 249, Kelly; *SC Disturbances* (1825), 386—7, O'Driscol; ibid., 211, Rev. Malachi Duggan.
51. De Tocqueville (1958 ed.), 142.
52. Arensberg & Kimball (1968 ed.), 208; *Poor Inquiry* (1835—37), App. A, 96.

Chapter 6
'VILE AND WICKED CONSPIRACIES'
(pp. 219—263)

1. For agrarian violence see Wall (1973); Lee, 'Ribbonmen' (1973); Broeker (1970); Lewis (1836). For urban riot see Brady ed. (1965), 49, 76, 80, 87, 88, 143; Caulfield ed. (1876), 468, 482, 485, 530, 531—2, 671, 779, and for sectarian violence pp. 11—15 above. There is as yet no serious analysis of faction-fighting, but see Ó Muir-

eadaigh (1961); Danaher (1966–67); O'Donnell (1975).

2. For prayers for the royal family see Brady ed. (1965), 129, 288–9; Raphoe statutes (1782) in Maguire (1920), II, 325; pastoral of Abp Butler, 20 Nov. 1788 (Cashel P, JBII 1788/6); Troy to Bray, 8 Dec. 1795 (ibid., Bray 1795/32); notice to the clergy of the diocese of Dublin, 26 May 1800 (ibid., Bray 1800/12). For prayers and fasts in time of war see Brady ed. (1965), 104, 212, 218–19; Moran ed. (1874–84), III, 365–6, 366–7, 369–70; pastoral of Abp Butler, 24 Feb. 1762 (Cashel P – wrongly placed with JBI 1757/1); Carrigan (1905), I, 185.

3. Brady ed. (1965), 78; pastoral signed by Troy and others, 25 Jan. 1793 (Cashel P, Bray 1793/4).

4. Brady ed. (1965), 143–4; address to the Catholics of Meath (1781), ibid., 213; pastoral of Abp Troy, 16 Feb. 1797, in Moran ed. (1874–84), III, 498; address from the altars of Dublin (1778) in Brady ed. (1965), 192.

5. Pastoral of Abp Troy, 16 Feb. 1797, in Moran ed. (1874–84), III, 496; pastoral of Bp Moylan, 26 Apr. 1798, ibid., III, 588; pastoral of Bp Dillon of Kilfernora and Kilmacduagh, 6 Apr. 1798, ibid., III, 581; lenten instructions for the diocese of Elphin, 1798 (Cashel P, Bray 1798/6); Troy to his clergy, 4 Mar. 1799 (Clogher P, 1/14/2).

6. Exhortation to the people of Ballyragget, Co. Kilkenny, 1775 (Cashel P, JBII 1775/5); Coppinger in Moran ed. (1874–84), III, 591–2; Moylan, ibid., III, 585.

7. Troy (1793, 2nd ed.), esp. 25–30, 4–5.

8. Doyle (1822), 22–3. For clerical involvement in politics in the 1820s and later see pp. 13–14 above.

9. See, for example, pastoral of Bp Doyle, *DEP*, 1 Dec. 1831; pastoral of Bp MacMahon of Killaloe, ibid., 14 Apr. 1831.

10. Hussey's pastoral, in England (1822), 315–26. For reactions to it see ibid., 200–5; Troy to Bray, 15 Apr. 1797 (Cashel P, Bray 1797/7); O'Farrell (1973), 93–6.

11. Brady ed. (1965), 191; Michael Peter MacMahon, Bp Killaloe, 4 Dec. 1798, 3 Dec. 1800 (RP 620/41/66, 620/9/99/2).

12. Hayes (1945), 258–70.

13. Ibid., 258–9; England (1822), 330.

14. RP 620/37/72, W. Smyth, Drumcrea, 13 May 1798; ibid. 620/37/134, Sir James Foulis, Mitchelstown, Co. Cork, 23 May 1798.

15. Troy to Bray, 12 Jun. 1798 (Cashel P, Bray 1798/13); Bp Caulfield of Ferns to ——, 15 Sep. 1798, in Moran ed. (1874–84), III, 571; Young to Bray, 4 Jul. 1798 (Cashel P, Bray 1798/6); Byrne (1863), I, 54–5.

16. Byrne (1863), I, 46; Kee (1972), 109; Pakenham (1972 ed.), 169–70; Hoban (1972), 362–6.

17. For the excommunication of rioters in Dublin see Brady ed. (1965), 49, 76, 80. The Whiteboys were excommunicated in Cloyne in 1762, in Ferns and Cashel in 1775, and in Ossory in

1779: see pastoral of Bp O'Brien of Cloyne, 30 Mar. 1762, in O'Conor (1813), App., xxvi–xxix; Brady ed. (1965), 174; pastoral of Abp Butler, in a newspaper cutting dated 25 Oct. 1775 (Cashel P, JBII 1775/6); Troy to the clergy of Ossory, 11 Oct. 1779, in Moran ed. (1874–84), III, 370–3. For the excommunication of the Defenders see pastoral by Troy, ibid., III, 476–9.

18. Pastoral of Bishop Sughrue of Kerry, *DEP*, 11 Dec. 1821.
19. *SC State of Ire.* (1831–32), 196, Nicholas O'Connor, PP Maryborough. But see p. 129 above.
20. Pastoral by Doyle, 5 May 1832, in *SC State of Ire.* (1831–32), App., 116–17; Fitzpatrick (1880 ed.), II, 413–14; p. 122 above.
21. 'Articles of General Discipline', 15–16 Oct. 1777 (Cashel P, JBII 1777/6); pastoral by Troy, 12 Dec. 1782 (ibid., JBII 1782/8); Wakefield (1812), II, 628.
22. Brady ed. (1965), 52, 82.
23. *SC State of Ire.* (1831–32), 215–16; *DEP*, 9 Aug. 1821; OSM 40/I/4 (1836), 32; Outrage P (1838) 6/82, R. Power, Schull, 19 Apr. 1838.
24. *DEP*, 27 Dec. 1821; *SC State of Ire.* (1831–32), 179; ibid., 251, 270, James Delany, PP Ballynakill.
25. *SC State of Ire.* (1825), 420, Thomas Costello, PP Abington; *DEP*, 27 Oct., 8 Dec. 1821, 3 Jan., 12 Feb. 1822; SOC 2345/57, Michael Creagh, 10 Apr. 1822; *DEP*, 26 Oct. 1819; ibid., 18, 23 Apr. 1822.
26. SOC 1031/28, Brigade Maj. Daniel Mahony, Killarney, 30 Apr. 1805; ibid. 2362/1, Lt Thomas Swyny, Mohill, 22 Feb. 1822; Outrage P (1836) 21/24, D. J. Barry, Swinford, 19 Apr. 1836; ibid. (1836) 25/4, Edward Spurling, Roscommon, 25 Jan. 1836.
27. *DEP*, 21 Oct. 1823; ibid., 12 Apr. 1831; *SC Crime* (1839), 244, J. H. Hutton, Chief Constable; *DEP*, 18 Oct. 1821; SOC 2352/12, A. Norcatt, Newcastle, 8 Apr. 1822.
28. SOC 2362/16, John P. Lyons, PP Kilmoremoy, 13 Feb. 1822; ibid. 2362/17, Lyons, 2 Mar. 1822; *DEP*, 23 Oct., 22 Dec. 1821, 5 Feb., 2, 11 Apr. 1822, 5 Aug. 1823, 21, 23 Jun. 1831; SOC 2345/51, Lord Doneraile, Apr. 1822; ibid. 2345/70, W. G. Crofts, Churchtown, 2 May 1822.
29. *DEP*, 22 Jan. 1822. See ibid., 31 Jan. 1824, for an incident where another Limerick priest took a leading part in the search for some stolen butter.
30. Ibid., 19 Mar., 16 Jun. 1831. See also ibid, 7 Mar. 1820.
31. *DEP*, 21 Feb. 1822; ibid., 29 Nov., 4, 11, 15, 27 Dec. 1821, 8, 15 Jan., 16 Feb. 1822.
32. Cashel P, Everard Visitation Book, 7–24, 30.
33. *DEP*, 29 May 1821; pastoral by Doyle, 5 May 1832, in *SC State of Ire.* (1831–32), App., 116; ibid, 183–4, 196, 256, 359; Outrage P (1832) 1086, Greene, Kilkenny, 9 May 1832.
34. Croly (1834), 29.

35. Lee, 'Ribbonmen' (1973); report on the state of Co. Limerick, 3 Nov. 1800 (RP 620/9/103/12); NLI, White MS, 177. See also Clark (1978).

36. *SC Crime* (1839), 29, 585, 1248, 545, 521; Kohl (1844), 32.

37. Pastoral, 5 May 1832, in *SC State of Ire.* (1831–32), App., 116.

38. *DEP*, 11 Dec. 1821.

39. NLI, White MS, 177; *Annual Register* (1775), quoted in Lewis (1836), 31; Brady ed. (1965), 179, 194.

40. Brady ed. (1965), 238, 241; Butler (1787), 25–7; Burns, 'Parsons, Priests' (1962).

41. Brady ed. (1965), 290; McAnally (1949), 33; *Candid and Impartial Account* (1794), 9, 34–5, 37.

42. RP 620/25/37, A. Cole-Hamilton, Beltrim, Co. Tyrone, 7 Sep. 1796; ibid. 620/9/100/6, Edmund Derry, PP Rathfriland, Co. Down, 6 Jun. 1800; ibid. 620/51/224, undated threatening letter; Moran ed. (1874–84), III, 596–7; B. Mackey, PP Emly, to Bray, 6, 10 Mar. 1798 (Cashel P, Bray 1798/4, 5); Young to Bray, 10 May 1798 (ibid., Bray 1798/10); Lanigan to Troy, 10 Mar. 1798, in *Castlereagh Corr.*, I, 161–2.

43. Pastorals by Troy, 6 Aug. 1795, 16 Feb. 1797, 1798, in Moran ed. (1874–84), III, 477, 497–8, 553; pastoral by Caulfield, 13 Sep. 1798, ibid., III, 576–7; pastoral by Moylan, 26 Apr. 1798, ibid., III, 587. Troy did in fact use his contacts with Dublin Castle in order to seek a position for his nephew: see Ronan ed. (1944), 3–4, 13–14, 22.

44. *DEP*, 13 Dec. 1821. For threatening letters sent to priests see *SC State of Ire.* (1825), 585–6, William O'Brien, PP Doneraile; *DEP*, 21 Feb. 1821, 10, 15 Jan. 1822, 7 Apr., 23 July. 1831. For MacMahon see ibid., 19 May, 16 Jun. 1831. For Kildare and Leighlin see *SC State of Ire.* (1825), 197, Doyle.

45. *DEP*, 19, 23 Nov 1819; SOC 2351/48, Keeper of Convict Penitentiary, Cork, 20 Mar. 1822.

46. *DEP*, 22 Dec. 1821; *LC State of Ire.* (1825), 181, Maj.-Gen. Bourke.

47. *DEP*, 11 Dec. 1821, 26 Feb. 1822, 19 Apr. 1823, 12 Apr. 1831.

48. Murphy (1965); Dr Walsh's letter in Townsend (1810), App., 84–8. For payments in kind and in work, and entertainment at stations, see pp. 49–50, 67 above.

49. Brady ed. (1965), 239, 234; Burns, 'Parsons, Priests' (1962).

50. Brady ed. (1965), 231, 241, 243; Burns, 'Parsons, Priests' (1962), 157; Gerard Teahan to Butler, 24 Apr. 1786 (Cashel P, JBII 1786/1).

51. Joint pastoral of the bishops of Cashel province, in Butler (1787), App. 1; Conway to Butler, 31 Jul. 1786 (Cashel P, JBII 1786/6; circular letter to the clergy of Cloyne and Ross, 4 Sep. 1786, in Brady ed. (1965), 245–7; regulations for the diocese of Ossory, 2 Sep. 1786, in Carrigan (1905), I, 192–4.

52. Brady ed. (1965), 239; Butler (1787), 21–2; Teahan to Butler,

24 Apr. 1786 (Cashel P, JBII 1786/1).

53. Joint pastoral in Butler (1787), App. 1; Brady ed. (1965), 239, 234, 231, 232. Some of these reports express the sums mentioned in Irish money, a notional currency, not embodied in any official issue of coins or notes, in which thirteen Irish pence were equal to one English shilling. Thus 1s 6d is often written as 1s 7½d, and 5s as 5s 5d.

54. Lord Westmorland, quoted in Lecky (1892 ed.), III, 218; RP 620/6/66/4.

55. Ridgeway (1807), passim; SOC 1092/3, Col. Harcourt, 28 Nov. 1806; Buckingham to Grenville, 11 Dec. 1806, in *HMC Dropmore*, VIII, 463–7; *relatio status* of Bp Plunket of Elphin (1826) in Larkin (1962), 480; SOC 1408/39, Lt.-Gen. G. V. Hart, Athlone, 25 Mar. 1812. For the agitation in Westmeath see *SC Disturbances* (1825), 188, Maj. Richard Willcocks.

56. Ridgeway (1807), 136ff, 226ff; Wakefield (1812), II, 562, 773; *SC State of Ire.* (1825), 259, Abp Kelly; SOC 1388/34, unsigned, 19 Oct. 1811; *SC Disturbances* (1825), 118, Maj. Willcocks.

57. SOC 1192/9, Lord Hartland, Strokestown, 7 Dec. 1808; Ridgeway (1807), 137, 145, 228, 230.

58. *DEP*, 8 Jan. 1822; *SC Disturbances* (1825), 448, James Lawler; *DEP*, 12 Feb. 1822; ibid., 17 Jan. 1822; SOC 2362/18, J. D. Ellard, Swinford, 18 Mar. 1822; *DEP*, 24 Feb. 1820; *SC State of Ire.* (1825), 259, Abp Kelly.

59. Outrage P (1843) 26/1973 on 26/2859, Robert Jones, JP, Fortland, 5 Feb. 1843; ibid. (1843) 21/5997, Const. Richard Roberts, 29 Jan. 1843; ibid. (1843) 21/159, 21/2389, 21/2391, 26/2529, 26/3085.

60. Notices regarding fees, ibid. (1843) 21/3045 on 21/4149, J. Strickland, 23 Feb. 1843; ibid. (1843) 21/5997, Const. Roberts, 29. Jan. 1843; ibid. (1843) 21/1901, Daniel Cruice, Ballina, 2 Feb. 1843. For the fee of one guinea see ibid. (1843) 21/2597. Ibid. (1843) 26/1973 on 26/2859, Jones, 5 Feb. 1843.

61. RP 620/51/224.

62. Ó Fiaich (1975), 48–51.

63. For a review of clerical attitudes see Murphy (1965), 117–19. For statements of the main arguments against accepting a state provision see Troy to Bray, 9 Apr. 1793 (Cashel P, Bray 1793/18); Young to Bray, 26 Dec. 1798 (ibid., Bray 1798/24); Townsend (1810), App., 91–3; *LC State of Ire.* (1825), 232–3, 256, 259, evidence of Bp Doyle and Abps Curtis and Murray.

64. S. Ó Súilleabháin (1963 ed.), 632; *Béaloideas* XXI (1951–52), 16–19.

65. Townsend (1810), App., 88–90.

66. 'Survey of Documents in Private Keeping', *Anal. Hib.* 20 (1958), 271; *SC Disturbances* (1825), 448, Lawler; *DEP*, 29 Jul. 1823; *LC State of Ire.* (1825), 181, Maj.-Gen. Bourke; *SC State of Ire.* (1831–32), 78, Col J. S. Rochfort.

67. *LC Disturbances* (1825), 237, O'Driscol; *SC State of Ire.* (1831–

32), 43, W. N. Despard; *SC Crime* (1839), 70, Warburton; *Poor Inquiry* (1835—37), Supp. App. E, 216; *SC State of Ire.* (1825), 258—9, Abp Kelly.

68. P. 232 above; *SC Disturbances* (1825), 28, Blackburne.
69. SOC 2352/35, Maj. Richard Willcocks, Rathkeale, 26 Apr. 1822. See also ibid. 2351/49, Col. William Thornton, Limerick, 20 Mar. 1822.
70. Ibid. 2345/60, W. H. N. Hodder, 18 Apr. 1822; ibid. 2352/35, Willcocks, 26 April 1822; *DEP*, 9 Apr. 1831.
71. For the Fenian period see Norman (1965), chap. 3. For some comments on the hostility created by clerical condemnation of the movement see also Ó Laoghaire (1973 ed.), 61—2. For clerical reaction to the Land League see Larkin (1975), and for Sinn Féin see Miller (1973), esp. chaps 18—20.

Chapter 7
PRIESTS, CHURCH AND PEOPLE — PRE-FAMINE AND POST-FAMINE
(pp. 264—278)

1. Doyle (1825), 58. For later ideas of Ireland as a country with a divinely ordained redemptive destiny see O'Farrell (1976), 60—2.
2. Pp. 88—90 above; for the English figures see Perkin (1969), 201.
3. Wakefield (1812), II, 555.
4. Thompson (1975), esp. 306—8.
5. Broeker (1970), 226—7; *SC Crime* (1839), 40—3, 769—71, 967—72.
6. Murphy (1969), 239.
7. Larkin (1972), 648—50; Miller (1975).

Appendices
(pp. 279—286)

1. *Devon Commission* (1845), Pt IV, 288—9. The number of holdings under and above 15 acres is taken from the adjusted set of figures calculated from the Devon Commission's data by Bourke (1965), 380.
2. *Cen. 1841*, 440. All figures relate to males 15 years old and upwards.
3. *Cen. 1831*, 343. The figures on the number of occupiers employing and not employing labour are seriously misleading: cf. *Cen. 1841*, xxiii; Cullen (1972), 110.
4. Lee (1968), 285 n. 1; Lee, *Modernisation* (1973), 2; Clark (1978), 25, 38.
5. The results of the 1732—33 enumeration were published in pamphlet form in 1736. For a discussion of the figures and their deficiencies see *Cen. 1861, Pt IV*, 2—3; Connell (1950), 4—25.
6. *Commissioners of Public Instruction, First Report* (1835), 1—7.
7. 'Report on the State of Popery', *Arch. Hib.* I (1912), 10—11.
8. *Castlereagh Corr.*, IV, 98—101.
9. *Commissioners of Public Instruction, First Report* (1835), App. II.
10. *Cath. Dir.* (1871), 211.

Bibliography

The principal manuscript and printed sources used in this study are set out in sections A and B. Since a complete bibliography of secondary sources relating to all the topics touched on in this book would be impractical, the list of books and articles in section C is confined to items cited in the footnotes.

The most important manuscript sources are the records of the Catholic dioceses of Cashel and Clogher, as well as the first of a series of letter-books belonging to Bishop Blake of Dromore; the scattered but valuable information on the activities of the Catholic clergy, particularly but not exclusively in relation to crime and outrage, in the Rebellion Papers, the State of the Country Papers and the Outrage Papers; and the mass of material relating to social life and popular custom in the Ordnance Survey Letters and the Ordnance Survey Memoirs. The second main body of sources is the considerable amount of documentary material relating to the Irish Catholic Church in the eighteenth and nineteenth centuries which has appeared in print, particularly in the journals *Archivium Hibernicum, Collectanea Hibernica* and *Reportorium Novum* and in the collections of documents edited by P. F. Moran and L. F. Renehan. Extensive use has also been made of the evidence given by Catholic churchmen and others before parliamentary inquiries into different aspects of Irish society in the first half of the nineteenth century.

Where modern historical writing is concerned the political history of the Irish Catholic Church in this period has been considerably better served than its social history (see Reynolds (1954), Broderick (1951), Norman (1965)). In recent years, however, Emmet Larkin (1962, 1967, 1972), D. W. Miller (1975) and J. A. Murphy (1965, 1969) have made important contributions to hitherto neglected areas, and their work has provided a valuable starting-point for many of the lines of thought developed in this book.

For abbreviations which might not easily be identifiable see p. 287.

A. MANUSCRIPT SOURCES

Belfast
Public Record Office of Northern Ireland
Clogher Diocesan Papers: Correspondence etc. of Catholic bishops and clergy, relating mainly to the period after 1800 (DIO(RC) 1 — xerox copies; originals in custody of bishop).
Copy letters of Edward Willes, Chief Baron, Irish Exchequer, to English correspondents, *c*. 1759 (Mic. 148; originals in Northumberland Record Office).
Letters of John Coyne, PP Tandragee, Co. Armagh, to Mme de Channes, Cistercian convent, Staplehill, Dorset, 1821–25 (T2830—modern typed copies; originals in Staplehill).
Foster—Massereene Papers: Some manuscripts relating to Catholic affairs, especially Maynooth College (D207/5).
Letter-book of Michael Blake, Bishop of Dromore, for 1833–34 (T3371 — xerox copy; original in custody of bishop).

Cork
Cork Archives Council
Newenham MSS: Papers relating to Newenham's efforts to carry out a census of religious affiliations with the assistance of the Catholic clergy.

Dublin
University College, Dublin
Irish Folklore Commission: A vast collection of material, though mainly relating to the later nineteenth century and after. Drawn on only very selectively for this study. Particular use was made of the replies to the questionnaire on matchmaking circulated on behalf of the late Professor Connell in 1956 (MSS 1459–61).

National Library of Ireland
Cashel Diocesan Papers: Subdivided into manuscripts of the different Archbishops of Cashel: Christopher Butler (1711–57), James Butler I (1757–74), James Butler II (1774–91), Thomas Bray (1792–1820), Patrick Everard (1820–21), Robert Laffan (1823–33), Michael Slattery (1833–57). (Microfilm P5998–6004; originals in Archbishop's House, Thurles).
White MSS: 'Annals of the City and Diocese of Limerick', composed by John White, a parish priest in Limerick city, *c*. 1755–68, with some later additions relating to events up to the 1790s and later. (MS 2714 — photostat; original in Maynooth College).
Registers of births, marriages and deaths (microfilm copies; originals in custody of parish priests)
  Nobber, Co. Meath, 1755–1865 (P4183)
  St Canice's, Kilkenny, 1769–1865 (P5029–30)
  Slieverue, Co. Kilkenny, 1767–1864 (P5031)

Public Record Office of Ireland
Newport Papers: Letters etc. of Sir John Newport (M482–3).
MS 'Hints towards a natural and topographical history of the counties Sligo, Donegal, Fermanagh and Lough Erne' by Rev. William Henry 1739 (M2533).

State Paper Office
Rebellion Papers, 1793–1808.
State of the Country Papers, 1795–1831.
Outrage Papers, 1830–54.

Royal Irish Academy
Ordnance Survey Letters (references are to the typescript copies prepared by Rev. Michael Flanagan 1926–28, available in NLI).
Ordnance Survey Memoirs: Draft reports on the topography, social economy, etc. of individual parishes, mainly in Counties Antrim and Londonderry, originally intended to be published as companion volumes to the first Ordnance Survey maps (1830–40).

B. PRINTED SOURCES

1. *Parliamentary Papers*
Papers presented to the House of Commons relating to the Royal College of St Patrick, Maynooth (1808; repr. 1812–13 (204) VI)
Commissioners of the Board of Education in Ireland, Eighth Report (1810 (193) X)
Abstract of Answers and Returns made pursuant to the Act for Taking an Account of the Population of Ireland [Census of 1821] (1824 (577) XXII)
Minutes of Evidence taken before the Select Committee Appointed to Inquire into the Nature and Extent of the Disturbances which have Prevailed in those Districts of Ireland which are now Subject to the Insurrection Act (1825 (20) VII)
Minutes of Evidence taken before the Lords' Committee on the Same (1825 (200) VII)
Select Committee on the State of Ireland, Report and Evidence (1825 (129) VIII)
Minutes of Evidence taken before the Lords' Committee on the Same (1825 (181.521) IX)
Commissioners of Irish Education, First Report (1825 (400) XII)
——, *Second Report* (1826–27 (12) XII)
——, *Eighth Report (on the Roman Catholic College at Maynooth)* (1826–27 (509) XIII)
Select Committee on the State of the Poor in Ireland, Report and Evidence (1830 (667, 589, 654, 665) VII)
Select Committee on the State of Ireland, Report and Evidence (1831–32 (677) XVI)
Abstract of Answers and Returns under the Population Acts, Ireland

[Census of 1831] (1833 (634) XXXIX)

Select Committee on Inquiry into Drunkenness, Report and Evidence (1834 (559) VIII)

First Report from His Majesty's Commissioners for Inquiring into the Condition of the Poorer Classes in Ireland (1835 (369) XXXII (Pt I))

——, *Second Report* (1837 (68) XXXI)

——, *Third Report* (1836 (43) XXX)

——, Appendix A and Supplement (1835 (369) XXXII (Pt I))

——, Appendix C (1836 (35) XXX)

——, Appendix D (1836 (36) XXXI)

——, Appendix E and Supplement (1836 (37) XXXII)

——, Appendix F (1836 (38) XXXIII)

——. Appendix H (1836 (41) XXXIV)

Commissioners of Public Instruction, First Report (1835 (45) XXXIII)

Commissioners Appointed to Consider and Recommend a General System of Railways for Ireland, Second Report (1837–38 (145) XXXV)

Select Committee to Inquire into the State of Ireland since 1835 in Respect to Crime and Outrage, Report and Evidence (1839 (486I, 486III) XI–XII)

Report of the Commissioners Appointed to Take the Census of Ireland for the Year 1841 (1843 (504) XXIV)

Royal Commission on the Law and Practice in Respect to the Occupation of Land in Ireland [Devon Commission], *Pt IV* (1845 [672] XXII)

Commissioners Appointed to Inquire into the Management and Government of Maynooth, Report and Evidence (1854–55 (1896) XXII)

Census of Ireland 1851: General Report (1856 [2134] XXXI)

Select Committee on the Births, Deaths and Marriages (Ireland) Bill, Report and Evidence (1861 (425) XIV)

Census of Ireland 1861, Pt IV (1863 [3204–III] LIX)

Thirty-Seventh Report of the Commissioners of National Education in Ireland (1871 [C. 360] XXIII)

Census of Ireland 1871: Abstract of Enumerator's Returns (1871 [C. 375] LIX)

Census of Ireland 1881: Pt II (1882 [C. 3365] LXXVI)

2. *Edited and Calendared Documents*

'Report on the State of Popery, Ireland, 1731', *Arch. Hib.* I (1912), II (1913), III (1914), IV (1915)

'An Sotach 's a Mháthair', *Béaloideas* VI, 2 (1936)

Bolster, Evelyn, ed., 'The Moylan Correspondence in Bishop's House, Killarney', *Collect. Hib.* 14 (1971), 15 (1972)

Brady, John, ed., 'Documents Concerning the Diocese of Meath', *Arch. Hib.* VIII (1941)

——, ed., 'Archbishop Troy's Pastoral on Clandestine Marriages',

Rep. Nov. I, 2 (1956)

——, ed., 'A Pastoral of Archbishop O'Reilly, 1788', *Seanchas Ardmhacha* IV, 1 (1960—61)

——, ed., *Catholics and Catholicism in the Eighteenth-Century Press*, Maynooth 1965

Memoirs and Correspondence of Viscount Castlereagh, 4 vols, London 1848—49

Caulfield, Richard, ed., *The Council Book of Cork*, Guildford 1876

Corish, P. J., ed., 'Bishop Caulfield's *Relatio Status*', *Arch. Hib.* XXVIII (1966)

——, ed., 'Irish College, Rome: Kirby Papers', *Arch. Hib.* XXX (1972), XXXI (1973), XXXII (1974)

Crawford, W. H., & Trainor, Brian, ed., *Aspects of Irish Social History 1750—1800*, Belfast 1969

Curran, M. J., ed., 'Archbishop Carpenter's Epistolae', *Rep. Nov.* I, 1 (1955), I, 2 (1956)

——, ed., 'Instructions, Admonitions, etc. of Archbishop Carpenter, 1770—86', *Rep. Nov.* II, 1 (1958)

Fenning, Hugh, ed., 'Some Problems of the Irish Mission, 1733—74', *Collect. Hib.* 8 (1965)

——, ed., 'John Kent's Report on the Irish Mission, 1742', *Arch. Hib.* XXVIII (1966)

——, ed., 'Clerical Recruitment, 1735—83', *Arch. Hib.* XXX (1972)

——, ed., 'Two Diocesan Reports: Elphin (1753) and Killaloe (1792)', *Arch. Hib.* XXX (1972)

Flood, W. H. Grattan, ed., 'The Diocesan Manuscripts of Ferns during the Reign of Bishop Sweetman', *Arch. Hib.* II (1913), III (1914)

Giblin, Cathaldus, ed., 'Catalogue of Material of Irish Interest in the Collection *Nunziatura di Fiandra*', *Collect. Hib.* 5 (1962), 9 (1966), 10 (1967)

Historical Manuscripts Commission, *Charlemont Manuscripts*, 2 vols, London 1891—94 (Report 12, Appendix, Pt X; Report 13, Appendix, Pt VIII)

——, *Manuscripts of J. B. Fortescue, Esq., Preserved at Dropmore*, 10 vols, London 1892—1927 (Report 13, Appendix, Pt 3; Report 14, Appendix, Pt 5; Vols III—X published separately (1899—1927))

——, *Manuscripts of the Duke of Rutland*, 4 vols, London 1888—1905 (Vol. III: Report 14, Appendix, Pt 1)

McGrath, Michael, ed., *Cinnlae Amhlaoibh Uí Súilleabháin (The Diary of Humphrey O'Sullivan)*, 4 vols, London 1928—31

MacLysaght, Edward, ed., *The Kenmare Manuscripts*, Dublin 1942

——, ed., 'Documents Relating to the Wardenship of Galway', *Anal. Hib.* 14 (1944)

Mac Suibhne, Peadar, ed., *Paul Cullen and his Contemporaries*, 5 vols, Naas 1961—77

Moran, P. F., ed., *Spicilegium Ossoriense*, 3 vols, Dublin 1874—84

O'Dwyer, Christopher, ed., 'Archbishop Butler's Visitation Book',

    Arch. Hib. XXXIII (1975), XXXIV (1976–77)
Ó Maolagáin, Pádraig, ed., 'Clogher Diocesan Statutes, 1789', *Arch. Hib.* XII (1946)
O'Shea, Kieran, ed., 'Bishop Moylan's *Relatio Status*, 1785', *Kerry Arch. Hist. Soc. Jn.* 7 (1974)
——, ed., 'Three Early Nineteenth-Century Diocesan Reports', *Kerry Arch. Hist. Soc. Jn.* 10 (1977)
Renehan, L. F., *Collections on Irish Church History*, 2 vols, Dublin 1861–74
Ronan, M. V., ed., 'Archbishop Troy's Correspondence with Dublin Castle', *Arch. Hib.* XI (1944)

3.   *Other Sources*
Statuta Synodalia pro Dioecesi Corcagiensi [Cork Diocesan Statutes] (1768), Cork 1810
Statuta Synodalia pro Unitis Dioecesibus Cassel. et Imelac. [Cashel Diocesan Statutes] , Dublin 1813
Synodus Dioecesana Dublinensis . . . 1879 [including Dublin Diocesan Statutes 1831] , Dublin 1879
Statua Dioecesana in Dioecesi Ardacadensi Observanda [Ardagh Diocesan Stautes] , Dublin 1834
Catholic Directory, Dublin 1836–
Dublin Evening Post, 1811–12, 1819–24, 1831

C. BOOKS AND ARTICLES

A Candid and Impartial Account of the Disturbances in the County of Meath, Dublin 1794
The Particulars of the Horrible Murder of Catherine Sinnott, London n.d.
A Report of the Trial of Edward Browne and Others for Administering and of Laurence Woods for Taking an Unlawful Oath, Dublin 1822
Report of the Trial of the Rev. John Carroll, Dublin 1824
Irish Priests: Their Education, Characters and Conduct Considered, Dublin 1821
Saint Columbkille's Sayings, Moral and Prophetic, Extracted from Irish Parchments and Translated by the Rev. Mr Taaffe, Dublin 1844
Parliamentary Gazetteer of Ireland, Dublin 1845–

Ahern, John, 'The Plenary Synod of Thurles', *Ir. Ecc. Rec.* ser. 5, LXXV (1951), LXXVIII (1952)
Akenson, D. H., 'National Education and the Realities of Irish Life, 1831–1900', *Éire–Ireland* IV, 4 (1969)
——, *The Irish Education Experiment*, London 1970
——, *The Church of Ireland: Ecclesiastical Reform and Revolution, 1800–85*, New Haven 1971
Archer, Joseph, *Statistical Survey of the County Dublin*, Dublin 1801
Arensberg, C. M., & Kimball, S. T., *Family and Community in Ireland*

(1940), 2nd ed., Harvard. 1968

Armstrong, E. C. R., *et al.*, 'The Reliquary Known as the Misach', *JRSAI* LII, 2 (1922)

Baker, S. E., 'Orange and Green: Belfast, 1832–1912' in H. J. Dyos & Michael Wolff, ed., *The Victorian City: Images and Realities*, London 1973

Barry, P. C., 'The Legislation of the Synod of Thurles, 1850', *Ir. Theol. Quart.* XXVI (1959)

Beames, Michael, 'Cottier and Conacre in Pre-Famine Ireland', *Jn. Peasant Studies* II, 3 (1975)

——, 'Peasant Movements: Ireland, 1785–95', *Jn. Peasant Studies* II, 4 (1975)

Beaumont, Gustave de, *Ireland: Social, Political and Religious*, ed. W. C. Taylor, 2 vols, London 1839

Begley, John, *The Diocese of Limerick from 1691 to the Present Time*, Dublin 1938

Bicheno, J. E., *Ireland and its Economy*, London 1830

Biggar, F. J., 'Local Historic Scraps', *Ulster Jn. Arch.* XIV (1908)

Blackall, Sir Henry, 'Lord Dunboyne', *Rep. Nov.* III, 2 (1963–64)

Blanchard, Jean, *The Church in Contemporary Ireland*, Dublin 1963

Bossy, John, 'The Counter-Reformation and the People of Catholic Ireland, 1596–1641' in T. D. Williams, ed., *Historical Studies* VIII, Dublin 1971

Bourke, P. M. A., 'The Agricultural Statistics of the 1841 Census of Ireland: A Critical Review', *Econ. Hist. Rev.* XVIII, 2 (1965)

Bowden, C. T., *A Tour through Ireland*, Dublin 1791

Bowen, Desmond, *Souperism: Myth or Reality?*, Cork 1970

——, *The Protestant Crusade in Ireland, 1800–70*, Dublin 1978

Brady, John, & Corish, P. J., *The Church under the Penal Code*: P. J. Corish, ed., *A History of Irish Catholicism*, IV, 2, Dublin 1971

Brenan, M. J., *Ecclesiastical History of Ireland* (1840), 2nd ed., Dublin 1864

Broderick, J. F., *The Holy See and the Irish Movement for the Repeal of the Union with England*, Rome 1951

Broeker, Galen, *Rural Disorder and Police Reform in Ireland, 1812–36*, London 1970

Burns, R. E., 'The Irish Penal Code and Some of its Historians', *Review of Politics* XXI (1959)

——, 'The Irish Popery Laws: A Study in Eighteenth-Century Legislation and Behaviour', *Review of Politics* XXIV (1962)

——, 'Parsons, Priests and the People: The Rise of Irish Anti-Clericalism, 1785–9', *Church History* XXXI (1962)

Butler, James, *The Most Rev. Dr James Butler's Catechism* (1775), 7th ed., Cork 1814

——, *A Justification of the Tenets of the Roman Catholic Religion*, Dublin 1787

Byrne, Miles, *Memoirs*, 3 vols, Paris & New York 1863

Byrne, P. F., *Witchcraft in Ireland*, Cork 1967

Campbell, Flann, 'Birth Control and the Christian Churches', *Pop. Studies* XIV, 2 (1960)

Campbell, Thomas, *A Philosophical Survey of the South of Ireland*, Dublin 1778

Carbery, Mary, *The Farm by Lough Gur: The Story of Mary Fogarty* (1937), Cork 1973

Carleton, William, *Traits and Stories of the Irish Peasantry* (1830–33), 2 vols, New York 1862

—, *Autobiography* (1896), London 1968

Carr, John, *The Stranger in Ireland*, London 1806

Carrigan, William, *History and Antiquities of the Diocese of Ossory*, 4 vols, Dublin 1905

Castlereagh, Robert Stewart, Viscount, *Memoirs and Correspondence*, see p. 317

Chadwick, Owen, *The Victorian Church*, 2 vols, London 1966–70

Clark, Ruth, *Strangers and Sojourners at Port Royal*, Cambridge 1932

Clark, Sam, 'The Importance of Agrarian Classes: Agrarian Class Structure and Collective Action in Nineteenth-Century Ireland, *Br. Jn. Sociology* XXIX, 1 (1978)

Cogan, Anthony, *Ecclesiastical History of the Diocese of Meath*, 3 vols, Dublin 1862–70

Cohn, Norman, *Europe's Inner Demons*, London 1975

Comerford, Michael, *Collections Relating to the Dioceses of Kildare and Leighlin* 3 vols, Dublin 1883–86

Connell, K. H., *The Population of Ireland, 1750–1845*, Oxford 1950

—, 'Peasant Marriage in Ireland after the Great Famine', *Past & Present* 12 (1957)

—, 'The Land Legislation and Irish Social Life', *Econ. Hist. Rev.* XI, 1 (1958)

—, 'Peasant Marriage in Ireland: Its Structure and Development since the Famine', *Econ. Hist. Rev.* XIV, 3 (1962)

—, *Irish Peasant Society*, Oxford 1968

Connolly, S. J., 'Illegitimacy and Pre-Nuptial Pregnancy in Ireland before 1864: The Evidence of Some Catholic Parish Registers', *Ir. Econ. Soc. Hist.* (1979)

—, 'Catholicism in Ulster, 1800–50' in Peter Roebuck, ed., *Plantation to Partition*, Belfast 1981

Coombes, James, 'Europe's First Total Abstinence Society', *Cork Hist. Arch. Soc. Jn.* LXXII, 215 (1967)

Coote, Charles, *General View of the Agriculture and Manufactures of the Queen's County*, Dublin 1801

Coulter, J. A., 'The Political Theory of Dr Edward Maginn, Bishop of Derry, 1846–9', *Ir. Ecc. Rec.* XCVIII (1962)

Coyle, Michael, 'Holy Wells in the Parish of Dunleer', *Seanchas Ardmhacha* II, 1 (1956)

Croker, T. Crofton, *Researches in the South of Ireland*, London 1824

Crolly, George, *Life of the Most Rev. Dr Crolly*, Dublin 1851

Croly, D. O., *Essay Religious and Political on Ecclesiastical Finance*,

Cork 1834

Crotty, R. D., *Irish Agricultural Production*, Cork 1966

Cullen, L. M., 'Irish History without the Potato', *Past & Present* 40 (1968)

——, 'The Hidden Ireland: Reassessment of a Concept', *Studia Hib.* 9 (1969)

——, *An Economic History of Ireland since 1660*, London 1972

Cunningham, T. P., *Church Reorganisation*: P. J. Corish, ed., *A History of Irish Catholicism*, V, 7, Dublin 1970

Curry, John, 'Ballycastle: The Social Geography of a North Mayo Parish' (unpublished MA thesis, University College, Dublin, 1968)

D'Alton, E. A., *A History of the Archdiocese of Tuam*, 2 vols, Dublin 1928

Danaher, Kevin, *The Year in Ireland*, Cork 1972

—— (as Caoimhín Ó Danachair), 'Faction Fighting in Co. Limerick', *North Munster Antiq. Jn.* X (1966–67)

Daunt, W. J. O'Neill, *A Life Spent for Ireland*, London 1896

de Brún, Pádraig, 'John Windele and Father John Casey', *Kerry Arch. Hist. Soc. Jn.* 7 (1974)

Donaldson, John, *A Historical and Statistical Account of the Barony of Upper Fews in the County of Armagh* (1838), Dundalk 1923

Donlevy, Andrew, *An Teagasc Críosduidhe . . . The Catechism or Christian Doctrine* (1742), 3rd ed., Dublin 1848

Donnelly, J. S., *The Land and the People of Nineteenth-Century Cork*, London 1975

——, 'The Whiteboy Movement, 1761–5', *IHS* XXI, 81 (1978)

Doyle, J. W., *Pastoral Address . . . against the Illegal Associations of Ribbonmen*, Dublin 1822

—— (as 'J. K. L.'), *Letters on the State of Ireland*, Dublin 1825

Drake, Michael, 'Marriage and Population Growth in Ireland, 1750–1845', *Econ. Hist. Rev.* XVI, 2 (1963)

Dutton, Hely, *Statistical Survey of the County of Clare*, Dublin 1808

——, *A Statistical and Agricultural Survey of the County of Galway*, Dublin 1824

England, T. R., *Life of the Rev. Arthur O'Leary*, London 1822

Evans, E. E., *Irish Folk Ways*, London 1957

Fahey, Jerome, *History and Antiquities of the Diocese of Kilmacduagh*, Dublin 1893

Faloon, W. H., *The Marriage Law of Ireland*, Dublin 1881

Farrell, William, *Carlow in '98: The Autobiography of William Farrell of Carlow*, ed. Roger McHugh, Dublin 1949

Faulkner, Anselm, 'The Right of Patronage of the Maguires of Tempo', *Clogher Rec.* IX, 2 (1977)

Finegan, Francis, 'The Irish Catholic Convert Rolls', *Studies* XXXVIII (1949)

Fitzpatrick, W. J., *Life, Times and Correspondence of the Rt Rev. Dr Doyle, Bishop of Kildare and Leighlin* (1861), 2nd ed., 2 vols,

Dublin 1880

Gallagher, James, *Sermons in Irish Gaelic* (1736), ed., U. J. Bourke, Dublin 1877

Gallagher, Patrick, 'Sources for the History of the Clergy of a Diocese: Seventeenth-Century Clogher', *Ir. Cath. Hist. Committee, Proc.* (1957)

Gamble, John, *Views of Society and Manners in the North of Ireland*, London 1819

Giblin, Cathaldus, *Irish Exiles in Catholic Europe*: P. J. Corish, ed., *A History of Irish Catholicism*, IV, 3, Dublin 1971

Guinan, Joseph, *The Soggarth Aroon* (1905), 2nd ed., Dublin 1906

Hall, James, *Tour through Ireland*, 2 vols, London 1813

Hall, Mr & Mrs S. C., *Ireland: Its Scenery and Character*, 3 vols, Virtue, London 1841—43

Hartnett, P. J., 'The Holy Wells of East Muskerry', *Béaloideas* X (1941)

——, 'Holy Wells of East Muskerry, Co. Cork', *Cork Hist. Arch. Soc. Jn.* LII (1947)

Hayes, Richard, 'Priests in the Independence Movement of '98', *Ir. Ecc. Rec.* LXVI (1945)

Healy, John, *Maynooth College: Its Centenary History, 1795—1895*, Dublin 1895

Hoban, Brendan, 'Dominick Bellew, 1745—1812: Parish Priest of Dundalk and Bishop of Killala', *Seanchas Ardmhacha* VI, 2 (1972)

Hogan, John, 'Patron Days and Holy Wells in Ossory', *JRSAI* II, 2 (1873)

Hoppen, K. T., 'Landlords, Society and Electoral Politics in Mid-Nineteenth-Century Ireland', *Past & Present* 75 (1977)

Hosp, Edward, 'Redemptorist Mission in Enniskillen, 1852', *Clogher Rec.* VIII, 3 (1975)

Humphreys, A. J., *New Dubliners: Urbanisation and the Irish Family*, London 1966

Inglis, H. D., *Ireland in 1834*, 2 vols, London 1834

Jones, F. M., 'The Congregation of Propaganda and the Publication of Dr O'Brien's Irish Dictionary, 1768', *Ir. Ecc. Rec.* LXXVII (1952)

Joyce, P. W., *English As We Speak It in Ireland*, Dublin 1910

Kee, Robert, *The Green Flag*, London 1972

Kennedy, T. P., *Church Building*: P. J. Corish, ed., *A History of Irish Catholicism*, V, 8, Dublin 1970

Kernan, Randall, *A Report of the Trial of an Action for Slander*, Dublin 1810

——, *Report of the Trials of the Caravats and Shanavests*, Dublin 1811

Kingston, John, 'Lord Dunboyne', *Rep. Nov.* III, 1 (1961—62)

Kohl, J. G., *Travels in Ireland*, London 1844

Large, David, 'The Wealth of the Greater Irish Landowners, 1780—1815', *IHS* XV, 57 (1966)

Larkin, Emmet, 'Church and State in Ireland in the Nineteenth Century',

Church History XXXI (1962)

——, 'Economic Growth, Capital Investment and the Roman Catholic Church in Nineteenth-Century Ireland', *Amer. Hist. Rev.* LXXII (1967)

——, 'The Devotional Revolution in Ireland, 1850–75', *Amer. Hist. Rev.* LXXVII (1972)

——, *The Roman Catholic Church and the Creation of the Modern Irish State, 1878–86*, Dublin 1975

Latocnaye, de, *A Frenchman's Walk through Ireland, 1796–7* (1797) trans. John Stevenson, Belfast 1917

Lecky, W. E. H., *History of Ireland in the Eighteenth Century* (1878–90), 5 vols, London 1892

Lee, Joseph, 'Marriage and Population in Pre-Famine Ireland', *Econ. Hist. Rev.* XXI, 2 (1968)

——, 'Irish Agriculture', *Ag. Hist. Rev.* XVII (1969)

——, 'The Dual Economy in Ireland' in T. D. Williams, ed., *Historical Studies* VIII, Dublin 1971

——, *The Modernisation of Irish Society*, Dublin 1973

——, 'The Ribbonmen' in T. D. Williams, ed., *Secret Societies in Ireland*, Dublin 1973

Le Fanu, W. R., *Seventy Years of Irish Life*, London 1893

Lewis, G. C., *On Local Disturbances in Ireland*, London 1836

Lewis, Samuel, *Topographical Dictionary of Ireland*, 2 vols, London 1837

Lowe, W. J., 'The Lancashire Irish and the Catholic Church, 1836–71: The Social Dimension', *IHS* XX, 78 (1976)

Luckombe, Philip, *A Tour through Ireland*, Dublin 1780

Lyons, F. S. L., *Charles Stewart Parnell*, London 1977

McAnally, Sir Henry, *The Irish Militia, 1793–1816*, Dublin & London 1949

MacCurtain, Margaret, 'Pre-Famine Peasantry in Ireland: Definition and Theme', *Ir. Univ. Review* IV, 2 (1974)

MacDonagh, Oliver, 'The Politicisation of the Irish Catholic Bishops', *Hist. Jn.* XVIII, 1 (1975)

McDowell, R. B., *Public Opinion and Government Policy in Ireland, 1801–46*, London 1952

MacEvoy, Brendan, 'The Parish of Errigal Kiernan', *Seanchas Ardmhacha* I, 1 (1954)

Macfarlane, Alan, *Witchcraft in Tudor and Stuart England*, London 1970

McGee, T. D'Arcy, *Life of the Rt Rev. Edward Maginn* (1857), 2nd ed, New York 1863

MacGeehin, Maureen, see Wall

MacGrath, Kevin, 'John Garzia, a Noted Priest-Catcher and his Activities, 1717–23', *Ir. Ecc. Rec.* LXXII (1949)

Mac Gréil, Mícheál, & Ó Gliasáin, Mícheál, 'Church Attendance and Religious Practice of Dublin Adults', *Social Studies* III, 2 (1974)

M'Kenna, J. E., *Diocese of Clogher: Parochial Records*, Enniskillen

1920

MacLysaght, Edward, *Irish Life in the Seventeenth Century* (1939), 3rd ed., Shannon 1969

MacNeill, Máire, *The Festival of Lughnasa*, London 1962

Maguire, Edward, *A History of the Diocese of Raphoe*, 2 vols, Dublin 1920

Maguire, J. F., *Father Mathew: A Biography* (1863), New York 1898

Maher, James, *Letters on Religious Subjects*, ed. P. F. Moran, Dublin 1877

Malcolmson, R. W., *Popular Recreations in English Society, 1700–1850*, Cambridge 1973

Manning, Michael, 'Dr Nicholas Madgett's *Constitutio Ecclesiastica*', *Kerry Arch. Hist. Soc. Jn.* 9 (1976)

Mason, W. S., *A Statistical Account or Parochial Survey of Ireland*, 3 vols, Dublin 1814–19

Meagher, John, 'Of the Genus Called "Discoverer" ', *Rep. Nov.* I, 2 (1956)

Meagher, William, *Notices of the Life and Character of . . . Rev. D. Murray, late Archbishop of Dublin*, Dublin 1853

Mercier, Vivian, *The Irish Comic Tradition*, Oxford 1962

Messenger, J. C., *Inis Beag: Isle of Ireland*, New York 1969

——, 'Sex and Repression in an Irish Folk Community' in D. S. Marshall & R. C. Suggs, ed., *Human Sexual Behaviour: Variations in the Ethnographic Spectrum*, New York & London 1971

Miller, D. W., *Church, State and Nation in Ireland, 1898–1921*, Dublin 1973

——, 'Irish Catholicism and the Great Famine', *Jn. Soc. Hist.* IX, 1 (1975)

——, 'Presbyterianism and Modernisation in Ulster', *Past & Present* 80 (1978)

Millett, Benignus, *Survival and Reorganisation, 1650–95*: P. J. Corish, ed., *A History of Irish Catholicism*, III, 7, Dublin 1968

Milner, John, *Inquiry into Certain Vulgar Opinions concerning the Catholic Inhabitants and the Antiquities of Ireland*, London 1808

Mol, Hans, ed., *Western Religion: A Country by Country Sociological Inquiry*, The Hague 1972

Morgan, Valerie, 'The Church of Ireland Registers of St Patrick's, Coleraine, as a Source for the Study of a Local Pre-Famine Population', *Ulster Folklife* XIX (1973)

Morris, Henry, 'Irish Wake Games', *Béaloideas* VIII (1938)

Murphy, Ignatius, *Primary Education*: P. J. Corish, ed., *A History of Irish Catholicism*, V, 6, Dublin 1971

Murphy, J. A., 'The Support of the Catholic Clergy in Ireland, 1750–1850' in J. L. McCracken, ed., *Historical Studies* V, London 1965

——, 'Priests and People in Modern Irish History', *Christus Rex* XXIII, 4 (1969)

'The Crime of Anonymity' in E. P. Thompson *et al.*, ed., *Albion's Fatal Tree*, London 1975

'Eighteenth-Century English Society: Class Struggle without Class?', *Social History* III, 2 (1978)

y, Mark, *Murroe and Boher: The History of an Irish Country Parish*, Dublin 1966

William, *Statistical Observations Relative to the County of Kilkenny, Made in the Years 1800 and 1801*, Dublin 1802

eville, Alexis de, *Journeys to England and Ireland* (written 1835), ed. J. P. Mayer, London 1958

, Patrick, 'Patrick James O'Byrne, Dean of Armagh (1810–19) and the Contemporary Scene', *Seanchas Ardmhacha* I, 1 (1954)

end, Horatio, *Statistical Survey of the County of Cork*, Dublin 1810

J. T., *A Pastoral Instruction on the Duties of Christian Citizens* (1793), 2nd ed., Dublin 1793

, G. S. L., 'Irish Fertility Ratios before the Famine', *Econ. Hist. Rev.* XXIII, 2 (1970)

eek, F., 'Roman Catholicism and Fertility in the Netherlands', *Pop. Studies* X, 2 (1956)

eld, Edward, *An Account of Ireland, Statistical and Political*, vols, London 1812

Maureen, 'The Rise of a Catholic Middle Class in Eighteenth-Century Ireland', *IHS* XI (1958–59)

The Catholic Merchants, Manufacturers and Traders of Dublin, 778–82', *Rep. Nov.* II, 2 (1960)

he Penal Laws, Dundalk 1961

The Decline of the Irish Language' in Brian Ó Cuív, ed., *A View of the Irish Language*, Dublin 1969

The Whiteboys' in T. D. Williams, ed., *Secret Societies in Ireland*, Dublin 1973

s Maureen MacGeehin), 'The Catholics of the Towns and the Quarterage Dispute in Eighteenth-Century Ireland', *IHS* VIII (1952–53)

homas, 'Archbishop John Carpenter and the Catholic Revival, 770–86', *Rep. Nov.* I, 1 (1955)

he Sign of Dr Hay's Head, Dublin 1958

T. J., 'Compulsory Irish in France', *Cork Hist. Arch. Soc. Jn.* VIII, 1 (1953)

on, John, Whitelaw, James & Walsh, Robert, *History of the City of Dublin from the Earliest Accounts to the Present Time*, vols, London 1818

aac, *Statistical Survey of the County of Roscommon*, Dublin 832

Patrick, 'Anthony Blake, Archbishop of Armagh, 1758–87', anchas Ardmhacha V, 2 (1970)

J. H., 'The Influence of the Catholic Clergy on Elections in neteenth-Century Ireland', *Eng. Hist. Rev.* LXXV (1960)

——, 'The Perspective of History' (typescript of no. 17 in the series of Thomas Davis Lectures, *Religion and Irish Society*)

Murphy, M. J., *Tyrone Folk Quest*, Belfast 1973

Murphy, P. J., 'The Papers of Nicholas Archdeacon, Bishop of Kilmacduagh and Kilfenora, 1800–23', *Arch. Hib.* XXXI (1973)

Murray, Patrick, Essay on William Carleton, *Edinburgh Review* XCVI (1852); repr. *Clogher Rec.* VII, 3 (1971–72)

Newenham, Thomas, *View of the Natural, Political and Commercial Circumstances of Ireland*, London 1809

Nicholls, George, *Poor Laws, Ireland: Three Reports*, London 1838

Nic Giolla Phádraig, Máire, 'Religion in Ireland: Preliminary Analysis', *Social Studies* V, 2 (1976)

Noonan, J. J., 'Intellectual and Demographic History', *Daedalus* XCVII, 2 (1967)

Norman, E. R., *The Catholic Church and Ireland in the Age of Rebellion, 1859–73*, London 1965

Nowlan, K. B., 'The Catholic Clergy and Irish Politics in the 1830s and 40s' in John Barry, ed., *Historical Studies* IX, Belfast 1974

O'Brien, J. A., ed., *The Vanishing Irish: The Enigma of the Modern World*, London 1954

Ó Coindealbháin, Seán, 'Holy Wells', *Cork Hist. Soc. Jn.* LI (1946)

O'Connell, Philip, 'The Plot against Fr Nicholas Sheehy: The Historical Background', *Ir. Ecc. Rec.* CVIII, 6 (1967)

O'Connor, Matthew, *A History of the Irish Catholics from the Settlement in 1691*, Dublin 1813

Ó Danachair, Caoimhín, see Danaher

O'Donnell, P. D., *The Irish Faction Fighters of the Nineteenth Century*, Dublin 1975

O'Donoghue, Patrick, 'Causes of the Opposition to Tithes, 1830–8', *Studia Hib.* 5 (1965)

——, 'Opposition to Tithe Payments in 1830–1', *Studia Hib.* 6 (1966)

——, 'The Holy See and Ireland, 1780–1803', *Arch. Hib.* XXXIV (1976–77)

O'Donovan Rossa, Jeremiah, *Rossa's Recollections*, New York 1898

O'Driscol, John, *Views of Ireland: Moral, Political and Religious*, 2 vols, London 1823

Ó Dufaigh, Seosamh, 'James Murphy, Bishop of Clogher, 1801–24', *Clogher Rec.* VI, 3 (1968)

O'Farrell, J. P., 'Francis Moylan, 1735–1815: A Bishop of the Resurgence' (unpublished MA thesis, University College, Cork, 1973)

O'Farrell, Patrick, 'Millenialism, Messianism and Utopianism in Irish History', *Anglo-Irish Studies* II (1976)

Ó Fiaich, Tomás, 'Irish Poetry and the Clergy', *Leachtaí Cholm Cille* IV (1975)

Ó Laoghaire, Peadar, *My Own Story* (1915), trans. Sheila O'Sullivan, Dublin 1973

O'Laverty, James, *An Historical Account of the Diocese of Down and Connor, Ancient and Modern*, 5 vols, Dublin 1878–95

Ó Muireadaigh, Sailbheastar, 'Na Carabhait agus na Sean-Bheisteanna', *Galvia* VIII (1961)

'Omurethi', 'Customs Peculiar to Certain Days, formerly observed in County Kildare', *Kildare Arch. Soc. Jn.* V (1906–8)

O'Neill, T. P., 'The Catholic Church and Relief of the Poor, 1815–45', *Arch. Hib.* XXXI (1973)

O'Reilly, Bernard, *John MacHale, Archbishop of Tuam*, 2 vols, New York 1890

O'Riordan, Michael, *Catholicity and Progress in Ireland*, London 1905

O'Rorke, Terence, *History, Antiquities and Present State of the Parishes of Ballysadare and Kilvarnet, in the County of Sligo*, Dublin [1878]

O'Shea, Kieran, 'David Moriarty', *Kerry Arch. Hist. Soc. Jn.* 3 (1970), 4 (1971), 5 (1972), 6 (1973)

Ó Súilleabháin, Amhlaoibh (Humphrey O'Sullivan), *Cinnlae (Diary)*, see p. 317, McGrath

Ó Súilleabháin, Pádraig, 'Catholic Sermon Books Printed in Ireland, 1700–1850', *Ir. Ecc. Rec.* XCIX (1963)

——, 'Catholic Books Printed in Ireland, 1740–1820, Containing Lists of Subscribers', *Collect. Hib.* 6–7 (1963–64)

——, 'The Library of a Parish Priest of the Penal Days', *Collect. Hib.* 6–7 (1963–64)

——, 'Sidelights on the Irish Church, 1811–38', *Collect. Hib.* 9 (1966)

Ó Súilleabháin, Séamus V., *Secondary Education*: P. J. Corish, ed., *A History of Irish Catholicism*, V, 6, Dublin 1971

—— (as J. J. Sullivan), 'The Education of Irish Catholics, 1782–1831', 2 vols. (unpublished PhD thesis, Queen's University of Belfast, 1959)

Ó Súilleabháin, Seán, *A Handbook of Irish Folklore* (1942), London 1963

——, *Irish Wake Amusements*, Cork 1967

——, *Irish Folk Custom and Belief*, Dublin n.d.

O'Toole, Edward, 'The Holy Wells of Co. Carlow', *Béaloideas* IV (1934)

Ó Tuathaigh, Gearóid, *Ireland before the Famine, 1798–1848*, Dublin 1972

Pakenham, Thomas, *The Year of Liberty* (1969), Panther ed., London 1972

'Pastorini', *The General History of the Christian Church, from her Birth to her Final Triumphant State in Heaven* (1771), 6th ed., Cork 1820

Paul-Dubois, Louis, *Contemporary Ireland*, Dublin 1908

Perkin, Harold, *The Origins of Modern English Society, 1780–1880*, London 1969

Plunkett, Sir Horace, *Ireland in the New Century*, London 1904

Pollard, Sidney, 'Factory Discipline in the Industrial Revolution',

Econ. Hist. Rev. XVI, 2 (1963)

Power, Patrick, *Parochial History of Water[ford] the Eighteenth and Nineteenth Centurie[s]*

——, *Waterford and Lismore: A Compendi[ous] Dioceses*, Cork 1937

Power, T. R., 'The Most Rev. James Butle[r]' *Ir. Ecc. Rec.* XIII (1892)

Prim, J. G. A., 'Olden Popular Pastimes in (1852–53)

Rawson, T. J., *Statistical Survey of the C[ounty]* 1807

Reid, D. A., 'The Decline of Saint Mond[ay]' *Present* 71 (1976)

Reynolds, J. A., *The Catholic Emancipation* New Haven 1954

Ridgeway, William, *A Report of the Proc[eedings]* *Commission*, Dublin 1807

Ronan, M. V., 'Priests in the Independen[ce]' *Ir. Ecc. Rec.* LXVIII (1946)

Sayers, Peig, *An Old Woman's Reflection[s]* Ennis, Oxford 1962

Senior, Hereward, *Orangeism in Ireland a[nd]* London 1966

Shanin, Teodor, ed., *Peasants and Peasant Soci[ety]* worth 1971

Shearman, J. F., *Loca Patriciana*, Dublin 1879

Simms, J. G., *The Williamite Confiscation* London 1956

——, 'Connacht in the Eighteenth Century', *I[HS]*

Smith, Charles, *Ancient and Present State o[f]* Cork (1750), new ed., 2 vols, Cork 1815

Solow, B. L., *The Land Question and the Iris[h]* Cambridge, Mass. 1971

Steele, E. D., 'Cardinal Cullen and Irish N[ationalism]' (1975)

Sullivan, J. J., see Ó Súilleabháin, Séamus V.

Synge, J. M., *The Aran Islands* (1907), Londo[n]

Teeling, C. H., *History of the Irish Rebellion o[f]*

Thackeray, W. M., *The Irish Sketch-Book* 1879

Thomas, Keith, 'Work and Leisure in Pre-In[dustrial]' *Present* 29 (1964)

——, *Religion and the Decline of Magic* (19 worth 1973

Thompson, E. P., *The Making of the Englis[h]* rev. ed., Penguin, Harmondsworth 1968

——, 'Time, Work Discipline and Industrial C 38 (1967)

——, 'The Appointment of Catholic Bishops in Nineteenth-Century Ireland', *Cath. Hist. Rev.* XLVIII (1962)

——, *Church and State in Modern Ireland, 1923–70*, Dublin 1971

Wilde, J. F., Lady, *Ancient Legends, Charms and Superstitions of Ireland* (1887), new ed., London 1899

——, *Ancient Cures, Charms and Usages of Ireland*, London 1890

Wilde, Sir W. R., *Irish Popular Superstitions*, Dublin 1852

Wood, Herbert, 'Report on Certain Registers of Irregular Marriages', *PROI, Rep. Dep. Keeper* 34 (1902)

Wood-Martin, W. G., *Traces of the Elder Faiths in Ireland*, 2 vols, London 1902

Young, Arthur, *Tour in Ireland* (1780), 2 vols, London 1892

Zimmermann, G.-D., *Irish Political Street Ballads and Rebel Songs*, Geneva 1966

Index